Bought to commemorate my last
family link with Swainson at the
death of my beloved Aunt Florence
Tunner. 5th July 1908 - 32nd July 1990.
Age 85ys. Cremated at Warrington Crematorium.
Signed by Shirley Dorothea Atkinson (niece)

SWANSEA
AN ILLUSTRATED HISTORY

SWANSEA

AN ILLUSTRATED HISTORY

Edited by

Glanmor Williams

CHRISTOPHER DAVIES

Published by
Christopher Davies (Publishers) Ltd.,
P.O. Box 403, Sketty, Swansea, SA2 9BE.

ISBN 0 7154 0714 7

*Printed in Wales by
Dynevor Printing Company, Rawlings Road, Llandybïe, Dyfed.*

CONTENTS

	Page
Acknowledgements	vii
List of Illustrations	ix
List of Figures and Tables	xv
Preface	xvii

Chapter 1: BEFORE THE INDUSTRIAL REVOLUTION
by Glanmor Williams — 1

Chapter 2: INDUSTRIAL DEVELOPMENT
by Paul R. Reynolds — 29

Chapter 3: THE PORT AND ITS WORLDWIDE TRADE
by David Boorman — 57

Chapter 4: LOCAL GOVERNMENT, ADMINISTRATION
AND POLITICS, 1700 TO THE 1830s
by John R. Alban — 85

Chapter 5: THE MAKING OF AN INDUSTRIAL
COMMUNITY by Ieuan Gwynedd Jones — 115

Chapter 6: RELIGION AND EDUCATION
by F. G. Cowley — 145

Chapter 7: ART AND ARCHITECTURE
by Prys Morgan — 177

Chapter 8: 'UNDER A RAINBOW': LITERARY HISTORY
by James A. Davies — 215

Chapter 9: THE ENTERTAINMENT OF THE PEOPLE
by Peter Stead — 245

Chapter 10: MUNICIPAL ADMINISTRATION AND
POLITICS, FROM THE 1830s TO 1974
by John R. Alban — 285

Chapter 11: TWENTIETH-CENTURY CHANGE
by Graham Humphrys — 321

Figures and Tables — 349

Bibliography — 357

Index — 365

ACKNOWLEDGEMENTS

We should like to express our warmest thanks to the following institutions and individuals for so kindly giving us permission to reproduce the illustrations which are included in this volume as follows:

Colour plates: Swansea City Archive Office, Guildhall, Swansea; The Trustees of the British Museum; University College of Swansea Library; Royal Institution of South Wales; Glynn Vivian Art Gallery, Leisure Services Department, Swansea City Council; Prys Morgan, Esq.

Other illustrations: Central Library, Swansea (pages 160, 169, 173); Century Hutchinson Ltd. (page 241); G. B. Davies, Esq. (page 175); Roger Davies, Esq. (page 219); Glynn Vivian Art Gallery, Leisure Services Department, Swansea City Council (page 223); H. Grenfell, Esq. (page 34); Hulton Deutsch Ltd. (pages 156, 331); Graham Humphrys, Esq. (pages 349, 350, 351, 352, 353, 354, 355, 356); Miss Pauline James (page 46); National Museum of Wales, Cardiff (pages 24-5); Public Record Office, London (page 2); Royal Institution of South Wales, Swansea (pages 27, 30, 33, 144, 147, 149, 149, 150, 155, 156, 158); South Wales Transport Co. Ltd. (page 345); Swansea City Archive Office, Guildhall, Swansea (pages 6, 9, 10, 22, 28, 39, 44, 51, 53, 56, 61, 62-3, 66, 69, 77, 83, 87, 88, 92, 94-5, 97, 106, 109, 112, 116, 121, 123, 131, 132, 134, 135, 138, 141, 142, 148, 157, 170, 185, 191, 193, 194, 195, 199, 203, 205, 206, 207, 208, 209, 211, 212, 233, 238, 247, 256, 258, 259, 260, 261, 262, 264, 265, 276, 289, 291, 293, 296, 301, 302-3, 312, 313, 315, 317, 318, 320, 323, 325, 328, 330, 334); *Swansea Evening Post* (pages 235, 277, 279, 280); University College of Swansea Library (page 45).

LIST OF
ILLUSTRATIONS

MONOCHROME PLATES

	Page
Charter of William de Newburgh, earl of Warwick, to the Burgesses of Swansea, 1158-84	2
View of Swansea Castle, 1838	6
Conjectural Reconstruction of fourteenth-century Swansea	9
Gable-end of the Cross Keys Inn, showing fourteenth-century windows, c. 1879	10
Colonel Philip Jones (1618-74)	22
View of Swansea, by Frances Place, 1678	24-5
Bishop Gore's House in High Street, late seventeenth century	27
The Swansea Town Crier, by Alfred Dixon, nineteenth century	28
View of Llangyvelach Copperworks, Landore, c. 1750	30
John Henry Vivian (1785-1855); Henry Hussey Vivian (1821-94)	33
View of the Hafod Copperworks, c. 1900	34
The White Rock Ferry, c. 1890	39
Sir John Jones Jenkins, M.P. (later Lord Glantawe) (1835-1915)	44
The Dyffryn Tinplate Works, Morriston	45
Group of Copperworkers at the Middle Bank Copperworks, c. 1910	46
View of Graig Trewyddfa, c. 1855	51
Blast Furnaces in the Lower Swansea Valley, 1881	53
The North Dock, 1881	56
Swansea and the Harbour, from a Daguerreotype, 1848	61
Fabian's Bay and the Ferry, looking towards the Beaufort Arms Ferryhouse, early nineteeth century	62-3
Vessels in the King's Dock, c. 1920	66
Aerial View of the Cambrian Dry Dock, c. 1920	69
Aerial View of the Eastern Docks, c. 1970	77
Aerial View of the Marina, 1986	83
The Town Hall of 1585	87
'Gabriel Powell's Chest'	88

Page

Gabriel Powell, 'King of Swansea'   92
The East View of Swansea Castle, by Samuel and
    Nathaniel Buck, 1741   94-5
The Oath of a Burgess, 1759   97
Swansea Corporation discussing Harbour Improvements, 1787 106
View of the Port and Bay of Swansea, by Thomas
    Rothwell, 1791   109
The Guildhall at the Burrows, 1829   112
Early nineteenth-century Swansea   116
The Bwrlais Brook at Cwmfelin, *c.* 1900   121
View of Morriston from the Wychtree Bridge, 1929   123
Mount Pleasant Chapel, *c.* 1900   131
The Design for the proposed New Market at
    Oxford Street, 1895   132
Entrance to the New Swansea Market in 1897   134
Interior of Swansea Market, 1906   135
Children at play in St Matthew's Graveyard, *c.* 1920   138
Sir Alfred Mond and Supporters, 1906   141
The Slip at Swansea Beach, *c.* 1929   142
The Reverend Joseph Harris (Gomer) (1773-1825)   144
The Old Chapel, on the Site of the Unitarian Church,
    High Street   147
St Mary's Church, mid nineteenth century   148
St David's Roman Catholic Church, 1856   149
Wesley Chapel, Goat Street   150
St Andrew's Church, formerly Presbyterian, now United
    Reformed Church   155
Worship at Bethania Chapel, Morriston in 1944   156
The Reverend Edward Squire, Vicar of Swansea, 1846-76   156
St Mary's Church, rebuilt 1955-9   157
The Royal Institution of South Wales, *c.* 1850   158
Swansea Grammar School, *c.* 1935   160
Swansea Municipal Secondary School, *c.* 1930   169
The National Schools, Oxford Street, 1847   170
Mayhill School   173
Seilo Newydd Chapel, Landore   175
Swansea Central Library, Alexandra Road, *c.* 1904   185
Sketty Hall, built *c.* 1758   191
Regency Houses in Cambrian Place   193
The Public Assembly Rooms, Cambrian Place, opened 1821   194
Hendrefoilan House, Sketty, built 1855   195

Page

Walter Road, *c.* 1910   199
Swansea Workingmen's Institute, built 1885   203
Head Post Office, Wind Street, opened 1901   205
Swansea Harbour Trust Offices, opened 1903   206
Swansea Central Police Station, Alexandra Road,
    erected 1912-13   207
The Exchange Buildings, built 1913-15   208
Council housing at Mayhill, 1936   209
Interior of the Brangwyn Hall, opened 1934   211
Aerial View of the Post-war Reconstruction of the
    City Centre   212
Walter Savage Landor in 1804, from a Portrait by
    George Dance   219
Dylan Thomas: a Drawing by Alfred Janes   223
Amy Dillwyn in 1904   233
At the Old B.B.C. Studio, The Grove, Swansea, October 1949.
    Standing: John Griffiths (Producer), Seated (Left to Right):
    Vernon Watkins, John Prichard, Alfred Janes, Daniel Jones,
    Dylan Thomas   235
At Rhosili, June 1940. Dylan Thomas, Swansea friends,
    Wyn Lewis, Vernon Watkins   238
Kingsley Amis   241
The Theatre Royal, Temple Street, *c.* 1891   247
The Albert Hall, 1929   256
The Grand Theatre, opened 1899   258
The Palace Theatre (later The People's Bioscope Palace),
    c. 1906   259
Oxford Street, showing the Empire Theatre and
    Carlton Cinema, *c.* 1930   260
The Plaza Cinema, Kingsway, opened 1931   261
The Regatta at Mumbles, 1929   262
Victoria Park and St Helen's Rugby and Cricket Ground   264
Crowd Scene at St Helen's Ground, early 1950s   265
The All Blacks *versus* a West Wales XV at St Helen's, 1967   276
Glamorgan celebrates victory at St Helen's   277
Tom Kiley playing before the uncovered North Bank
    at the Vetch Field, 1952   279
Ivor Allchurch, 'The Golden Boy'   280
The Old Guildhall at Somerset Place, extended 1848   289
Slum Clearance at Cross Street, 1879   291

Page

Swansea Infirmary and Workhouse on the Burrows,
    originally built as the Bathing House   293
Swansea General Hospital, opened 1864   296
Election Card in support of Sir John Talbot Dillwyn
    Llewelyn, 1892   301
The Central Library, opened 1887, within its Townscape   302-3
The Swansea Corporation Electricity Power Station at the
    Strand, built 1899-1901   312
Works for the Construction of Main Drainage Scheme at the
    Corner of Bryn-y-Mor Road and King Edward Road, 1934   313
The Guildhall, opened 1934   315
Post-war Town Centre Reconstruction at the Kingsway, 1950   317
H.R.H. The Prince of Wales presenting the Charter of
    City Status at the Brangwyn Hall, 15 December 1969   318
Old Swansea Slums: Rosser Court, York Street, 1929   320
Advertising the Importance of Swansea for Coal Exporting
    and Patent Fuel Making, 1915   323
Women at Work in a Swansea Tinplate Works in the 1920s   325
Aerial view of the Main Entrance to the University College,
    Swansea   328
Industrial Dereliction in the Lower Swansea Valley, 1960s   330
Kitchen in a Council House at Cwmrhydyceirw, 1944   331
Electric Tramcar at Pentre Estyll, *c.* 1903   334
A City Mini-bus at Penygraig Road, Mayhill, 1989   345

COLOUR PLATES

Between pages 6–7:

Swansea Market Square, by John Nixon, 1799. (Trustees of the British Museum).
Map showing the Beaufort Coal Holdings at Trewyddfa, 1845. (University College of Swansea Library).
View of the Beaufort Bridge and Fforest Copperworks, *c.* 1790. (Royal Institution of South Wales, Swansea).

Between pages 22–3:

William Adolphus Knell, Copper Clippers off Mumbles. (Glynn Vivian Art Gallery, Leisure Services Department, Swansea City Council).
Coal Vessels in the North Dock, *c.* 1900. (Swansea City Archive Office, Guildhall, Swansea).

Between pages 182–3:

Dillwyn Cup and Saucer. (Glynn Vivian Art Gallery, Leisure Services Department, Swansea City Council).

Seascape with Three Barques, by James Harris. (Glynn Vivian Art Gallery, Leisure Services Department, Swansea City Council).

Swansea for Pleasure, by W. Grant Murray. (Glynn Vivian Art Gallery, Leisure Services Department, Swansea City Council).

Temple Street, by Will Evans, 1941. (Glynn Vivian Art Gallery, Leisure Services Department, Swansea City Council).

Between pages 198–99:

'And Death Shall Have No Dominion', by Ceri Richards. (Glynn Vivian Art Gallery).

Hafod Copperworks, by James Harris. (Glynn Vivian Art Gallery).

The Plas House, *c.* 1835. (Prys Morgan, Esq.).

Swansea Bay, Colts Hill, and Underhill, *c.* 1800, by Benjamin Barber of Bath. (Prys Morgan, Esq.).

Ann of Swansea, by W. J. Watkeys. (Glynn Vivian Art Gallery).

Between pages 294–5:

The Reservoir at Brynmill Park. (Swansea City Archive Office).

Cockle Woman, by Evan Walters. (Glynn Vivian Art Gallery).

Swansea Marina from Dylan Thomas Square, 1989. (Graham Humphrys, Esq.).

Between pages 310–11:

Hancocks Brewery, Little Wind Street, *c.* 1969. (Graham Humphrys, Esq.).

The Grand Theatre, after Modernization, 1989. (Graham Humphrys, Esq.).

List Of Figures And Tables

Page

Figure 1: The distribution of major industries in Swansea
in 1908 — 349

Table 1: Occupations of workers aged 10 or over in
Swansea County Borough in 1911 — 349-50

Table 2: Population, Housing, and Welsh-speaking in
Swansea, 1931-81 — 350

Figure 2: The Employment Structure of Swansea in 1911
and 1931 — 350-1

Table 3: Employment in Industry in Swansea County
Borough in 1931 — 352

Figure 3: The Employment Structure of Swansea in 1961
and 1981 — 353

Figure 4: The Growth of Housing in Swansea from 1915
to 1989 — 354

Table 4: Employment in Industry in Swansea County
Borough in 1961 — 354-5

Figure 5: The Urbanized Area of Swansea Bay City
in 1989 — 355

Table 5: Employment in Industry in Swansea and Morriston
Employment Exchange Areas + in 1981 — 356

PREFACE

Of all the cities and towns of Wales, Swansea has a history unsurpassed in length, importance, variety, and interest. Until now, however, there has been no handy account of its modern development available for the interested reader. This volume aims to fill that gap by presenting the history of the city with particular emphasis on the last and most formative two hundred and fifty years. It has been written by a team of authors, some of them Swansea-born and all of them having worked, lived in, and loved the city for many years. Compiling it has been a great joy for all of us.

In the Middle Ages Swansea was the capital of the Marcher Lordship of Gower, and for centuries it flourished as a small administrative centre, port, and market-town. Though there were early signs of its future industrial greatness, it was not until the coming of the Industrial Revolution in the first half of the eighteenth century that it really began to 'take off'. In the next hundred to a hundred and fifty years it became a metallurgical centre and port of world importance, expanding rapidly in size and population. Faced with all the complex and fearsome problems of a fast-growing industrial community, it pioneered the way and set new standards in urban government, public health provision, parks and housing, educational and cultural facilities, and the amenities of modern life. It also evolved a dynamic artistic and literary life and a vigorous popular culture, in Welsh and English, of rare interest and achievement. More recently, it has adjusted to the pressure of two world wars and painful economic and social change, but stands confident to face the challenge of the twenty-first century.

Editing this book has been an enormous pleasure for me, if only on account of the splendid co-operation I have had from all my collaborators. I should like to thank them one and all for their immediate readiness in responding to my invitation to contribute to the volume, and for the enthusiasm and punctuality they showed when writing their chapters. I am deeply grateful to them. Two among them deserve my special thanks. Mr Peter Stead took the initiative in proposing the volume and was kind enough to write his chapter thousands of miles away across the Atlantic when he was teaching at the University of North Carolina. Dr John Alban, the City Archivist, has been of quite exceptional assistance. In spite of ill-health, he not only wrote two chapters himself but also read all of them in typescript and made many useful suggestions. In addition, he was extra-ordinarily helpful over the bibliography and the choice of photographs. I should also like warmly to thank our publisher, Mr Christopher Davies. From the outset he has been tremendously enthusiastic about the project, which has benefited hugely as a result of his experience, skill and kindness. The craftsmen at our printers, Dynevor Printing Company, deserve our best thanks for the care and expertise they have shown in producing so handsome a volume.

Last, but not least, I must thank the Swansea City Council, and especially its leader, Councillor E. Tyssul Lewis, for the enlightened and public-spirited support and encouragement they have given this project.

Glanmor Williams

BEFORE THE INDUSTRIAL REVOLUTION

Glanmor Williams

Swansea is not one of those Welsh towns — Caerleon, Caernarfon, Caerwent, Cardiff, Carmarthen among them — whose origins may be traced back to a Roman settlement once existing on its site. Although Roman coins and pottery have been discovered within the bounds of the later medieval town of Swansea, no Roman fort ever previously stood there, because no military presence would have been needed between the forts of Neath and Loughor on the Roman road along the coast of south Wales. Nor, again, could Swansea claim to have been an ancient *llan* ('church, enclosure') founded by a Celtic saint, such as that associated with Illtud at Llantwit Major or Teilo at Llandeilo, even though early saints laboured earnestly in its vicinity. Throughout the Dark Ages, the *aber* or estuary of the Tawe remained, in Sir John Lloyd's evocative phrase, 'the haunt of gull and plover'. The simple and largely self-sufficient agrarian communities of that era had little trade and small need for urban centres. In so far as the lords of the commote of Gŵyr (Gower) needed some sort of primitive court to rule their subjects it may well have been sited at Loughor.

Not until the coming of the energetic and enterprising Scandinavian sea-rovers, from the tenth century onwards, did the situation begin to change. Operating from their bases in Ireland, the Norsemen thrust boldly into the Bristol Channel, bent on trading as well as raiding. With their keen eye for maritime advantage, they were quick to spot the possibilities of natural harbours and commercial potentialities. Among the places they lighted upon was the mouth of the Tawe, where they seem to have established a small community of traders. To it, as to other places along the south Wales coast, they gave a

Willelmus Comes Warwik omnibus Baronibus z Burgensibus z hominibus tam anglicis quin Walensibus z tam presentibus quin futuris salutem. Sciatotum sit omnibus vob z francis z anglicis tam presentibz quin futuris me concessisse z carta mea confirmasse burgensibus de Sweinesse has consuetudines. scilicet, unicuiquz burgensi burgagium cu omnibus suis pertinentiis scilicet, von assartis z unicuiquz septem acras ultra nemur z sup Burglakeshroc z pascua usqz Hadedebwye z usqz Thu z usqz ad fossam Sci David. z sic qd nullus actiam inde heat fit me z psatos burgenses z nemora undiqz circa burgum meum ad pascenda pecora sua quin longi in die ire potint z eadem nocte Ad domos suas redire. z porcos suos in nemore meo libe z quiete absqz consuetudine heant. Quic aute ad domos suas z sepes z naues suas faciendas reddendo de naue vii denar. z omne aliud nemur ad ignem eorum z ad omnia aisiamenta sua z ferend z ad uendend ubicunqz voluerint z potint. Omnes bestias salua z capra z senglario et marquina. Et insup infra Pulkanan z Blakepulle omne arenam ad piscarias suas faciend illis concessi. Et si forte Porpeys aute storgoun in alia piscaria captum sit, meu e. z ego dabo illi cui piscaria est xii denar ul unam summam frumenti. Et si burgenses ert polam piscem aliq in cape potint illorum sit. Et si mari recedente wrek ert polam inue nerint dimidium meum sit z dimidium illorum sit. Et si wrek inuenerint in suam terram meu sit totum. Et viuarien armigeri mei herbam ad equos meos capiant burgenses simul mei capiant cum ille, exceptis pratis meis. Et si in exercitu summoniero burg meos siue ad aliud effectu meu ibunt cum dispensa sua ita ut eadem nocte ad domos suas redire possint. Et si longi illos duxerim sup dispensam meam erunt. Et si lucrati fuint mediettate cont me heant. In dominibus suis z ert domos suas spacium von pedum in ripe ante hostia sua pace illis concessi z sup burgagia sua furnu bonu z ostre z omnia pertinentia sua libere z quiete. Et si burgens forfecerit z in curia mea ducti fuint, usu nemor eorum z no sit rogat p vad z pleg tunc placitabit in curia mea. Et si p pleg z vad roga fuint aute in curiam mea ducti fuit placitabit in hundred suo. Burgensis no debet alibi placitare ni in hundredo ni calumpnietur de tacione corpis mei aut opidi mei. Et si burgensis heat tacione calumpniat fuit purgabit se sexta manu p iur iurand ni in curia mea loqui uoluero Justicia mea ni placitabit hecense qin burgense teste pro hoc, alicui de cibo meo z de pane testificari con burgens. Qui effudit sanguine a nona diei sabbati usqz ad mane diei lune xl solid de forefco. Et a mane diei lune usqz ad nona sabbati vii den de forefco, excepto assaltu mediciato z forestall quis illud incurrat aduena scindat pannos ad detaillie ni emat pelles ni carnes ni de burgense qui burgens uult discede z uendit burgag suu z domu sua det iiii den theloneo z quiet sit z si nollet phendiiet p und inse p illud theloneu z si domu sua uend ni potuit faciat de hoc qd e sup tra uelle suu z si burgens uadit in negociu suu ibuat alic domni sua q reddat uirga sua z eat z reddat qin noluit iit ad ppa sua. Hec aute preditt concessi burg meis de Sweinesse z heres, con ad tenend de me z hed meis hereditarie singqz con reddendo in singlis annis xii den. Et ut hec concessio rata sit z irrefragabilis hos adhibui fore testes. Willm London z c.

La charte le Conte Willam de Warwik des burgeys de Sweinesse.

Scandinavian name, made up of two elements: *'Sveinn'*, an Old Norse proper name, plus *'sae-r, sja-r, sjo-r'* = 'sea', or, more probably, Old Norse *'ey'* = 'island' or 'inlet'. The name appears in a number of early forms, such as 'Sweynesse', 'Sueinesea', or 'Sweinesei'. Clearly, the origin of the name 'Swansea' — *pace* the local football club — had nothing to do with 'swans' and may have had little to do with 'sea' either. The instinct of the native-born Swansonian, who cannot bear to hear the name pronounced with a hard medial 's', is sound; for the true pronunciation has always been as though the name were spelt 'Swanzey' — as indeed it was, by John Miles in the seventeenth century when he founded the town of 'Swanzey' in Massachusetts, or by Daniel Defoe in 1722 *(see page 57)*. Who the original Sveinn or Swein may have been, we can only speculate. It has been suggested that he was Swein Forkbeard, king of Denmark 986-1014, who may indeed have had contacts with south Wales. But whether it was he or some one else who gave his name to Swansea, and when that happened, remains uncertain. Neither can we be sure of the nature of the first Scandinavian community or how long it lasted. Along with the Norse name, interestingly enough, two Welsh names for Swansea — Abertawe and Seinhenydd — also appear in the documents at an early date.

Only with the Norman conquest of south Wales early in the twelfth century does Swansea emerge plainly into the light of history. At that time the estuary of the Tawe lay within Gŵyr, the largest commote in Wales, a territorial unit bounded by the rivers Loughor, Aman, Twrch, and Tawe. Hitherto, Gŵyr had usually been linked with the commotes of Carnwyllion and Cydweli further west, and in 1106 was in the possession of a Welsh ruler, Hywel ap Goronwy, who was killed in that year. The king of England, Henry I, anxious to safeguard the interests of the Crown in south Wales by ensuring that Welsh territory came into safe Norman hands, conferred Gŵyr upon one of his most prominent and trustworthy vassals, Henry de Newburgh, earl of Warwick. The latter proceeded to transform the former commote into the marcher lordship of Gower and set about organizing and consolidating the Norman position there. Within his own lordship a marcher lord was virtually an independent ruler, and one of de Newburgh's first and most essential tasks, therefore, was to choose a *caput* or headquarters. The obvious choice for the lordship of Gower was Swansea and here de Newburgh erected his chief castle. It was not a stone building but a strongly-fortified timber one, built on the summit of a mound (motte), natural or man-made, and surrounded by

Charter of William de Newburgh, earl of Warwick, to the Burgesses of Swansea, 1158-84.

a flat area (bailey), defended by a ditch, bank, and palisade, and manned by his vassals, who held their lands from him on condition of performing castle-guard. This castle was the nerve centre of his lordship; serving as military citadel, barracks, seat of justice and administration, financial headquarters (evidence exists of coins being minted at Swansea in the twelfth century), prison, and, when he and his family were in residence, home.

Strategically, Swansea was admirably placed to oversee both the Gower peninsula and the hilly hinterland to the north; it controlled the main routes through the lordship, and, together with the castles of Loughor and Llandeilo Talybont, dominated the vital middle area. Remains of the trading community established earlier by the Norsemen probably still existed and could be used to protect the lordship against those continuing sea-borne raids known to have gone on long into the twelfth century. The harbour safeguarded both the mouth of the river and the vital ferry at its lowest crossing-point. The Tawe itself provided an excellent means of supplying the needs of castle and community and partly providing for their defence. A river offered further advantages which the Normans were quick to exploit wherever they built castles: it provided water for mills and early industries, sites for weirs and fish-traps, and a supplementary drinking-supply in times of low rainfall. The wisdom of the choice of site, made first by the Scandinavians and confirmed by the Normans, has been reinforced by the passage of time, even if the early founders could not possibly have foreseen many of the later advantages accruing to Swansea.

To be still more secure and flourishing, however, a *caput* like Swansea castle needed an adjoining community of traders and artisans. Hence the marcher lords' habit of capitalizing on their right to found boroughs — a privilege denied to an ordinary manorial lord and usually reserved to the Crown — in order to encourage immigrants to settle within them. Many of the oldest boroughs of south Wales were founded in just this fashion. Inhabited by non-Welsh settlers who were attracted by the inducements held out to them, these boroughs were just as integral a part of the pattern of Norman conquest as the castles. Swansea was typical of them; and though its earliest charter dates from some time between 1158 and 1184 — an early document by the standards of Welsh towns — it seems reasonable to assume that its borough status was first conferred upon it early in the twelfth century. Another characteristic Norman practice accompanying the found-ation of a borough was to set up, in or near the town, a Benedictine monastery, peopled by alien monks and endowed with the former possessions of the local Welsh church. As it happened, however, de Newburgh did not follow this custom in Gower; instead, he established a little priory at Llangenydd, a daughter cell of the abbey of St Taurin in Evreux. Later, the Order of St John was endowed with land and founded a church dedicated to St John (now St Matthew's in High St.) on the northern outskirts of Swansea.

From early in the twelfth century, accordingly, the essential pattern of the life of the town for the next four hundred years — in some respects the next seven hundred years — had already been laid down. It consisted of four component elements, all interlocking with one another. First and foremost, it served as the *caput* of the lordship; this was its basic *raison d'être*. Second, it formed a focus of agricultural activity and the venue of the most important markets and fairs held within the lordship. Third, it acted as a centre of crafts, services, and early industries. Finally, it was a port; the base of merchants, mariners, fishermen, and boatbuilders. Its variety of roles attracted many people to it on military, legal, commercial, social, and other business. Infinitely small in size and population as compared with modern towns, it represented, nevertheless, the main concentration of people and wealth, however modest, within the medieval lordship of Gower.

Swansea served as local headquarters for a succession of eminent Norman families during the Middle Ages. For most of the twelfth century the lordship of Gower was ruled by the de Newburgh family until, in 1184, it passed into the hands of the King. For virtually the whole of the thirteenth century it was held by the oppressive and less than scrupulous de Braoses, from whom it passed in 1326 by the marriage of the last of their heiresses, Alina, to one of the Mowbrays. Eventually, in the fifteenth century, it came to a family of Welsh origins, the Herberts, with whose heirs, the Somersets, successively earls and marquesses of Worcester and dukes of Beaufort, it has remained until today. These grandees were rarely resident in Swansea and were content to entrust their day-to-day authority to their chief official, the seneschal or steward. The *caput* was always referred to in documents in such a way as to suggest that it ranked as being of equal significance with the lordship. The town of Swansea, on the other hand, was seen as an inferior part of the lordship of Gower, 'whilst its castle was superior, capital, metropolitan' (W. H. Jones). One of the largest in south Wales, the castle dominated the town. The first motte-and-bailey structure, centred on what is now Worcester Place, was constructed of timber, and not until the thirteenth century was that

Swansea Castle.

View of Swansea Castle,
1838.

part of it known as the 'Old Castle' rebuilt in stone. Further extensions, called the 'New Castle', were added in the fourteenth century. Some doubt exists as to who was responsible for these later works. They have usually been attributed to Henry de Gower, bishop of St David's (1328-47), a native of the area, on account of the elegant arcaded parapets, which characterized a number of his buildings and were almost unique to him. But is has also been suggested that the Mowbrays may have built the 'New Castle' using masons previously employed by the bishop. As the most awesome and obvious expression of Norman power and alien rule in the neighbourhood, Swansea castle, like other similar strongholds, was the target of fierce Welsh hostility and was attacked and savaged on many occasions in the Middle Ages. The last of these occurred during the furious Glyndŵr Rebellion (1400-10), when castle and town were seized and the lordship ravaged.

Economic and social aspects of Swansea's medieval existence were

Swansea Market Square, by John Nixon, 1799.

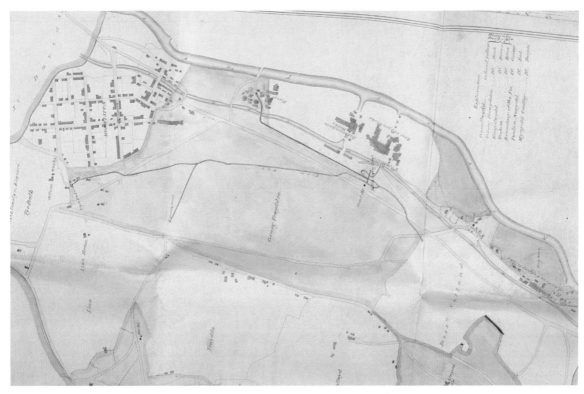

Map showing the Beaufort Coal Holdings at Trewyddfa, 1845.

View of the Beaufort Bridge and Fforest Copperworks, c. 1790.

determined largely by the borough charters granted to it by its over-lords. The latter were well aware that in order to attract settlers to their foundation they had to offer them incentives, while those who migrated there had every reason to want to see the terms on which they took up residence presented and defined. Both sides stood to benefit from such an arrangement, and the town's charters stipulated the conditions of the contract between overlord and burgess — what each could expect on the part of the other. The three most important charters were: the one granted by William de Newburgh between 1158 and 1184; King John's grant of freedom from the necessity of paying tolls elsewhere in the realm (1215), renewed in 1234 and 1322; and the lengthy and elaborate charter of 1306, arrived at after a long period of friction between lord and townsmen. The principal right enjoyed by the burgesses was burgage tenure, for which they paid a standard annual rent of 1s.0d. This freed them from any of the burdens normally attaching to feudal tenure and conceded to them the privilege of having their own ovens and brewhouses on their burgages. It also allowed them to claim the right to be tried in their own borough courts and not in the usual manorial courts for any offences they committed. The charters further conferred upon them freedom to exploit the natural advantages of the lands allocated to the borough: to till its fields; pasture livestock in its meadows, woods, and waters; make forest clearances; and take wood for building and repairing their homes, constructing ships, and for fuel. They were also allowed to trade freely through the port and within the lordship and to fish along the shore. The charter of 1306, in its provisions for the protection of burgesses against irregularities in court procedures and illegal financial exactions, brought to light the oppressive and inequitable practices of which the Braose family had long been guilty in relation to the townsfolk and offered safeguards for their future. It recognized their privilege of making an annual choice of a reeve, who would be con-firmed by their overlord. It also restated their right to utilize the common lands and mine coal for their own use, though they were not allowed to sell it to strangers.

For most of the activities of Swansea's burgesses during the Middle Ages information is painfully thin. But they were, undoubtedly, active cultivators and herdsmen, taking full advantage of the borough's extensive lands, which stretched from the sea along the River Tawe as far as the Burlais Brook (Cwmbwrla = the valley of the Burlais), and from there all the way round to the Clyne Valley and down to the sea again at Blackpill. They were as anxious as most medieval communities to ensure their own food supply as far as possible and not to have to depend on others for it, though it seems likely that they may have had to import some of their corn supply from English sources. Another link between the town and the agriculture of the surrounding lordship was forged by Swansea's right to hold weekly markets and annual fairs — one of the most highly prized prerogatives of any medieval town. The borough would, moreover, have been the local centre of specialists and artisans of all kinds — lawyers, scriveners, shopkeepers, innkeepers, millers (there would have been a town mill where all were obliged to grind their corn), blacksmiths, carpenters, boatbuilders, craftsmen in wool and leather, sailors, fishermen, and the like. Apart from agriculture and its associated crafts, the two kinds of early industry which loomed largest were the trades in leather and in wool and cloth. Additionally, no small part of the town's prosperity derived from its being a busy little port. An indication of the importance of shipping was the right granted to the citizens in the charter of 1306 to build four 'great ships' every year and an unlimited number of small boats, many of which might have been used for inshore fishing as well as trade. In the absence of documentary evidence of any significance, we can do little more than conjecture about the commercial activities in which townspeople might have been engaged. Trade was likely to have been similar to that of Carmarthen and Milford Haven, which are known to have maintained close and regular contacts with ports along the Bristol Channel, south-west England, Ireland, and even France. Corn, cloth, and manufactures might have been expected to be shipped in from Bristol and the Severn ports, fish and cloth from Ireland, and wine and salt from France. Evidence of such imports from France and Bristol comes in the form of finds made in Swansea of pottery originating from France and of particularly large quantities of it made in Bristol, the emporium of the south Wales coast for centuries. Exports from Swansea, like those from other south Welsh harbours, probably included butter, cheese, hides, wool, and timber, and in the later medieval period, woollen cloth, coal, and lime. At the time of Edward I's Welsh wars, in 1276 and 1282-3, Swansea was sufficiently well-established as a port to have been required to take part in the king's plans for assembling men and supplies destined for his campaigns against the last independent princes of Wales.

Down to about the middle of the fourteenth century the story of Swansea would appear to have been one of modestly successful growth. In spite of frequent and damaging attacks by hostile Welsh

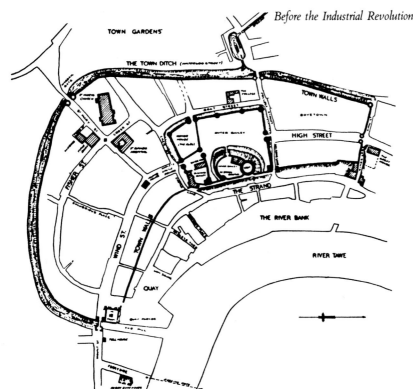

Conjectural reconstruction of fourteenth-century Swansea.

princes and people in the course of the twelfth and thirteenth centuries, the town, like many medieval boroughs, had shown surprising resilience and powers of recovery. Its buildings, except for the castle and churches, were mostly unpretentious affairs, made of timber, wattle and mud; easily burnt, they could also be rebuilt without too much trouble. Not that medieval Swansea was ever anything more than a small town — no bigger than a modern village. Its population probably never numbered more than about 1,000-1,500, though that was bigger than most Welsh towns in an age when most of the market-towns in Europe ranged between 500 and 2,000 in the number of their inhabitants. The conjectured street plan of about the year 1400 shows a small, rough semi-circle of buildings extending outwards a short distance from the Tawe and the castle. To these should probably be added two tiny 'suburbs'; the one clustered outside the north gate, and the other on the east bank of the Tawe at the ferry crossing. In 1317 and 1338 the authorities felt sufficiently confident — or apprehensive, perhaps! — to raise money, by means of murage tolls, to build town walls, a few fragments of which still remain. In 1332, also, Bishop Henry de Gower showed enough pride in Swansea, as well as his deep concern for the aged and infirm among priests and laymen, to found the Hospital (almshouse we might call it) of the Blessed David (the Cross Keys public house still stands on part of the site) to house them.

Gable-end of the Cross Keys Inn, showing fourteenth-century windows, c. 1879.

Did the city fathers of the period but know it, however, Swansea, like most parts of Europe, was on the brink of a long spell of economic and social turmoil. For the best part of a century after *c.* 1335 the age was one of economic decline, depopulation, war, and rebellion. Severe famines early in the century, from 1315 to 1317, were followed by the Black Death of 1349-51 and other visitations of pestilence at intervals later. It is impossible to tell precisely how Swansea was affected; but since plagues are certainly known to have had dire consequences for the lordship of Gower and since ports and estuaries generally suffered more severely than the surrounding countryside, the chances are that Swansea's population fell alarmingly. The problems were aggravated by the Crown's repeated demands in the course of its periodic campaigns during the Hundred Years' War (1337-1453), which led to heavy taxation, depreciation of the currency, and inflation. All these difficulties were drastically compounded by the ravages of the destructive and protracted Rebellion of Owain Glyndŵr (1400-10), in the course of which the lordship of Gower was devastated. In most parts of Wales this long succession of disasters left in their wake malign consequences, from which Swansea was almost certainly not immune. It may be symptomatic of the borough's exigencies that its burgesses made no attempt for two centuries after 1332 to secure any renewal or extension of their privileges by means of a new charter.

As it so happens, three major sets of accounts relating to the town have fortuitously survived for the years 1367, 1400, and 1449, respectively, to give us some inkling of Swansea's situation during the later Middle Ages. At first sight, they appear to reveal a catastrophic drop in income and prosperity. Revenues recorded from a number of sources fell alarmingly: the rent from the corn mill went down from £16.13s.4d. in 1367 to £9.6s.8d. in 1449; revenue from tolls plummeted from £12.1s.3d. to £2.6s.8d.; and that from the Hundred Court, even more calamitously, was decimated from £34.7s.0d. to £3.10s.9d. Swansea was not exceptional in this respect; income from many other towns and lordships in the Welsh March slumped equally disastrously during these years. Yet the drop was only partly caused by decline and adversity; by the mid fifteenth century there is other evidence of recovery and restructuring in economic life. The Marcher lords, however, having relaxed their grip over their financial and judicial administration in the course of earlier crises, had in most instances quite failed to recover anything like full control of their officials. Income which ought to have been accruing to them was either being witheld, or not being collected, on specious grounds. Deficiencies which were usually attributed to the dislocation caused by plague, war, or rebellion, were in reality being caused by the slackness and/or dishonesty of officials and tenants. In Swansea, for example, the fifteenth century had witnessed the setting up of at least four new and highly lucrative fulling mills, from which the lord was not receiving the income to which he was entitled. This could well have been only one example of fraudulent practices out of many. Similarly, it is known that by the second half of the century Swansea, along with a number of other south Welsh ports, enjoyed distinctly profitable contacts with Bristol and other trading centres. Again, by 1532 the burgesses of the town were alert and active enough to arrive at an agreement with their overlord, the earl of Worcester, designed to safeguard their interests in relation to the cloth and leather trades. All

in all, it seems reasonable to conclude that by the beginning of the
sixteenth century Swansea had recovered to some extent from the
crises which may earlier have beset it and was poised to take advantage
of the opportunities of a new age.

That new era in the history of Wales generally was initiated partly
by the policies of the Tudor dynasty. Its second representative, Henry
VIII, and his Parliament enacted legislation during the years 1536-43,
usually known as the Act of Union, which integrated Wales
completely into England, swept away the outmoded legal and
administrative arrangements of the Marcher lordships, and replaced
them with a régime based on English law and the English shire system.
The former lordship of Gower was merged with that of Glamorgan to
form the new county of Glamorgan. Viewed in the light of earlier
history, this was an 'unnatural' union, since Gower's traditional links
had always tended to lie with areas in west Wales not in the south-east.
In the process, the lordship of Gower lost its quasi-autonomous status,
which meant among other things that Swansea's role as its *caput* was
extinguished too; nor was it compensated by becoming Glamorgan's
shire-town, a distinction which instead devolved upon Cardiff. Such
downgrading might conceivably have been a fatal blow to Swansea's
future. Writing of the fate of other former capitals of lordships, that
intelligent observer, George Owen of Henllys, commented how,
'being placed in wild and obscure places inapt for any trade', 'they fell
into ruin and utter decay'. Fortunately for Swansea, however, it was
one of those towns that was convenient 'for a market town, or else had
some good port or habour fit for trading by sea'. Consequently, 'it fell
to some good trade and so flourished' and was able to uphold itself 'in
some reasonable wealth'. In other words, the economic functions fulfilled by Swansea since its inception, as market-town, regional centre,
and port, heavily outweighed the loss of its former position as *caput* of a
lordship.

Though no longer a *caput*, Swansea still retained its status as a
borough. The structure and operation of its municipal government
become much more intelligible from the sixteenth century onwards,
thanks mainly to the careful way in which its town records have been
preserved. The municipal archives, apart from a handful of charters,
begin in the Tudor period and constitute one of the best collections of
their kind in Wales. They provide a surprisingly clear picture of how
and by whom the town was administered. A decisive voice was still
exercised by the lords of Gower, the earls of Worcester. This they
contrived through the medium of their stewards, normally chosen

from among the more prominent families of local gentry, like the imperious Sir George Herbert (d. 1570) in the first half of the sixteenth century. The steward presided at the two Courts Leet, attended by the burgesses and held on the Feast of St Philip and St James (1 May) and at Michaelmas (29 September), when the borough officials were appointed and burgesses admitted. The steward chose the portreeve (the equivalent of mayor) annually from two aldermen nominated by the burgesses. The council of the borough was composed of twelve aldermen, chosen for life by the burgesses. The latter, with whom ultimate power in theory lay, formed only about 8 to 10 per cent of the total population. They became burgesses by one of four routes: inheritance, marriage to the daughter of a burgess, apprenticeship to a burgess, or by gift of the corporation. Below the portreeve, aldermen, and burgesses came a series of officials, some appointed for life, some for a year only. Most important among them were the common attorneys, who administered the corporation finances. There were a number of others, including such picturesquely-named minor dignitaries as 'ale-tasters', 'waiters of the market', and 'steward of the mountain'. The records of the aldermen in council and the burgesses in Common Hall were concerned with two matters principally — the regulation of trade and the treatment of the poor. During this period the relief of the poor became increasingly shared with the parish and its officials. The parish was the other ruling body of the town, also presided over by the portreeve and operated under his control. Theorectically it was made up of all the inhabitants of the parish, but it, too, was dominated by the same small group of leading citizens. Among its responsibilities were the upkeep of highways and bridges, the relief of maimed soldiers and distressed sailors, the relief of the poor, the supervision of the gaol, and the extinction of vermin.

The minority of burgesses was concerned to limit its own numbers at this time because the privileges resulting from burgess status were still of considerable value. Only burgesses were free from those tolls on merchandise entering the town by land or sea which non-burgesses or 'sensers' were strictly required to pay. They also had the right to trade free of charge within the borough — again in marked contrast to the non-burgesses. Another of their prerogatives was communal trading: all cargoes brought into the port must be offered for sale to the burgesses in the first instance, and only when their needs had been satisfied was the residue made available for purchase by others. Borough property, too, could only be leased to burgesses, usually at an advantageous rental. Finally, there were the minor delights of corporation feastings and merrymakings, held annually at Easter and Michaelmas and on other special occasions for national rejoicing. Quite apart from the burgesses' desire to keep down their numbers, their overlord had his own reasons for not wishing to see them increase. Under the terms of the Act of Union, Swansea became one of the boroughs whose burgesses participated in the return of a Member of Parliament for Glamorgan Boroughs. The fewer the burgesses, the smaller the number of voters, and the easier they were for the lord to control in the interests of his own favoured candidate.

There were, however, some few indications of an incipient spirit of independence on the part of the burgesses. Whereas in 1548 they appeared to be suitably deferential to the steward, the autocratic Sir George Herbert, referring to him obsequiously as their 'chief head and governor' and humbly beseeching him 'in the way of charity and for God and love' to allow their by-laws to be put in force, by 1566 their attitude seems markedly to have changed. The earl of Worcester then complained to his steward, Sir Edward Mansel, 'for that the Corporation will bear their money against me in any suit, I think they might as well come to cut my throat . . . I take them to be careless but only to serve their own turn'. A few years later, when enacting an important set of by-laws, the burgesses declared spiritedly, if somewhat unhistorically, that the 'custom and usage of the Town of Swansea long before time of memory hath been that the Aldermen from time to time have used and had authority to make and erect laws and ordinances for the well government of the public estate and wealth of the said town'. The independence of the townsfolk ought not, however, to be overemphasized. Overlord and corporation still had need of one another and would continue in that state for a long time to come. The lord had an enduring interest in overseeing the affairs of a borough from which he derived considerable income and prestige and where he had a dominant voice at election times. The town, on its side, was small and glad to have a protector with influence at Court and in high places. Both parties stood to gain from harmonious mutual interdependence in an age of economic growth and expansion.

Contemporary Tudor governments were concerned to give what help they could to advance the economic welfare of their subjects. They encouraged agriculture, industry, and trade by paternalistic measures like the Navigation Acts, which provided for the carrying of goods in British ships. The Act of Union, too, provided for the absorption of Wales into the realm, thus bringing the country and its resources more fully under such rudimentary economic direction as the state was able to provide. An early example was an Act of Parliament of 1544 which included Swansea among other Welsh towns described as being in decay and in need of rehabilitation. At the beginning of Elizabeth's reign came an attempt to rationalize the customs organization along the Welsh coast for the first time. Swansea was placed under the head port of Cardiff but was given its own customs house in 1573. The new system, disliked by the locals — especially by bigwigs like the earl of Worcester, who saw themselves losing revenue to the Crown — took a long time to settle down, and even as late as 1615 the deputy controller of customs at Swansea was accused of accepting bribes and favours in return for turning a Nelsonian eye to illegal imports and exports at the port.

It was not royal policy, all the same, which principally accounted for the remarkable expansion of economic activity during the century from *c.* 1540 to 1640. The main stimulus was the steep growth in demand brought about by a big increase in population during those years, when the population of Wales rose from about 250,000 to about 400,000 and was accompanied by an equally swift rise in prices, which went up five- or six-fold. Nearly all Welsh towns benefited as a result, and Swansea more than most. Its earlier role as market-town, centre of crafts and services, and as a port above all, was vigorously enhanced during this century. The 'king's antiquary', John Leland, *c.* 1536-9, referred to it as 'the market town and chief place of Gower'. Markets were held there twice a week, on Wednesdays and Saturdays, to which the farmers from round about came to sell and buy. Many of the townspeople themselves continued to have a vital interest in the market so it is not surprising that a new and improved market house should have been built in the town in 1651. Swansea was also the centre for three annual fairs, which attracted traders from far and near for the sale of livestock, on which the economic life of the whole area largely depended. It also maintained its function as a centre of crafts and trades. Thanks to the municipal records we are able to trace a remarkably wide and varied range of wares and services being offered there. The three most important interests represented among them were clothing, building, and food and drink, in which many traders and craftsmen were engaged — shoemakers, tailors, hatters, glovers, tanners, and tuckers in clothing, for example; carpenters, tilers, masons, paviers, and glaziers in building; or bakers, butchers, vintners, millers, and fishmongers in food and drink.

But Swansea's most important function, on which its growth and prosperity were coming increasingly to depend, was that of a busy

port. In 1655, in Oliver Cromwell's charter to the town, he could refer
to it with more than a little pride as 'an ancient port town and
populous, situate on the sea-coasts towards France, convenient for
shipping and resisting foreign invasions'. For a century beforehand the
municipal authorities had been paying more minute attention to the
state of the harbour and the welfare of shipping. Careful regulations
had been laid down for the repair of the quay and the disposal of ballast
so that the waterways should not become cluttered up. Throughout
the first half of the seventeenth century enterprising individuals like
Walter Thomas of Danygraig had been engaged on improving the
quay and building small docks. A new quay was built in 1652 and considerable sums were subsequently spent on repairing and extending it.
Symptomatic of the growth in trade was the marked increase in boat
and ship building along the riverside. In 1642 a graving dock had been
constructed; and by 1652 so much boat building was going on at the
quay that it had to be rigorously controlled because it was in danger of
seriously impeding traffic in the port.

What had partly contributed to the rising volume of trade was the
development of the traditional commerce characteristic of the Middle
Ages — the import of salt, wine, corn, fruit, and fine cloth, and the
export of the typical products of south Wales like butter, cheese, hides,
leather, wool, and so on. But the decisive factor had been the
prodigious growth in the export of coal. Coal was king and by the
seventeenth century it had made Swansea the busiest port in Wales.
Happily, the rise of the trade is illustrated in the port books of the
period, which have been preserved from Elizabethan times onwards.
Although they are a financial not a trading record, noting the amount
paid in customs dues — which were often evaded — and not the total
volume of goods carried, and though there are many years for which
they no longer exist, they nevertheless contrive to provide a far more
detailed picture of contemporary trade than anything available for the
Middle Ages. Thus, between 1591 and 1600, some 3,000 tons of coal
were exported from Swansea in an average year, whereas by the
decade from 1631 to 1640 that had increased four-fold to an average of
12,000 tons in a year. This swiftly growing demand for coal arose from
its wider use as fuel in a whole range of industries, in agriculture where
it was used to burn lime in lime-kilns before spreading it on the land,
and for domestic purposes. Demand for coal in south Wales was
limited and most of what was being mined in or near Swansea was
destined for export. Of the comparatively large quantities leaving by
sea, much was dispatched coastwise to a variety of ports along the

Somerset, Devon, and Cornwall shore of the Bristol Channel and the south coast of England; and further amounts were exported to France and the Channel Islands. The trade was seasonal in character, being confined mainly to the summer months, with the period from November to February ruled out on account of the unfavourable weather and the short hours of daylight. Though much of the cargo was carried in ships from the importing ports, local vessels were also prominently engaged; the 40-ton *Jonas* of Swansea, for instance, made at least half a dozen round trips from Swansea to Rochelle in 1587-8, and in the year 1629-30, 42 out of 57 shipments from the port were carried by local ships.

The little coalpits around Swansea had been able to meet this demand for two reasons. First, the coal in the vicinity outcropped near the surface and was easy to work in an age when technology was too rudimentary to allow it to be mined at any depth. Second, the coal lay relatively near the sea and could be transported by water, the only way of moving it any distance when the roads were primitive and inadequate. So, wherever coal could thus be won, men were busily engaged in mining it. Even gentry families of standing, like the Mansels of Margam or the Thomases of Danygraig, were eager to become involved in this profitable activity. Smaller men also became active entrepreneurs, and there is evidence of the remarkably early emergence in the town and district of an embryonic proletariat of full-time colliers. Attracted by the possibility of profit or employment, people were moving into Swansea from the surrounding countryside and even further afield — some from as far away as Ireland. The foundations of the future industrial greatness of Swansea and its environs were already being laid in Tudor and Stuart times and the way being prepared for the coming of the Industrial Revolution.

It is not only the nature of the town's economic activity that becomes clearer during this era but its social structure as well. It now becomes possible to make estimates of its population that are far less hazy than ever before. A Chantry Certificate of 1545 gives the number of Swansea's 'houseling people' (i.e., adults over the age of confirmation) as 600, which, multiplied by a half, would yield a total population of roughly 900. A bishop's certificate of 1563 returns the number of households as 180 and, allowing an average of 5 per household, that also gives a total of 900. Both sets of statistics are no more than rough-and-ready round figure guesses; but a population of 900-1,000 for Swansea would not be much out of line with what is known of other south Wales towns at the time. Calculations for 1631 and 1639 made by

Dr W. S. K. Thomas on the basis of the births, marriages and deaths recorded in the parish registers render estimated population totals of 1,390 in 1631 and 1,887 in 1639. Taking a median figure of, say, 1,650, would give us an increase of the order that might be expected over this period. A survey of the town taken in 1650 shows that its population was housed in only about ten or a dozen streets, including High Street, Wind Street, West Street, Fisher Street, Castle Bailey Street, Frog Street, Cross Street, Goat Street, and Wassail Street. The survey reveals in all about 162 tenements in Swansea at this time; but there must have been about twice as many households. Of the tenements, 136 were inside the walls and 26 outside. It was still a tightly-knit little community; small enough for everyone to know everyone else, and one where everybody knew his place in society and was expected to keep to it. One of the features of the composition of the Tudor population had been the marked increase in the proportion of Welsh people. Medieval Swansea had been an Anglo-Norman town, from which the Welsh had been largely excluded. That had been changed by the Act of Union, which placed the Welsh on an equal footing with the English and encouraged many of them to migrate into the towns. By the 1590s there were enough of them in Swansea to demand their church services in Welsh. In speech and culture, however, it remained mainly English, like most market towns in Wales, though then as now a good deal of Welsh must have been heard when people came in to shop and trade.

As far as the social structure was concerned, the townspeople were divided into four groups, broadly speaking. At the top of the tree came a small group of local gentry families and, closely associated with them, a handful of the wealthiest merchants. It is not easy to distinguish between them because many of the gentry were engaged in trade or industry as well as landed pursuits, while many of the merchants had farming interests, and in the lists of their goods and chattels made when they died are abundant references to their crops, livestock, and farming implements. These groups, as would be expected, lived in the best houses. During the century or so after 1560 Swansea, like other Welsh towns, underwent something of a housing revolution, in the course of which the well-to-do built themselves new houses or dramatically remodelled medieval dwellings. They now lived in commodious houses, containing a number of rooms, all well-furnished and boasting glazed windows; dwellings which provided them with more warmth, comfort, light, and privacy. Swansea's biggest and finest house was Plas Newydd or New Place, which stood until Victorian times, when it was pulled down to make way for Ben Evans' store on the corner of what is now Castle Gardens. Built originally by Sir Matthew Cradock early in the sixteenth century, it was much extended by his grandson, Sir George Herbert, when he acquired the former Hospital of the Blessed David in 1549. The degree of material comfort enjoyed by the richest members of the community is well illustrated by the will and inventory of John Morris, gentleman, who died in 1608, leaving behind him a large list of luxurious furniture and fittings, including a Spanish bed, Turkish carpet, rugs, carved and embroidered chairs, cushions of gilded leather, taffeta curtaining, silver plate and cutlery, and a mass of clothing.

Below this élite came the smaller traders, farmers, and craftsmen, who would understandably be far less wealthy and live in much more cramped surroundings. Their shops or workplaces would normally form part of the house in which they dwelt, and most of their capital would be tied up in the tools and materials of their trade. Their standard of living was much more modest in terms of accommodation, furnishing, clothes, and diet, but would, all the same, have enabled them to live a reasonably comfortable existence.

It is, nevertheless, reliably estimated that about half of the population of every town lived on or below the poverty line, and this was no doubt true of the poorer craftsmen, general labourers, colliers, and seafarers who lived in Swansea. At the best of times there existed among them a good deal of insecurity and unemployment; and, having no social security system as a safety-net against hard times, sickness, or adversity, they were often dependent on charitable relief and voluntary hand-outs. Their diet tended to be monotonous and inadequate; sickness and disease were commonplace; infant and child mortality was rife; and the expectation of life was low — 30-35 years. Their housing tended to consist of one- or two-roomed hovels, and many had to survive as best they could in other people's cellars, passages, and outhouses. Subject to the usual evils of overcrowded, insanitary, and squalid conditions, the poorest among them were under-nourished and wretchedly clothed, a ready prey to the epidemic diseases which were not infrequent visitors.

Right at the bottom of the scale came the paupers; those who were unable to make their own living, however inadequately, and had to depend on the charity of others. They included the old, the unemployed and unemployable, the chronically sick and disabled, and very young orphan children. The problem of poverty emerged on a greatly enlarged scale in the sixteenth century and raised nightmares of fear and anxiety in the minds of local and national governors. In 1603 the burgesses of Swansea voiced their profound concern about what they described as paupers of 'evil lives and ungodly living' who frequented 'disorderly alehouses to the great loss of the burgesses'. The corporation took draconian measures to try to check the entry of such people into the town and insisted on removing even cripples and pregnant women from other parishes so that they should not become a burden on the Swansea rates. To relieve their own poor, the corporation kept down the price of corn in time of scarcity, bought food and clothing for the destitute, and administered charitable gifts and bequests. But many of the paupers still depended on the benevolence of their own more fortunate neighbours; a paragon of such charitable virtue was Hopkin David, according to a verse on his gravestone:

> The relics of a saint here lie
> Who spent his days in piety;
> The poor come here and raise their cry
> To feel their alms deeds with him die.

A major social change of the period imposed by statute on the whole population, rich and poor alike, was the Reformation. Following some uncertainty when the country swung first to Protestantism under Henry VIII (1509-47) and Edward VI (1547-53) and back again to Catholicism under Mary I (1553-58), a Protestant régime, which proved to be permanent, was established under Elizabeth I in 1559. These Reformation changes swept away the pope's authority, the monastic orders, the medieval hospital, the Latin rite, and the medieval appearance and practices of church, clergy and people; altars, roodscreens, images, vestments, pilgrimages, mass, and the rest, all now disappeared. They were replaced by the royal supremacy, a Protestant prayer book, vernacular services, and a simplified church order. If there was any opposition in Swansea to such sweeping alterations, no evidence of it has survived. By the early seventeenth century, indeed, there are indications that moderate Puritan sympathies were taking root in the town. The corporation paid for the delivery of a number of sermons, some of which were preached by Puritan sympathizers; and a number of citizens took to giving their children Old Testament names, hitherto unknown in Swansea and usually a sign of Puritan inclinations.

Mention of Puritan sympathies is a timely reminder of those convulsive upheavals of the 1640s and 1650s in which Swansea, together with the rest of the kingdom, was caught up: the wars between King Charles I's supporters and those of Parliament from 1642-51, which ended in a defeat for the royalists and the short-lived triumph of the Puritan régime between 1648 and 1660. When the civil wars broke out, Swansea appeared to be solid in its support for the king's cause. The lord of Gower, the earl of Worcester, was one of Charles' richest and staunchest supporters, whose influence was thrown in heavily on the king's side. So was that of the rest of the local gentry and even the leading merchants. But from the outset there was a potential opposition, small but determined, drawn from among some of the minor gentry and yeomen; men like Philip Jones of Llangyfelach, who held Puritan convictions, fought in the parliamentary armies, and were to be prominent in the government of Swansea and south Wales after the war was won. During the campaigns themselves Swansea was a base of some importance for the royalists: a garrison town, royal arsenal, and port of entry from the Continent. In 1645, however, it fell to Parliament and Col. Philip Jones became its governor. Two years later, Oliver Cromwell himself was made lord of Gower and in 1648 came to Swansea in the course of the second civil war. The overall impact of the conflicts on the town was very damaging. Trade was disrupted, many markets were closed, and its prosperity was further reduced by the need to convoy ships and the heavy taxes imposed on coal exports. It was not to be wondered at that, in the 1650s, much solicitude should be shown in adopting measures to revive the port, reinvigorate shipping, and re-establish the well-being of markets and fairs. At this time, with Cromwell's Protectorate firmly in the saddle nationally, a number of individuals and families new to government emerged to take control of the town's destinies.

Along with the political changes went far-reaching modifications of the church and religion. Even before the civil wars, Swansea was one of the few places in Wales where Puritanism had taken root, and a small independent Puritan church was founded there in 1642, just before the war broke out. Not until about 1645, however, when the parliamentary armies had won sweeping victories, could the Puritans hope to make much real progress in Wales. From then on, and throughout the 1650s, a number of leading ministers were active in Swansea. Independents, Presbyterians, Baptists, and Quakers, all revelling in governmental encouragement, were able to form vigorous congregations in the town. Side by side with these activities went interesting experiments in education. The Propagation Act of 1650

*Colonel Philip Jones
(1618-74).*

made provision for the setting up of a number of schools in Wales; the first time that the state had ever assumed responsibility on this scale for the education of its subjects. One such school was founded in Swansea but does not appear to have been an outstanding success; the main reason for its limited effectiveness being the strong subterranean prejudice against Puritanism among whole sections of the townspeople. The majority among them showed their real feelings in 1660, when they rapturously welcomed the restoration of the monarchy in the person of Charles II and the re-establishment of the Anglican church.

William Adolphus Knell, Copper Clippers off Mumbles.

Coal vessels in the North Dock, c. 1900.

With the fifty or sixty years that followed the Restoration we reach the last phase in the history of old Swansea before the dawn of the industrial age proper. The Restoration was followed by a long period of relative peace and stability that provided conditions ripe for an age of commerce that preceded the age of industry. Swansea's earlier history of economic enterprise and activity made it one of the Welsh towns best fitted to take advantage of this era of expansion. The agricultural production of the neighbourhood continued to thrive, finding a ready market across the Bristol Channel as well as at home, and was reflected in some of the mixed cargoes dispatched from the port. A ship sailing to Bridgwater in 1682, for example, as well as carrying a cargo of about 80 tons of coal had on board 20 gallons of butter, 60 Welsh pigs, and 40 sheep; and another vessel at about the same time carried 80 tons of coal, 60 gallons of butter, 20 bushels of oatmeal, 16 cattle, and 40 sheep. Industries linked to the products of agriculture, like clothmaking or tanning leather, were still buoyant, as were soapmaking or glass working, which depended on the ashes derived from burning kelp or seaweed. But the vital industry, still growing fast, continued to be coal; between 1700 and 1740 at least sixteen collieries are known to have been at work in the neighbourhood of Swansea, with more and more of their colliers being employed full time. Coalmining also had a valuable 'knock-on' effect in providing other kinds of non-agricultural employment for farmers, glad to use their horses and carts for the transport of coal, as well as for the labourers who manhandled it into boats at the river side. By the early eighteenth century Swansea had developed into an extremely busy coal harbour, with many 'coal places' ranged along the quays. Daniel Defoe, a shrewd and lively observer, commented on it in admiring terms in 1722 (*see page 57*) and his description is attested by statistics drawn from the contemporary port books. Coastwise shipments of coal from Swansea in the years 1709, 1710, and 1711 amounted to 9,861 tons, 8,694 tons, and 8,940 tons, respectively, with another 2,532 tons and 3,195 tons going to Ireland in 1709 and 1710; Ireland having now taken over from France as a major market. Many Swansea ships are also recorded in the same port books, with the total tonnage of coasting vessels belonging to the port amounting to 2,148 tons in 1709.

It was the success of the coal industry which led directly to the beginnings of the large-scale smelting of metals in the locality of Swansea during the first quarter of the eighteenth century. Already, late in the seventeenth century, Sir Humphrey Mackworth had begun

View of Swansea by Francis Place, 1678.

smelting metals at Neath. In 1717 a works for the smelting of copper and lead ores was established on the banks of the Tawe at Landore by Dr Lane of Bristol. His example was followed in 1720 at the junction of the Burlais brook with the Tawe, when James Griffiths and other local Quakers set up the Cambrian Works. When Lane went bankrupt his works were acquired by Morris, Lockwood and Co. in 1727. These smelters came for the most part from Cornwall, Bristol, London, or other older-established areas. They were attracted to Swansea by its convenient harbour facilities and still more by the ample coal supplies which the successful local coal industry was making available. What they dubbed 'the cheapness of coals and labour' was crucial, since it took some eighteen tons of fuel to smelt four tons of copper ore in order to produce one ton of copper. It was therefore manifestly more convenient to bring the copper ore to the coal than vice versa. These years saw the foundations being firmly set in place for the future metallurgical greatness of Swansea. Some of the 'big names' among the industrial entrepreneurs — Mackworth, Lane, and Morris — had already appeared on the scene; but links presaging the future close contacts between Swansea people and the West Country were also

already in place, in the shape of contemporary wills in which testators made provision for their kinsfolk across the Bristol Channel as naturally as if they lived in Glamorgan.

As a result of the economic growth already noted, the population of Swansea continued to grow apace. The returns made in 1670 in connection with the Hearth Tax record 325 households in the town. Allowing an average of 4.5-5 per household that would give a population of 1,460-1,625. Tax returns, however, notoriously tend to underestimate the population, since the tax-net was not normally close-meshed enough to catch all those who ought to have paid; so we might reasonably add, say, another 100-200 to allow for tax-evasion and other errors, giving us a total of 1,750-1,800. For the 1690s and the 1710s it is possible to use the parish registers again, using the same statistical basis as that employed by Dr Thomas. For the years between 1690 and 1697 the average figure based on births and deaths works out at about 1,840, and for the years 1712-20 at 1,830 — a surprisingly consistent total. However, it is necessary to remember that a large proportion of the population were now Dissenters by conviction and so would not have their births or deaths recorded in Anglican registers.

In 1676 no fewer than 298 Dissenters were recorded in the Swansea area and even that figure is considered to be on the low side. It therefore seems likely that by the beginning of the eighteenth century, allowing for a Dissenting population (including their children) of 400-500, the population of Swansea was in the region of 2,250-2,400. It continued to expand throughout the eighteenth century and by the time of the first Census of 1801 had reached 6,099, the second highest figure for a town in Wales, being exceeded only by Merthyr Tydfil (7,000+).

The number of burgesses was not increasing to anything like the same extent. In proportion to the total population, the ratio of burgesses was actually falling, since most of the Dissenters, who included in their midst some of the most enterprising and radical elements among the inhabitants, were excluded from the government of the town. The burgesses were tending to become a narrower 'closed shop' all the while, having apparently lost much of the drive and initiative which had characterized them in the sixteenth and early seventeenth centuries. They were content to be ruled more and more by their overlords, whose powers had been underlined and augmented in the charters issued to Swansea by Cromwell (1655) and King James II (1685). Authority passed increasingly into the hands of the lord's stewards and a confined circle of their cronies among the leading burgesses *(see pages 96–102)*.

The Restoration of 1660 had brought back not only the monarchy and the traditional ruling classes but the Anglican church as well. The effects of the Puritans' attempts to propagate their own doctrine and ethos in Wales had not been lost on Anglicans. In 1682, a leading establishment figure, Bishop Hugh Gore, who had actually kept a private school in Swansea in the 1650s, established his grammar school in the town to encourage 'virtue and good literature' among its youth. The school was no doubt intended to train and discipline intellectual and moral qualities and to give promising boys an avenue by which they might enter trade and the professions. It may also have sought to defend the church against Dissenters, though it is worth remembering that Anglicans and Dissenters could often work together to remove what they both regarded as a 'mountain of ignorance and immorality'. Another religious figure hard at work during much the same period as Bishop Gore was a leading Dissenter, Stephen Hughes, 'the Apostle of Carmarthenshire', who lived in Swansea and laboured mightily in the cause of religion and education in south Wales through the medium of the charity known as the Welsh Trust. Hughes was one of no fewer

Bishop Gore's House in High Street, late seventeenth century.

than four or five Dissenting ministers who made Swansea a 'city of refuge' for their fellow-believers, though strictly speaking, according to the law of the land, they had no right to be domiciled within five miles of a chartered borough.

By the first quarter of the eighteenth century Swansea was admirably equipped to face its commercial and industrial future. It was a flourishing town, with a busy harbour, an active and expanding coal industry, and an embryonic smelting industry in its vicinity. Its population was lively and enterprising, and their entrepreneurial enthusiasm was shared by the local gentry, from the Mansels downwards. Within a century the Industrial Revolution would turn the town into a highspot of fashion and culture, the busiest port in Wales, and a centre of metallurgical manufacture of world significance. Swansea was truly coming of age.

*The Swansea Town Crier, by
Alfred Dixon, nineteenth
century.*

INDUSTRIAL DEVELOPMENT

Chapter 2

Paul R. Reynolds

Had the burgesses of Swansea been gifted with the ability to foresee the future, they would have known that history was about to be made when a certain doctor from Bristol arrived in their town one day in 1716. His reasons for coming were entirely unrelated to his profession, for he had not come to practise medicine, but to supervise the erection of a copperworks a mile or two to the north of the town. John Lane was a distinguished physician and surgeon, who enjoyed a high reputation among his contemporaries, but nothing he did in the field of medicine had such far-reaching consequences as his decision to build the Llangyvelach copperworks. Lane's copperworks was the first of fourteen such works in the Lower Swansea Valley which made Swansea the centre of the copper smelting industry, not only in Britain but in the whole world, in the eighteenth and nineteenth centuries. Copper smelting led to zinc and lead smelting, and the pool of metallurgical expertise so built up in the district resulted in Swansea becoming in turn the centre of the tinplate industry in the nineteenth and twentieth centuries.

Swansea no longer has a non-ferrous metals industry, and steel and tinplate have migrated to its periphery, but the character of the city and its physical environment still bear testimony to the two hundred years during which it dominated — and was dominated by — the copper and tinplate industries. During that time Swansea was the centre of one of the most important industrial areas of Britain. It was also one of the places in which the Industrial Revolution was born; for copper smelting was an established and flourishing industry here well before the first iron furnace at Merthyr was tapped and when the Rhondda Fawr and Rhondda Fach had another century to wait until their Sabbath calm was disturbed.

It was far from chance that led Lane to Swansea. He selected the town as the site of his copper venture because it had all the features that

View of Llangyvelach Copperworks, Landore, c. 1750.

he was looking for, and especially an abundant supply of cheaply worked coal. Swansea was already the centre of an active coal industry which dated back almost literally to time out of mind. The earliest reference to mining in the area is in 1306, and by Elizabethan times there was a flourishing export trade. Nearly all the coal raised in Swansea until the introduction of copper smelting was shipped away as domestic fuel, but there were already a number of small local industries which made use of it.

Swansea's industrial revolution, therefore, lay not so much in the sudden transformation of the basic pattern of economic activity. Rather it was the intensification of the existing coal mining industry, coupled with diversification into large-scale metal working. The real revolution was in the scale of industrial activity and even more in its social implications. Leadership within the community passed from the landowning gentry families to a new class of industrial entrepreneurs, the origins of many of whom lay outside Swansea, while an industrial working class grew out of the heterogeneous band of unskilled labourers who had worked indifferently at either agrarian or industrial tasks as the occasion arose.

Copper Smelting

The main direction of Swansea's industrial development was determined by the introduction of copper smelting, for which it formed an ideal location. Despite the well publicized efforts of Ulrich Frosse at Aberdulais in the 1580s, copper smelting had never been successfully developed in Britain and most of the country's requirements had been imported from Sweden. This changed in the 1680s with the discovery of large reserves of copper ore in Cornwall, at about the same time as a process was successfully devised for smelting the ores in reverberatory furnaces by means of coal. The new technology was first applied at Bristol and then at Neath, but the advantages of Swansea soon outweighed the claims of both.

The Welsh process of copper smelting, which was already in use by the second quarter of the eighteenth century, involved a series of repeated roastings and meltings to remove impurities from the ores. It was thus voracious in its demands for coal: in the eighteenth century the proportion of coal to ore was generally about three to one, although by the middle of the nineteenth century this ratio was down to about two to one as the process was simplified and fewer stages were required. Demands for coal of this order called for a coalfield location rather than one at the source of the ore. South Wales is the nearest coalfield to Cornwall and within south Wales the coal measures come down to the coast only in the western part of the coalfield. The cost of land transport in the eighteenth century totally ruled out an inland site. Given these factors, Swansea was clearly the most eligible location. It is approached through sheltered water and the River Tawe is navigable for several miles. On either side of the river is flat land offering sites for industrial development with any amount of easily worked coal in the immediate vicinity. Thus ore-bearing vessels from Cornwall could sail up the river and tie up immediately alongside a smelting house. Coal could be transported to the furnaces at very little cost and, equally important, it provided a cargo for the return voyage to Cornwall where it found a ready sale, not least to power the pumping engines that were needed to drain water from the deepening copper mines. The importance of a site beside navigable water is clearly shown in the location of the Lower Swansea Valley copperworks, which were all without exception close to the banks of the Tawe.

Lane's Llangyvelach copperworks was built on a site beside Neath Road just to the north of the present Landore railway viaduct.

Production started in 1717. The works were said at the time to have been 'larger and more useful' than any of the existing works in Neath or Bristol. Lane appears to have been less than competent as a business-man and in 1724 Robert Morris was brought in from Shropshire to supervise the undertaking, an event of great significance, for the Morris family was to be one of the leading industrial dynasties in Swansea for the next hundred years or more. It is only in com-paratively recent times that the family's links with the city have been severed. A memorial to the great influence which they once had remains in the name of Morriston, which was founded as an industrial township by Robert's son, John Morris I, in the 1780s.

Control of Llangyvelach works passed to Robert Morris, following Lane's bankruptcy in 1726 as a consequence of unwise involvement in the South Sea Bubble. Morris founded a partnership, Lockwood, Morris & Company, who were to be a major force in copper smelting and coal mining for two generations until the partnership was dissolved in 1800. Copper smelting was moved to the Fforest works, near what is now Morriston, in about 1748 and again, in 1793, back to new works in Landore.

Further entrepreneurs entered the industry, and by the end of the eighteenth century there were seven copper smelting houses in pro-duction in the Lower Swansea Valley with an additional one at Penclawdd. Together with a few other firms in the region, their combined output was around 7,000 tons of refined copper *per annum*, which represented about 90 per cent of the total United Kingdom output. The fact that copper — mining and smelting together — was Britain's principal metallurgical industry at this time gives some indication of the importance of Swansea within the national economy.

Two large but comparatively late entrants to the industry were Vivian & Sons and Williams, Foster & Company. The founder of the former, John Vivian, entered the smelting industry at Penclawdd in 1800 as a partner with the Cheadle Brasswire Company. In 1809 he built his own copperworks at the Hafod. The Vivian family was to remain in possession of the works through four generations until 1924 and, in the person of such figures as John Henry Vivian (1785-1855) and Henry Hussey Vivian (1821-1894), was to dominate the copper industry of Swansea and indeed the world. The firm of Williams, Foster was one of the last new entrants to the industry. Their Morfa works, built on a site adjacent to the Hafod works in 1835, was to develop into the largest of all the Swansea copper smelting works. By the middle of the nineteenth century these two firms had become by far the most important in the industry and were eventually to be its last two survivors.

The product of the Swansea copper smelters took the form of fine copper ingots which were sold to manufacturers and merchants elsewhere, especially in Bristol, Birmingham, Liverpool, and London. Manufactured copper goods were not a major component of Swansea's output until smelting went into decline in the twentieth century. The refined copper was then used for a variety of purposes. One of the earliest was in the manufacture of domestic goods, and this was the area in which the Birmingham tradesmen specialized. An increasingly important use during the eighteenth century was for components in the manufacture of steam engines. Also starting at this time was the use of copper to sheath the underside of ships' hulls beneath the waterline, so as to prolong their seaworthy life. This practice was first applied to ships of the Royal Navy in the 1770s and was subsequently adopted by the merchant marine. Copper goods were also in demand for the slave trade — hence the Bristol and Liverpool markets. One of the largest customers was the East India Company, whose annual contract in the closing years of the eighteenth century was generally in the region of 1,500 tons. The home government, too, could be expected to buy large quantities of copper for coinage (although on an occasional rather than an annual basis) and for naval and military supplies.

John Henry Vivian (1785-1855).

Henry Hussey Vivian (1821-94).

The copper smelting industry was thus important and one that could rely on a ready market for its produce. It was therefore attractive to a would-be entrepreneur, but at the same time it demanded a considerable level of capital investment. At the beginning of the nineteenth century it appears that each of the works then in production had a fixed capital of around £40,000 and in the middle of the century it was calculated that it would take £45,000 to set up even a small copperworks. At this time a small colliery could be got into production for perhaps less than £10,000. This sort of wealth could not be found in south Wales in the eighteenth century, with the result that nearly all the entrepreneurs responsible for the development of the smelting industry came from outside the area. However, industrialization was certainly encouraged by local landowners and the owners of mineral rights, for copperworks demanded constant supplies of coal, the delivery of which would increase the income from their estates.

The entrepreneurs fall into a number of categories. Initially, they were men of property who were looking for a profitable investment, such as John Lane (Llangyvelach, 1717), Thomas Coster & Company

(White Rock, 1737), or Chauncey Townsend (Middle Bank, 1755; Upper Bank, *c.* 1757). Townsend's origins were in London, but both Lane and the Coster partners were Bristolians. The involvement of Bristol capitalists in the growth of Swansea's copper smelting industry is significant. Before the development of cheap land transport in the form of canals and especially railways, the Bristol Channel formed a major means of communication. The Bristol Channel province was an economic entity comprising south Wales and the west of England, and dominated commercially and financially by Bristol at the apex of the triangle. Not for nothing was the city known as 'the Welsh metropolis'.

Once copper smelting had been successfully established at Swansea, entrants were attracted from mining and manufacturing, *i.e.,* from the processes both before and after smelting. John Vivian, the founder of the Hafod works, was a Cornishman who came to prominence as an agent for the Cornish miners and who had himself an interest in several mines. Similarly, Michael Williams, of Williams, Foster, and the Grenfell family, owners of Middle Bank and Upper Bank in the nineteenth century, had Cornish origins. Besides Cornwall, the other main ore producing area in the United Kingdom was Anglesey, where copper was discovered in 1768, and two companies associated with

View of the Hafod Copperworks, c. 1900.

mining in this county acquired smelting houses in Swansea, the Parys Mine Company at Upper Bank in 1782, and the Stanley Company at Middle Bank in 1787 and at Penclawdd soon afterwards. Among the copper manufacturers who entered the smelting industry were the Birmingham Mining & Copper Company (1793) and the Rose Copper Company (1797). Both of these were formed by copper manufacturers in the Birmingham area as a reaction to the monopolistic prices which the existing smelters charged. They were co-operative in nature and were intended to supply their members with refined copper at a lower price than they would otherwise have had to pay.

As has been noted, it was the convenience of Swansea for the copper mines of Cornwall that led to the establishment of the smelting industry in the town, and until well into the nineteenth century Cornwall remained the main source of the ores. The Parys Mountain on Anglesey provided an additional source, especially when its output was at its peak in the late eighteenth century. However, with a decline in output from Anglesey, together with an increasing demand for copper, it became necessary to look farther afield. From the 1820s Latin American countries, especially Cuba and Chile, started to supply ore to Swansea, and subsequently Australia, Canada, South Africa, and Spain were all drawn upon. Later in the nineteenth century it became increasingly common for these countries to supply regulus, or partially smelted ore. Initially undertaken in order to save transport costs, the production of regulus was often the first step towards the creation of a fully formed smelting industry in the country of origin of the ores, one of the factors which was to lead to the eventual collapse of the Swansea smelting industry. Cornwall continued to be the principal supplier until the 1870s, when its reserves finally started to approach exhaustion. For the next twenty years the amount of copper ore imported into Swansea continued to rise, but then imports tailed off as the copper smelting industry went into decline. Swansea's enforced dependence on imported ores was a factor that contributed to the ultimate failure of its smelting industry.

The labour requirements of the copper smelting industry were comparatively small compared with those of the coal and iron industries, although within Swansea itself copper workers always formed a high proportion of the labour force. In the eighteenth century an individual concern seems rarely to have employed more than 100 workers. In the nineteenth century this figure increased, and the largest of the works, the Morfa, employed around 600 or 700 at its height. Workforce statistics are hard to establish before 1851, but from then onwards it becomes possible to extract figures for employees in the different industries from the census reports. In Swansea, employment in the copper industry remained very much the same from 1851 right through to 1911, averaging around 1,200. In 1851 copperworkers, with a total of 1,146, formed the largest single component of the labour force. They retained this position among land-based workers until 1891, when tinplate workers first started to outnumber them (3,442 to 1,192), although in every census year but one from 1861 the number of seamen was greater.

If the labour force employed on copper smelting was comparatively small, it included a high proportion of skilled men, perhaps as many as 25 per cent. This was a direct result of the nature of the Welsh process of copper smelting. It has been described as 'tedious and intricate' (although also as 'some of the finest examples of skilled metallurgical art'), and it called for skill and judgment in implementing the various stages of the process, and in deciding when a particular batch of ore was ready to pass from one stage to the next. Wages were not particularly good, and generally less than in tinplate. There were, however, other incentives offered by employers to their key workers to encourage them to remain loyal and resist poaching by other employers. One of these, especially in the earlier years of the industry, was the provision of either houses or building plots at advantageous rents. Morriston, created by John Morris I in the 1780s, is the best known example of a planned industrial settlement in Swansea, but similar housing can be found in Vivianstown, for workers in the Hafod, and Grenfelltown, for Upper Bank and Middle Bank employees. Morris Castle, the ruins of which still dominate the Lower Swansea Valley, is another example: it was built as a block of industrial flats by John Morris I in about 1775.

The working life of the copper smelter was an arduous one. As well as skill and agility, physical strength and long shifts were required. The heat of the furnaces was intense and the atmosphere in which the men were expected to work was highly polluted. However, medical opinion of the time did not appear to regard conditions in the copperworks with any great concern. In 1854 a Dr Williams, after describing the alternation between extreme heat and extreme cold to which furnace workers were subjected, concluded that the copperman 'seems, however, to be a happy man; for we are told that the contented copperman merrily whistles as he alternately sweats and shivers'; and the veteran coppermen, who may apparently have spent thirty or forty years before the furnace, 'are generally as hale, florid and corpulent as their neighbours'.

Even more of a hazard, and not just to the coppermen in the smelting houses, was the all-pervasive smoke, laden with sulphur, which constantly rose from the copperworks. By the 1820s it had blighted the vegetation on Kilvey Hill and had caused the gentry to move up-wind to the more salubrious environment of Sketty. The Morrises moved from Clasemont to Sketty Park, and the Smiths from Gwernllwynchwith to Derwen Fawr. Only the Grenfells remained close to their works, at Maesteg House overlooking St Thomas. Legal action to prevent the nuisance was taken by landowners and farmers, and J. H. Vivian attempted to reduce the emission of smoke, if only to avoid the heavy costs of litigation. However, it was of little effect because Swansea knew that the economic advantages that came with copper smelting far outweighed the environmental disadvantages. Smoke continued to be poured out and, in combination with the mountainous heaps of discarded slag, its effect was to produce a blighted and derelict landscape which has only begun to recover within the past twenty years.

If the smoke had such an effect on vegetation, one can imagine what it must have done to the human constitution; yet again the medical men seemed little concerned. John Gutch, who was works surgeon at the Hafod in the 1830s, was 'certainly . . . disposed to say, that the men employed in the copper works, and living constantly in the smoke, are not more subject to disease than in other localities, where there is a dense and crowded population': and to reinforce his point he went on to mention 'two women upwards of ninety, who were not in their early years brought up to or inured to its effects' (*i.e.,* copper smoke), 'but who are now living in the midst of it, and enjoying excellent health'. But perhaps Gutch had to say that. After all, as well as being works surgeon, he was also a friend of the Vivians in private life.

Other Non-ferrous Metal Smelting

While copper smelting was certainly the largest of the Swansea non-ferrous smelting industries, it was by no means the only one. Second in importance came zinc (or spelter), which Chauncey Townsend was the first to attempt to smelt in Swansea on a regular basis. His Middle Bank works was started in 1755 to smelt lead, followed by Upper Bank (*c.* 1757), at which both lead and zinc were treated. However, both works went over to copper smelting under later owners. It was to be another eighty years before zinc smelting really became established at Swansea. This followed two technical developments in both of which zinc played an important part. The first was the invention by G. F. Muntz of his so-called 'yellow metal', which he patented in 1832. This was an alloy of copper and zinc which proved suitable for sheathing the hulls of ships in place of the more expensive copper which had hitherto been used for this purpose. Muntz manufactured the metal himself at Upper Bank from 1838 to 1842, and subsequently it was manufactured under licence by Vivians. The second new process which gave zinc an added importance was the invention by H. W. Crauford of galvanized iron, which he patented in 1837. These familiar sheets of iron, or later steel, coated with zinc, were found to be ideal for housing and industrial purposes in newly developing countries, especially in arid areas such as South America, South Africa, or inland Australia, which lacked adequate resources of timber.

These two new processes of the 1830s resulted in a number of existing copper works being converted to zinc smelting and in the construction of entirely new zinc works. The Vivians converted the old Birmingham copperworks to zinc smelting (under the name of Morriston spelter works) in 1841, and from about 1850 Pascoe Grenfell & Sons were smelting zinc at Upper Bank in addition to copper. Of the new works, the first to be set up was that of the Cambrian Smelting Company in 1836. It did not last long, but the site was subsequently taken over in 1858 by L. Ll. Dillwyn, M.P. for Swansea. He and his successors smelted zinc there until 1926. Further new concerns ·followed in the 1860s: the Crown (later English Crown) works was set up in 1866 at Port Tennant, followed by Jennings & Company (1866), the Villiers Spelter Company (1873), the Swansea Vale Company (1876), and the Swansea Zinc Ore Company (before 1887). The last four works were all located on the eastern side of the valley on sites close to the South Wales Railway and the Swansea Vale Railway, in interesting contrast to the earlier copperworks whose sites had all been determined by the availability of water transport. All these zinc works were to change hands several times and by 1930 all had closed, with the exception of the Swansea Vale works, which survived until 1971, latterly as the property of the Imperial Smelting Corporation. But even though the output of zinc increased, it was still far from enough to meet the demand and until World War I Britain imported twice as much zinc from Germany as was produced by the small and inefficient domestic industry.

Employment in zinc was never as great as in copper smelting, but it rose steadily during the nineteenth century. The process used originally was the English process of downward distillation. It required a large input of coal but was more sparing of labour. Because of the quantities of coal required in this process (as much as 27 tons for each ton of zinc produced) the more economical Silesian and Belgian processes, which used the principle of upward distillation, were introduced. The Vivians had introduced Belgian-style furnaces by 1848 and, at all the works which were set up after this date, either the Belgian or Silesian process was used. But while these continental processes were more sparing of fuel, they made greater demands on both the skill and labour of the workers and it was not always easy to find local men to take the jobs. This, together with the need to import workers with the necessary skills, led to the migration of Belgian and German workers to Swansea. The descendants of these little colonies, now completely integrated, can still be found in the city.

The White Rock Ferry, c. 1890.

Of the other metals produced at Swansea, lead came third in importance. Attempts by Lane and Townsend to smelt this metal in the eighteenth century do not appear to have met with any great success. In 1870 White Rock copperworks was acquired jointly by Vivian & Sons and Williams, Foster. It was adapted for lead and silver production and continued thus for the next fifty years, although the numbers employed never rose above 100. In 1874 it became the sole property of Vivians. The industry peaked in about 1890 when 11,400 tons of ore were imported, but thereafter decline set in and by 1910 the industry was on the point of collapse. The war gave it a temporary reprieve, but lead smelting at White Rock ceased in 1923. The main reason for this decline was that good quality ores could no longer be purchased and Vivians were reduced to dependency on an irregular supply of low grade ores.

Among other metals to be produced were arsenic, nickel, silver, and gold. Arsenic was extracted from copper ore at works in the Clyne Valley and elsewhere, while gold and silver were produced as a by-product of copper smelting at the Hafod works from 1850 onwards. L. Ll. Dillwyn also smelted silver at Landore from 1853 for a number of years. Nickel and cobalt were produced at the Hafod Isha works by a company set up in 1855 by H. H. Vivian as a separate venture from the family copper smelting business.

Tinplate and Steel Manufacture

The smelting of copper and other non-ferrous metals was one of the distinctive industries of the Swansea district. Equally so was the manufacture of tinplate — thin sheets of iron, or later steel, coated with a wash of tin. The invention of this material appears to have taken place in medieval Germany, but by the end of the eighteenth century Great Britain had become by far the most important tinplate producing country in the world. At that time the industry was located in two areas, the Midlands and south Wales, although it was not until 1845 that the first tinplate works was erected in Swansea. The industry then became increasingly concentrated on the western half of the coalfield, with Swansea as its main centre — although that claim might have been challenged by Llanelli, otherwise known as 'tinopolis'. By 1891, out of a total of 525 mills in the whole of Britain, 502 were located in south Wales: and of those 502, about three-quarters lay within twenty miles of Swansea. Communities such as Gorseinion or Pontarddulais depended almost entirely on the industry for their livelihood, and within Swansea itself Morriston, in particular, came to be dominated by it.

One of the most important factors in attracting the tinplate industry to Swansea was the existence of a work force in which a variety of metallurgical skills were present as a result of over a century of metal smelting. In turn, the growth of a pool of skills specific to tinplate manufacture attracted further investment in the industry, which thus became self-perpetuating. Also important were Swansea's geographical position and natural resources. Pig iron for conversion into wrought iron tinplate bar could be obtained from the ironworks of the *Blaenau* (upland Glamorgan), and until the 1860s most of the tin used in the industry came from Cornwall. New sources for both of these materials were employed later in the nineteenth century, but this served only to consolidate the position of Swansea in the tinplate industry. Iron produced from domestic ores at inland furnaces was replaced by steel produced from imported ores, while tin from Malaya and Australia replaced Cornish tin, both of which changes gave economic advantages to a coastal location for tinplate manufacture. Finally, in addition to its convenience as the point at which the various ingredients could best be brought together Swansea had the advantage of two basic raw materials required for any industrial process in the nineteenth century, coal and water. Coal was of course important, although not required in the same quantities as in the smelting industries, while water was required in abundance by the traditional pack mill process. Initially it was required to power the rolls by which the iron bar was reduced to sheets as a preliminary to tinning, but even after steam power had been introduced for this purpose, water was used for the various cleaning processes which formed part of tinplate manufacture.

The first tinplate works in the Lower Swansea Valley, the Upper Forest, was erected by Hallam & Company in 1845. It comprised five hand mills and had its own forges and puddling furnaces, which typifies the trends which were then beginning to appear in tinplate manufacture. Hitherto, the industry had been conducted on a small scale, with producers only operating one or two mills. It had also been the practice to buy bar iron ready forged rather than to buy pig iron for conversion into bar in an integrated puddling furnace. But during the nineteenth century, with the growth of demand, there was a tendency for a tinplate works to contain a larger number of mills and to carry out the three connected processes of forging, milling, and tinning within the same establishment.

Altogether, eleven tinplate works were built in the Lower Swansea Valley. The dates at which they were erected reflect the fluctuations of the tinplate market, which followed a cyclic pattern of distinct troughs and peaks of demand. Because so much of the output was exported to the United States, this cycle reflected economic conditions on that side of the Atlantic as much as in the home market. Swansea's second tinplate works was the Landore (1851). It was followed by three works which reflect the high level of demand in the late 1850s, due in part to the Crimean War and the increased confidence in canned food to which it led. These were Cwmfelin (1858), Beaufort (1860), and Cwmbwrla (1863). Over-production and the collapse of the American market during the Civil War led to recession, but with Reconstruction, demand started to rise again and in the resultant market upsurge Worcester (1868), Morriston (1872), and Duffryn (1874) were opened. Again, over-production led to a fall in prices during the 1870s, but in 1879-80 there was a further boom during which three more works opened, the Midland (1879), Aber (1880), and Birch-grove (1880). No further new works were opened in the valley, although Baldwins built their King's Dock works in 1909 and the adjacent New Elba in 1925, the last new works to be built for the traditional pack mill process. The dockside location of these last two is significant in view of the dependence of tinplate on export markets. Altogether, the number of individual mills in Swansea increased from five in 1845 to 106 in 1913.

The market for tinplate was predominantly overseas, especially in the United States. It could almost be said that the West was won only because of Welsh tinplate. It provided a cheap and portable material for all the domestic utensils of a homesteading family — plates, pans, buckets, kettles, bowls, even the roof of their house. To this were added two important new uses, cans for food and containers for petroleum. The first bully beef from the meat factories of Chicago was almost certainly packed in Welsh tinplate, and petrol from the oil wells of Texas was distributed in drums of the same material. An idea of the growth of tinplate production in response to the demand from America can be conveyed by figures. In 1865 total United Kingdom production of tinplate was around 84,000 tons: of this, over half, 49,000 tons, went to the United States. In 1891 production was up to 586,000 tons, of which 325,000 tons went to the United States. In both years a quarter of the total output, or less, was sold on the domestic market.

However, the Welsh tinplate trade was succeeding too well in America for its own good. In response to pressure from protectionist politicians and from representatives of the iron and steel industry of that country, who wanted to stimulate the development of their own tinplate industry, the McKinley Act, passed in 1890, placed a duty on all imported tinplate. The effect on the Welsh industry was dramatic. After a frenetic burst of activity to beat the tariff, which came into effect in 1891, production fell from 586,000 tons in 1891 to 445,000 tons in 1898. The more enterprising workers emigrated to the United States where their skills were at a premium in the nascent tinplate industry, and some Welsh entrepreneurs attempted to establish works in that country so as to transfer their production to within the tariff barrier. For those who remained there was unemployment, reduced hours and wages, and considerable distress. The industry began to emerge from depression in the late 1890s, and by 1902 output had returned to the level of 1891 as new markets were found in the Empire and on the Continent. However, despite the McKinley tariff, the United States remained the biggest single customer until 1911.

Whereas copper smelting was an industry that called for a large input of capital, a tinplate works could be set up for a comparatively small sum. In the middle of the nineteenth century it required about £3,500 for each mill, although by 1870 this had doubled to around £7,000 and by 1910 it had doubled again. Nevertheless, these were sums within the capacity of small entrepreneurs, especially when, as was often the case, they combined to form a group of investors to finance the erection of a tinplate works. The very nature of the traditional pack mill process made it possible to enter the industry with a small amount of capital, for there were virtually no economies to be gained by large-scale working. The converse of this was that a business established with the minimum of capital could only yield low profits, which in turn made expansion difficult. The nature of the industry and the origins and expectations of its investors meant that it became locked into a cycle of small works, little capital, and low profits. It also led to a market distinguished by pronounced fluctuations of boom and stagnation. Because entry was easy, entrepreneurs were enticed in at a time of rising demand. This resulted in over-production, the collapse of the market, falling prices, and business failures. The resultant reduction in output caused prices to rise, which led to further new entrants being attracted into the industry and a repetition of the whole cycle.

Initially, capital tended to come from ironmasters, who saw in tinplate an outlet for their product, or from merchants who wanted some control over the source and costs of their stock. Much of the mer-

Sir John Jones Jenkins, M.P.
(later Lord Glantawe)
(1835-1915).

cantile capital originated in Liverpool or Birmingham, but from the 1870s an increasing amount of investment came from the savings of middle-class traders and professional men. At the same time a change can be seen in the area from which capital was drawn, with industrial south-west Wales becoming the predominant source.

Among those who were responsible for the development of the tinplate industry in Swansea, two names in particular stand out. One is that of John Jones Jenkins (1835-1915), later the first Baron Glantawe, the other, Daniel Edwards (1835-1915). Both were born locally to families in modest circumstances, Jenkins at Clydach and Edwards at Morriston. Jenkins became manager at Hallam's Upper Forest works in 1858 and the following year he formed his own company, the Beaufort Tinplate Company, which built its works on the site of the former Fforest copperworks battery. He was later active in the promotion of the Prince of Wales Dock, opened in 1882, which resulted in Swansea replacing Liverpool as Britain's major tinplate shipping port, and in the creation of the Swansea Royal Jubilee Metal Exchange in 1887, which had the effect of making Swansea the main centre for dealings in tinplate, again at the expense of Liverpool. He entered local politics, becoming Mayor of Swansea on three occasions, and was later M.P. for Carmarthen during the course of one Parliament. He was raised to the peerage in 1906.

Jenkins' exact contemporary, Daniel Edwards, was the son of a stonemason and at first followed his father's trade. His entry to tinplate was as an employee of Hallam at Upper Forest and of Jenkins at the Beaufort works. In 1868, with two other partners, he formed the Llansamlet Tinplate Company, which built the Worcester works, a small two-mill concern with a capital of £6,000. In 1873 he, too, formed his own company which built the Duffryn works at Morriston. Edwards has been described in rather florid terms as 'Morriston's own Welsh Captain of Industry', and his presence can still be felt in that township in tangible form. The tinplate works with which he was associated have all been demolished and their sites cleared, but three of his houses still stand, as does Tabernacl Chapel, Morriston, the building of which was supervised by Edwards. He may have become a tinplate entrepreneur by 1870, but he had not forgotten his original trade of stone dressing.

The careers of Jenkins and Edwards are interesting, not simply as exemplars of the Smilesian process by which a man of determination could rise from a cottage in Clydach to the House of Lords, but because of what they show of the nature of the Welsh tinplate industry. It was a highly localized industry, both in the geographical sense and in the sense that finance was generated locally and control was exercised locally. It was essentially an industry of small units, which was why it was possible for a man to form and control his own company without any great personal capital.

If the traditional pack mill process of tinplate manufacture did not require large capital resources, it was unquestionably labour intensive. The process involved repeated handling of the materials in a lengthy and potentially dangerous sequence of operations, with between fifty and seventy employees required for each mill. In its essentials the process remained unchanged between the early eighteenth century and the introduction of the continous hot-strip mill. The first such mill in Britain was erected at Ebbw Vale in 1938, but in Swansea the traditional pack mills remained in operation until well after World War II.

However, while the basic processes remained unchanged, technical improvements were, of course, made. Partly as a result of these, the size of the average unit of production increased from one or two mills at the beginning of the nineteenth century to as many as twelve by mid century. Of these innovations the first was the introduction of steam

The Dyffryn Tinplate Works, Morriston.

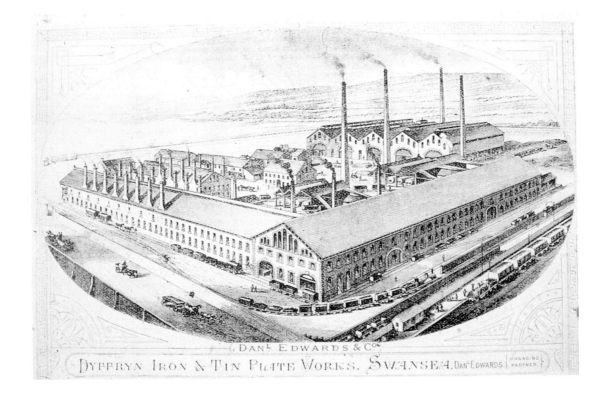

DYFFRYN IRON & TIN PLATE WORKS, SWANSEA. Dan¹ Edwards & Cº.

power to drive the rolls, by means of which the bars of iron were reduced to sheets of the thickness required, and the shears by which they were cut to shape. Landore tinplate works, built in 1851, used steam power from the outset and an engine was erected at Upper Forest in 1853. However, many of the smaller works continued to use water power, a symptom of the low-capital character of the industry.

Another significant improvement was the introduction of mechanical tinning pots. The first patent is dated 1843, but it was not until the 1860s that they started to make any great impression on working methods. They producd economies by reducing the amount of tin that was deposited on a plate and also by making it possible to dispense with a washman in the tinhouse. Various different types of tinning pot were used. In one of them, the invention of Daniel Edwards, first used at the Duffryn works, zinc chloride was first regularly used as a flux in place of palm oil.

But by far the most far-reaching innovation was the use of steel in place of wrought iron. During the 1880s tinplate makers changed *en masse* from iron to steel, with the result that an entirely new industry

Group of Copperworkers at the Middle Bank Copperworks, c. 1910.

was born in Swansea, the open-hearth steel industry. During the nine-teenth century two different steel-making processes were developed. The first of these was the Bessemer process, discovered in 1856, the other the open-hearth process of Sir William Siemens. Following experiments in his own works in Birmingham and by the Martin brothers in their ironworks in France, Siemens was able to patent his process in 1867. The same year he obtained a site at Landore, just to the south of the railway viaduct, on which his company, the Landore Siemens Steel Company, built its first works. It started to produce open-hearth steel commercially in 1869 and expanded onto a larger site on the eastern bank of the Tawe in 1871. At first the principal product was steel rails, but open-hearth steel was not able to compete with Bessemer steel in this market on account of its higher production costs. In 1875, therefore, Siemens went over to making tinplate bar, the market for steel nearest to hand.

Mild steel from the open-hearth furnaces was quickly adopted by the tinplate industry. It was ideal for rolling, and its manufacture did not call for any elaborate machinery, which commended itself to an industry dominated by small capitalists. The sheets produced from steel bar were smoother than those made of iron and therefore required less tin to give an acceptable coating. After Landore the open-hearth process was next introduced at works in Gowerton and Llanelli, followed by Birchgrove (1880), Cwmbwrla (1882), Cwmfelin (1885), and Upper Forest (1886), although in some of these steel manu-facture did not last for very long.

Open-hearth steel remained the staple of the tinplate industry so long as the pack mills survived, but with the modernization of tinplate production after World War II the demand for open-hearth steel declined. In Swansea the last place at which it was made was the Duffryn works, which closed in 1961, although open-hearth pro-duction continued elsewhere in Britain until the late 1970s.

Coal Mining

Underpinning all this metallurgical activity, and a fundamental factor in its location in the Swansea region, was coal. Coal had been mined in the region since medieval times and by the sixteenth century Swansea had become a successful coal port, third only to Newcastle and Sunderland in the tonnage which was handled. The main market was in France, the Channel Islands and the west of England, where it was used almost entirely for domestic heating.

At the beginning of the eighteenth century output was averaging at least 30,000 tons a year. Mining was still firmly in the hands of the local landowners, who tended to regard coal as just another product of their estates, like crops or fisheries. It was something that they could use for their own purposes, or allow the tenants to work as a perquisite, but above all it was a cash crop, a commodity to be produced far in excess of their own requirements and sold to raise money. Of the landowners the largest producers, not only in Swansea but in the whole of Wales, were the Mansels, from whose Briton Ferry estate in the parish of Llansamlet as much as 15,000 tons of coal could be raised in a good year. Also important as mineral landlords were the successive dukes of Beaufort: the family did not directly own any great quantity of land around Swansea, but as seignorial lords of Gower and Kilvey they were possessed of the mineral rights over all copyhold and common land in the lordship, a point which could lead to bitter disputes between the dukes and their agents on the one hand and the local land-owning families on the other, notably the Prices of Penllergaer and the Popkinses of Fforest. Wherever coal was easily worked, and even more important, wherever it lay close to navigable water, landowners exploited it and were already starting to lease new land simply for the sake of its coal. At this period the main coal producing areas were on either side of the Swansea valley, the Clyne valley, and north Gower; in every case districts within easy reach of navigable water. Coal that had to be carried overland for any distance was virtually valueless, for land transport was difficult and expensive.

The coal industry of Swansea was also well aware of technical developments which were taking place elsewhere in the country. The first Newcomen atmospheric pumping engine was erected at Dudley in 1712, an innovation of the greatest importance for the coal industry, and within five years Thomas Mansel had installed a similar engine on his estate. Mansel also had a 'water engine' for pumping his collieries by 1720, and in 1731 James Griffiths of Swansea took delivery of another Newcomen engine, probably for pumping at Mynyddbach. There is no evidence for waggonways at Swansea at this period, but this is perhaps more a reflection on the surviving records than any indication of technical backwardness. Sir Humphrey Mackworth had wooden waggonways at Neath in the 1690s and it would be surprising if the Mansels did not use them too.

Thus, at the start of the eighteenth century, there was a well established coal industry at Swansea which was capable of producing a large annual output at a reasonable cost. This was an important factor in attracting copper smelting to the town. Copper smelting in turn led to a great increase in the demand for coal and this brought about a change in the character of the coal industry, which became dependent more on supplying the needs of the smelters than on the export market. At the same time the landowners tended to cease working their coal themselves, choosing rather to grant leases to industrialists, in many cases the same men who were the owners of the copperworks. Thus, Lockwood, Morris & Company soon saw the necessity of a source of coal under their own control after suffering from the inability of their landlord, Thomas Popkins, to maintain an adequate supply. Eventually, they took the duke of Beaufort's coal in the Landore area under a 99-year lease from 1746, which made them one of the largest colliery undertakings in south Wales. Similarly, on the eastern side of the valley, Chauncey Townsend took a mineral lease of the Briton Ferry estate from the last of the Barons Mansel, and also of Gwernllwyn-chwith, both in 1750. Lockwood, Morris continued to operate an integrated copper and coal business until 1800, but Townsend soon gave up his smelting works and he and his successors, the Smith family, concentrated on coal mining alone. The effect of copper smelting on the demand for coal can be seen in the increase in output from about 30,000 tons a year at the beginning of the eighteenth century to at least 300,000 tons a year at its end. Of this total by far the largest part was produced by Lockwood, Morris and the Smith family, who between them dominated the Swansea coal industry from 1750 to 1800.

As a result of a complex rearrangement of the affairs of Lockwood, Morris in 1800, coal production on the western side of the valley was mainly in the hands of two producers during the first forty years of the nineteenth century, the Penvilia Vein Company and John Morris II, who between them worked the Beaufort taking and the Pentre estate of Calvert Richard Jones. The only other producer of any consequence in this area was Richard Mansel Phillips, the last of the squire coalowners, who continued to work the coal under his estate, the site of the modern Manselton. On the eastern side of the river two further generations of the Smith family continued to work the Llansamlet colliery, but it was a colliery that had passed its peak. Output had reached an annual figure of perhaps 200,000 tons in the late 1790s, but by 1843 it was down to about 70,000 tons a year. Even so, it was still the largest of the Swansea coal undertakings. The last of the Smiths, Charles Henry, sold up in 1872 and retired to Tenby.

If Lockwood, Morris and Chauncey Townsend had both preferred only to work coal and had moved out of metal smelting, the Vivians on the other hand, who had entered smelting at a comparatively late date, were very anxious to acquire a supply of coal under their own control. When John Vivian set up his Hafod works in 1809 all the coal within easy reach had been taken and the firm was dependent on John Morris II for its coal. Normally this was an arrangement that worked harmoniously enough, for each party knew that it was in its interest to keep on good terms with the other. Nevertheless, John Vivian and his son, John Henry, both hankered after their own coal, and finally in 1839 the opportunity presented itself. The Penvilia Vein Company had been working the duke of Beaufort's Five Foot Seam for nearly forty years and needed capital to bring new areas into production. When it was unable to raise the money itself, J. H. Vivian took advantage of the situation to form the Swansea Coal Company, in partnership with Williams, Foster of the Morfa copperworks, to take over the leases of the Penvilia Company. The new company also acquired the mineral takings of John Morris over the following few years and soon became one of the largest coal companies in Swansea. It was dissolved in 1863, with most of the assets going to Vivian & Sons, who continued in the coal business until the company ceased to exist in 1924. They owned a number of pits, the largest being Mynydd Newydd, from which they raised coal of various different types. In this way they were able to use a blend of coal in the copper furnaces, a practice which led to better results than by using one type only.

To an increasing extent the centre of gravity of the Swansea coal industry was moving out of the Lower Swansea Valley, for by about 1850 its reserves were largely depleted and the coalowners were having to look farther afield for workable reserves of coal. The actual number of collieries on the western side of the valley did not start to decline until the 1880s, and somewhat later on the Llansamlet side, but the most productive new collieries were increasingly to be found on the western edge of Swansea, at first at Cockett and Fforestfach, where there was steady growth from around 1850, and later in the Gorseinion area, which became the most productive part of the Swansea district from the 1890s. There were also smaller collieries in north Gower, the Clyne valley, and in the Dunvant area.

By the end of the nineteenth century the coal industry of Swansea had dwindled to a position of no great consequence in comparison with eastern Glamorgan. Less than 10 per cent of Glamorgan's pits were located around Swansea, and only about 3 per cent of the total number of miners in Glamorgan were employed in them. In about 1900 the average-sized pit in the area employed around 100 workers, compared to 281 in Glamorgan as a whole, although both figures rose in those boom years of the south Wales coal industry leading up to 1914. Even so, the largest pit in the Swansea area in 1911, Garngoch No. 2, at which 520 men were employed, ranked only 109th in size in the whole of Glamorgan. The centre of gravity of the industry had shifted east. The demand for steam coal was such as could only be met by opening up the unworked seams of the Mid Glamorgan valleys. Swansea had been exploited too much in the past to be able to compete. There was, however, one division of the coal industry in which Swansea was the market leader, and that was patent fuel manufacture, a useful outlet for small coal which could be combined with pitch to form briquettes for both the domestic and export markets.

Apart from Vivian & Sons, the coalowner of most importance in later nineteenth century Swansea was John Glasbrook (1816-1887), whose career exemplifies the trends noted above in the location of the industry. He was born into a Llangyfelach farming family and entered coal mining in the 1840s when he opened two collieries in the Cockett area. In 1854 he took the duke of Beaufort's Trewyddfa coal, the previous lease of which had expired in 1845. There was still coal to be worked there, despite its long history of intensive exploitation, and

View of Graig Trewyddfa, c. 1885.

there is even evidence for investment by Glasbrook in improved facilities in the 1870s. He worked a variety of collieries in addition to the Beaufort lease until he embarked on his last major undertaking, the Garngoch collieries near Gorseinion, at a time when this area was increasing in importance. Coal was struck in Garngoch No. 1 in 1878 and sinking at Garngoch No. 2 started in 1884. John Glasbrook himself died in 1887, but the business was carried on by his sons under the title of Glasbrook Brothers.

Glasbrook and Vivians were the two largest of numerous colliery concerns in the second half of the nineteenth century. Unlike earlier times, when the industry had been dominated by a few major partnerships or individuals, from 1850 onwards it was much more the preserve of the small investor. There were solicitors and tradesmen, engineers and colliery agents; just the same sort of men as were financing the contemporary tinplate industry. It reflected the decline in the Swansea coal industry: reserves of virgin coal were few and activity was now more a matter of extracting pockets of coal left behind by earlier working, or scraping out thin seams that had hitherto been beneath consideration. Like tinplate, this sort of colliery activity was a low-capital business, especially if the coal could be won by level or by re-opening an earlier shaft, and it attracted the same sort of investor.

The Eclipse of Swansea's Traditional Industries

So far, in considering the various industries which formed the character of Swansea, the story has not been taken consistently beyond the early years of the present century. In the final paragraphs of this chapter a brief attempt will be made to describe their decline and to offer a few explanations.

The years of prosperity leading up to 1914 helped to mask the *malaise* which was affecting all of Swansea's traditional industries in one way or another. Employment in each of them was showing an increase, or at least was not declining. Copper smelting continued to be profitable and the output of tinplate rose to new heights. However, as soon as depression set in after World War I the true situation of these industries was revealed. They were in no position to compete effectively and many of them succumbed.

In the case of copper smelting, decline had set in from about 1890. The principal cause was undoubtedly a reduction in the quality of the ores which were available to the Swansea smelters. So long as the metal content remained high (20 per cent or more) it was economic to

Blast Furnaces in the Lower Swansea Valley, 1881.

ship the ores to Swansea for smelting; but with a reduction in the metal content of the ores it became increasingly the practice to smelt the ores at the point of extraction. With fewer ores being imported, Swansea concentrated increasingly on copper fabrication, producing goods to the specification of ship builders and railway companies. A further contributory factor to the decline of copper was a weakening of control in Vivian & Sons, one of the two surviving businesses, after the death of Henry Hussey Vivian in 1894. His successors took the profits from the business without making adequate provision for renewal of plant or for innovation, with the result that the processes and equipment became increasingly old-fashioned. Copper smelting ceased in 1921, and in 1924 Vivian & Sons amalgamated with Williams, Foster to form British Copper Manufacturers Limited. BCM was in turn acquired in 1928 by Imperial Chemical Industries, who continued to fabricate copper goods at the combined Hafod and Morfa works through their subsidiary, Yorkshire Imperial Metals. The works closed in 1980 when, after more than 250 years, Swansea finally severed its connection with the copper industry.

At the beginning of the twentieth century the prospects for the tinplate industry looked bright enough. It was beginning to recover from the effects of the McKinley tariff and almost every year from 1898 until 1913 annual output increased. After the war, however, the situation was very different. The international market for tinplate was saturated through over-production, and the tinplate manufacturers of Wales found it increasingly difficult to sell their product. Output showed an increase from 848,000 tons in 1912 to 958,000 tons in 1937, but it was in an erratic series of fits and starts with sharp alternation of boom and depression. At the same time exports declined from 57 per cent of the total output in 1912 to 35 per cent in 1938, again with many fluctuations. In 1912 British tinplate production was approximately equal to that of the United States, but by the end of the war, American production was four times greater and rising. Britain still had the greater share of the export market but by 1938 the gap had become very small.

The reason for the success of the United States tinplate industry compared to that of Britain was twofold: it was technically more advanced and it was better organized. By the 1930s it was clear that the British industry needed to be radically re-equipped and reorganized. Amalgamation had already reduced the number of firms in south Wales to 34, of which Richard Thomas & Company was by far the largest with nearly half the productive capacity, including four of the works in Swansea. This firm opened Britain's first hot-strip mill at Ebbw Vale in 1938. World War II served to accelerate the process of rationalization. Small, uneconomic works were closed under the tinplate redundancy scheme and production concentrated on a few large works. Pack mill production continued into the 1950s; but with the opening of the modern strip mills at Trostre (near Llanelli) and Felindre (north of Swansea) it was quickly phased out. Upper Forest & Worcester works closed in 1958 and Duffryn in 1961, the last two of the old tinplate works to make their own steel. At the King's Dock and Elba works hand rolling in the traditional way continued until 1964, and the tinning pots remained in use at these works into the early 1970s, making them the final survivors of the traditional pack mill process in Swansea.

In the case of coal, the main reason for the industry's demise was simply that after centuries of exploitation all Swansea's reserves had been worked out. High demand in the years before World War I made it economic to work the remaining thin, deep seams, such as the Two Foot and the Hughes Vein, but after the war, when the market contracted, this was no longer viable. An end to mining on the western side of the valley was hastened in 1925, when Vivians sold their mining interest to a small local syndicate. Hitherto, all the collieries on this side of the valley had been drained through Calland's Pit at Landore. Pumping had been carried out by Vivians but the new owners could not afford to continue, with the result that the water rose and within a few years all the collieries as far north as Tirdonkin, near Llangyfelach village, had been flooded out. On the eastern side of the valley Llansamlet Collieries Limited continued to work until 1930, and in north Gower a few small concerns carried on until shortly before the war. The last active pit within the boundaries of Swansea was Felin Fran, which worked a pocket of coal in the extreme north-east of the borough. It was sunk as late as 1931 and survived until 1965.

Chapter 3

THE PORT AND ITS WORLDWIDE TRADE

David Boorman

'In speaking of Swansea, one must not think of the beautiful, but of the useful with a capital U. Nobody talks of sea views and mountains here, but of how many ships were entered, and what the export and import returns were, and the like . . . The soul of the town is in her docks.' (*Daily Telegraph*, 6 December 1882).

Early Developments

'The chief sea port is Swanzey, a very considerable town for trade, and has a very good harbour. Here is also a very great trade for coals and culmn, which they export to all the ports of Sommerset, Devon, and Cornwall, and also to Ireland itself; so that one sometimes sees a hundred sail of ships at a time loading coals here; which greatly enriches the country, and particularly the town of Swanzey.' The maritime possibilities of the town had been recognized long before Daniel Defoé's description of the port in the early eighteenth century rightly drew attention to its pride of place among the ports of Glamorgan, the importance of the export trade in coal and culm, and the well-established links with the ports on the English side of the Bristol Channel and the fast developing trade with southern Ireland. Although the absence of relevant records for the late medieval period makes it impossible to assess with any precision the volume of trade handled by the port during that period, it is probable that Swansea's maritime trade was similar in pattern to that of Carmarthen and Milford and that there would already be strong links with the ports of the Severn and of south-west England together with a limited trade with Ireland and even with the French ports of La Rochelle, Bordeaux, and Bayonne.

From such port books as survive for the seventeenth and early eighteenth centuries, a clearer picture of the port's trade begins to

The North Dock, 1881.

emerge, highlighting especially the growing importance of the export trade in coal, increasingly in demand for both industrial and domestic uses. The fact that, at Swansea, the coal mines were located in the immediate hinterland of the town, and thus within easy reach of the port, gave a tremendous boost to the local coal industry. In 1709, 1710 and 1711 the coastwise shipments of coal and culm from Swansea amounted to 9,861 tons, 8,694 tons, and 8,984 tons respectively; a further 2,532 tons were shipped to Ireland in 1709 and 3,195 tons in 1710. Swansea coal was also finding its way to the Channel Islands, to France, Spain, and Portugal. Among a variety of commodities brought into the port were tobacco, wine, apples, pears, prunes, raisins, figs, hops, cheese, onions, pepper, salt, tar, pitch, oakum, iron, and cloth. Although much of the trade was carried on in vessels from the Devon ports, from Ireland, the Channel Islands and abroad, local shipping was increasingly involved. In 1709 the total tonnage of coasting vessels belonging to the port of Swansea was 2,148 tons.

If coal was the foundation of the port's economic prosperity for much of its history, it was to be joined from 1717 onwards by another group of minerals, the non-ferrous ores, and especially copper ore. The ready availability of the coal needed in the smelting process and the fact that about eighteen tons of coal were needed for the production of one ton of copper ensured that the copper smelting industry came to be located in the Neath area and in the Lower Swansea Valley rather than in Cornwall from where, for about a century, the bulk of the copper ore was to come. As the river Tawe was navigable for small vessels for about three miles upstream from its mouth, 60-ton boats were able to carry copper ore up to the quay at Landore. Initially, the smelters had difficulty in obtaining sufficient supplies of the ore, leading Robert Morris to remark: 'It (the amount of copper manufactured) would not employ a vessel of 60 tons four voyages a year to London but that other contributions must be found for its cargo such as stone coal, butter, oats, and other grain which will sell better in London, unless the Company was to enter into the Lead Trade'. However, as the industry began to expand, new sources of ore-supply were sought, especially in Ireland and in Anglesey. Some copper ore came from much further afield and at least one vessel brought a cargo of copper ore from New York in the early eighteenth century.

Whereas the ready availability of coal and the growth of the smelting industries, combined with the advantages of a bay which provided a safe anchorage for shipping and of a harbour enclosed from the open bay, worked to the benefit of the port, navigational problems threatened to act as serious deterrents to further expansion. There was a very real danger of the river being rendered unnavigable not only by the scourings brought down in times of flood and by the silting and drifting of sand but also by the behaviour of irresponsible traders who, as they entered the harbour, discharged their ballast into the river. The Corporation had taken steps as early as 1555 to prevent such practices, and in 1583 had issued a regulation to the effect that ballast was to be discharged either at the town quay or at the coal lading place itself. The appointment of a layer keeper from the late sixteenth century onwards was another measure designed to prevent obstructions in the harbour as well as to provide safe layerage for all craft, especially on the mud-bank of the river where vessels 'would lie high and dry and suffer no strain or damage when the tide ran out' (Jones, 1922).

In the sixteenth and seventeenth centuries the Corporation had also been active in providing quays at its own expense as well as leasing at low rentals sections of the river bank to individuals for the construction of docks. However, by the eighteenth century the Corporation seemed content to leave developments in the hands of private enterprise and viewed the port more as a source of income, in terms of rentals, moorage and quayage dues, than as a facility requiring regular expenditure. There was increasing dissatisfaction among local merchants at the Corporation's failure to take a constructive approach in dealing with the problems of the port. Consequently, in 1768 a public meeting was called to consider, in the words of Charles Collins, one of a number of burgesses concerned about the situation, 'some means of improving the harbour, as the bar below the Ferry was evidently increasing, and consequently the navigation of vessels of burden rendered more difficult except on the top of high spring tides'. Although the spring tides made it possible for relatively large ships to enter the harbour, the time needed to discharge and load such vessels resulted in great delay, as they could not clear the port on the ensuing neap tides. The problem became more acute with the growth in the size of vessels in the copper ore trade. One expedient adopted to get over this difficulty was that of unloading cargoes from larger vessels anchored in the roadstead into lighters and barges which would bring the ore to the riverside quays owned by the copper smelters. However, this operation was not only time-consuming but also expensive, adding greatly to the costs incurred by the town's growing smelting industry.

The champions of improvement faced a formidable opponent in the person of Gabriel Powell, steward to the duke of Beaufort, the borough's lord. It is possible that Powell's opposition is to be explained in terms of the fact that he wanted Swansea to develop as a fashionable seaside resort and not as a centre of trade and industry; but a more likely explanation is that he feared that the setting up by Act of Parliament of an independent body to administer the harbour would result in a consequential loss of revenue to both the duke and the corporation. However, the decision by the advocates of improvement not to apply to Parliament for an Act was taken not out of fear of Powell but because 'upon procuring a Return from the Custom House it appeared that in the year 1768 only 690 vessels had entered the Port, the Tonnage of which amounted only to 30,631, which was judged too small a Fund to raise an useful Income on'. Three years later there was further talk of an application to Parliament; but, again, this course of action was passed over, on this occasion in favour of opening a subscription for the purpose of removing from the harbour the 'Paddocks or Banks of Gravell and Sand gathered in the River'. Even this modest proposal seems not to have resulted in any positive action.

Further concern about the state of the harbour was expressed at a meeting held at the Mackworth Arms Hotel in October 1787. When the matter came before the burgesses in November a determined attempt to block any action was made by Powell and his supporters on the grounds that 'if any act be passed by Parliament to carry the said resolutions into a law it would be very prejudicial to this Town and Borough, and may tend to the manifest destruction of many of our most valuable rights and privileges'. Passions ran high and Charles Collins was knocked to the ground, kicked, and lost his wig before Powell carried the day by 10 votes to 5. It was not until late 1789, some months after Powell's death, that the Corporation as a whole began to show a readiness to co-operate with traders and industrialists in seeking a sensible solution to the pressing problems of the harbour. Although still opposed to promoting a bill in Parliament, the Corporation agreed to join with others in a subscription for 'Imploying some judicious persons conversant in Imbanking of Rivers and Navigations to Come to this Town to inspect into and point out the best Methods of Improving the Harbour of this Borough'. By the end of 1790 the Corporation had changed its mind about applying to Parliament and had united with other interested parties in petitioning 'for leave to bring in a Bill for the Improvement of the Harbour and River of Swansea'. The application to Parliament was successful and resulted in the Swansea Harbour Act of 1791, which placed the responsibility for the harbour in the hands of trustees.

The Port under the Harbour Trustees, 1791-1923

Although the long-established interests of both the duke of Beaufort and of the Corporation were recognized in that clause of the 1791 Act which provided for the appointment of trustees, there were also places for Sir Herbert Mackworth and for the chief agent of the Briton Ferry estate, as well as for twelve persons to 'represent the interest of the present and future proprietors and lessees of Collieries, Mines and Minerals, and of Persons engaged in Copper Works, Potteries, Salt Works, or any other works and manufactories whatsoever within the said River, Port and Harbour of Swansea, and the owners of ships and vessels frequenting the same'. The 1804 Harbour Act reduced the burgesses' representation from twelve to six, increasing by the same amount the number of representative or proprietary trustees. A further six representative trustees were added by the Swansea Harbour Act of 1836. Further changes to the composition of the Trustees were made by the Swansea Harbour Act of 1854: henceforth the Trust was to consist of two nominees of the lord of the seignory of Gower, his steward and his coroner, the chief agent of the Briton Ferry

Swansea and the Harbour, from a Daguerreotype, 1848.

*Fabian's Bay and the Ferry,
looking towards the Beaufort
Arms Ferryhouse, early
nineteenth century.*

estate, nine Corporation representatives, and twelve proprietary
trustees representing the interests of trade, industry, and shipping.

The size of the task confronting the Trustees was highlighted in the
report which Captain Joseph Huddart, a leading marine surveyor,
prepared at their request in 1794. Not only was it essential to remove
the bar but piers would also have to be constructed at the mouth of the
river to prevent further silting. The trustees adopted Huddart's
recommendations but it was not until 1810 that the work on building
the piers and deepening the channel was completed. No steps at all had
been taken to carry into execution the powers given under the 1791
Act 'to make all such Works as shall be necessary in an effectual
Manner to stop up the Water in the said River, and make the same a
Floating Harbour'. Huddart alluded to this matter in a further report
which he drew up in 1804, advising the Corporation against letting
their property along the west bank of the river mouth, 'for should
foreign trade be introduced, and ships employed that would not take

the ground well, the most eligible site for a wet dock is from the upper end of the western pier towards the Ferry pool, and if taken from the harbour executed at the least expense'.

Vessels would continue to lie on the mud in the river at low tide for almost another fifty years. Before then, the other leading ports of the Bristol Channel would have constructed floating harbours; Bristol in 1809, Llanelli in 1828, Cardiff in 1839, and Newport in 1844. This is not to suggest that traders and trustees were blind to Swansea's need of a floating, or wet, dock to diminish the risks to which the larger vessels, often laden with heavy and valuable cargoes of copper ore, were continually exposed. Pamphlets were published, letters written to the Trustees or to the *Cambrian*, and public meetings held; and few would have disagreed with the remarks of Thomas Telford, the eminent engineer, in a report which he prepared for the Trustees in 1827: 'The Harbour of Swansea is, in my opinion, singularly well situated for being rendered capacious, convenient, and safe; but that this can only be effectually accomplished by converting both the river and the harbour into floats, totally independent of each other, and yet so as to be occasionally connected'. However, the Trustees were slow to move, and it was not until early 1832, after some pressure from the prominent local industrialist and M.P., J. H. Vivian, that they adopted a plan for a floating harbour submitted by Jesse Hartley, Chief Engineer of the Liverpool Dock Company. In its final form the scheme comprised a half-tide basin at the mouth of the river leading to a twelve-acre dock, with a navigable cut giving direct access to the upper river.

There followed three years of what the historian of the port, W. H. Jones, has described as 'painfully-drawn-out discussions', before an application was submitted to Parliament for powers to proceed with the work. Although an Act was obtained in July 1836, nearly four years of lengthy and costly negotiations over land were to elapse before work on the new cut began in the late spring of 1840. At that time the cut was intended only for waste water but, in January 1843, the Trustees decided to make it a navigable tidal cut. Just over two years later, on 11 March 1845, the barque *Charles Clarke* became the first vessel to sail through the new cut, making her passage 'amidst the firing of guns . . . in most gallant style without touching either sides or bottom, or meeting any obstruction to her free navigation'. Work on floating the old course of the river began in earnest in September 1849, an event which 'caused the leading ships in the harbour to hoist their colours in honour of the undertaking'. On New Year's Day 1852 the Float was formally opened. 'No public demonstration was made on the occasion; indeed, the event — all-important as it is to the town and district — was not signalised in any way, beyond the waving of a few banners from some of the adjoining premises, and the hoisting of flags on some of the vessels in the harbour.' Despite the absence of celebrations, the *Swansea Herald* rightly remarked that 'it may now be said that Swansea has a floating harbour'.

While work was proceeding on the new cut at what must have seemed a snail-like pace to local traders and industrialists, an initiative was taken independently of the meetings of the Trustees to enhance the port's facilities. J. H. Vivian had already envisaged a floating dock on the Burrows, an area of prime residential properties immediately to the west of the river Tawe. It became known in February 1840 that a group of promoters, with Vivian as one of the principal backers, were proposing to build a railway from Loughor to Swansea, to terminate at floating docks on the Burrows. Although nothing came of the project at that time, its desirability was not to be lost sight of, and in January 1846 the *Cambrian* was able to announce the formation of the Swansea Dock Company with a proposed capital of £200,000. An advertisement placed by the company in that newspaper rightly drew attention to the fact that, despite a growing and direct trade between Swansea and Cuba and the west coast of South America, 'many vessels, being too sharp to lie aground, object altogether to chartering for Swansea, and all demand a largely-increased freight in chartering from South America to Swansea, above the current freight to Liverpool, the practical result of which is, that Copper Ores are shipped from South America to Liverpool, from whence they are trans-shipped, at great cost and loss, to Swansea, in coasters'. The want of suitable harbour facilities also threatened the development of the copper ore trade from Australia,whence the first shipments reached Swansea in 1846.

The company's bill passed the Commons in the following year in the face of strong opposition from the Corporation, which had earlier expressed its support of the scheme, and from the Harbour Trustees. It appeared that a golden age of prosperity lay before the town and port, with Swansea likely to become a second Liverpool before the end of the century! In fact, what lay before the company was a decade of difficulties and frustration. An acrimonious dispute between the London and the Swansea Boards of Directors was not resolved until April 1848. It made shareholders reluctant to pay calls on their shares, and the general investment crisis of 1848 only compounded the company's problems. However, the company must have felt that the tide had turned in its favour when the marquess of Worcester, the duke of Beaufort's son and heir, and the Corporation rallied to its support in 1849. Three years later, on 26 February 1852, the marquess of Worcester raised the first sod on the Burrows site, watched by a crowd of nearly 80,000 people.

Excavation of the dock basins, which began in May 1852, brought a resumption of conflict; on this occasion between the champions of the new dock and those who were indignant that their access to the beach for riding and bathing was under threat. Although this dispute was eventually resolved to the satisfaction of both parties, it had caused some delay, as did two strikes by the labourers employed on the project in August 1853 and March 1854. Despite these interruptions the work proceeded until January 1855, when it came to a complete standstill because of lack of funds. The money market was nervous at the time of the Crimean War, and the pace of investment slackened. It was then that the Harbour Trustees, at first informally, and subsequently officially, put forward the suggestion that they should buy the Dock Company's Act and so take over the building and the management of the South Dock. Although the negotiations did not proceed smoothly, an agreement was eventually reached, the Trustees securing the appropriate powers under the 1857 Harbour Act. The Trustees showed what the *Cambrian* called 'rare energy' in bringing the works to completion, and when the South Dock was officially opened on 23 September 1859 the same newspaper hailed the occasion as 'incomparably more important to us, as an industrial and commercial community, than any event that ever transpired in our midst'.

By the early 1870s it was evident to the Trustees that even the North and South Docks, with a quay frontage of 10,000 feet, the whole of which was traversed by a low level railway directly connected with the Great Western, London and North Western, and Midland Railways, were insufficient to cope with the expanding trade of the port. Their consulting engineer, James Abernethy, recommended the provision of an additional dock on the eastern side of the river, taking up the whole of Fabian's Bay and the greater part of Port Tennant. The suggestion that the eastern side should be developed had been can-

Vessels in the King's Dock, c. 1920.

vassed for about fifty years but had hitherto been resisted as likely to work against the best interests of the town. Now, however, it was taken up and incorporated in the Bill which became the Swansea Harbour Act of 1874. The urgent need for a new dock was obvious when work on the project began in 1879. The port was so overcrowded with shipping that it has been suggested that 'thanks to the growth of the copper-smelting, zinc spelter, steel, iron, tinplate, and other works, . . . there was probably no other harbour in the kingdom worked by docks where such an amount of traffic was carried on a given water space as in Swansea' (Jones, 1922). Moreover, not only the number of ships clearing the port but also the tonnage was increasing. Whereas in 1851 3,616 vessels with a tonnage of 269,545 had cleared from Swansea, the figures for 1879 were 5,745 and 761,708 respectively. Many of the vessels calling at the port in 1879 were steamships, whose registered tonnage was well below their gross tonnage and the weight of the cargo which they carried. Work was sufficiently well advanced on the new dock to permit of its official opening by the Prince of Wales, after whom it was named, on 18 October 1881. However, a day of splendid pomp and pageantry was to be followed by several months of irritation and impatience while the dock was completed. Not until June 1882 was it opened to shipping. It was jocularly remarked of one of the first craft to enter the dock — a small smack called the *Atlas* — that her name should have been the *At Last,* because of the delay in getting the dock ready for shipping. However, once in use, it soon proved its worth, especially in the expansion of the export trade in Welsh tinplate to America.

It was not long before the Trustees realized that even the Prince of Wales Dock could not handle either the ever-increasing amount of trade passing through the port or the size of steamship that was being built towards the end of the century. Following a visit to Glasgow in 1900 to see at first hand the facilities of a modern port they decided to go ahead with the construction of a new deep dock to the south of the Prince of Wales Dock. The Corporation agreed to guarantee the interest on the expenditure for the first decade; the Trustees, in turn, undertaking to repay any such advances during the following ten years. Powers to construct the new dock and to borrow £2,000,000 were given to the Trustees by the Swansea Harbour Act, 1901. Three years later, in July 1904, King Edward VII turned the first turf. Work on the King's Dock was completed in 1909, the Chairman of the Harbour Trust, Sir Griffith Thomas, formally opening it on 22 November.

Successive Harbour Acts from the 1850s to the outbreak of the First World War had enabled the Trustees to raise about £4,500,000 for the improvement of the port. If, at times, progress had been painfully slow, not all the blame could be attached to the Trustees, and they could point to an impressive record of work achieved. If pride of place must be given to the new docks built during these years, passing reference should be made to some other achievements: an extensive railway system; the half-tide basin to the North Dock; the extension of the western pier; deepening the channel leading to the Prince of Wales Dock; an extension to that dock; the construction of new locks; the provision of a new deep entrance to the North Dock; the erection of a fish market and of a coaling stage for trawlers; and a host of other works, all designed to enhance the facilities of the port and so contribute to its prosperity.

Although there were nine privately-owned dry docks in the port by the end of the nineteenth century, Swansea had never become a major shipbuilding centre. In the era of wooden ships the availability locally of good oak timber, coupled with suitable sites provided by sheltered beaches and the river Tawe, had led to some activity in this industry. Probably the most important eighteenth-century shipyard in Swansea was that owned by three generations of the Squires family. Towards the end of that century John Mills was building ships in Swansea, as was Charles Llewhelling, who was followed by his son, George. Early nineteenth-century shipbuilders included John Tucker and, especially, the firm of Meager and Richards. Ships were built not only for local owners but also for customers in such ports as Barnstaple, Bideford, and St Ives. However, the ports of North Devon were themselves centres of shipbuilding and, as Swansea's output decreased, theirs increased, many nineteenth-century Swansea-owned vessels coming from their shipyards. In the mid-nineteenth century both the Neath Abbey Company and Swansea Iron Ship-building Company turned out several fine iron-built vessels, the latter company launching, in June 1849, the steam-yacht *Firefly*, which made the journey to Coquimbo, on the coast of Chile, in 64 days. There was a further flurry of shipbuilding between the late fifties and the seventies, associated especially with the Richardsons, leading merchants in the copper-ore trade as well as shipbuilders and owners, and George Blaney Meager. Among vessels built by the Richardsons, either at what had formerly been Meager's dry dock on the town side of the river or at the old patent slip on the east side of the North Dock, were the oak-timbered and copper-fastened barques, the *Duke of Beaufort*, the *Marquis of*

Worcester, and *Owen Glyndwr*, all three originally used in the Cuba and Chile copper-ore trade and, subsequently, in the same trade from Port Nolloth, Cape Colony. However, from the mid-seventies onwards wooden shipbuilding virtually ceased at Swansea.

In fact, for some fifty years, vessels built in the Maritime Provinces of Canada, and especially in Prince Edward Island, predominated in the Swansea-owned fleet. One of the leading shipbuilders on the Island, William Richards, was a Swansea man, and once his brother, Thomas Picton Richards, gave up his career as a ship master and established himself in Swansea as a shipowner/broker, vessels built of softwood in Prince Edward Island were bought in ever-increasing numbers by Swansea shipowners. Although inferior in quality to ships built of Welsh oak, they were considerably cheaper. The dominance of Prince Edward Island-built vessels is illustrated in an analysis of the 263

Aerial view of the Cambrian Dry Dock, c. 1920.

Swansea-owned vessels listed in Lloyd's Register of Shipping for 1876-77: 112 of those vessels (43 per cent) were built in Prince Edward Island, compared with 37 built in north-east England, 34 in North Devon, 14 in the Glasgow area, and 11 in Swansea.

Swansea shipyards were no more successful in making the transfer into the building of iron or steel ships. This was a matter which did not escape the criticism of the *Cambrian*. The edition for 6 January 1882 insisted that 'Swansea should start at once in the building of iron and steel ships . . . We have the means, we have the men, we have the metals too, for the building of iron and steel ships on the banks of the Tawe; and if we do not take advantage of our position and opportunities it is our own fault.' In the previous year the newspaper had raised hopes that great steel shipbuilding works were to be established in the port, but the project came to nothing. During the seventies and eighties a few iron-screw steamships were built in Swansea yards but these vessels were all small in size. Unlike their opposite numbers in Cardiff, Swansea shipowners preferred wooden sailing ships to iron steamships, a fact accounted for by the nature and demands of the trade in which their ships were engaged. Whereas coal exports constituted the basis of Cardiff's trade, the importation of non-ferrous ores, and especially of copper ore, lay at the heart of Swansea's trade. For that trade, sailing ships were particularly suitable, and with its decline in the late nineteenth century Swansea shipowners were deprived 'of the necessary incentive to adopt the steamship with enthusiasm' (Craig, 1979).

Until the end of the age of sail Swansea was relatively important as a shipowning port. Although the ownership of ships was never the preserve of a few, from the 1850s onwards certain names predominated. The Baths, the Richardsons, and Henry James Madge owned many of the ships which they employed in the deep-sea copper ore trade and were already owners, part owners, or joint owners of 1000 tons of Swansea-registered shipping by 1859. Eighteen years later, in 1877, there were twenty-three individuals and two limited liability companies owning 2,000 or more tons of shipping in the port. Among the individuals were the Richardsons, James Edward and James Henry Burgess, George Shaddick, John and William Harris, Bernard Rudkin Hennessey, Henry Hoskin, George Blaney Meager, Thomas Ford, Thomas Picton Richards, Lawrence and Gilbert Tulloch, and William Henry Tucker, all of them influential men in the commercial life of the town. Some of them, like Thomas Ford and Thomas Picton Richards, had themselves been sailors before settling to life ashore as merchants and shipowners. Others, like the Burgesses and George Shaddick, were shipbrokers as well as owners. The Tullochs were ship chandlers, Hennessey a chronometer- and watch-maker, Meager and the Harris Brothers ship builders and dry-dock owners. Alongside these individual owners were the two limited liability companies floated in 1873 to operate sailing ships, the Swansea Shipping Company Limited, in which the Burgesses and George Shaddick were the main investors, and the Swansea Merchant Shipping Company Limited, in which Jeremiah Clarke Richardson and Edward Bath were heavily involved. Between 1877 and 1900 a further 32 such companies were floated in Swansea, with a total share capital between them of £348,240. These, however, were single-ship, and generally steamship, companies.

1876 saw the registration of shipping, in terms of tonnage, reach its peak in the port. As the steamship came more and more to replace the sailing vessel, the port declined in importance as a shipowning centre. Even in 1914 the tonnage owned by the leading steamship owners in Swansea, the Harris Brothers, was only 11,483, whereas ten Cardiff shipowners owned steamship fleets of 23,000 or more tons. The new entrepreneurs in Swansea turned increasingly from the sea to the land, and especially to the fast-expanding tinplate industry, when they came to make their investments.

The cruel sea, dangerous or badly loaded cargoes, and, less frequently, negligent officers or owners greedy of gain at the expense of safety, combined to take a heavy toll of Swansea-registered shipping. Between January 1873 and December 1899 over 200 Swansea vessels were reported as totally wrecked or missing. Although just over half of the casualties took place in the North Atlantic, the South Atlantic and the waters of the South Pacific were also the graveyards of many Swansea-owned ships. The fate of Swansea ships can be illustrated by reference to the Board of Trade's annual return of wrecks for the twelve months from July 1878 to June 1879. During that period five Swansea ships foundered, six were stranded, three were lost as a result of collisions with other vessels, one was abandoned following the spontaneous combustion of its cargo, and two were reported missing. The first to founder, early in October 1878, was the brigantine *Emily*, carrying super-phosphate from Charleston, South Carolina, to Newcastle. Later that month the brigantine *Nelson* foundered on a voyage from Puerto Cabello, Venezuela, to Swansea with a cargo of copper ore, to be followed on 5 November by the brig *W. H. Tucker*, laden with phosphate rock, from Bull River, South Carolina, to Belfast. On Christmas Eve the brigantine *Erycina* foundered while carrying phosphate of lime from Coosaw, South Carolina, to Birkenhead, while in January 1879 the brig *Argo*, bound from Swansea to Dakar with a cargo of coal, met a similar fate. In the previous July the barque *Record* had been stranded in Ceara harbour, Brazil, having sailed from Liverpool with a general cargo. The barquentine *Curlew* and the brigantine *Creole* were stranded in January 1879, the first north of Capbreton, on the south-western coast of France, almost at the end of her voyage to Bayonne from Baltimore with grain, and the latter off the Brazilian coast with a cargo of bone-ash from Rio Grande do Sul for Falmouth. In March it was the turn of the brigantine *Irene*, stranded off Maranham, Brazil, whither it was bound with a cargo of coal from Cardiff. Another brigantine, the *Iberia*, met with a similar fate in May while carrying a general cargo from Buenos Ayres to the Argentine port of Laguna de los Padres, as did the brigantine *Mabel* in June, in the bay of Old Fort, St Lucia, whither it was sailing in ballast from Barbados. The schooner *Leader*, carrying zinc from London to Swansea, collided with the North Shields steamship *Ben Ledi*, in December 1878, twenty miles north of St Ives, Cornwall. A month later the barque *Diadem*, en route from Swansea to Cape Town with coal, was in collision with a United States ship in the North Atlantic, and in February 1879 the brig *Delta*, taking coal from Swansea to Bahia, Brazil, collided with the French steamship *Equateur* eighty miles north of the Brazilian coast, with the loss of five lives. In July 1878 the crew of the barque *Stranger* had been forced to abandon their vessel some forty miles off the South African coast following the spontaneous combustion of the cargo of coal which was being carried from London to Port Nolloth. The two ships reported missing were the *Corsair* and the *Glynllifon*, both carrying cargoes of phosphate rock from South Carolina to Britain.

Throughout the nineteenth century the trade of the port revolved around non-ferrous ores — copper ore in particular — semi-refined copper produce, and coal, although by the end of the century the export trade in tinplate was becoming increasingly important. If in the late eighteenth century Swansea could be referred to as 'the Brighton of Wales', 'Copperopolis' was a far more appropriate name in the century which followed. From Vivian's Hafod works northwards along the banks of the river Tawe there stretched a succession of copper smelting works with a seemingly insatiable demand for copper ore. For the first thirty or so years of the nineteenth century the great bulk of copper ore came from Cornwall, with lesser amounts from Ireland, Devon, the Isle of Man, and Anglesey. The 1823 *Swansea Guide* stated that 70,000 tons of copper ore, almost entirely from Cornwall, were imported each year into Swansea. It was not long before ore began to arrive from more distant places. Among the most important sources of supply at various times during the century were Sweden, Norway, Spain, Italy, Algeria, British South Africa, Australia, Newfoundland, Venezuela, Cuba, Chile, and California, a number of which later became leading exporters of regulus (partially smelted ore) once some part, at least, of the smelting process took place in the vicinity of the mines. Copper ore imports from overseas through the port reached a peak of 95,361 tons in 1889, falling twenty years later to 17,345 tons; regulus imports peaked at 56,812 tons in 1900 but had dropped to 17,284 tons by 1913.

Although never rivalling the trade in copper produce in value, imports of iron ore, zinc ore, pitwood and timber, and foodstuffs, especially grain, were by no means insignificant, especially from the early 1880s onwards. Foreign iron ore came almost exclusively from Spain, much being shipped through the northern Spanish port of Bilbao. Until the late 1860s imports of zinc ore were not distinguished in the annual returns of the Trust from those of other non-ferrous ores. However, within fifteen years zinc ore imports were accounting for over a fifth of all non-ferrous ore imports, and by 1913 for over a third. Ships carrying zinc ore arrived from a number of Southern European and North African ports, including Bordeaux, the Sardinian ports of Carloforte and Cagliari, and Bougie in Algeria. The local coalmines created and sustained a demand for pitwood, of which considerable quantities were imported from France, while Canada, Russia, and, to a lesser extent, the Scandinavian countries supplied timber for building purposes. Grain imports first topped 100,000 tons in 1903. A third of these came from the Argentine, which maintained its leading position in the years before the War, although significant quantities also came from Russia and, in some years, from Roumania, the United States of America, and Australia.

Exports far exceeded imports in volume, and whereas imports only trebled in the period from 1862 to 1913, exports increased sevenfold. Although Swansea fell behind Cardiff in the amount of coal exported, the trade in that commodity was still considerable. Annual shipments of coal coastwise, which had hovered around the quarter of a million tons mark from 1854 to 1880, reached 486,138 tons in 1913. In the same year the port's foreign shipments of coal exceeded three and a half million tons, whereas in the mid-1850s they had been only just over 80,000 tons. Not only was locally mined coal in demand as fuel in the world's naval and mercantile fleets, in rail transport, and in domestic and industrial institutions but the use of anthracite coal for central heating and other purposes also resulted in a large-scale exploitation of the south Wales anthracite field after 1890. Of the 1,999,687 tons of anthracite coal exported from south Wales in 1907, 1,761,687 tons passed through the port of Swansea. Manufactured or patent fuel was another important item in the port's export trade, rising from 99,000 tons in 1855 to 925,000 tons in 1913. France was the principal importer of coal and patent fuel from Swansea. Other important markets included Italy, Germany, Spain, Sweden, Algeria, the United States of America, and Brazil.

The growing importance of tinplate exports from the early eighties onwards was recognized by the Trust in its *Annual Return* for 1885 which, for the first time, carried statistics relating to that trade. Initially, the main overseas outlet was the United States of America, to which almost 130,000 tons, out of total exports of 191,373 tons, were shipped in 1886. Another outlet from 1887 onwards was Batum, the Black Sea port which was the centre of the Russian petroleum industry. However, the local tinplate industry and trade seemed likely to suffer a serious setback when, on 1 July 1891, the McKinley Tariff, designed to protect the American industry against foreign competition, came into operation. Initially, the tariff appeared to have little effect but, as less and less tinplate was shipped to the United States, there was a sharp fall in exports in the closing years of the century. New markets were needed and were eventually found, with the result that the trade not only recovered its former level but soon surpassed it, exports overseas climbing to 350,300 tons in 1913. No single country provided a market which matched the American one in importance. Success lay rather in finding a number of smaller markets in various parts of the world: Japan, China, and the Straits Settlements in the far East; the Argentine and Brazil in South America; with Sweden, Russia and Roumania, Holland and Belgium, France and Germany, Italy and Portugal all playing their part.

The peak year in the history of the port under the administration of the Trustees was 1913. Exports coastwise and overseas exceeded six million tons for the first time, and combined imports and exports amounted to more than seven million tons. However, storm clouds were already gathering over Europe, and the outbreak of war in August 1914 marked the beginning of a period of decline in the port's fortunes. Trade with Germany, Austria, and Belgium, which had amounted to over half a million tons in 1913, ceased altogether in 1915, the first full year of war. As men were called up to serve in the armed forces, the output of coal from the south Wales pits was seriously affected. For days at a time the work of the port came to a complete standstill as a result of embargoes on the movement of shipping. An application to the Board of Trade to make Swansea a controlled port, which would have put it on the same footing as the railway-owned ports in the Bristol Channel and made the government responsible for making good deficiencies in the balance sheet, was unsuccessful. This was a severe blow, as continual increases in wages and in the costs of materials were putting an impossible strain on the Trustees' revenues.

In 1918 imports and exports fell to a little over four million tons, the lowest level since 1904. The Trustees found themselves unable to meet their obligations to their bondholders and, eventually, two receivers were appointed to manage the harbour's affairs. However, the Trust's General Manager, P. W. Phillips, was able to sound a note of hope in his preface to the *Annual Return* of the trade of the port for 1917, informing his readers that the Anglo-Persian Oil Company had completed its negotiations for valuable frontage in 'the King's Dock Extension'. Although the war's insatiable demand for men and materials had resulted in the withdrawal, for the time being, of the licence for the work, the Company expected rapid and unbroken progess once the restrictions were removed. The decision of the Anglo-Persian Oil Company to locate refining works at Llandarcy was a major factor in bringing about a change for the better in the fortunes of the port. An appropriate area of water-way was available, and this, opened by Queen Mary in July 1920, became the Queen's Dock. Before long, crude oil was being imported in considerable quantities from the Persian Gulf while the refined petroleum played an important part in the export trade. The other factor which helped to ensure a return to prosperity was the transfer in 1923 of responsibility for the management and operation of the port from the Trustees to the Great Western Railway Company.

A Great Western Railway Port, 1923-1947

At a special meeting of the Harbour Trustees in May 1922 the Executive Committee reported on recent negotiations with the Great Western Railway Company with a view to transferring the trust's docks and undertakings to that company. The trustees were assured that 'in the event of the proposal for the vesting of the undertaking of the Swansea Harbour Trust in the Great Western Railway materialising, it is the intention of the Company to do their utmost to work, with the maximum of efficiency, the unified system of docks which will be formed in South Wales. In all matters affecting the various towns and docks their aim and object will be to hold the balance evenly between the various interests. In furtherance of this policy the Great Western Railway Co. will maintain in a full state of efficiency the tipping and other shipping appliances at Swansea Docks.' The GWR would take over the trust's financial liabilities (mortgages, arrears of interest on them, and arrears of interest on the trustees' stocks) and discharge them in cash. Holders of Harbour stock would receive an equivalent amount of GWR preference stock. To a hard-pressed trust which had not recovered from the financial problems occasioned by the war this was a lifeline, and it was not surprising that the trustees should agree that the proposals would be in the best interests 'not only of the Stock and Mortgage holders but also of the Harbour and the Town generally'. The proposals found statutory expression in the Great Western Railway (Swansea Harbour Vesting) Act of 1923, when the Swansea Harbour Trust came to an end after 132 years of responsibility for the port.

As a GWR port, it became part of what was at the time the largest dock system in the world. No major changes took place in the docks in the inter-war years with the exception of the closure of the North Dock in 1928, the result of a decline in use partly due to the increase in the size of vessels frequenting the port. The North Dock Basin was retained for vessels coming up to Weaver's Mills. By the late twenties the South Dock Basin was the centre of the port's fishing industry. Extensive fish wharves had been provided there for the use of a fleet of about forty deep-sea steam trawlers operated by Consolidated Fisheries Limited. However, whereas some 15,000 tons of fish had been landed in 1928, by the mid-thirties the annual catch was nearer 10,000 tons. Most of the port's trade was handled by the three docks to the east of the river Tawe. The Prince of Wales Dock, used chiefly in connection with various lines of regular sailings to continental ports, had a deep-water area of twenty-eight acres and was equipped with nine coal hoists, thirty-five cranes, and 226,120 square feet of warehouse space. At the King's Dock, which handled the larger cargo-carrying vessels, there were seven coal hoists, sixty-five hydraulic and electric cranes, and transit sheds with 453,142 square feet of floor space. Adjoining the entrance to this dock was an oil-bunkering jetty where the largest vessels could replenish their bunkers. Discharging berths along the eastern side of the Queen's Dock, which had a water space of 150 acres, were equipped with storage tanks and pipe lines, providing a

direct connection with the refinery at Llandarcy. The 10,000-ton tankers bringing crude oil not only from Abadan but also from Haifa and Tripoli could discharge their cargoes in twelve hours.

In nearly every year between the wars Swansea's exports were twice as valuable as its imports and exceeded them by nearly as much in volume. Coal, especially anthracite, towered over the port's export trade, accounting in peak years for about four-fifths of the tonnage shipped out through the port. However, both peaks and troughs in this trade were closely related to events outside the port's control. The strike in the United States coal-producing areas in 1922 and the French occupation of the Ruhr in 1923 worked to the port's advantage, whereas the prolonged stoppage in the British coal industry following the General Strike of 1926 not only led to a sharp drop in coal exports that year but also resulted in a loss of some foreign markets to overseas competitors. Throughout the 1930s the demand for Welsh anthracite

Aerial View of the Eastern Docks, c. 1970.

coal ensured a level of exports which was generally higher than that of the more uncertain twenties. Coal shipped out of Swansea found its way to many parts of the world but especially to France, Italy, and Canada.

Second in importance to coal exports were those of refined petroleum, although these fell off sharply after reaching a peak of more than eighty million gallons in 1925. The decline in oil exports was the direct result of the decision by the Anglo-Persian Oil Company to refine crude oil nearer to the oil-fields in the Persian Gulf. However, as the refinery at Llandarcy reduced the amount of heavy fuel made there, it concentrated on the production of high-grade motor spirits, burning and incubator oils, diesel oils, and lubricating oils. Swansea's exports of lubricating oil in 1937 were twice as great as those of 1932. Eire, Denmark, Argentina, and Germany were the principal importers of lubricating oil, and Eire, the Channel Islands, Norway, Denmark, Holland, and Spain of kerosene and motor spirit.

Although exports of coal and oil dominated the port's export trade, iron and steel manufactures, and especially tinplate, played an important role. The best year was 1929, when the total of all iron and steel products exported amounted to nearly three-quarters of a million tons, half a million tons of which were accounted for by tinplate exports. However, throughout the thirties increasing foreign competition resulted in a fall in demand for Welsh tinplate, and the trade became heavily dependent upon demand from other countries within the British Empire. The rapid growth of the Canadian food-canning industry and a growing Australian market were of especial importance in keeping the port's shipments of tinplate at a reasonable level. The combined shipments of coal, coke, and patent fuel, of iron and steel goods, and of oil accounted for all but two or less per cent of the port's outward shipments in the years between 1929 and 1937.

Although never as important as the port's export trade, its import trade in the years between the wars was considerable. At its height in 1927 it exceeded two million tons and almost reached £10 million in value. In other years, however, it barely exceeded one million tons. As in the nineteenth century, so in the years before the outbreak of the Second World War a high proportion of the imports consisted of materials required by the exporting industries of the district. The local iron and steel industry could not produce tinplate, terne, tubes, and galvanized steel for the export market without foreign scrap-iron, pig-iron, and steel billets, relying heavily, therefore, on imports from France, Belgium, Luxemburg, Germany, India, and the U.S.A. Zinc ore concentrates for the galvanizing industry and for a variety of other commodities, tin bars for the tinplate industry and for manufacturing bronze and other alloys, lead for lead piping and for coating steel sheets, copper bar for the copper fabricating plant in the area, and iron pyrites for use by the small chemical factories in the neighbourhood featured regularly, albeit in varying quantities, among the port's imports. Crude petroleum and, from 1931 onwards, refined petroleum figured prominently among the imports, as did the large quantities of pitwood required by the local coal mines. Sawn timber for the building industry, for packing cases for the tinplate trade, and for rail-wagon repair and construction came into the port from Sweden, Finland, Russia, and Canada. Among imported foodstuffs wheat, barley, maize, and oats were well to the fore, but there were also small amounts of potatoes from France and the Channel Islands, as well as tinned milk, beer, lard, and meat.

The volume of shipping calling at the port for overseas cargoes was closely related to the fluctuations in the import and export trade. Likewise, as the markets for the products of the area's industries changed, so did the direction of the export trade. A comparison of the departures of vessels from Swansea in 1932 and 1937 shows little or no change in the number of sailings for Eire, and for the ports reached via the Suez Canal, an increase in departures for Australasia and for Europe, and a falling-off in sailings for the Americas. Incoming cargoes from overseas were dictated by the needs of Swansea and its hinterland for raw materials and foodstuffs. The greatest change that occurred between 1932 and 1937 was in the number of ships coming from East Africa, India, the Persian Gulf, the Far East, and the Pacific Islands. Whereas in 1932 only 44 vessels with a net tonnage of 182,675 had come from ports in those regions, the corresponding figures for 1937 were 137 and 817,030. What might be termed the coastal liner services of the port in the late thirties were provided by Coast Lines Limited with its bi-weekly service to Liverpool, and weekly services to almost every port of importance in the United Kingdom, and by W. Sloan and Company's weekly service to Clydeside. Much of the coasting trade and part of the overseas trade was handled by tramps, the larger ones of over 1,000 tons gross being mainly used in the coal trade while the smaller ones carried a wide variety of cargoes. Two-thirds of the coasters coming into Swansea arrived in ballast. Whether coming in ballast or with cargo, most left with cargoes of coal.

The coming of war in September 1939 brought to local industry 'a plethora of war production orders, especially concerning munitions

manufacture' (Arthur, 1988). Before long the docks were busy handling weapons of war and troop reinforcements, initially from and to
the countries of the British Empire and later from the United States. It
was not surprising, therefore, that Swansea became a target for
German air raids designed to inflict severe damage on local industries
and on the port. In July 1940 an enemy plane in a daylight raid dropped
four high explosive bombs at the 'Mole' end of the King's Dock,
causing extensive damage to sheds and workshops, killing twelve dock
workers and injuring a further twenty-six. Over the next few months
further bombs were dropped on various parts of the docks although
damage was only slight. On the occasion of the 'Three Nights' Blitz' in
February 1941, when the destruction of water mains made the task of
local fire-fighters virtually impossible, many miles of hose stretched
from both the North and South Docks in an attempt to keep up a
supply of water. Anti-aircraft guns were erected in the area of the
North Dock Basin and the Prince of Wales Dock, and a Swansea
Docks unit of the Home Guard was formed. The shortage of dockers
during the war was alleviated to some degree by making use of British
and American troops to help with the traffic passing through the port.
In readiness for the D-Day landings, troops and equipment were
ferried in, and later the port was busily involved in handling the war
materials needed to keep the battle-front supplied.

Post-War Developments, 1948-1988

The Transport Act of 1947 brought the railway-owned docks under
the control of the British Transport Commission, which placed responsibility for their administration in the hands of the Docks and Inland
Waterways Executive. On the dissolution of the British Transport
Commission in 1963, the control of thirty-one harbour undertakings,
including Swansea, was vested in the newly-created British Transport
Docks Board.

The post-war years were difficult ones for British docks in general,
and Swansea was no exception. Enemy attacks during the war had
caused damage calling for an extensive programme of rehabilitation,
and there were, inevitably, considerable arrears of maintenance and
replacement. The difficulties were compounded by restrictions on
capital investment and by Government controls on the supply of raw
materials. However, a programme of investment gradually got under
way, even if, in Swansea's case, it amounted initially to no more than a
modest £11,700 in 1949 for repairs to shed roofing. Two years later, the

Commission was able to report that it had authorized the expenditure of some £500,000 for the electrification of the pumping machinery at the Cardiff and Swansea Docks and for the modernization of the electrical distribution systems at Swansea, Cardiff and Newport. By 1960 schemes of major improvements and modernization costing almost £8,000,000 had been sanctioned at the Commission's south Wales ports. At Swansea one quay, forming two berths, and equipped with nine electric cranes, was provided for bulk cargo traffic. Four other quayside electric cranes were also installed elsewhere in the port. A new 1,000-feet long approach jetty was built at the entrance to the King's Dock, while the quayside fronting 'A' and 'B' sheds of that dock, together with its Phoenix Wharf and the West Wharf of the Prince of Wales Dock, were reconstructed. Private firms were also responsible for some works, the most notable of which were the construction by the Prince of Wales Dry Dock Company, Swansea Ltd., of a new dry dock, 670 feet long, for vessels up to 32,000 tons deadweight, and the provision by B.P. Refinery (Llandarcy) Ltd. of additional facilities at the Queen's Dock for the reception of ocean-going tankers, with separate facilities for coastal vessels, and the erection of extensive dockside oil installations.

The facilities of the port continued to improve under the Docks Board. Among an impressive list of works undertaken were the reconstruction of the West Pier, the provision of new facilities for dealing with fish traffic, the transfer of two coal hoists from Cardiff to the King's Dock, the making of new roads within the docks, the reconditioning of the eastern breakwater at the dock entrance, and the overhaul of the outer lock gates. Of particular note was the construction in the late sixties of a roll-on/roll-off terminal at the East Pier in the tidal waters of the Tawe. This included the provision of a hinged bridge ramp 250 feet in length with a 20-feet wide roadway and operating machinery, a hard-standing area of about five acres, an access roadway, and a customs and reception hall. Officially opened in May 1969, the ferryport had a dramatic effect on the passenger traffic of the port. Whereas just under 11,000 passengers passed through the port in 1968, for 1969 the figure was almost 150,000.

Sadly, the ferryport closed ten years later as a result of the decision of the B and I Company, on economic grounds, to transfer its Irish service to Pembroke Dock. Despite the closure of the ferryport, there was a small amount of passenger traffic in the early eighties. The *Prince of Brittany*, owned by Brittany Ferries, brought 400 passengers on a day trip from France in October 1982 while, in 1983 and again in 1985, the

Russian firm, C.T.C. Lines, used the port as a picking-up and setting-down point for some of its cruises. Far more significant was the bringing back into use of the ferryport in April 1987 with the introduction of a new ro-ro service to Cork operated by Swansea Cork Ferries Ltd. In its first six months of operation, the ferry *Celtic Pride* carried 82,986 passengers and for the corresponding period in 1988 96,488 passengers.

1969 saw not only the opening of the ferryport but also the closing of the South Dock, the culmination of what has been described as Swansea's 'slow spiral of declining competitiveness'. The dock soon became derelict and was partly infilled. However, in the mid-seventies the City Council, which had purchased the dock on its closure, decided to reactivate it and transform it from being a public eyesore into something which would benefit both visitors and local inhabitants. The dock was re-excavated and the sea admitted once more in order to create a 600-berth yacht marina. This became a central feature of a Maritime Quarter, which also included a waterfront village, restaurants, an art gallery, a theatre, sailing and sea-angling schools, and a maritime museum. By early 1988 about £25,000,000 of public money and a further £28,000,000 of private money had been spent in developing the Maritime Quarter.

In the course of the sixties and seventies, twelve of the ports run by the British Transport Docks Board were sold or transferred to other port authorities. From 31 December 1982 the remaining nineteen ports, of which Swansea was one, were placed under the control of Associated British Ports. During the first six years for which the port was administered by ABP, about £1,000,000 was invested in improving facilities. Sheds and cranes were renovated, and surface work carried out in the King's Dock area in order to provided open storage space for drums, heavy items of cargo for overseas construction projects, and containers. However, there was considerable concern as to the future of the port. Although British Coal's trade in anthracite duff was not wholly diverted to Barry, as had seemed likely at one stage, the amount of coal shipped out through the port continued to fall. Some of the steel traffic previously handled at Swansea was diverted to un-registered ports where handling charges were much cheaper. The two most promising developments were the opening of the Cork ferry service and the provision of containerization facilities at the port. The first container ship sailed out of Swansea in February 1987, when the *Brynmore* left the King's Dock for Belfast with a containerized cargo of west Wales anthracite coal. In August 1988 the operating company,

Aerial View of the Marina, 1986.

the Belfast-based Coastal Group, announced that work had begun on a £4 million multi-user container terminal at the King's Dock. Cargo on the twice-weekly Dragon Shipping Line service from Swansea to Belfast had diversified from coal to general trade, and there was a strong possibility that a container service would be established with the Mediterranean.

Throughout the period of public ownership the port's trade continued to be dominated by the import of crude petroleum and the export of refined petroleum and, to a lesser and decreasing extent, of coal and coke. From 1962 to 1971 inclusive the total inward cargoes passing through the port amounted to almost 14,500,000 tons, of which just over half was accounted for by crude petroleum. Of the total outward shipments of some 57,000,000 tons during the same period, petroleum accounted for 38,000,000 tons, and coal and coke for a further 13,000,000 tons. No other commodities approached these in importance, although the value to the port of the trade in iron and steel, including tinplate, in non-ferrous ores and the inward trade in dredged sand and gravel should not be overlooked. Changes in both the volume and pattern of trade since the early seventies indicate some of the problems faced by the port in the late twentieth century. Whereas its total trade exceeded seven million tonnes in 1973 and six million tonnes in each of the three following years, the highest figure in the period from 1977 to 1986 was 5,809,000 tonnes in 1977. The amount of coal shipped out through the port last exceeded one million tonnes in 1980, falling dramatically to 177,000 tonnes in 1984, the first year of the prolonged national coal strike. The subsequent recovery was slight and slow as some markets were lost to foreign competitors. However, the decision to restructure the refinery at Llandarcy as a specialist refinery in 1985 and the closure of the pipeline to it from Angle Bay in West Wales was reflected in the great increase in the import of foreign petroleum products. Whereas these had amounted to only 347,000 tonnes in 1984, the amounts for the three years 1985, 1986 and 1987 were 732, 000, 1,662,000, and 1,354,000 tonnes, respectively. Conversely, there was a decline in the outward shipment, whether overseas or coastwise, of petroleum products.

Trade with countries on the deep sea routes, which exceeded a million tonnes in 1972, had fallen to 130,000 tonnes by 1986. In the latter year there were no imports from those countries, and the export trade would have been very small, had it not been for markets in the Indian sub-continent for manufactured iron and steel goods. The port had to look increasingly to countries on the near and short sea routes, and especially to countries within the European Economic Community, as outlets for its exports and as sources of its imports. Of a total 1,800,000 tonnes of goods imported from overseas in 1986, 1,500,000 tonnes came from EEC countries, the Netherlands supplying nearly one million tonnes, while of the 1,120,000 tonnes exported, 860,000 tonnes went to countries within the Community, France taking 380,000 tonnes. Increasing trade with Europe was a feature of many British ports during the 1980s, and not just of Swansea; however, it tended to favour ports on the south and east coasts at the expense of those in the west.

Despite the fall in its trade, Swansea was headed only by Port Talbot in the amount of trade handled by Bristol Channel ports in 1986. Associated British Ports refused to share in the pessimism about the port's prospects, choosing rather to highlight the developments of the decade and to insist that 'Swansea's advantageous geographical position, combined with extensive cargo-handling facilities, . . . ensures that the port maintains an excellent service for all existing and potential users'.

LOCAL GOVERNMENT, ADMINISTRATION AND POLITICS, 1700 TO THE 1830s

Chapter 4

J. R. Alban

The present system of administration in the City of Swansea dates from 1974, when the Local Government Act, 1972 (1972, *cap.* 70) came into force. This legislation provided Swansea, as indeed other areas of England and Wales, with a two-tier system of local government based on the division of major functions between a county council (in the local case, West Glamorgan) and a district council (the City of Swansea). Such a bilateral system had applied to rural areas since 1894; but, for the first time, it was now also applied to major towns. Certain other essential functions, however, were left outside the scope of these two new main authorities: for example, responsibility for health care, the supply of electricity and water, and the provision of a police force are today in the hands of separate bodies.

For many inhabitants of Swansea, the reorganization of 1974 seemed to be a strange new departure. Indeed, to some it was even seen as a retrograde step resulting in a decline in efficiency. At the date of reorganization, most Swansea people — in contrast to those who lived in the surrounding rural areas — associated local government and administration with a single, all-purpose authority, the County Borough of Swansea. Immediately before reorganization, the county borough had had almost sole responsibility for most of the aspects of local administration which touched upon people's daily lives: its functions in 1974 included education, libraries, housing, weights and measures and public protection, roads, markets, museums, parks, town planning, rating, and public health. Some years earlier, the county borough had also been responsible, among other things, for policing the town, licensing motor vehicles, administering Quarter Sessions and Assizes, and for the supply of electricity and water. Those with longer memories would perhaps recall that the county borough had, at some time, administered poor relief and, for a short period, had even run the town's municipal telephone system. In the course of the twentieth century, these various functions and others had been transferred to other types of authority or had been taken over directly by central government.

However, the system which disappeared in 1974 did not have a long tradition behind it. The County Borough of Swansea had, indeed, only come into existence in 1889 and at the time of its creation, moreover, it was the heir to a tradition of 'democratic' modern local government which dated back only to 1835. Furthermore, although widely regarded as an all-purpose authority, for much of its life the county borough was only one of a number of organizations reponsible for different aspects of local government within the town. Most of these bodies, variously concerned, for example, with poor relief, education, and public health, had emerged in the latter half of the nineteenth century, as the result of legislation which stemmed from constant experimentation aimed at improving the quality of life in the growing towns of Victorian Britain. Local government and its administration in Swansea today are a direct continuation of this nineteenth-century tradition of improvement, and the bilateral system adopted in 1974 retains many features introduced in the nineteenth century. However, the present City of Swansea is also the heir to a far older tradition of municipal government, which ultimately had its roots in the middle ages, but which was changed dramatically in the 1830s. This chapter therefore seeks to trace the evolution of local government administration and politics from 1700 to the 1830s, while chapter 10 continues that story from the 1830s to the 1970s.

The Unreformed Corporation

The borough of Swansea had grown up around the castle which the Norman conquerors of the Welsh commote of Gŵyr had erected near the mouth of the river Tawe at the beginning of the twelfth century. The castle was almost certainly there by 1116, and one may assume that a small settlement already surrounded it by that date. In common with the practice in most marcher lordships in Wales, the new Norman lord of Gower encouraged the residence of traders, merchants, and

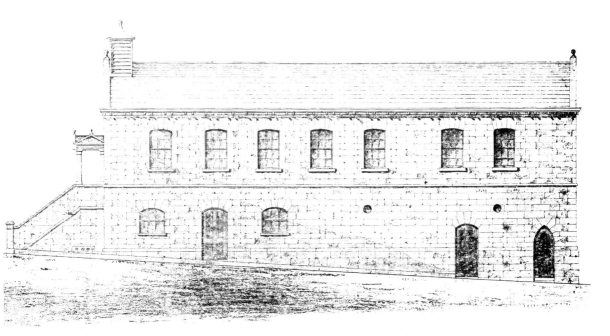

The Town Hall of 1585.

craftsmen, initially to supply the needs of the castle's garrison. By the middle of the twelfth century, the settlement around the castle seems to have developed into a thriving little borough, which was given its first charter by William de Newburgh, lord of Gower, at some time between 1158 and 1184. In the course of the next two hundred years, other charters of privileges were granted by several kings of England and, in 1306, by William de Braose, lord of Gower. In the seventeenth century, three further charters were granted, two by Oliver Cromwell and one by James II.

While the medieval charters of the lords of Gower and those of the seventeenth century granted certain rights of self-government, it is clear that by the modern period there was 'little resemblance to the constitution prescribed by any of those charters', as the Commissioners on Municipal Corporations noted in their report of 1835. By the eighteenth century, the administration of the borough was mature, and, as in many other British towns, the practical workings of its constitution had developed mainly through custom, although in some small points certain provisions of the charters had a bearing.

At the beginning of the eighteenth century, Swansea was still a small coastal town of about 2,000 inhabitants. In its built-up extent, it was scarcely larger than it had been in the middle ages, with the bulk of its population still living within the area delineated by its former town walls. The town may have lost its pre-eminence as the autonomous capital of the marcher lordship of Gower in the 1540s, but its strong economic position, as the market town for peninsular and upland Gower, its embryonic extractive industries — coal had been mined there since the fourteenth century — and, not least, its importance as as port, had all contributed to its thriving survival when other former marcher capitals had declined into becoming sleepy backwater villages. Indeed, in 1700, Swansea was a town of great potential, where the first steps in serious industrial development were about to take place, based upon the centuries-old trade in coal and the advent of new metallurgical industries. Well could Daniel Defoe remark twenty years later that 'Swanzey is a seaport, and a very considerable town for trade . . . so that sometimes may be seen a hundred sail of ships at a time loading coals here; which greatly enriches the country and particularly this town'. Defoe was writing just at the start of Swansea's

'Gabriel Powell's Chest'.

industrial expansion. Coal had attracted copper-smelting to the lower Swansea Valley in 1717, and this new industry was to expand rapidly during the next 150 years, to be joined in the nineteenth century by a host of other metallurgical industries. The twin impetus of the growing Industrial Revolution and the needs of foreign war in the eighteenth century gave an enormous boost to Swansea's economic development, and this process was intensified by the more rapid industrial expansion of the nineteenth century. One tangible result of industrial growth was an increase in population. By the time of the first census in 1801, Swansea's population stood at 6,099; by 1831 it was 13,265, while by 1851 it had increased to 16,993.

However, while the population of Swansea increased over seven-fold between 1700 and 1831, the administration of the town during the same period remained virtually unchanged. Before 1835, control of the town's affairs lay chiefly in the hands of an unreformed corporation which, in essence, had changed little over the centuries. Many of the organs through which this corporation operated were, in fact, also the administrative organs of the seigneurial manor of Swansea, whose lord, the duke of Beaufort, dominated borough affairs through his local agents.

The corporation of Swansea before 1835 only superficially resembled a modern local authority. Unlike modern councillors, the burgesses were not elected, nor did they therefore have any responsibility to an electorate for any actions which they took. The influence of the lord was an extremely important factor in the town's affairs before 1835. In most instances, as we shall see, his word was final, and although such a state of affairs seemingly nullified any notions of 'democracy' in the town, usually the burgess body were prepared to accept such controls. In fact, in many respects, the interests of the lord and the burgesses were mutual: for example, both parties were keen to limit the number of burgesses, the lord so that he could exercise closer control, the burgesses so that each one would share in a larger slice of the borough's economic cake — the privileges which went with the freedom of the borough.

The corporation of the eighteenth and early nineteenth centuries comprised a Steward, a Portreeve, twelve Aldermen, a Recorder, two Common Attorneys, a Layer Keeper, two Sergeants at Mace, some minor officials, and an indefinite number of burgesses. Although nominally the Portreeve was the head of the corporation, it was the Steward who wielded the greatest power. The Steward was the representative of the lord — the duke of Beaufort — within the

seigneurial borough of Swansea, and in all aspects of borough administration the influence of the lord, through his principal agent, the
Steward, was paramount. In practice, the Steward controlled all
appointments to corporation offices; for example, at the Leet Court he
selected and swore in the Portreeve, aldermen, and officials of the
corporation. He could therefore ensure that no burgess whom he or
the lord regarded as unsuitable could hold office. This power over
appointments gave the Steward a great deal of direct influence, while
he could also apply indirect influence, which most Stewards exercised
successfully. Together with the Portreeve, the Steward presided over
the Court Leet which was held in the borough twice a year, on the
feast of St Philip and St James (1 May) and at Michaelmas (29
September). They also presided over the two civil courts of the
borough: the Court Baron, which heard causes of under 40*s*., and the
Court of Pleas, which dealt with causes exceeding that amount.

The Portreeve was the head of the corporation, and was elected
annually at the Michaelmas Leet. On the eve of the court's meeting,
the aldermen met to choose four from their number, whose names
were presented to the burgess body meeting in Common Hall on the
following day. From the four, the burgesses selected two, whose
names were then submitted to the Steward, who chose one to be
Portreeve for the ensuing year. By this method, the lord could
determine who would hold the office, but by the early nineteenth
century, it appears that the aldermen shared the office in rotation. The
duties of the Portreeve were numerous. As well as presiding over the
courts and acting as 'chairman' in Common Hall, he was the coroner
and chief constable of the borough, was clerk of the market, and had
custody of the borough archives and the standard weights and
measures. He was also involved in the distribution of charity to the
poor and was the billeting officer whenever troops came into the
town. After the passing of the respective legislation, he also became *ex
officio* a harbour trustee and an improvement commissioner for
Swansea.

To support himself in office, the Portreeve received emoluments
from four traditional sources within the borough: ancient rents known
as 'free rents'; tolls of quayage, wharfage, and markets, the first two
being dues levied on all merchandise imported into Swansea; keelage
dues, a toll on all ships entering or leaving the port; and the assize of
ale, a small tax imposed annually on all the inns in the borough. By
1833, the revenues from these sources came to about £750 a year, a not
inconsiderable amount.

The Recorder, who was elected by the aldermen and burgesses, held office during his good behaviour and acted as the corporation's solicitor. As his name suggests, his main role was to attend the meetings of the corporation and to record the proceedings. There was no fixed salary for the office, but the Recorder was entitled to take certain fees. For instance, as the officer of the Court of Pleas, he received fees which, by the early nineteenth century, amounted to approximately £60 a year. As the corporation's attorney and solicitor, he also took legal fees, which came to about £300 a year, while he was also entitled to a fee of one guinea upon the admission of every burgess. The office was therefore lucrative and one of great importance. Small wonder, then, that for most of the eighteenth and early nineteenth centuries successive Stewards made sure that they held their office jointly with that of Recorder.

The financial matters of the borough before 1835 were under the control of two officials known as the Common Attorneys. Their general duties were to superintend the property of the corporation, to collect rents, and to receive and pay all moneys. In other words, they acted as the treasurers to the corporation. Officially, the Common Attorneys' term of office was one year, at the end of which the outgoing officials returned the names of four burgesses to the Steward, from whom the latter selected two to serve as Common Attorneys for the following year. However, by the nineteenth century, it was usual for one of the outgoing officials — known as the 'acting' Common Attorney — to have his appointment renewed so that he would serve for a number of years. This practice provided a continuity essential in financial matters. At an earlier period, when the Common Attorneys had been changed annually, serious problems had often occurred, mainly through the lack of continuity, but also because of a lack of enthusiasm and erratic accounting practices on the part of the office holders. Thus, in 1790 it was reported that no accounts had been submitted by the Common Attorneys for the previous five years, while there were also several instances of the corporation's having repaid the same debt twice because defective records had been kept. One reason for this lack of efficiency was that many burgesses regarded the post of Common Attorney as onerous. By the nineteenth century it was realised that a sound financial reward would offset this burden, and this was thus another reason for the appointment of a semi-permanent 'acting' Common Attorney, who took for his exclusive use the poundage of five per cent on all rents collected, which had hitherto been traditionally shared between the two Common Attorneys.

Gabriel Powell, 'King of Swansea'.

Because of Swansea's importance as a port, the corporation appointed an official known as the Layer Keeper. His title was derived from the 'Layer' or mud bank in the river Tawe and Fabian's Bay which was exposed at low tide, when ships' bottoms 'laid up' on it. The Layer Keeper's main task was to ensure that no ballast or other offensive material was thrown into the river and to remove tree trunks and other obstructions to navigation from the river and from Fabian's Bay. The indiscriminate dropping of ballast had been a constant problem since at least the sixteenth century, assisting in the silting up of the river and bay, thereby making it difficult for ships of any size to enter the harbour. Indeed, from that century onwards, the records of the corporation abound with ordinances directed against the dropping of ballast. The Layer Keeper was also responsible for the navigation of the harbour bar and the river and for ensuring that the mooring posts on the quayside were kept in good order. Persons transgressing against the river ordinances were presented before the borough courts by the Layer Keeper.

It appears that, originally, the borough had appointed several Layer Keepers, but by the beginning of the eighteenth century, one burgess was appointed to the office annually. In recompense for his services, the Layer Keeper was entitled to take a portion from the revenues raised by the keelage dues levied within the port, the remainder being shared between the Portreeve and the duke of Beaufort's Water Bailiff. Nineteenth-century returns show that the Layer Keeper took the smallest portion, e.g.:

Category	Keelage	Portreeve	Water Bailiff	Layer Keeper
Foreign vessels	7s.	3s. 4d.	2s.	1s.
British vessels going to foreign ports	3s. 6d.	1s. 8d.	1s. 4d.	6d.
British vessels above 100 tons going to or coming from any port in the U.K. or Ireland	2s.	10d.	8d.	6d.

The Layer Keeper was elected at the annual Easter Court Leet, the jury nominating two burgesses, from whom the Steward selected one to serve for the ensuing year.

Few burgesses wished to be nominated for the two posts of Sergeant at Mace, which were regarded as onerous and of little financial reward. The duties of the Sergeants, who were appointed annually, were to attend the Portreeve, to execute the processes of the Court Leet and Court Baron, and to supervise the common pound. In other words, their duties were partly ceremonial, but they acted mainly as the bailiffs of the borough courts, collecting fines, arresting miscreants, and seizing goods as distresses. Their selection took place annually at the Michaelmas Leet and followed the standard practice:

the names of four burgesses were submitted to the Steward from whom he chose two to serve in office. The sergeants each received an annual salary of two guineas, but supplemented that with a fee of 5s. for every arrest which they made, while they also took a portion of the fees received in court (6d. where the amount was under 40s. and 2s. 6d. where it was above 40s.). By the early nineteenth century, the annual emoluments from all these sources amounted to under £10 for each sergeant.

Among the several classes of minor officials were constables, who were appointed each year at the Michaelmas Leet, while two haywards were selected at every Easter Leet. In origin, these last

THE EAST VIEW OF SWANSEA CA

To the most Noble **HENRY SOMERSET** *DUKE of Beaufort.* Marquefs and Earl *of Worcefter.* Earl *of Glamorgan,* Vifcount *Grofmont.* Baron Herbert, Lord *of Ragland, Chepstow and Gower. and* Baron *Beaufort of Caldecot Castle in the County of Monmouth. This* Prospect *is humbly Inscrib'd by may it Please Y*.*Grace Y.*.*Graces most humble and Obedient Serv.*.* *Sam*.*& Nath*.* Buck.*

The East View of Swansea Castle, by Samuel and Nathaniel Buck, 1741.

named were purely manorial officials whose duty it was to supervise the common lands of the borough. The Hayward for the Mountain was responsible for the common of Townhill, while the Hayward for the Burrows looked after the extensive tract of land lying immediately behind the foreshore and stretching from the western side of the river mouth to the Brynmill stream. The duties of these officials became negligible after the enclosure of the Townhill and Burrows in 1762.

Of this multitude of officials, the two most important were the Steward and the Portreeve, of whom the Steward, as the lord's agent, was the pivot of local administration in the borough of Swansea before 1835. Below the Steward and Portreeve was an 'aldermanic council',

IN THE COUNTY OF GLAMORGAN.

THIS Castle was built by Henry Beaumont Earl of Warwick, about A.D. 1113. Soon after which Griffith ap Rhys ap Theodore Prince of South Wales came before it, and burnt down great Part of the out Buildings. It is the Property of his Grace the Duke of Beaufort, Lord Paramount of Gowerland. —
Sam.l & Nath.l Buck delin et Sculp. Publish'd according to Act of Parliam.t March 25, 1741.

or executive body, which consisted of twelve aldermen. The decisions of this council seem to have been subject to the approval of the general body of burgesses. When a vacancy occurred among the aldermen, the survivors selected two of the burgesses and submitted their names to the Steward, who, if they were acceptable, chose one of them and swore him in as an alderman. The office of Alderman was held for life, although a member could be disenfranchised if he were absent from the borough for a year and a day or if he behaved in a manner which was detrimental to the interests of the corporation. Loss of office, however, was not necessarily permanent, and, on payment of a fine, a dismissed alderman could be reinstated. Being a member of the aldermanic council was an important privilege, since only aldermen could be chosen for the lucrative office of Portreeve.

The general burgess body was composed of an indefinite number of members, who met from time to time in Common Hall, where they determined the corporation's general policy. The apparent democracy in such meetings was virtually nullified in practice by the influence which the Steward exerted. Moreover, by the eighteenth century, the burgesses formed only a small percentage of the town's total population. There were thirty-five burgesses in 1789, fifty-three in 1802, and 104 in 1833, while the population of Swansea stood at 6,099 in 1801 and 13,256 in 1831. Taking the population as a whole, it is therefore very clear that local government in Swansea before 1835 was in the hands of an oligarchy, and a self-perpetuating one at that. The burgesses were not elected in the same way as modern councillors, but themselves controlled admission to the corporation in the strictest fashion. Admission to the burgess body was a very important privilege, since only burgesses were eligible for the offices of the corporation, some of which were lucrative (although, as we have seen, others were regarded as onerous). Furthermore, since the 1540s, only burgesses had the right to vote for the member of parliament. Most importantly, however, burgesses were exempt within the borough from payment of all tolls and dues — tolls and dues which were stringently exacted from non-burgesses. Allied to this were the almost exclusive trading rights which burgesses enjoyed within the borough. Burgesses also had an almost complete monopoly of leases of corporate land, usually at extremely low rents, while from 1763 onwards, senior members of the corporation received annuities from the profits of the enclosed lands on the Townhill and Burrows. By the original resolution, the two senior aldermen received £4 each and the eight senior burgesses £2 from the sum of £24 set aside annually for this purpose from the

The Oath of a Burgess, 1759.

Town and Borough
of Swansea
The Oath of a Burgess.

You shall true Burgess be of this Town and
Borough of Swansea..... You shall be obedient
to the Steward and Portreeve thereof for the Time
being..... You shall pay all ~~Taxes~~ lawfully Rated
and Taxed on you..... You shall maintain the
Priviledges and Liberties with all laudable
accustomed orders used or to be used within this Town,
to the best of your endeavours, and if there shall
happen to come any thing to your knowledge that
shall or may in any wise be prejudicial to the
Liberties of the said Borough, You shall not only acquaint
the Portreeve for the time being, and other the Aldermen
of the same but also shall defend it to the utmost of
your Power and likewise do all things that becomes
good Burgesses for to do.

So help you God &c.

Richard Awbrey Senr. was admitted a Burgess of this
Town the Fifth day of December, One Thousand seven
Hundred and Fifty nine as appears by the Records of the said
Borough, on Payment of the Composition Money.

Gab: Jeffreys
Dy. Recorder there

receipts of rent from the enclosed lands. These payments were discontinued in 1792, but resumed in 1796. The number of senior burgesses entitled to receive them was increased to twelve in 1821, while in 1825, the amount of each annuity was increased to £10.

Since there were many valuable privileges attached to burgess-ship, it was in the corporation's interests to keep its numbers as low as possible. Admission to the burgess body was therefore strictly controlled, as it had been for centuries. In the middle ages, possession of a burgage plot had been an essential prerequisite, although by the end of the fifteenth century, this had been reduced to possession of part of a burgage plot. The property qualification had disappeared by the sixteenth century, and by the eighteenth there were four means by which a burgess could be admitted: by birth, as the son of a burgess; by marriage. However, a burgess's daughter who married whilst still a or, less frequently, by gift. Admission by these four avenues was very strictly regulated, and the slightest discrepancy in a claim could invalidate it.

Candidates claiming their freedom by any of the above means had to have attained the age of twenty-one and had to be married. Admission by birth was only open to those sons of burgesses born *after* their fathers' own admissions. Sons born before the father had been admitted had therefore technically not been born as sons of burgesses, and so their claims were invalid. Again, only daughters born after their fathers' admission could transmit the freedom to a husband on marriage. However, a burgess' daughter who married whilst still a minor could transmit her claim to a husband who had attained his own majority. The husband of a burgess's daughter who failed to claim admission during his wife's lifetime was debarred from claiming by marriage, although in at least one case the burgesses relaxed this ruling. In 1789, a William Jones was granted the freedom of the borough on payment of fifteen guineas. Jones had been married to the daughter of a burgess and therefore 'had an undoubted claim to be admitted', but since he had not claimed during his wife's lifetime, his claim by marriage was extinct, and admission on payment of the fine was, in effect, admission by gift.

Admission by apprenticeship or 'servitude' was limited to those who had served a seven-year apprenticeship with a burgess. During his period of indenture, the apprentice had close links with his master and would usually have lived within his household. In many ways it was therefore logical that such a person should become eligible for admission as a burgess once he had qualified in his profession or trade.

However, the rules for admission by this method were very strict. For instance, if the indentures had not been enrolled correctly in the corporation's records, the apprentice's claim was invalid. Moreover, as a means of limiting admissions by this route, no burgess was allowed to keep more than two apprentices at one time. Perhaps because of the stringency of the admission process, apprenticeship was never a popular method of gaining the freedom of the borough, only eight apprentices being admitted between 1734 and 1834.

Before 1835, the corporation also had the power to bestow the freedom of the borough by gift, although this was the least common method of admission. In most cases where admission was by gift, a payment had to be made. In 1613, the burgesses had resolved that all who received the freedom by gift should pay 20s., while in 1698, this fee was raised to £3. In the eighteenth century, there were consequently few admissions by gift and none between 1726 and 1768. By the end of the century, fees for such admissions were usually high. In 1789, as we have seen, William Jones paid fifteen guineas, while in the same year, Thomas Urmson paid £50 for admission. The relative smallness of Jones's fee suggests that some 'discount' may have been allowed him in respect of his formerly having a claim by marriage. After 1789, admissions by gift became more frequent, although they were still considerably fewer than admissions by birth and marriage. Occasionally, the burgesses granted the freedom to eminent persons: Lord Nelson and Sir William Hamilton, for instance, received it in 1802. Persons who performed good services for the borough might also be given the freedom as a reward. On 22 June 1792, Edmund Estcourt was admitted 'for his friendship . . . as the Corporation's solicitor in London' and also for having presented the town with a clock, which was mounted on the wall of the castle. Another lawyer to be thus honoured was the barrister, Henry Sockett, of Gray's Inn, who was admitted in November 1830 'in consideration of his many and valuable services afforded to the Town and Borough of Swansea'. Nevertheless, the freedom of the borough was not there for the asking, and important local industrialists, such as John Henry Vivian, had to wait many years before receiving the freedom. Indeed, Vivian was admitted only in 1834, one year before the demise of the unreformed corporation.

A person claiming admission as a burgess, by whatever route, initially asserted his claim before the burgesses in Common Hall. If the claim were undisputed, an entry was made in the books by the Recorder and at the meeting of the Court Leet next following, the claimant was presented by the jury to the Steward and Portreeve as a person fit to be admitted as a burgess. The claimant was then duly sworn and admitted. From 1789 onwards, the claimant was required to obtain a certified copy of the order for his admission, at a fee of 1s., and to show this to the jury at the Leet Court before he could be presented.

On admission in the Court Leet, all burgesses had to pay fees, which comprised composition money to the borough and a court fee to the Recorder. The composition paid by those admitted by birth or servitude was 5s., while for those admitted by marriage it was £1 10s. As we have seen, the composition paid by persons admitted by gift varied. However, all applicants paid the same fee to the Recorder. By 1833, this was one guinea. On admission, the new burgess swore an oath of obedience to the Steward and Portreeve, although burgesses who were Quakers could affirm instead of swearing.

The administration of the borough operated both individually, through its officials, and corporately, through a series of meetings. Periodically, the burgesses met at their 'Common Hall', the proceedings of which were recorded in the 'Hall Day Minute Books', a series which runs from the sixteenth century to the demise of the corporation in 1835. The hall in which the burgesses met was on the upper floor of the town hall which had been erected on the north-west side of the ruins of the 'new castle' in 1585. It was a stone-built, two-storey building, with its main accommodation on the first floor, and the ground floor divided into at least three separate sections, to include a weighing house, a store room, and a 'dark house' or gaol. It was on the ground floor that the burgesses stored the 'privileged goods' and 'thirds' taken under a practice laid down by sixteenth-century borough ordinances which ensured that all goods entering the town should be first offered to the burgesses for sale, and only then would the residue be made available to the public at large. At first-floor level, the building had two main rooms: the Guildhall and the court room on the northern end, and the Grand Jury Room on the southern end. It was in this northern room that the burgesses met for the Hall Days, while the borough courts, and the county courts of Petty Sessions and Quarter Sessions, were also held there. The town hall was used for such purposes until 1829, when the business of the corporation moved to a new Guildhall, built 1825-9 at Somerset Place, a far larger and grander building than the old town hall, which was ultimately demolished in 1856 to make room for a new Post Office.

The meetings of the burgesses in Common Hall must not be equated with those of a modern local authority. True, it was one of the main organs of town government and administration, and it was in Common Hall that the burgesses discussed matters relating to the borough. But there the similarities ended. Unlike those of local authorities today, the meetings in Common Hall were not regular. In fact, the frequency of meetings varied over the years. For instance, until 1759, three or four were held a year, but in 1770 and in 1788, a meeting was convened only once. However, in some years, as many as thirteen meetings could take place, although by the early nineteenth century meetings averaged five or six a year. Furthermore, unlike modern councillors, the burgesses were not elected; thus they had no responsibility to an electorate or, indeed, to the population of Swansea at large. To be a burgess meant the enjoyment of privileges denied to non-burgesses. Small wonder, then, that the matters dealt with in Common Hall usually reflected the interests of the burgess body as a whole. They were mostly concerned with financial matters, such as the market, the corporation estate, and the granting of leases to burgesses, to the almost total exclusion of measures which could have benefited the town as a whole. For instance, whenever the question of town or harbour improvement was raised before the 1790s, the decision taken was always negative.

Moreover, while the Hall Day Minute Books at first sight suggest a democratic process, in practice such democracy was superficial. It has been noted above how the Steward always had the final word in appointments to office, but his influence and patronage were even wider, as the *Report of the Commissioners on Municipal Corporations* clearly revealed in 1835:

> The corporation has for a long time been wholly under the control of the lord of the borough exercised through his steward.
>
> The lord's steward having the power of rejecting an alderman from the valuable office of portreeve (in addition to that of preventing the admission of any obnoxious burgess into the body of aldermen in the first instance), his influence in that body is all prevailing.
>
> Again, the lord's steward having the power of rejecting any burgess from the office of layer keeper, common attorney, or other inferior offices in the corporation, as well as that of alderman, a considerable number of burgesses are immediately influenced in this way.

While these influential weapons were wielded by any person holding the office of Steward, a determined one, like Gabriel Powell, who held the office from 1745 to his death in December 1788, exercised even greater sway through the sheer force of his personality. Indeed, Powell had a further hold over the burgesses. Over a period of many years, he had loaned several sums of money to the corporation, taking as security the town chest which contained the borough archives. The chest was kept in Powell's house in High Street, the relevant minute books being brought to Common Hall by him and then taken home again after the meeting. Powell died in December 1788 and, early in the following year, his executors refused to return the items to the burgesses until the debts, by this time amounting to £1,000, had been repaid. The Portreeve was therefore empowered by the burgesses to raise the money 'as expeditiously as possible' and they were also compelled to purchase a new minute book to replace the current one, which was detained by Powell's executors. Even from beyond the grave Gabriel Powell's influence was felt. Small wonder, then, that during his lifetime he should have been known as 'the King of Swansea'.

The resolutions taken at Common Hall were often therefore no more than formalities, the outcome having been decided by the Steward beforehand. However, there were a few rare occasions when certain burgesses did not accept such foregone conclusions with docility. For example, in November 1787, when Gabriel Powell attempted to make the burgesses approve a resolution, the text of which they had not seen, he was challenged by certain members of the corporation, but without success, as was usually the case.

The other main organs of administration and the dispensation of justice were the courts of the borough. The Court Leet, earlier called the 'Dourne Court', was, in origin, a manor court which, as in many other boroughs, had developed into an organ of local administration.It met twice a year, on the feast of St Philip and St James (1 May), and at Michaelmas (29 September). As we have seen, it was in this court that borough officials were elected, where the admission of burgesses was regulated, and where the indentures of apprentices were enrolled. In many respects, it formalized decisions previously taken by the burgesses in Common Hall.

There was no criminal court as such within the borough, although Swansea did become an assize town in 1835, on the abolition of the Court of Great Sessions, and, occasionally, county courts met in the town. However, two civil courts were held in Swansea every third Monday. These were the Court Baron (originally a manorial court) and the Court of Pleas. The charters of Oliver Cromwell and James II had provided for a court of record to be held every Monday, but by the eighteenth century, that had lapsed, although traces of its functions were to be seen in the Court Baron.

The Court Baron, which was presided over by the Steward and the Portreeve, had jurisdiction over causes under 40s. This court concerned itself mainly with cases of minor debt, and, occasionally, slander or libel. In contrast, the jurisdiction of the Court of Pleas was unlimited in amount and it had the power to try all manner of civil suits. In practice, however, actions in this court were chiefly for debt, concerning sums rarely exceeding £20 in total. A high proportion of cases were settled out of court once a writ had been issued. For example, out of thirty-one actions commenced in 1832, only twenty were entered in court, and of these, fifteen judgements went by default and only two cases were actually tried. This suggests a lack of impartiality within this court, where judge, jury, and officials were all members of the burgess body. A non-burgess suing a burgess for debt could therefore expect little sympathy. In this court, as in the Court Baron, the Steward and the Portreeve sat as judges by custom. However, since the Steward was usually a solicitor by profession, in practice, he sat as the presiding judge.

Because of the nature of oligarchical government in Swansea before 1835, 'politics' in the modern sense did not play a dominant role. Burgesses were not elected but selected according to their individual qualifications for admission. They therefore did not need to canvass for votes nor follow any party line. In fact, in the eighteenth and early nineteenth centuries, politics entered mainly into the sphere of parliamentary representation, and even then, the majority of burgesses were prepared to follow the lord's will in such matters.

Before the Acts of Union of England and Wales in the sixteenth century, Swansea, in common with other Welsh towns, had had no representation in parliament. From the 1540s, Swansea had a member of parliament, although, apart from a short period in the 1650s, it had to share its representation with seven other towns in Glamorgan until the parliamentary reform of 1832.

The Acts of Union had provided the new county of Glamorgan with two members of parliament: the knight of the shire for the 'body of the county' and the member for the boroughs of Glamorgan. The latter represented the county town of Cardiff and seven 'out-boroughs': Aberavon, Cowbridge, Kenfig, Llantrisant, Loughor, Neath, and Swansea. The idea of contributory boroughs was unique to Wales and in some parts it survived until 1944. The presence of so many towns in the consituency meant that no elections were held in Swansea before 1832. For the whole of the eighteenth century, uncontested elections were held at Bridgend, while polling for contested elections was held in the county town of Cardiff, although from 1815 to 1832, *all* elections were held at Bridgend.

The only exception to Swansea's political situation before 1832 occurred in the late 1650s. Under the terms of Oliver Cromwell's second charter to the town in 1658, Swansea was granted the privilege of electing 'One able and discreete person . . . to be a Burgess of the Parliament'. In the following year, William Foxwist, a justice of the Court of Great Sessions, sat as the member for Swansea for the four-month term of Richard Cromwell's parliament. Thereafter, the privilege fell into abeyance, as did so many Protectorate grants after the Restoration.

Before 1832, both the county seat and the contributory borough seat came strongly under the influence of the great county families. The eight towns which made up the borough seat were controlled by four main groups of patrons in the period under consideration. As in the case of the dukes of Beaufort in Swansea, the patrons chiefly exercised their power as lords of the manor or borough. Thus, because of the contributory nature of the seat, the selection of a candidate was not an affair exclusive to Swansea, and the influences at work in the other contributory towns were also of importance in this respect. In the eighteenth century, the main groups with influence over the borough seat were the Mansel family, with their control of Kenfig and their influence in Aberavon; the Mackworth family, who controlled Neath and had some power in Aberavon; the so-called 'Cardiff Castle interest', operated initially by the Herberts and later passing to the Lords Windsor and through them to the Butes, was an important force in Cardiff, Cowbridge, and Llantrisant; finally, the dukes of Beaufort had control over Swansea and Loughor.

In general, the patrons consulted one another rather than put up rival candidates. Consequently, before 1832, elections to the borough seat were usually unopposed. Contested elections took place only in 1734, 1818, and 1819. The politics of the borough members reflected the interests of the controlling magnates; thus they were usually Tories, or independents with Tory inclinations. In fact, between 1700 and 1832, only three Whigs were elected to the seat. The influence of the various patrons was reflected in the persons chosen as members. For example, in the early eighteenth century, the Mansel family held wide political power in Glamorgan, thus it is not surprising that the occupants of the seat between 1700 and 1734 were either members of the Mansel family or persons with close Mansel connexions. After 1790, the 'Cardiff Castle interest' was in the ascendancy, a fact reflected in the tenure of the seat from 1790 to 1832 by the Butes or their nominees. In fact, the 'Cardiff Castle interest' had controlled the seat between 1734 and 1739, although two Mackworth M.P.s had held it from 1739 to 1790.

Patrons like the Beauforts and Butes exercised control in the boroughs by trading the controlled votes of burgesses. In Swansea, as in many of the other boroughs, only burgesses were entitled to vote for the borough candidate. In boroughs such as Kenfig, it was possible for patrons to admit large numbers of burgesses at election times so as to increase the votes for a particular candidate. However, there is little evidence of this practice in Swansea, where the admission of burgesses was so strictly controlled, and where, in any case, the dukes of Beaufort found they could exercise tighter control over a smaller burgess body. There is not much information on the interaction between the burgesses and the lord in Swansea with regard to parliamentary elections, but generally the burgesses were prepared to vote as the lord directed. To do otherwise would be to risk his displeasure.

If the burgesses formed an oligarchy in local government, they also formed a minority electorate in Swansea. In 1801, only fifty-nine persons out of a total of 6,099 in Swansea were entitled to vote, and, indeed, the total number of voters for the whole of the eight boroughs in 1820 amounted to 700, of whom forty-seven came from Swansea. To counteract such inequalities, not just in Swansea but in the nation as a whole, the first Reform Act was passed in 1832. This introduced significant changes in Swansea's parliamentary representation and affected political developments, in ways which will be discussed in chapter 10.

The Harbour Trustees

Although the corporation was the main body concerned with the administration of borough affairs before 1835, by the early nineteenth century, two other administrative bodies had come into being in Swansea, one of them concerned with the harbour, the other dealing with urban improvements.

With the development of Swansea's industries, the trade of its port grew at least six-fold during the eighteenth century, but harbour facilities had not kept in step. For example, a nine-foot high bar of sand and gravel across the mouth of Fabian's Bay meant that only vessels of

Swansea Corporation discussing Harbour Improvements, 1787.

small burden could enter the port. The poor facilities had given rise to several attempts at harbour improvement, for instance in 1762 and 1771, but these had been thwarted by Gabriel Powell and Iltid Thomas. On 10 October 1787, a group of committed burgesses held a general meeting at the Mackworth Hotel in Wind Street to discuss 'Improving the navigation of the port of Swansea', and resolved to obtain a harbour improvement act. They had not reckoned on the continuing opposition of Gabriel Powell to any kind of change which he felt was not in the lord's interest. At the meeting of Common Hall on 2 November, Powell proposed mortgaging the corporation's estate for £500 in order to oppose the harbour bill's passage through parliament. This led to unseemly scenes of fisticuffs in Common Hall, which were the subject of a notorious contemporary cartoon by Moses Harris. Powell's blocking bid was successful, nonetheless.

The death of Gabriel Powell late in 1788 removed the greatest obstacle to harbour improvement and left the way open for reform. Thus, from October 1789, the corporation began to take an active interest in developing the port. Ultimately, in 1791, an Act of

Parliament was obtained for this purpose, the bill having been presented jointly in the name of the corporation and the duke of Beaufort. The act established a statutory body of Harbour Trustees to improve and manage the port of Swansea, thereby taking the harbour effectively out of the control of the corporation. Nevertheless, the corporation continued to possess rights and interests on the riverside, including the old privilege of levying the dues of quayage, wharfage, and keelage, until 1835. The borough's Layer Keeper continued to operate until the same date, and, indeed, the Court Leet of the manor of Swansea continued to appoint an honorary Layer Keeper until the 1920s.

The constitution of the Harbour Trustees, as established by this act, took into account the various local interests in the port. The original trustees included the duke of Beaufort, his eldest son, and his Steward, Recorder, Water Bailiff, Coroner, and Bailiff; the borough interests were looked after by the Portreeve, aldermen, and twelve burgesses; while twelve persons represented 'the interests of . . . proprietors . . . of Collieries, Mines, and Minerals, . . . Copper Works, Potteries, Salt Works, or any other works and manufactures within the said River, Port, and Harbour of Swansea, and the owners of ships and vessels frequenting the same'. Several prominent landowners were also appointed trustees by the act.

The trustees were to meet on the first Monday of each month at the Guildhall of the borough. In fact, they had no separate offices until 1858, when a house in Mount Street was leased. Their first purpose-built offices, at the corner of Adelaide Street and Mount Street, were not opened until 1901.

The act empowered the trustees to improve the harbour and to build a lighthouse at Mumbles. To enable these works to be carried out, they could borrow up to £12,000 and could also levy rates on vessels entering the port. The first act empowered them to elect one of their number as a Treasurer and to appoint a Layer Keeper, although, with expansion in the nineteenth century, the trustees provided themselves with professional staff, which included a Clerk, a Treasurer, a Harbour Master, and a Surveyor and Engineer.

In the course of the nineteenth century, further harbour acts were obtained, which enabled the trustees to build a large complex of docks on both sides of the river. The first of these, the North Dock, opened in 1852, and by 1920 there were five docks, two on the western side of the river and three on the eastern side. The Harbour Trustees continued to run the port of Swansea, with its docks and complex system of railways, until 1923, when the undertaking passed to the Great Western Railway Company under the terms of the Great Western Railway (Swansea Harbour Vesting) Act (13 and 14 George V, *cap.* 19). In 1947, the port was nationalized and was managed by the British Transport Docks Board until 1983, when it was privatized, and today it is under the control of Associated British Ports.

The Swansea Paving Commissioners

Before 1835, the general obligation for town improvement in Swansea rested with two bodies, the Court Leet and the parish. As such, the corporation had no legal obligation to carry out works of improvement, although it could have done so if it wished. Under the Court Leet's manorial jurisdiction, residents could theoretically be presented and fined for failing to keep the town and its streets in a proper state of repair and cleanliness. The Leet appointed constables to watch the streets and to enforce the requirements for maintaining them, but while the number of constables increased from eight to twelve between 1780 and 1815, they appear to have been highly ineffective. Records from the end of the eighteenth century show that there were numerous presentments for non-compliance, but there is little evidence that any works were carried out as the result of presentments and fines. Such an inefficient system made it difficult to maintain the *status quo*, let alone effect additional improvements.

The other body with a responsibility for streets was the parish. Since the sixteenth century, the obligation for the upkeep of roads had fallen upon the parish and its official, the Surveyor of Highways. Eighteenth-century surveyors in St Mary's parish were generally ineffective, while the problem was compounded by the fact that in Swansea's immediate vicinity there were several parishes, each of which had its Surveyor of Highways, few of whom worked in conjunction with their neighbours. Indeed, in the 1840s it was reported that some local Highway Surveyors were even working at cross purposes with others.

The apathy of such bodies was not a problem unique to Swansea. Many other towns in England and Wales were experiencing difficulties stemming from the fact that their local administrations had not kept pace with the needs of the age. One means of tackling improvement, popular in the eighty years after 1750, was to place the responsibility in the hands of special Improvement Commissioners. In order to do this, an Act of Parliament was usually required.

Attempts to obtain an improvement act for Swansea had been made, for instance, in 1774 and 1778, but, as with early attempts at harbour improvement, these had been of no avail. Many burgesses were apathetic, but others felt that any changes would be unwelcome. The chief exponent of the latter view was Gabriel Powell, who wished to keep Swansea as a small, pleasant, prosperous seaside town. He felt that any change for change's sake would be detrimental, particularly to the interests of the duke of Beaufort. In all things, Powell acted first and foremost as the duke's loyal servant. However, on some occasions he did the borough a good service. For example, in 1761, he supported an act for the enclosure of the Townhill and Burrows, which brought distinct financial advantages both to the burgesses and to the duke. Incidentally, the act also brought personal benefit to Powell, who acquired fifty-five acres of leased land on Townhill. But whenever he felt that the interests of the borough did not coincide with those of the duke, he did not hesitate to oppose them; thus few attempts at reform

View of the Port and Bay of Swansea, by Thomas Rothwell, 1791.

PORT and BAY of SWANSEA. *Glamorganshire.*

escaped his vigilance. For instance, in 1787, he personally went to London to oppose a scheme for a local improvement bill. Giving evidence before a Commons committee at the time, he stated that 'Swansea is a poor town mostly inhabited by colliers, but as well paved as most country towns are'. These words were immortalized in a satirical cartoon by Moses Harris, entitled 'The Steward', which pictured Powell standing near a dilapidated well in a filthy street in which swine rooted. By also showing him standing outside a building captioned 'Swansea Theatre', the cartoon attacked another of his prejudices. In his evidence to the committee, Powell had also declared, 'I know of no theatre there; I may have heard of one; I was never at it'.

While a harbour act had been obtained shortly after Powell's death, an improvement act was many years coming. In some ways, this delay was somewhat surprising. From the 1780s to the 1830s, Swansea had great pretensions to becoming a seaside resort of some standing. 'The Brighton of Wales' or a 'Welsh Weymouth' were some of the comparisons made by contemporaries. During that period, the town was provided with bathing houses, bathing machines, public gardens, circulating libraries, public assembly rooms, theatres, and a newspaper; in fact, all the accoutrements needed to make it a genteel and fashionable place of resort. However, all these assets would have been to no avail if the town were generally dirty and unpleasant. While many visitors sang Swansea's praises, there were some, like the Reverend John Evans, who commented adversely on the state of the town, while in 1804, the *Cambrian* newspaper remarked that an improvement act would 'tend more to the comfort, convenience, and respectablity [of Swansea] than almost any other measure'. Nevertheless, the act was still slow in coming, and it was not until 1809 that royal assent was granted to 'An Act for better Paving, repairing, cleansing, lighting and watching the several streets . . . of Swansea . . . and for removing and preventing nuisances . . . therein'.

The act named 116 commissioners, who were appointed for life, but who could be disqualified by non-residence or by having connexions with contracts placed by their number. The Paving Commission was a body legally separate from the corporation. It had its own Clerk, and its administrative offices in York Place were physically separate from those of the borough. None the less, the interests of the borough were well represented on the commission from the start. The Portreeve, Recorder, and Steward were *ex officio* members of the commission, while the list of original commissioners included many persons who were already burgesses. Vacancies on the commission, as they arose, were to be filled by co-option, although intending candidates had to have substantial property qualifications.

The responsiblities of the Paving Commissioners were to repair, maintain, scavenge, light, and watch the streets of Swansea. To enable them to carry out these undertakings, they were empowered to levy a rate of 1*s*. in the pound, based on the Poor Rate evaluation. On the strength of the yield of this rate, they were also able to borrow up to £10,000. The product of the 1*s*. rate amounted to about £2,000 a year, and this was soon found to be woefully inadequate to cover the costs of improvements. Thus, while the establishment of the Paving Commission was hailed in Swansea as a step of significant progress, almost from the start inefficiency was the hallmark of its activities. To begin with, none of the original commissioners had had any experience in the realm of urban improvement, so there was never any overall plan of action devised. As time went by, the commissioners began to learn through experience, but their records nevertheless testify to their almost continuous helplessness. Many resolutions were passed, but could not be acted upon, largely through restricted and inadequate finances. Furthermore, many of the commissioners' schemes were ill-conceived. For instance, in 1819, scavenging of the streets was undertaken by female paupers, who collected the refuse into piles, which were left at specified points in the streets for farmers to cart away. Not surprisingly, there were numerous complaints when the piles remained unmoved.

During the forty-one years of the Paving Commission's existence, very little of note was actually achieved. The body's inadequacies were apparent to contemporaries, and several measures were taken in an attempt to improve matters. For example, in 1836, under a permissive clause of the Municipal Corporations Act, 1835, the Paving Commission transferred its functions to the reformed corporation. Nevertheless, although elected members sat on the commission from that date, it still remained a legally separate body. In the same year, the responsibility for policing the town was transferred from the commission to the newly constituted borough Watch and Ward Committee under the provisions of the same legislation.

Despite these amalgamations, the commission's track record after 1836 was little better than it had been previously. Thus, in 1844, a second Improvement Act was obtained to extend the powers of the commission, but, again, this proved to be of very little practical effect. When George Thomas Clark surveyed the town of Swansea on behalf of the General Board of Health in 1849, he clearly underlined the

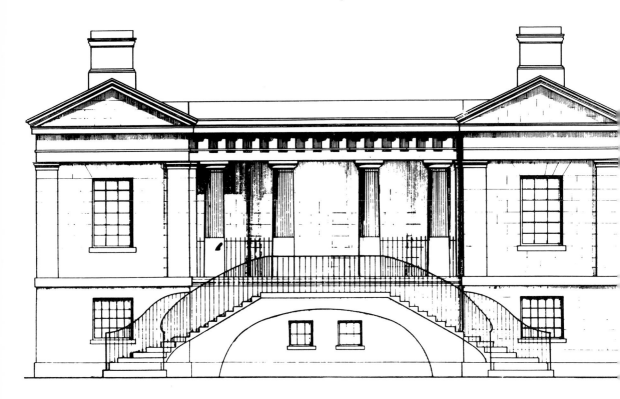

The Guildhall at the Burrows, 1829.

deficiencies of the Paving Commissioners. For example, they only operated within 80 yards of public lamps, which meant that most of the town lay outside their direct control, since there were only 183 street lamps in an area of about 5,000 acres, of which 230 acres were built up.

Another area in which the Paving Commissioners were inactive was that of water supply. For centuries, the main source of water for the town had been wells, springs, and the river Tawe itself. The borough water map of 1854 clearly shows that even by that late date these were still the main sources of water for most of the built-up area of the town. Indeed, the earliest concern for a proper water supply had been the initiative of private enterprise, again a grim indictment of the Paving Commission. In 1837, a group of people led by W. H. Smith (who was known locally as 'Waterworks Bill') banded together to obtain an Act of Parliament (7 and 8 William IV, *cap.* 52) for the establishment of a waterworks company and to build a reservoir at Brynmill. This scheme was not a great initial success: the reservoir was too low-lying to permit a sufficient, constant pressure of water, thus, by 1845, only 470 houses out of a total of 3,369 had a piped supply, while as late as 1854, no houses north of the High Street station were connected to the mains. Nevertheless, the Waterworks Company's pioneer work laid the foundations for a massive municipal involvement in water supply later in the century.

Perhaps the most serious indictment of the Paving Commissioners was their impotence in preventing epidemics or in dealing effectively with them when they occurred. The rapid and unplanned urban growth in Swansea in the first half of the nineteenth century spawned insanitary conditions and occasional epidemics. But to say that the Paving Commission never reacted to emergencies, as some commentators have suggested, is not true. For example, during the serious cholera outbreak in 1832, the commissioners established a temporary 'Board of Health' for the town, and appointed investigators to visit houses where deaths had occurred, to arrange for their fumigation, and also to supervise burials and destroy infected clothing.

Indeed, it would be equally wrong to write off the Paving Commission as a total failure. There were some areas of operation in which they achieved limited success. For instance, in 1821, it was they who first illuminated Swansea's streets with gaslight. In an agreement with the newly-formed, private gas company, the commissioners laid on mains and erected lamp posts while the gas company manufactured the gas. They displayed lack of foresight in the following year, however, in turning down the gas company's offer to be bought out, and again, in 1837, when the corporation was invited to buy the gas undertaking, the offer was rejected. Thus, in contrast with many other towns, gas supply never became a public utility run by the local authority. Laudable as the gaslighting scheme may have been, it was not without its drawbacks. The gas was very expensive to manufacture and the mains were costly to maintain. Moreover, with the gasworks originally situated above the town at Dyfatty, it was difficult to get the supply down to the town centre. Finally, the first gas lamps, spaced at 72 yards apart, did not give adequate illumination.

The Paving Commission also brought into existence Swansea's first regular body of watchmen in 1825, thereby filling a gap left by the corporation's inactivity. This corps consisted of seven officers who patrolled the streets by night. Policing the town in the daytime was left to three constables supplied by the Glamorgan magistrates. In 1833, these nightwatchmen were dismissed and three full-time constables were appointed in their place. This state of affairs continued until the establishment of a borough Watch Committee in 1836, which was followed soon afterwards by the creation of a proper police force.

By the 1840s, the commissioners had also repaired many of the town's main streets, although shortage of funds meant that side streets were neglected and that the work was, in the main, that of repair and not of improvement. Some success was also achieved in the provision of sewers. By the 1840s, the Paving Commission had constructed five covered sewers, but these emptied their untreated filth directly into the river Tawe, while the former town ditch served as a sixth open sewer. Moreover, relatively few houses in the town were actually connected to the sewers, the majority having soak-away privies which, in their turn, contaminated the water supplies from adjacent wells and springs.

It was therefore clear that the Paving Commission was never capable of effective action in Swansea, but it continued to exist until 1850. By that date, national events had overtaken the commissioners, and the reforms of the Public Health Act, 1848 replaced them with a more efficient Local Board of Health.

If the Paving Commission had proved its inadequacy by the 1840s, the same can be said for the corporation at an even earlier date. An oligarchical system of local administration whose roots lay in the middle ages was, by the early nineteenth century, an inefficient anachronism incapable of meeting the needs of the emerging industrial conurbation which Swansea was becoming. The corporation, too, underwent reform in the 1830s, as a result of national legislation. The story of how that happened is dealt with in a later chapter.

THE MAKING OF AN INDUSTRIAL COMMUNITY

Chapter 5

Ieuan Gwynedd Jones

By whichever route one approached Swansea in the second half of the nineteenth century, whether by the old turnpike road from Carmarthen and the west through the villages of Fforestfach and Gendros — the road by which so many hundreds of Swansea people or their parents had first come to settle in the town; or down the Tawe Valley along the Swansea Canal from the upland counties of mid-Wales; or else by road or rail through neighbouring Neath and Llansamlet from east Glamorgan and Monmouthshire; or even by that less familiar but older and most important route of all, by way of the harbour from the Bristol Channel and the world's oceans beyond and so directly into the town itself — by whatever route or mode of transport the traveller came, he would see immediately that here was a great centre of industry. Even the approaches through the rural solitudes of Gower along the gentle curve of the Bay could not obscure this fundamental fact. The perpetual clouds of smoke by day and the flames by night from the many hundreds of furnace stacks could be seen from great distances, and they formed a variegated backcloth to the newly laid-out streets and squares of the middle-class terraces and villas of Sketty and the Uplands. And always the Bay was filled with hundreds of ships awaiting their turn to tie up and discharge their cargoes in the harbour and alongside the river wharves. Smoke, flames, and ships indicated the sources of the wealth so conspicuously displayed in the mansions and parks and the well-to-do housing of the people who lived in these pleasant parts of the town within sight of the bay but away from the smoke and the flames.

Along none of these routes into the town would one be deceived into believing that this place in any way resembled the industrial towns of comparable size and importance in Wales. What struck visitors to Merthyr Tydfil, for instance, or indeed to any of those iron towns which had grown up recently along the northern rim of the south Wales coalfield, was the stark monotony, the poverty, and the featurelessness of their architecture, and the simple uniformity in the appearance of their inhabitants. In fact, appearances were deceptive and one needed to live in Merthyr to understand the complexities underlying its apparent simplicities. Not so Swansea. To pass down the Tawe Valley by road or canal (or by rail after 1865) from Morriston was to experience the changing variety of the place. Morriston itself was a self-sufficient township, proud of its origins as a planted town set down there besides the splendid new bridge over the river, canal, and turnpike by the Morris family whose name it bore. To proceed thence down the valley was to pass through a succession of other smiliar communities, each with its own characteristic, unmistakable features, all linked organically to their neighbouring industrial undertakings in the

Early nineteenth-century Swansea.

valley bottom below or on the slopes of the hills above. From Morriston to Brynhyfryd, Plasmarl, and Landore, to Hafod or Tre-Vivian on the right bank of the river, and on the other bank, echoes of the same kinds of places — Llansamlet, Winsh-wen, Bon-y-maen, Pentre-chwyth, Foxhole, and Pentre-guinea. All these places on the left bank looked down and across at the communities the other side, at their common places of work, and down to the mouth of the river and the sail-filled port.

To proceed into the town was to move into a different world again. This was a place of business and trading, of getting and spending, of commerce and banking on an international scale. It was a town of shops of a breathtaking variety that amazed and confused the newly-arrived peasant or visitor from the less favoured towns of the county. It was a town for staying in; a hive of hotels and hostels and lodging houses, of eating places, coffee houses and restaurants. And everywhere, underlying a furious contemporaneity and modernity, was antiquity; the very new cheek-by-jowl with the very old, ancient buildings and structures long laid down. The streets around the castle and down towards the mouth of the river proclaimed the medieval origin of the place, yet at the same time displayed the confident growth of recent times. Further down, flanked by the Burrows and the river mouth, forming a kind of promontory of fashionable elegance in the midst of business and commerce, was the seat of government and law, the Guildhall and the Law Courts and those other splendid buildings, the Assembly Rooms and Royal Institution, Swansea's proudest possessions. It was a complex town in ways deeper and profounder than these, but the appearance of things proclaimed a mature and self-confident urbanity.

It was a town full of movement and change. It could no longer claim to be the largest town in Glamorgan and Wales: that dubious honour had passed to Merthyr Tydfil early in the century, but it was growing very rapidly in size. Just over 8,000 in 1811, it reached 73,000 in 1891; a growth rate of nearly three per cent per annum. But rapid growth was not only, or even the most important, distinguishing mark of Swansea's development: other mineral and manufacturing towns on the south Wales coalfield were growing at a comparable and even greater pace. What distinguished Swansea's growth from all these others was its regularity from decade to decade and from year to year. Its expansion had none of the spasmodic spurts and sudden declines that were so characteristic of the iron and colliery towns, and this was a consideration of fundamental importance in the shaping of the society being formed therein. It provided a more or less stable framework for the orderly creation of individual and distinctive communities within the larger whole, and it was a major factor in shaping the basic assumptions and expectations about society of the people most involved.

This even and regular increase of the whole nevertheless concealed some sharp differences and variations in the growth patterns of the constituent parts of the Municipal Borough. It is important to understand that the Town and Franchise, the parish of St. John's, the chapelry of St. Thomas, and the Upper Division and the Lower Division of St. Mary's parish developed differently. The Town and Franchise experienced a growth of between a quarter and a third in its population in each decade of the century from the beginning to its end: 6,000 in 1811, it was 21,500 in 1851, and 48,000 in 1891. The internal movements within its very restricted areas which this caused were very complex. They lay at the root of many of the governmental reforms of the century, and were especially important in the huge changes that took place in the administration of Public Health. There were two related aspects to these causal changes. First, they led to an increasing, indeed a novel, segregation of the different social classes, the main feature of which was the migration of the old upper-class gentry families and the newer commercial middle-class families to the western fringes of the town. Second, they led to the gross over-crowding, with all its attendant dangers, of the central core of the old town. Once started, these pressures resulted in the creation of new middle-class suburbs in Brynymor, Uplands, and Sketty, and along the main roads leading out of the smoke-laden air and dirt of the town into the fresh breezes and green pastures of the west.

The migration of the old bourgeois families from their elegant terraces of houses and their pleasant public gardens and riverside walks became inevitable once it had been determined by the very progressive Harbour Trust to link the main-line Railway Station in the High Street with the docks on the west bank of the river and, at a slightly later date, to excavate the South Dock on the Burrows served by the new Llanelly Railway Station on Sandfields. But this had unexpected benefits for the prestige of the Borough and for its image of itself, for it meant that this very pleasant quarter, which had survived virtually unscathed a hundred years of industrialization, would now become the nerve centre of the constantly expanding commercial life of the town. It became the most highly admired location for business, for legal and professional firms, for agents and brokers, and the all-important

Exchange. More than any other change, this symbolized the final victory of the conquering bourgeoisie and the shape of things to come.

The town had a private and concealed aspect as well as a public one, and those who stayed to admire the latter were as often as not in ignorance of the former. To walk along Wind Street and Castle Street into the High Street was to be impressed by the width of the pavemented thoroughfares, and to admire the excellent taste and good sense manifested in the handsome buildings on either side of the street. Here, there were fine shops with stylish, plate-glass frontages of the most up-to-date kind, intermingling with the older Welsh houses with their characteristic low elevations and peaked gables. One passed shops that were also the workplaces of a great variety of craftsmen in wood and metal and precious stones. There were makers of clocks and ships' chronometers, ironmongers, merchants of all kinds, sellers of wine and food and clothes. Many of these craftsmen and tradesmen and shopkeepers lived above their premises, and they were the heads of households which included not only their immediate families but also their servants, apprentices, and even journeymen.

But behind the public faces of these main thoroughfares were the courts and labyrinthine streets and alleys inhabited by a different class of people altogether. It was a quarter still in process of formation as the pressure on space led to the building of yet more houses on what had once been open spaces. This was the private, the least-known face of the old borough, and it was in these anonymous places, in dark and noisome courts, that the inexorable effects of the growth of population were most evident. Here dwelt the bulk of the old town's inhabitants, the majority of them in two-roomed cottages, often in conditions of gross overcrowding. Hardly any houses had fewer than five occupants and many had more than ten. In the Irish area of Greenhill and the fringes of Dyfatty some of these little cottages contained four families with fourteen or fifteen residents. This was a world and a mode of existence as different from that of the shopkeepers and merchants as was theirs, in turn, different from the refined, leisured and cultivated life of the old gentry and the new professional men.

It was likewise a world removed, if not concealed, from the visitors who continued to holiday in this 'Brighton of Wales'. The transformation of the old Swansea and the loss of the picturesque qualities of the harbour and the foreshore was Mumbles and Oystermouth's gain. But deeper and more significant than the partial loss of one personality was the winning of another, as Swansea became increasingly the seaside resort for the working-class suburbs and the industrial towns of the Swansea and Neath valleys and, with the building of railways to the mid-Glamorgan coal valleys, of many other similar communities. Oystermouth Road, with its single terrace of large apartment houses looking out across the road and railway and tramway to the sea and the wide stretch of sands beyond, came to typify for more and more people the quintessential Swansea. But it was the industrialized valley, its working-class suburbs, and its decayed and increasingly revolting core which determined its future.

Yet this six-fold growth of the Town and Franchise was dwarfed by the scale of growth in other constituent parts of the municipal borough. St Thomas, on the left bank of the river, grew more than thirty-fold. This was due to the building of Port Tennant in the second decade of the century, following the enclosure of Fabian's Bay and its connection by canal and, later, by railway with the collieries of the Neath Valley and eventually of the Rhondda Valley. The New Cut and the opening of the North Dock, in 1845 and 1851 respectively, further hastened the development of St. Thomas as a dockside community. It became one of the most important suburbs of Swansea to which it was tied, despite the intervening river, by increasingly powerful economic and administrative links. Here, in this most cosmopolitan part of the town, were experienced the first stirrings of working-class radical movements.

Of a different nature was the expansion of population in the old parish of St John's. This ancient parish extended from the top of High Street, where the ancient church had been located, to the outskirts of Morriston four miles to the north. In it, and on the fringes of the adjacent parish of Llansamlet across the river, were located the great copper, zinc, and iron works, together with their associated undertakings, such as chemical works. Here were the smelting works of the Vivians, of Pascoe Grenfell, and of Williams, Foster & Co., and here, on the slopes above the works, were the homes of the hundreds of persons employed in them.

Like most industrialists who, out of business calculation if not of benevolence towards their fellow men, provided accommodation for the key-workers, the Vivians planted what soon became a new industrial village at Hafod-Isha — or Tre-Vivian or Vivianstown. By the middle of the century there were more than sixty terraced houses there which, judged by the standards of the time, provided superior accommodation for their workers. Tre-Vivian consisted of two classes of houses, the smaller renting (in 1850) for 2s. (10p) and the larger for 3s. (15p): this at a time when a furnaceman earned roughly 30s. (150p)

The Bwrlais Brook at Cwmfelin, c. 1900.

per week. Other industrialists had already pioneered this kind of paternalism — notably the remarkable Sir John Morris at Morriston — and the Grenfells also built houses of the same utilitarian pattern for their workers at Pentre-chwyth. Of Vivian's houses it was said that they were 'ample in room, sound in structure, floored with dry bricks, roofed with tiles and partitioned into convenient compartments'. The Hafod houses were also provided with small gardens with privies and pig-styes at the bottom. A correspondent of *The Morning Chronicle*, who was visiting Swansea in 1850 to report on the condition of the people, expatiated on the excellent conditions enjoyed by workmen fortunate enough to occupy such houses. He found 'the same wealth of furniture, the same love of display, the same neatness and cleanliness' that he had remarked upon as characteristic of the workmen living in ironmasters' cottages in Merthyr Tydfil.

Certainly, if all the housing had been of this quality, Tre-Vivian and the other suburbs would have been fortunate places. But this was not the case. Most of the houses had been built, and were all the time being built, by agencies and persons whose immediate concern was to profit from them. Vivian, as a good businessman, expected his properties to show a profit: in 1809 J. H. Vivian expected a return of 12 per cent from his cottages, enough to reimburse the outlay and keep the houses in good repair. In 1908-9 the rents brought in £4,500. Cottage owners were not concerned with standards of building or repair, and might, for political reasons, prefer to own properties with rateable values below the sum at which their occupiers would qualify for a vote in local elections. As in other parts of the coalfield also, the workmen had a passion for owning their own homes, and many houses were built by terminating, as well as permanent, building societies. What proportion of this housing was adequate is doubtful, for all the legislation regarding the housing of the poorer classes, like most of the sanitary legislation until the great Public Health Act of 1872, was adoptive rather than compulsory, and it is certain that much of the housing put up in this critical period of population expansion would have been such as a later generation would regard as very inadequate. In this way the villages of the Industrial Revolution were formed, growing not according to any plan, but haphazardly in response to market demands. In none were there public amenity buildings, except the religious ones, but where, as in Hafod and Pentre-chwyth, the industrialist also put up schools, well-planned and built, there existed the beginnings of an infra-structure which would enormously assist in the creating and sustaining of a sense of community.

Praise for the paternalistic industrialists was the common currency of the time. The objective reports of Inspectors of the Board of Health were less complimentary. The Reports of De la Beche in 1845 and of G. T. Clark, himself an industrialist (and historian) of Glamorgan, in 1849 recognized that the suburbs were not the exclusive preserve of the copper masters. All were over-crowded, in certain places as badly as the old town centre. It was one thing to have outside lavatories, another to have efficient systems for the disposal of sewage and refuse. They pointed out that many of the cottages, as was the case in Foxhole and St Thomas across the river, were 'truly Celtic'. They were either thatched and close, or cold and damp, and they were in cheerless contrast to the houses being put up by the masters anxious to retain their labour force.

These suburbs were largely self-contained towns in respect of their location and their dependence upon particular works and industries. Tre-Vivian and Landore, with their streets of terraced houses and square chapels, looked down upon the smoke-engulfed works on the

floor of the valley. To get to the point of labour the workmen walked down the steeply-sloping streets and across the main Neath Road and the canal. All went in the same direction, at the same time, depending upon the shift, and all came back together up the sloping streets to their homes when the shift was done, having shared the same dangers, endured the same circumstances. As individual places they seemed no different from other places on the coalfield, and the disciplines they accepted were the same. Proximity to work was a vital consideration to all workers whatever their occupation, and remained so until the coming of public transport. Only then did the workers become mobile. Middle-class individualistic critics who condemned the traditional immobility of the workers and their alleged failure to respond quickly to the needs of the labour market rarely understood the force of such considerations as these. Coppermen, in any case, had no choice but to remain with the employer with whom they had entered into a

View of Morriston from the Wychtree Bridge, 1929.

contractual agreement as a condition of obtaining employment. Since the secrets of the various smelting and calcining processes existed not on paper but in the skills of the furnacemen, it was necessary to secure their loyalty and prevent their migration to competitor undertakings. The same considerations applied to some of the tinning processes, and the general effect was to create a generation of workmen and their families as rooted to the place of work as any agricultural worker on a landed estate. This was strengthened by the complimentary need to employ whole families, sons following fathers in the slowly-mastered hierarchy of skills. Often, also, women and girls were given unskilled, but frequently laborious, work to perform, and in this way the bond of obligation stretched over the generations, weaving virtually all the inhabitants into a nexus of relations between place of work and place of residence. Such was the case also in some of the related industries, notably the tinplate works, and to a lesser extent in transport, but the fact that it obtained in the major industries, upon which the employment rhythms of the places depended, undoubtedly gave to the whole a character and a cohesion which they might not otherwise have possessed.

These considerations applied almost as powerfully in the colliery villages to the north of the Borough. By the third quarter of the century, gone were the days when the collieries were small undertakings content to exploit only the surface and shallower seams of coal for the regular market of the smelters. With increasing local demand from other industries, such as tinplate works, chemical works, and the expanding patent fuel works on the docks and, above all, an expanding export market, they were now working at great depths in the famous high-quality Graigola seams. Cockett, Treboeth, and Fforestfach developed as colliery villages. These also shared the same characteristics of relative stability and ordered, peaceful growth, for they were not, on the whole, producing solely for a highly volatile and unpredictable market but also for an industry which had its own, separate rhythms.

Colliers and coppermen had much in common. The labour demanded of each group was both arduous and dangerous. Strength and agility were the requisite qualities in the complicated processes of roasting, refining, and calcining, and the collier needed not only strength and endurance but also a variety of skills to enable him to survive in such unnatural environments. Both learned to work in teams, to rely upon each other, to trust each other and to think of the good of the whole rather than the rights and benefits of the individual.

Both worked in poisoned atmospheres, both tested their constitutions to the uttermost. 'The pulse of the copperman working before his furnace', wrote the Medical Officer of Health in 1854, 'beats at 120 degrees, his chest heaves to and fro in strained respiration, muscular action is exerted and vigorously the skin pours forth floods of water.' Working before the banks of furnaces was extremely hazardous, and accidents and disfigurements were frequent. Shifts at one time had been of twenty-four hours in the arsenic- and sulphur-laden atmospheres, but since the 1850s were of twelve hours, except in some spelter works. It is no wonder that the men were of sallow countenances, desiccated, wiry and thin. It was said that men coming from a distance to work in the copper works either acclimatized within a few months or died.

The furnacemen were skilled men, key workers, and they were paid appropriately high wages. They were at the top of a rigidly maintained hierarchy, in which it was accepted that promotion from one grade to another and from one wages level to another should be by seniority. Furnacemen earned about twice the amount paid to labourers, and their status in the community might be correspondingly high, though this did not necessarily follow, for other things conferred status as well as income and occupation. Coppermen were also paid weekly; there was no truck, and they were given concessionary coal. All the workmen likewise paid a poundage for the schools and for the medical services provided in the works.

It is important to bear in mind that smelting, tin-plate manufacture and the mills and foundries associated with them were not the only industries in Swansea. Dafydd Morganwg's *Hanes Morganwg* (1874), which is one of the best and most comprehensive contemporary guides to mid-Victorian Glamorgan, lists, in addition to the eighteen iron and brass smelters, nine brass foundries, four chain works, two alkali works, a crucible factory, a drainpipe manufactory, and, not to be forgotten, a tobacco pipe factory. To these should be added the ship building and ship repair yards, and the makers of a multiplicity of things like ropes, sails, and the gear required by the largest fleet of ocean-going ships in the Bristol Channel west of Bristol itself. Hence, the labour force in Swansea was a very diverse one, far more complicated in structure than those of other industrial towns of the coalfield.

The largest single occupation group was that of the labourers who were required in great numbers in every undertaking, but who were especially numerous in the docks. Here, they were employed as trimmers and stevedores, work which was classified as unskilled but which in fact required more than brute muscle-power. As the *Workers' Journal* pointed out, 'Every class of work requires a greater or lesser amount of skill or discernment in its operation . . . a docker may not have studied the intricacies of cubic and other measurements but he acquires a marvellous skill in stowing and unloading cargo'. Yet it was in the docks that the labourer was least esteemed. His wages were low, his labour casual, and he suffered the humiliation of the hiring system. Some of the dock labourers lived in Pentre-guinea and Port Tennant and had shipwrights and riggers and other craftsmen as neighbours, but many more appear to have lived in the old town centre, where dilapidation and decay were greatest and sanitation most deficient, and where, according to the Medical Officer of Health in 1875, mortality rates were as high as 39 per 1,000. Such workers constituted almost the lowest grade of society, only paupers lying between them and the bottom line of destitution.

For measured by income, earned and unearned, by occupation and residence, Swansea recognized itself to have a structure of society into which all persons could be slotted with more or less certitude. At its apex — a real if rarely visible presence — was an aristocrat, the duke of Beaufort, in whose lordship Swansea lay. He owned substantial parts of the borough and its environs, and had rights over much of what he did not own. Below him was an upper middle class whose composition, for most of the century, was probably unique to the Municipal Borough. It included the old urban gentry, descendants of wealthy tradesmen and professional men, who had interests, but no direct involvement, in industry. They were a class of *rentiers*, annuitants, relics of Swansea's *ancien régime*, fulfilling the role of a social and cultural élite. The antiquary, Col. Grant Francis, was one of this class. It also included persons and interests of a different origin and style of life. These were the landed proprietors of the region, closely associated with the town's industrial development, but themselves benefiting indirectly through mineral royalties, way-leaves, and such like. The Llewellyn family of Penllergaer were leading members of this class. Finally, there were the industrialists, like the pottery owner, Lewis Weston Dillwyn, who married into the families of the local gentry and themselves acquired status thereby.

The most powerful members of the middle class were the capitalists, great and small. The Vivian family, the Grenfell family, and the Morris family were the most powerful in this group. All had come from outside, all had found their own capital, and together they had set the pace of industrial development in the valley. All had created totally integrated concerns: they owned not only the means of production but also much of the infra-structure of the communities they planned and created. They were capitalists of the stamp of Josiah John Guest of Dowlais and of the Crawshays of Cyfarthfa. Their greatest social asset was that they suffered none of the disadvantages of humble origins and other impediments to the realization of their social aspirations. They had, as it were, dual rights to Singleton Abbey or Sketty Hall, Maesteg House or Clasemont, or the other mansions; their families were old and their wealth, though new, was sufficient.

Below these were the other, lesser industrialists, of whom there were increasing numbers, whose interests did not necessarily coincide with those of the class above. Below these, again, were growing number of agents, managers, accountants, lawyers, and other professional men. There were also a substantial class of businessmen, bankers and financial agents, brokers and stockbrokers, who were the nerves of the financial operations of the borough and the conduits along which flowed the supply of essential information and the myriads of decisions on which business depended. These were the men who were building their villas and terraced houses on the western outskirts of the town, thereby not only associating themselves spatially with their social superiors but also putting a distance between themselves and the unfortunate classes below them elsewhere in the borough.

Such movements in the residential patterns of the town were symptomatic of profound changes taking place in the cultural life of the community at large and of the lesser constituent communities of the town and suburbs. First, religion and language were increasingly being seen as the most important elements in this new culture. Second, consciousness of class difference was coming to be recognized as an integral part of that culture. Third, as the century drew to a close, this class consciousness was coming to be expressed in new ideologies and in demands for new forms of political organization.

From the earliest stages of industrialization there had been a distinct inclination for immigrants to settle among people of their own language and culture. Throughout the century English immigrants tended on the whole to settle in the town itself, and the Irish likewise formed distinct communities, while the Welsh immigrants overwhelmingly preferred the northern parts of the borough. Hafod, Cwmbwrla, Plasmarl, Glandwr (Landore) and Treforus (Morriston) were as Welsh in language and culture as any of the new industrial villages of the Upper Swansea Valley. Nor should this surprise us, for all these places had been peopled by immigrants from neighbouring parishes. They continued to settle from these same parts throughout the century and after, fed by an inexhaustible reservoir of ready labour. The stream slackened only when the rural parishes of upland Carmarthenshire and beyond began themselves to be industrialized and to develop villages and towns almost identical in character with those of Mynydd-bach, Llan-giwg and Llangyfelach.

It speaks volumes for the innate ability, intelligence and adaptability of these men and women from deep rural parishes that, so soon after the initial foundation of the works, they should have mastered the relatively sophisticated technologies and skills required of them. Nor, properly considered, is it strange that, shift after shift, week in and week out, year by year, they should have endured the appalling conditions in which they were required to work. For their perspectives were different from ours, and for most of their history, as has been the case with working classes everywhere, they were powerless to change them for the better. For the vast majority there was no alternative. Behind them in the countryside they loved so intensely and whose charm and beauty they never ceased to sing, was the deepest poverty, as deep as the examples they could see about them in Hafod or Landore, and a helplessness in the face of privilege almost more hopeless than that they endured in the discipline of the works. Nor could they, with respect to atmospheric pollution, believe otherwise than what their masters and betters, the doctors, the scientists, judges and elected rulers told them, and apparently believed themselves, that the impure air they breathed was in fact beneficial to them. Everyone in Swansea, high and low, was entrapped in his own self-deception with regard to what was happening to the environment and to its social consequences.

More important to them was the undoubted fact that their standards of living were higher than those they and their parents had experienced in the country. As we have explained, they earned more, some of the housing they occupied, though by no means all of it, was adequate, their clothing was good by comparison with that of their cousins in the country, and their food abundant. There were other benefits of which they were highly conscious. More problematic was their vulnerability to disease, especially the endemic diseases associated with primitive forms of sewage and drainage, and the very inadequate water supplies. Typhoid, diarrhoea, and scarlatina were killer diseases, and it was these which had kept the average mortality rates as high as 23.6 per thousand between 1866 and 1876, and infant mortality at a horrifying 149 per thousand live births. Sometimes these diseases reached epidemic proportions, the cholera was never far away in people's imagination, and as a port Swansea was particularly vulnerable to infectious diseases brought in from abroad. Nevertheless, these communities were of a richness and variety hardly to be found elsewhere. In particular, the cultural achievements of these working-class communities must be understood as being the most characteristic contribution of Swansea to the intellectual and spiritual life of Wales. What was this culture of the working classes?

Towards the end of the 1860s, at a time when the town seemed to be in the prime of its maturity, a very intelligent and sensitive observer had this to say about the place:

> I climbed, one Sunday morning, on to the heights which overhang the town of Swansea, consigned on that one day to silence and rest. Two kinds of buildings alone evinced any signs of life; the high chimney shafts, towering over the iron foundries, gave vent to black serpents of smoke, curled round by the wind into spiral coils, chasing one another over the tiled roofs; and from the church steeples I heard the sound of bells inviting to worship. Labour and Prayer — these were the elements which seemed to float in the air over this town, spread out as it is on the edge of the resounding sea . . . Religion and Industry.

For him, the black serpents of smoke and the sound of bells did not symbolize hostile forces in inevitable confrontation, but an alliance in which industry enhanced the material bases of life, while religion led to liberty of thought and the enhancement of human values. Probably most thinking people in Swansea, including working-class people, would have agreed with him. All would have known that, as a matter of historical fact, industry and religion had grown up together, and that the flourishing state of the one had somehow been a condition for the growth of the other.

As Dr Cowley explains in chapter 6, the seeds which had been planted at the time of industrialization had borne fruit sixfold by the end of the century, by which time also the Nonconformist denominations outnumbered the Church of England by three to one. Yet what is revealing about the changing nature of society was not merely this growth in provision but the way it had taken place in different parts of the Borough. These differences in pattern between the town and its suburbs suggest that there were different impulses at work, that they were responding to different demands, or had different perceptions of their respective needs. The chapels of Old Dissent — Baptists, Independents, Unitarians and Quakers — in the old town, which could trace their proud, unbroken descent from the Puritans of the seventeenth century, looked like and were middle-class institutions, supported on the whole by tradesmen, businessmen and farmers. As one contemporary historian put it, 'The working class (at the beginning of the century) was almost wholly in the hands of the devil whom they served to the best of their ability'. In less picturesque words, the working class had not yet been captured for religion, with the implication that not much effort had been made to do so. When these chapels multiplied with the westward drift of the respectable classes they reproduced themselves in the same architectural dress as their parents, and were as a rule quickly paid for by the munificence of benefactors. Mount Pleasant Baptist chapel, the foundation stone of which was laid on the day that Swansea's greatest Baptist, the Rev. Joseph Harris (Gomer), died, was built by day-work 'everything in the most substantial manner . . . no scrimping, no unseasoned wood or untempered mortar'. It cost a staggering £4,510. There were 54 members at the time, and the costs were cleared as they built. By the end of the century they had spent another £9,000 or so on improvements of one kind and another (including the classic façade that now graces the centre of the town), much of it given by the brothers Walters 'out of the spoils won in the battle of industry and business'.

How different were the circumstances of the congregations in the industrial, working-class suburbs! How different their histories! There, in Hafod or Landore, Cwmbwrla or Morriston, establishing a congregation, building a chapel, and maintaining a ministry were, by comparison, tasks of heroic proportions. Until the third quarter of the century, they were invariably working-class or popular churches, unpretentious in appearance and character, almost always heavily in debt, often sharing ministers. Yet, relatively to the incomes and the prosperity of the communities involved, they were at least as costly as the middle-class temples of the town, and many a plain façade belied the riches of the experience within.

Of course, these early Nonconformist churches were aided by benefactions of well-to-do sympathizers — sometimes more well-to-do than sympathetic, as in the case of Lewis Weston Dillwyn and the Morriston Baptists. Told by the agent that under no circumstances would Mr Dillwyn grant them land for building a chapel, one of the

Capel Bethesda deacons, Daniel Davies, went to see his son, the young and ambitious Lewis Ll. Dillwyn, and gently suggested that his father's mean and prejudiced attitude would be unlikely to assist his candidature were he at some future date to stand for parliament for the borough. The matter was settled immediately in favour of the congregation, and the future member for Swansea had learned a valuable political lesson.

Mount Pleasant Chapel, c. 1900.

The capture of the working class for nonconformity was an enterprise undertaken largely by the working classes themselves. The scale of the enterprise ought not to be underestimated, nor its pace exaggerated. Only from the end of the 1860s was its success assured. By then the ethos of nonconformity had become an important, if not the dominant, element in the artistic and intellectual life of the borough as a whole. Its physical presence was overwhelming even in the old town, and in the suburbs it had virtually exclusive control of the media: pulpit, platform and press. It was a culture in which the lines between the sacred and the secular seemed to its middle-class critics to be deplorably confused and blurred and not good for society as a whole. In this they were of one mind with the members of the Secular Society who, however, were peculiarly weak and ineffective in the district. But the mix of Nonconformity with a community's readiness to adapt and absorb old traditional forms of popular culture was itself a creative force in society. If, as was largely the case, the provision of libraries, museums, art galleries, and public parks was a typically middle-class motivated movement, but one in which the working class, as rate-payers, gladly co-operated, the development of the eisteddfod, choral societies and that now forgotten pastime, the public lecture, was the creation of the working class themselves. Its heart in Swansea was the industrial suburbs: the town merely provided additional facilities, when superior facilities, such as the Albert Hall, were required for conferences, demonstrations, and other public meetings.

The Design for the proposed new Market at Oxford Street, 1895.

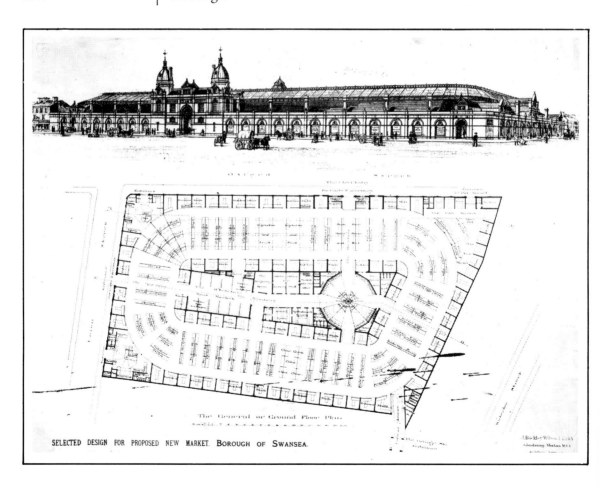

SELECTED DESIGN FOR PROPOSED NEW MARKET. BOROUGH OF SWANSEA.

The Church of England was also active in these areas. By the end of the century it had not only built new churches and rebuilt old ones, it had also planted many iron churches where it judged the need to be greatest. In few places in Wales were the evidences for the renewal and reform of the Church and the ability of its hierarchy to achieve their aims more evident than in Swansea. It was in the industrial suburbs that these divergent ways of dealing with the same problem of irreligion were most clearly to be seen.

It is necessary also to bear in mind the strong intellectual and literary traditions which it was all the while absorbing. The Rev. Joseph Harris (Gomer) was a link between the old and the new. His periodical, *Seren Gomer*, founded in 1814 and edited by him until his death in 1825, provided a platform for the new writers who were emerging, a forum for the discussion of religious, philosophical and critical questions, a kind of clearing-house for information about the eisteddfod movement and, in the writings of Gomer himself and some of his contributors, standards of literary excellence. The theological debates of the time were of the essence of this religious culture. No doubt, much of it was of dubious quality, but it was through discussion and debate that more than theological questions were decided: it accustomed people to the idea of agreement not to fiat from above but by discourse among each other.

One can see how the intense competitiveness which developed between these communities, as conditions of life gradually improved in the third quarter of the century, had the paradoxical effect of encouraging local differences while enhancing the sense of community of the whole. The chapel culture was itself strongly competitive, in the conditions of the time necessarily so. Emulation promoted the desire to excel, not only in outward appearance and architectural style but also in the richness and range of the different facilities they each offered. The size of the buildings, which to us appear to have been excessive, was determined not by the ordinary needs of the congregations as much as by their extraordinary and recurrent ones and by the necessity to display their commitment to the community by means of these ritual occasions. The great round of festivals of preaching, song, concerts and performances of oratorios, sacred and secular, was sustained in this way, and was complimented, not contradicted, by the equally important sporting contests between rival teams, and the pride of a locality in the exploits of its own players.

This popular religion produced leaders of men at a time when they were most needed. It released the innate capacities of people to

Interior of Swansea Market, 1906.

manage their own affairs. As an experienced industrialist, who also possessed the objectivity of an historian, G. T. Clark of the Dowlais Iron Company, explained to the Royal Commission on Trades Unions in his evidence in 1867, that 'the Welsh especially have a great capacity for organization and self-government, as shown in their Friendly Societies and in their ecclesiastical arrangements'. The institutions being developed in the coalfield by and for the men and their families made great demands on the relatively few who possessed the necessary degrees of literacy to run them. Burial and Sickness Societies, Friendly Societies, Building Societies and Trade Unions required the services of devoted and intelligent men. Executive committees carried heavy responsibilities; the multiplication of minor offices may have been a response to practical administrative needs as well as a desire to involve as many persons as possible in their affairs.

All this was particularly true of the resurgent self-help movements when increasingly they came under the scrutiny, sometimes hostile, of government and the law. They were handling very considerable sums of money. In 1873, for example, there were more than 170 lodges of Friendly Societies in the Swansea district, with funds totalling nearly

Entrance to the New Swansea Market in 1897.

£40,000. According to the evidence collected for the Royal Commission, from which these figures have been taken, most of these lodges were very rickety affairs which, if one took a long view — say, twenty years — were probably bankrupt. But it was a constant preoccupation of workpeople that they and their families should be supported during sickness and in old age, and in the end be saved from the disgrace of a pauper's grave. This is why lodges affiliated to the great Orders, especially the Manchester Unity of Odd Fellows and the Foresters, were increasingly popular in the district. These 'English' Orders in fact were bilingual organizations and many were thoroughly Welsh in their proceedings. The Welsh Order of Ivorites — *yr Iforiaid* — which had been founded with the dual aims of providing the usual benefits together with the furtherance of Welsh culture, was also strong in the district, especially, of course, in the Welsh suburbs. They were particularly active in sponsoring and in publishing the transactions of local and regional eisteddfodau. This was a development of great significance; men whose essays or poems appeared thus in print acquired a very high status in the community; they brought to their communities a kind of fame and were greatly honoured for so doing. They embodied the community's highest values.

Whatever may have been the radical and secular origins of these self-help organizations in Swansea, possibly more so than in other coalfield towns, the links with the chapels were strong. The partial dependence of the societies on lower middle-class persons for the necessary expertise in running them; teachers, shopkeepers, clerks, often carried the burden of secretaryships, for example, and these were always, necessarily so, respectable members of society. But this did not negate their essential nature as working-class organizations serving the common people.

What was true of Friendly Societies was also true of the trade unions: indeed, they were often the same organizations fulfilling the same social benefit purposes. Until the late 1880s and the slow, spasmodic, and largely ineffective irruptions of militancy into the even tenor of industrial relations, and the rise of the New Unionism, Swansea's trade unions were confined to craftsmen. They were few in number, not more than between 5 per cent and 10 per cent of the total work force. They were confined to the élite 'high earners' who, as often as not, also enjoyed the inestimable advantages of regularity of employment. Shipwrights, engineers, boilermakers, rollermen, printers, carpenters, and masons, some of the town's craftsmen anxious to restrict entry to their crafts and to protect their shifting membership — such were the men who belonged to unions. In some respects they seemed very advanced: Swansea's trade unions were the first in Wales to come together to form a Trades Council in 1873; but this had more sound than meaning, it was largely ineffective, and there was no reason why the commercial men of the town should take any particular note of its proceedings. Most copper and smelter workers, all seamen, all dockside workers, all transport workers until 1887, and all general labourers lay outside any kind of trade union organization. Commenting on this situation in 1887 the *South Wales Daily News* wrote, 'Now, if trade unionism is weak anywhere, it is weak in Swansea. There are few such centres of industry as Swansea, and there are fewer still where so many of the toiling masses neglect to combine for their general well-being.'

The tinplate workers were something of an exception. Elsewhere in south Wales they joined the ironworkers, but in Swansea and the west, they formed their own union, the Independent Association of Tinplate Workers, but its history showed how weak an institution it was and how ineffective in the face of the intransigence of the masters. Its secretary was William Lewis (Lewys Afan), and by 1871 it had over 4,000 members, and was strong enough, it seemed, to challenge the employers on a claim for wages uniform with those of tinplate workers elsewhere. The ensuing strike lasted for two months, but the settlement was made over the heads of the leaders, both the men and the employers ignoring them. The settlement agreed the existing rates but also enshrined the customs of the works, and the '1874 List', as it was known, remained in force and the basis of all subsequent negotiations until the depression at the end of the century. It was an example of what could be achieved without formal union organization, and thus came to be regarded as both an example and a warning.

It is extraordinary how alike in respect of social origin, education, and culture these leaders of the craft unions were. A few were Secularists, a few were members of the Socialist Society: William H. Morris, for example, of the Engineers was an active member of the Social Democratic Federation. But these were the exceptions that proved the rule, and the rule undoubtedly was that their connections were mainly with the chapels. David Wignall, the copper worker who became the first District Secretary of the Dockers Union, was for years the unpaid pastor of the little Tabernacle Baptist Chapel in Tontine Street. David Williams, secretary of the Boilermakers, was a Sunday School teacher and a strong temperance advocate. David

Children at Play in St Matthew's Graveyard, c. 1920.

Jones, son of a working tailor whose family endured great poverty when he died, went to work in Dillwyn's Pottery at the age of eight and as a young man helped to build Mount Zion, where he became joint pastor with Ben Davies, another trade unionist. David Jones was secretary of the Carpenters and became the first working man JP. The outstanding example in the area was William Abraham (Mabon) of Waunarlwydd, collier and executive member of the ill-fated Amalgamated Association of Miners who, having moved to east Glamorgan during the great strike of 1875, became the acknowledged leader of the south Wales miners. It was Mabon and H. H. Vivian who were largely responsible for the introduction of the Sliding Scale in the industry, and it is easy to see that this attempt to replace strikes and other forms of confrontation and militancy with conciliation and arbitration according to agreed rules was the embodiment of the spirit and doctrine advocated and taught in the chapels. Mabon's deaconship, his fervent patriotism and his leadership of the union blended together without contradiction, and it was his philosophy which dominated industrial relations until the coming of the South Wales Miners Federation. The underground chapel and the weekly prayer meetings in Tynewydd Colliery, introduced by the colliers themselves in 1845 after a particularly costly explosion, typified, and perhaps generated, the somewhat submissive readiness of the men to accept 'the iron laws of economics' and the market economy, and to give their support to Mabon rather than to the advocates of a more militant attitude to industrial relations.

There was one area in the life of the community, however, which was of the greatest importance to all classes in the community. This was local government and politics. In the early part of the century this had been the preserve of properly qualified burgesses, and the rules governing the admission of burgesses were such as effectively to exclude all whom the Corporation for the time being wished, for whatever reason, to exclude. The Municipal Corporations Act of 1835 introduced a measure of democracy, and subsequent legislation, especially in the field of Public Health and education, further widened the opportunities for democratic participation in the government of the Municipal Borough. The key consideration for those reformers who desired to make the system truly democratic was the restricted nature of the franchise, which made it difficult, if not impossible, for ordinary workers to break into the magic circle of government. There were no specifically working representatives on the Municipal Corporation and its numerous committees, no working-class Guardians of the Poor, no working-class members on School Boards, and no magistrates drawn from the lower classes. Government was a middle-class monopoly, though not therefore necessarily government by a class for that class. On the contrary, it was industrialists and businessmen, like Thomas Ford, Frank Ash Yeo, John Jones Jenkins, and William Thomas, who pushed forward schemes for public service, town improvements, cultural and recreational amenities, and the municipalization of key services. Also, as prosperity returned after the depressions of the 1870s, there was a resurgence of the older radicalism aimed at taking advantage of the increasing opportunities of those years for greater participation. Various pieces of legislation from the 1850s onwards, especially the extension of the vote to £10 occupiers in 1888, increased the total municipal electorate to an enormous degree: 747 electors in 1839, there were 2,012 in 1854, 6,416 in 1870, and 15,103 in 1889. This was also the date when Swansea became a County

Borough, and the time when the drive to capture the government of the borough began in earnest. By the late 1890s many of the working-class wards were being contested by trade union candidates calling themselves Labour and having agreed platforms and a common electoral strategy. At the same time, they were pressing non-elected bodies, such as the Hospital Board of Management, for seats for their nominees. These peaceful and orderly changes were of revolutionary significance in the history of the borough. The industrial community could be said to have emerged when elected representatives of all its social constituent parts were sharing in its government.

Such changes presupposed the politicization of the unions and the making of a Labour Party in the constituencies. Trade unionism itself changed in fundamental ways during those years of advance in local government. There was an explosive growth in unions catering for the unskilled, especially among the dockers. The gasworkers, seamen, railway servants, and most of the occupations which had hitherto been unorganized now came to be unionized. This undoubtedly reflected and was stimulated by the growth in the country as a whole of the New Unionism, but there were sufficient resemblances between what was then happening in Swansea and the developments which preceded it to lead some to think that developments in Swansea were intelligible in terms of its own history, and that the activities of national leaders, such as Ben Tillett and Will Thorne, in the borough were stimulant rather than novel. However supine the Trades Council had been in the past, it was in the 'nineties no longer 'the lazy watchdog that gives one bark and then runs into its kennel and growls', but a very different kind of animal indeed. Gone were the days when the craft unions ruled the roost and dictated policy, for they were themselves revitalized and using the Trades Council as an instrument for the solidarity of the working class who were being recruited indiscriminately into the new general unions, like the Dockers Union (for that in effect was what it had become). Before the end of the century the Trades Council had become a power in borough politics, intent on turning to the political advantage of the emerging Labour Party this dramatic heightening of class consciousness. The fruits were swift to ripen. David Williams won a seat (at his second attempt) for the St Thomas ward in 1898, Labour had five seats two years later, and so began the struggle for control of the Corporation, which was finally achieved in 1927.

I have put local politics first, not because parliamentary politics were unimportant, but because it was in the politics of the municipality that these industrial boroughs first came to understand

Sir Alfred Mond and Supporters, 1906.

themselves as political communities. National politics were of the greatest interest to Swansea people, as had always been the case. The radical political movements of the early decades of the century, which had brought south Wales to the very edge of rebellion, were now things of the past. In any event, the disorders of the 1830s, especially the Merthyr Rising of 1831 and the March on Newport by the Chartists in 1839, had been distant from Swansea both ideologically and geographically. There had been no concurrent rioting in Swansea, no Scotch Cattle, and the Chartism which had set down roots in the district never wavered from the constitutional ways of political reform. The mature and sophisticated social structure of the town and its deep-rooted Dissenting tradition had ensured that this should have been so then, and equally that it should persist into the future. Now, at the end of the century, the constituency ranked high in the calculations of politicians in the two great parties and the emerging Labour Party.

*The Slip at Swansea Beach,
c. 1929.*

But only rarely had national affairs impinged on local affairs in such a way as seriously to disturb the constituency; and, because they had had to do with issues of popular education, disestablishment, and the like, the deep and firm consensus which characterized the life of the constituency remained unimpaired. Swansea had been emphatically Liberal throughout the century, and the Liberalism of its representatives had been such, until the end of the century, as to accommodate the radicalism of their constituents. Now, with the rise of Labour, that consensus was breaking down and there was a certain impatience with the official Liberal Party for what Labour supporters regarded as the irrelevance of its policies. The official organ of the Trades Council complained in 1899 that during a Liberal Party rally in the Albert Hall in 1899, not a word was said about Labour represent-ation, the payment of MPs, the Eight Hour Day, and other equally pressing issues. But most political activists, including some of those who called themselves Labour, were content to work within the existing structures of the Liberal Party. Not until the eve of the First World War was it practical, or prudent anyway, to be otherwise than 'Lib Lab'.

More to the point, there was not much that the voters in the two constituencies, Swansea Town and Swansea District, could do about the representation except hope for the emergence of a radical candidate to vote for. The numbers of electors had gone up substantially in the course of the century, rising from just over 10,000 in 1883 to nearly 21,000 in 1901, but the trade unionists and other radicals among them could do little to break the grip of the Liberal establishment on the choice of candidate. Neighbouring Gower, with its strong Welsh Nonconformist radical majority in the coal valleys, offered a more realistic hope. Moreover, the division of the parliamentary borough into two distinct constituencies was not conducive to the return of a member more representative of the opinions of the working-class majority. The new constituency boundaries recognized the social fact that in political terms there existed two different political communities, a conservative-inclined Town Division with a penumbra of radicalism, and a thoroughly radical, Labour-inclined District Division embracing most of the industrial suburbs and centred on St Thomas. Such has been the reality ever since, but equally the structure of the County Borough and the nature of the wider franchise offered a real hope that democracy would one day triumph in the locality as a whole.

Today, as industrial archaeologists carefully map the course of old roads, railways and canals, and methodically trace the remains of the works they once served, the memory of those times slides into the dark backward of the past. The industrial suburbs on either side of the river still gaze across at each other, but in less comprehending ways than when they both looked out at the energy, the smoke and the fire, which had brought them into being and sustained them for so many generations. Yet enough remains in the towns and the villages themselves to remind the traveller on his way down the valley to the city and the harbour, with its marinas and pleasure boats, of the nature of the communities that ordinary working people created here, and the richness of the heritage we have inherited from them.

Chapter 6

RELIGION AND EDUCATION

F. G. Cowley

The Established Church and Dissent in the Early Eighteenth Century

On 20 May 1739 the roof of the nave of St Mary's collapsed 'just before Divine Service began, by which particular instance of divine guidance the lives of many people were saved, and only one person wounded'. The vicar, Charles Davies, was late, delayed by the unpunctual arrival of his barber to shave him, and most of the congregation were outside waiting for him to appear. This dramatic incident was one in what was to be a long history of fabric problems at St Mary's. But it was also symptomatic of much that was wrong with the Church, not only at Swansea but elsewhere in the eighteenth century.

St Mary's was a twelfth-century foundation and, since it had served the *caput* of the medieval lordship of Gower, was the premier church of Gower and the largest. Yet the church was miserably poor, assessed at a mere £30 per annum at the beginning of the eighteenth century. Much of its income had been appropriated in medieval times to support the Hospital of the Blessed David founded by Bishop Henry de Gower in 1332, and when this property was acquired by Sir George Herbert in Edward VI's reign something like two-thirds of the tithes which should have formed part of the income of St Mary's were permanently lost to it. Swansea's only other church — St John's — was more a chapel of ease than a church and situated at the north end of the town on the site of the present St. Matthew's church. Founded by the Knights Hospitallers about 1165, the church was worth only £2 per annum, *c.* 1708 and was generally used by the Welsh-speaking inhabitants of the town and served either from Llangyfelach or Llansamlet.

The classic method for dealing with fabric defects was to raise a church rate and the churchwardens of St Mary's resorted to it on a number of occasions. As the eighteenth century advanced it became increasingly difficult to collect, mainly because the growing body of

The Reverend Joseph Harris (Gomer) (1773-1825).

Dissenters was refusing to pay. There was thus little money available to the Church in Swansea during the eighteenth century for securing the fabric or enlarging the accommodation, still less for mounting major pastoral initiatives.

Dissent had put down early roots in the Swansea region. Its growing strength in the later seventeenth century was due partly to the policy of the central government during the Long Parliament and the Interregnum (1640-60), partly to the complaisant attitude of the civic authorities and the supportive action of sympathetic landowners during the period of persecution, and partly to Swansea's position as a port in contact with what one historian has called 'the great Dissenting nerve centre of Bristol'. The Toleration Act 1689 allowed Dissenters (with the exception of Unitarians and Roman Catholics) to worship freely in licensed premises and the Dissenters of Swansea now acquired meeting houses in the town. A congregation of Presbyterians or Independents (they were hardly distinguishable at this time) acquired a meeting house in a court off the eastern side of High Street. By 1697 it had proved too small for their needs and they built a new chapel on the site of the present Unitarian chapel. Dr John Evans in 1715 estimated an average attendance of 250 for the Swansea Independents. The Baptist community at Swansea, a branch church dependent on Ilston Church which John Miles had founded in 1649, assumed the mantle of the parent church when Miles was ejected in 1660 and in 1698 rented the meeting house just vacated by the Independents and this, from long association, came to be known as Baptist Court. A recent historian, T. M. Bassett, has suggested that Swansea Baptist church and its branches had about 80 members in 1690. The Quakers, the élite of the Dissenters, had their meeting house to the north of Baptist Court on the site of the burgage now occupied by High Street Post Office (behind which a Quaker burial ground still remains). The site was given them in 1656 by the prosperous merchant William Bevan, one of Swansea's earliest Quakers, and was occupied by Quakers continuously until 1960. In the early eighteenth century the membership could not have been more than 20.

One early congregation of Dissenters, though its centre was three miles north of Swansea, should be mentioned here because it played such a significant role in the history of the Independent cause in Swansea in the late eighteenth and early nineteenth centuries. A mixed congregation of Independents and Baptists met at Cilfwnwr farm, near Llangyfelach, at least as early as 1666. By 1692 the congregation had become exclusively Independent and in 1700 moved to

Tirdwncyn. In 1715 Dr. John Evans gave a figure of 1,006 for the combined membership of the churches of Neath, Tirdwncyn, and Blaen-gwrach. A purpose-built chapel was erected at Mynyddbach in 1762 on the site of the present chapel. This chapel, wrote the Rev. T. Sinclair Evans, 'exerted all the attractive influence of the ancient Jerusalem whither the tribes went up'. Members came on foot and on horseback from as far afield as Baglan in the east and Loughor in the west. The chapel was eventually to become the mother of many Independent causes in the Swansea area.

The Old Chapel, on the site of the Unitarian Church, High Street.

The Methodist Revival

North of the Old Duke Public House in Upper High Street is a mound overlooking the Prince of Wales Road and the Hafod. It is now crowned with the ruined walls of houses, the burnt-out shell of an

St Mary's Church, mid nineteenth century.

Anglican mission church, and the foundations of a recently-demolished chapel. In the early eighteenth century this green hillock — Crug-glas — was the resort of drunkards, card sharpers, prize fighters, and all the riff-raff of the fairground for which the area was frequently used. It has entered the legendary lore of Calvinistic Methodism because it was here that the great Howell Harris preached on a number of occasions in the late 1730s and early 1740s and faced some of the most hostile audiences of his preaching career. It was at Crug-glas, too, that an attempt was made on his life. The would-be assassin, a drunkard egged on by Harris's enemies, aimed a pistol at him. When the pistol misfired, the assailant went to sleep off his intoxication in a lime-kiln, was overcome with fumes, and died.

Howell Harris was, and remained, a staunch member of the Church of England; but after a conversion similar to that experienced by the Wesleys and George Whitefield, determined to devote his life to winning souls for Christ as an itinerant preacher. He was no theologian and was refused ordination on a number of occasions, mainly because of his irregular preaching activities. He had a powerful presence, a thunderous voice, and great gifts as an orator. When, to use his own expression, he had 'the liberty and the power', he was able to sway an audience and evoke feelings ranging from the depths of remorse to the heights of spiritual exaltation. He was also a great organizer and sought not merely to preach and effect individual conversions but to establish societies or fellowship meetings of committed Christians, which were to act as cells re-invigorating the flagging religious life of the parish and supplementing the worship of the parish church.

The town was not the natural habitat of the early Methodist societies. They took root and flourished best in the hamlet and village; and their meeting places were the cottages and farm houses of middling sort of people. There was a flourishing society at Llansamlet dating from at least as early as 1742 and its meetings were first held in the farm houses of Trewern and Waunllysdy. The society then moved to two cottages called 'Y Cwm' and worshipped there for forty years until the establishment of a purpose-built meeting house in 1782-3. This building, Salem, Capel-y-Cwm, still survives next to the bigger chapel which replaced it in 1905.

In the 1780s a well-to-do brewer, David Thomas, who had been a member of the Independent congregation at Mynyddbach, moved to Swansea. He worshipped in a mixed meeting of Independents and

St David's Roman Catholic Church, 1856.

Wesley Chapel, Goat Street.

Methodists in a room in Castle Street known as 'The Old Room'. After a disagreement he decided to build his own chapel at Crug-glas. It was opened in 1799 by the famous supporter of the Methodist cause, David Jones, vicar of Llan-gan. David Thomas had planned to make his chapel available to various denominations but through the influence of his friend, David Jones, it was eventually given over absolutely to the Calvinistic Methodist body.

John Wesley, though a friend and admirer, differed in his theological stance from Howell Harris. The latter based his religious thought firmly on the theology of John Calvin, stressing the absolute corruption of man's nature, the election by God of whose who are to be saved, and justification by faith alone. By contrast Wesley was an Arminian. He emphasized man's free will and rejected the doctrine of predestination which, to him, turned God into a tyrant and took away man's responsibility for his own salvation. Wesley's missionary activities in Wales were more limited than Harris's because of his inability to speak Welsh. He was forced to confine his activities to the English-speaking areas. In the Swansea region this meant the town itself and also peninsular Gower, where he established a number of very successful village societies. Wesley first visited Swansea and preached there in 1758 but a successful society was not established until 1769. It met at this time in that 'Old Room' in Castle Street which provided accommodation for Calvinistic Methodists as well as the old Dissenters. The Wesleyan society, after acquiring their own exclusive meeting house in the 'upper end of the town', moved in 1789 to Bunkers Hill (Banc Caer Hill) in Goat Street.

Another group of Methodists in the Castle Street Room, unable perhaps to accept the Arminian views of the Wesleyans, were worried about their future. Selina, countess of Huntingdon, took pity on this 'remnant of Israel' and gave them the site for a chapel on the Burrows which was built in 1787 and opened in 1789.

Both Harris and Wesley had from the first protested their loyalty to the Church of England and insisted that members of their societies should attend Sunday service in their parish church. But towards the end of the century pressure grew for the Methodists to ordain their own ministers. The Wesleyans resisted this pressure until after the death of their leader in 1791 and the Calvinistic Methodists until 1811. These dates mark the formation of two new denominations which, as the nineteenth century advanced, became increasingly identified with the nonconformists of the older Dissent in their criticism of the Established Church and, later, in political pressure for its disestablishment.

The Circulating Schools

Methodism would not have attained the success it did unless the people had been sufficiently literate and religiously attuned to respond to its message. Education at the beginning of the eighteenth century was still theoretically, and largely in practice, the province and preserve of the Church. The ideal (not always realized) was a school in every parish in which a schoolmaster, licensed by the bishop, would provide for the common people a basic literacy to enable them to read the Bible and Catechism and would inculcate in them the social virtues of hard work, deference, and acceptance of their lot in life. The Welsh Trust and the Society for Promoting Christian Knowledge had already attempted to establish such schools on a permanent basis and to distribute Bibles and religious literature to those who could profit from them. But it was not until Griffith Jones, rector of Llanddowror, established his Circulating Schools that a real degree of success was achieved. The schools were set up in the winter months (the least busy period for agricultural workers) and served by itinerant schoolmasters who would, if requested, return year after year. The school held in Swansea in 1745-6 had 201 pupils; but schools were also held at farms, hamlets and villages in the vicinity — at Cwm, Llansamlet, Pentre Estyll (St John's parish), Cnap Llwyd and Graig Trewyddfa (Landore), Olchfa, and many other locations.

The schools were successful because the schoolmasters concentrated solely on teaching their pupils to read the Bible and Catechism and used as the medium of instruction the language with which their pupils were most familiar: Welsh in the Welshry north of Swansea, English in Swansea itself and in the anglicized villages of Gower. The hours of instruction were flexible and could be fixed to cater for adults at night and children by day. The colliers of Trewyddfa were keen pupils of the school held in their area, even after a hard shift at the coal face, and asked the Rev. John Price, vicar of Llangyfelach, to plead with Griffith Jones that the school should not be discontinued.

The Circulating Schools flourished between 1738 and 1777 and made many industrial and agricultural workers literate, attuned to theological argument, and receptive to the message of the new Methodism as well as the old Dissent. It is hardly a coincidence that many of the schools were located in areas like Cwm, Llansamlet and Cnap Llwyd, and Landore, where thriving Methodist societies were established.

Urbanization and Triumph of Dissent

The large, widely-scattered membership of central 'Jerusalems' like Mynyddbach had already begun to break up before the end of the eighteenth century. Lewis Rees, minister of Tirdwncyn/Mynyddbach between 1759 and 1795, had vigorously resisted the pressures for independence exerted by members of his branch churches, and insisted that members worship at the mother church every Sunday morning. To complain of the distance was, in his view, a sign of slackening fervour if not of downright laziness. He reluctantly allowed the building of Bethel in Sketty in 1770 and Libanus in Morriston in 1782. But after his death a new plantation took place within the town of Swansea. David Davies, Rees's successor, established Ebenezer in 1803 and in 1808 relinquished his pastorate at Mynyddbach to concentrate his energies exclusively on Ebenezer and Bethel. The growth of dissent within the town was now greatly assisted by a major increase in population caused by immigration. Many of the immigrants were committed Independents, Baptists, and Methodists who had come into Swansea from neighbouring rural parishes. Growth was also boosted by doctrinal conflicts within congregations. In 1798 a group of fifty members of Baptist Court broke away after a doctrinal disagreement to form their own church in Back Lane. It was this congregation over which Joseph Harris (Gomer), the founder of Wales' first successful Welsh periodical, *Seren Gomer*, was to preside with such distinction between 1801 and 1825. In 1813 a similar split occurred in the congregation of Independents in High Street over a successor to the minister, William Howell. One party removed to found the Congregational church of Castle Street, which opened in 1814. The group remaining appointed Richard Awbery as their pastor and the church became Unitarian. The Old Dissenters, noted in the eighteenth century for their 'dryness', now became imbued with a new spirit. The Methodist revivalists 'warmed the air' for them and revitalized them with missionary zeal and a desire for expansion.

After Joseph Harris's death in 1825 it was decided to honour his memory by amicably dividing the English and Welsh congregation at Back Lane and establishing new chapels for each. The first English Baptist church, now known as Mount Pleasant, opened in 1827 and the Welsh Baptist chapel, Bethesda (Prince of Wales Road) in 1831. The latter building could seat 1,000 people and cost £1,600, an indication of the expansionist hopes which the Baptists now entertained. The Calvinistic Methodists at Crug-glas were also finding their accommodation becoming cramped and their search for a new site ended in the establishment of Triniti chapel on the Ropewalk Field (later Park Street). Only a few thatched cottages stood in the area at this time but, as the planners had foreseen, it would soon become a central one in the rapidly expanding town. The chapel with seating for 1,500 was opened in 1829. The Wesleyans built their first real chapel on the site of their Goat Street meeting room in 1825, but in 1844 embarked on a much more elaborate building. The original builder went bankrupt and the building remained roofless, with grass growing from its walls for many years — misguided visitors mistook it for Swansea Castle! But eventually, two chapel members, William Morgan, manager of the Hafod Copper Works, and Thomas Evans, a well-known chemist, took over the building operations and it was finished and opened in

1847 'under the challenging stimulus of a huge debt'. The chapel became the 'cathedral of Methodism in west Wales' and was undoubtedly the finest chapel yet erected by a Nonconformist sect in Swansea. It survived until the blitz of 1941 reduced it to a shell.

In 1851 a religious census was taken in England and Wales. Its object was first, to count the number of places of worship and the number of sittings available in each, and secondly, to count the number who attended the services on Census Sunday, 30 March 1851. The returns for Swansea show that by 1851 the town had become predominantly Nonconformist.

CENSUS OF 1851: SWANSEA, INCLUDING TOWN AND FRANCHISE
AND PARISHES OF ST. JOHN AND ST. THOMAS

Denomination	Number of Places	Number of Sittings	Attendance Number
Church of England	4	4,021	2,717
Independent	7	3,965	3,958
Baptist	5	2,384	2,936
Calvinist Methodist	4	2,167	2,013
Wesleyan Methodist	4	1,416	1,232
Primitive Methodist	1	300	410
Lady Huntingdon's	1	650	1,050
Unitarian	1	400	328
Quakers	1	35	35
Roman Catholic	1	412	500
Jews	1	72	80
Mormons	1	200	320

(Based on figures published by Professor I. G. Jones, in *Morgannwg* XII [1968]).

In the second half of the century Nonconformity consolidated its position of ascendancy by a policy of chapel building and re-building which more than matched the efforts of the now renewed Established Church. This period saw the building of chapels on an aggressively monumental scale, both within the town and in its suburbs. Ebenezer was rebuilt in 1862 but the integrated frontage comprising the Sunday school and manse was not completed until 1896. St Andrew's, Swansea's only Presbyterian church, was built in 1864 by Scottish immigrants engaged in the drapery trade. They displayed their wealth in a large building with twin towers and Perpendicular-style windows which still dominates the sky-line of St Helen's Road. The façade of Mount Pleasant Baptist chapel, with its four Corinthian columns, was built when the chapel was extended in 1875. Triniti (Park St. 1865-75),

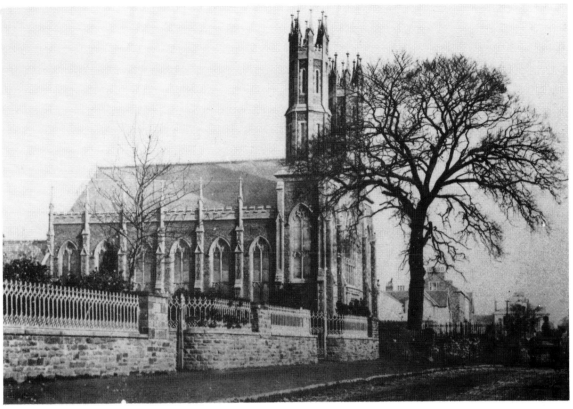

Bethesda (*c.* 1870), Siloh Newydd (Brynhyfryd 1878) and Tabernacl (Morriston 1872) were among the architecturally most prominent chapels rebuilt in this period of Nonconformist triumphalism.

The chapels were now dominating the religious, social, and cultural life of Swansea, for they had become more than places of worship. They were also centres of instruction and entertainment. Workmen learned to read music, using the tonic sol-fa system, and took part in the oratorios and other musical performances put on by the larger chapels. Ebenezer was fortunate in having the noted musician, Joseph Parry, as its organist between 1881 and 1888. Many, too, gained experience in the art of public speaking and in the procedures of committee work through teaching in Sunday school and officiating at chapel meetings. The chapels were nurturing articulate and capable administrators, many of whom were to be recruited by the new unions and the new Labour party in the first half of this century. In the later nineteenth century, however, Nonconformists were still firmly allied to the Liberal Party. They campaigned vigorously for temperance causes, securing the passing of the Sunday Closing Act in 1881, and kept up political pressure for the disestablishment of the Welsh Church.

St Andrew's Church, formerly Presbyterian, now United Reformed Church.

Worship at Bethania Chapel, Morriston in 1944.

The Reverend Edward Squire, Vicar of Swansea, 1846-76.

Impressive buildings, superb pulpit oratory, elaborate musical performances, and local eisteddfodau were all signs of vigorous life and expressions of Nonconformity's growing confidence. But many were aware of how deceptive the façade of strength could be. Was not music deflecting the chapel from its true purpose and introducing divisions? 'When music comes through the chapel door', it was said, 'the devil comes with it.' Others were conscious of the threat to Nonconformity posed by the growing monoglot English population of Swansea. Unless more chapels were provided for English speakers, it was feared that Nonconformity would die out. No one was more alive to this danger than the Rev. Thomas Rees, Independent minister of Ebenezer (1861-85). Rees was one of Swansea's most prominent Nonconformists. He was the author of *A History of Protestant Nonconformity in Wales* (2nd ed. 1883) and joint-author of *Hanes Eglwysi Annibynnol Cymru* (1875). He was no Anglophile. 'Swansea is to a great extent an English town', he declared at the opening of St. Andrew's church, 'and it was a fact that wherever the English language prevailed in Wales the advancement of pure religion diminished.' Nevertheless, no-one devoted more energy than he to fund-raising to provide Swansea with English Independent chapels. He cultivated the generosity of the tobacco magnate, H. O. Wills, who contributed handsomely to the building of Walter Road English Congregational chapel, which was opened in 1869. Other denominations followed the lead of the Independents and in the last quarter of the century the growing residential suburbs of Swansea became well provided with chapels for English speakers.

'The Age of Voluntaryism': Education 1800-1870

This period in educational history has been conveniently labelled by historians as 'The Age of Voluntaryism' because the elementary schools established during it were initiated, supervised, and maintained by the voluntary efforts of denominations, societies, and private enterprise, with little or no assistance from the State. The Nonconformists were for the greater part of the nineteenth century

St Mary's Church, rebuilt 1955-9.

opposed to state assistance or supervision on principle. They feared it would operate to their detriment in favour of the Established Church. The State, in fact, did little in this period to interfere in the field of education but from 1833 did make small annual grants which went mainly to two major voluntary societies: the non-sectarian British and Foreign Schools Society and the Anglican National Society for Promoting the Education of the Poor in the Principles of the Established Church. The British Society was established in 1814 and took over the supervision of schools initiated by Joseph Lancaster.

Lancaster hit on the idea of founding schools in which the teacher would train older pupils to act as monitors. These monitors would in turn teach the younger children and thus enable one teacher to cope with a school numbering a hundred or more pupils. Lancaster visited Swansea in 1806 and a boys' school using his methods was established in Goat Street in the same year. It was the first Lancasterian school to be established in Wales. A girls' school in York Place followed in 1811; but when this came under the controlling interest of Anglicans, another girls' school founded on the strict principles of non-sectarianism favoured by the British Society was set up in Queen's

The Royal Institution of South Wales, c. 1850.

Street in 1821. These schools were under the auspices of the British Society after 1814, and many more were to be founded in the town and its suburbs in the pre-Board School period. The best of them, like the Hafod Copperworks School founded by J. H. Vivian in 1847 for the children of his workmen, provided the model for the new Board schools which were built after 1870.

A cursory glance at the evidence in the celebrated 'Blue Books' on Welsh education in 1847 would give an immediate impression that Swansea was well provided with elementary schools. There were after all some 53 schools listed, of which 47 were private. But the commissioners did in fact find much to criticize with regard to provision and conditions in the schools. They drew attention to cramped and unsuitable premises, lack of books and equipment, unqualified teachers, and pupil absenteeism. Many pupils withdrew through sheer economic necessity after a brief period of schooling. All these short-comings took time and money to remedy. Increasing financial aid from the State and local authorities, and legislation and by-laws compelling attendance and a strictly-defined period of study for children, were to remedy some of them. The problem of poor teaching could not be solved before more training colleges were opened. Swansea opened its first permanent training establishment in Nelson Terrace in 1872, where it remained until it removed to its more lavish premises on Townhill in 1913.

The early history of two institutions deserves special mention here because of their long and intimate connection with the cultural and educational life of Swansea: the Swansea Grammar School and the Royal Institution of South Wales.

The Swansea Grammar School, 1682-1870

The Swansea Grammar School was founded in 1682 by Hugh Gore, bishop of Waterford and Lismore, to provide a free classical education for twenty sons of the poorer burgesses. The school flourished in the eighteenth century but gradually changed its character and began catering for the better-off burgesses and gentry families of south Wales, who paid fees for their sons' tuition and board. Non-fee paying foundation scholars became rare. The school entered on a period of decline with the appointment of the Rev. John Oldisworth in 1801. He was a convivial ex-naval chaplain, probably an alcoholic, and author of Swansea's first guide-book. But Oldisworth's conduct was not solely to blame for the decline. The endowments were insufficient to

*Swansea Grammar School,
c. 1935.*

attract really competent masters and keep the buildings in repair, while the major English public schools were now exerting an attraction which well-to-do families in south Wales found it difficult to resist. There was also unease among the townsfolk because of the classical bias of the curriculum and the difficulties their sons experienced in mixing with boys of a richer and more sophisticated background. The school was originally situated in Goat Street; but in 1816 this site was abandoned and the school held in various private houses. In 1842, on the death of the master, the Rev. Evan Griffiths, when pupil numbers had fallen to a mere handful, the school closed. Largely through the efforts of George Grant Francis, the Court of Chancery sanctioned a new scheme, with a wider curriculum and special provision for the twenty sons as enjoined in the original charter, which enabled the school to re-open in 1852. The pupils entered the newly-erected buildings on Mount Pleasant in 1853. A new block comprising a library, science laboratories, lecture room, gymnasium, and art room was added in 1869, and pupil numbers rose from 71 in 1857 to 130 in 1887.

The Royal Institution of South Wales

The Royal Institution of South Wales was founded in 1835 as the Swansea Philosophical and Literary Society, having as its objects 'the cultivation and advancement of the various branches of natural history, as well as the local history of the town . . . the extension and encouragement of the fine arts and the general diffusion of knowledge'. The building which became its headquarters was opened in 1841. The society had arisen 'phoenix-like' from the ashes of a previously defunct society, the Cambrian Institution, founded in 1821; but the immediate stimuli for its establishment were the founding of the British Association for the Advancement of Science in 1831 and of the Neath Philosophical Society in 1834. The Swansea society was set up by George Grant Francis, then only twenty-one years of age, and by a group of remarkably gifted industrialists and professional men who were also amateur scientists. Among the founding members there were three Fellows of the Royal Society: Lewis Weston Dillwyn, John Henry Vivian, C. R. M. Talbot, and four who were to become Fellows: John Dillwyn Llewellyn, William Edmond Logan, John Gwyn Jeffreys, and William Grove. The founders hoped that the new society would fulfil the functions of an embryo university and in its earliest years it did valuable scientific research and attracted the interest and support of scientists like Faraday and De la Beche. But this period was short-lived and it had already ceased to be involved in primary scientific research when it acted as host to the British Association in 1848. Thenceforward, such serious scientific work as it sponsored was undertaken by specialist off-shoot groups like the Swansea Geological Society. It continued to provide popular lectures on literary, historical, and scientific subjects for what was predominantly a middle-class membership and achieved some degree of success in organizing science classes for the public at large at a time when there was little or no science or technology in the curriculum of local schools. It served as a museum, as an educational centre, and as a meeting place for many of the town's cultural societies; functions it continues to discharge to the present day.

Reform and Renewal in the Established Church

In the early nineteenth century the fortunes of the Established Church were at an extremely low ebb. Miles Bassett, vicar of St Mary's from 1757 to 1813, was, like many of his clerical colleagues, a pluralist and in addition to his vicarage of Swansea (then worth only

£90) held that of Aberafan, together with the perpetual curacies of Oystermouth, St Ismael (Ferryside), and Bonvilston. In the later years of his ministry he had witnessed the secession of the Wesleyans and the Calvinistic Methodists — a grave blow to his own morale as well as a major loss to the Church. In his visitation return for 1804 he reported with an air of resigned helplessness the strange break-up of his Sunday school. It was a long-established institution with a large attendance 'but owing either to a wicked or absurd report that the children were all to be sent to Botany Bay', the scholars 'all abruptly absented themselves and it has never since been resumed'. Confirmations at this period were rare events, as Bassett boldly reminded his diocesan: 'We have had no confirmation here since 1789', and 'this parish and the two adjoining ones of Llangyfelach and Llansamlet are the most populous in your lordship's diocese'. The fabric was again in a poor condition and in 1812 the churchwardens of both St Mary's and St John's were cited to the ecclesiastical court 'on account of the dilapidated and indecent state of their respective churches'. In 1816 the churchwardens feared that St Mary's was facing bankruptcy.

Unlike the Nonconformists, the Church was unable to respond quickly to the needs of the rapidly-growing population of Swansea. A chapel could release members to establish a new cause without difficulty. All that was required initially was to rent a suitable meeting room to house the nucleus of a future congregation. The Church was unable to operate with similar ease and speed, for at the beginning of the century it still required an act of Parliament to create a new parish.

But by the 1830s the tide was turning. The Established Church at national level, largely through government initiative, started to set its house in order. A series of parliamentary statutes began the process of removing long-standing abuses like pluralism and non-residence and provided the Church with more efficient machinery to discharge its pastoral functions. The Ecclesiastical Commission was set up in 1835 to manage the estates of the Church and to make a more equitable distribution of its income. A less cumbersome procedure was also devised to speed up the creation of new parishes in populous areas. Even so, progress at Swansea was initially slow. One looks in vain for any concrete achievement during the vicariate of Dr. William Hewson (1813-45). 'He was', wrote a later curate of St Mary's, 'more at home on the bench than in the pulpit and more frequently seen in the lady's drawing room than in the widow's cottage.' The establishment of Holy Trinity church in 1843 seems to have owed little to Hewson and was not a strategically wise contribution to church extension anyway.

His successor, the Rev. Robert Shirley Bunbury, an ardent evangelical, did not live long enough to see any of his visions realized.

The Church in Swansea really owed its transformation to the leadership of two great vicars of St Mary's: the Rev. Edward Burnard Squire (1846-76) and the Rev. Prebendary J. Allan Smith (1885-1902). Squire had had a colourful career before his ordination in 1841. He had served in the East India Company, the Indian Army and Navy, had commanded two sloops in the first Burmese War (1824-26), and been an agent for the Church Missionary Society in China until expelled on the outbreak of the Opium War. After training for the ministry at St. Bees, he entered on his new duties at Swansea with great energy and zeal. He paced around Swansea as though he were still on the quarter-deck of one of his sloops, but his stern appearance and gruff manner belied his innate kindness. He was a compassionate man with a genuine concern for the poor. During his vicariate, St Mary's thankfully lost its reputation as the church of the rich and respectable, and its clergy and laymen began to make contact with the poor and destitute in the warren of alleys and courts in the areas of High Street, Back Street, and the Sandfields. The Swansea Parochial Visiting Association was set up and each visitor was allocated forty houses. At the height of its activities the Association was relieving 2,000 cases a year with blankets and baby clothes.

The parish church had long had an accommodation problem, mainly because large blocks of seats had been earmarked and paid for by prominent laymen. The problem became more urgent as residential building expanded westward towards the Brynmill boundary of the parish and eastward across the river into the district of St. Thomas. During the vicariates of Squire and J. Allan Smith the work of church extension made great progress. St Paul's, Sketty, funded by the Vivians, was consecrated in 1850 and soon became a separate parish. Christ Church, which started in a schoolroom in the Sandfields in 1863, was financed by the wine merchant, John William Clark. It was consecrated in 1872 and became a separate parish two years later. St Peter's, Cockett, was consecrated in 1856 on a site provided by John Dillwyn Llewelyn and became a separate parish in 1878. St James, Walter Road, was consecrated in 1867 but, unlike other churches, it remained as a chapel-of-ease to St Mary's until 1985. Canon Smith on his appointment in 1885 was determined to push forward the work of church extension and his vicariate saw the establishment of the churches of St Mark (consecrated 1888), St Thomas (1888), and St Gabriel's (1889). St Matthew's was built in 1887 on the site of old St

John's, after its dedication had been taken over by a new church built by the Vivians in the Hafod. Canon Smith was an indefatigable fund raiser. In 1901 he claimed he had raised no less than £66,742 for the work of church extension. His crowning achievement was the building of a new church of St Mary's between 1895 and 1899. The new church was designed by Sir Arthur Blomfield and consecrated before its completion by Frederick Temple, archbishop of Canterbury, in 1898.

The work of church extension was one manifestation of the new spirit which was animating the Established Church; another was the movement to found church schools. The National Society was founded in 1811 and its ambition was to see a church school in each parish. Little was done at Swansea until Squire became vicar of St Mary's. He lost no time in reviving the Sunday school and in establishing the first National Schools at Oxford Street. They were opened in 1848 with accommodation for boys, girls and infants. Within weeks, 400 children were in attendance and 'were receiving such instruction as may fit them to be useful members of the community, and such religious knowledge as through Divine grace may prepare them for eternity'.

The Oxford Street Schools became model schools, but really catered for the better-off classes who could afford the scale of fees charged. Squire was more concerned with the poorer children who wandered the streets of Swansea bare-footed and uncared for. Unless the Church addressed itself to these, he wrote in one of his annual reports, 'multitudes must remain in darkness and ignorance who will grow up in crime and become the pests of society, the inmates of our gaols'. Squire founded two schools to meet the needs of the poor in what were then considered to be tough areas of the town. The first was a Ragged School organized in Recorder Street in the Sandfields area. Opened in 1857, it was replaced in 1862 by the Parochial Schools, Oystermouth Road, on a site opposite the Gaol. The schools were badly sited for infants who had to cross the track of the Mumbles Railway but their needs were soon to be catered for by the St Helen's National Infants School which was opened in 1864. It is now better known as Christ Church Infants and is the sole surviving Church school in Swansea. A second school for the poor was opened in 1864 in Powell Street (off High Street) in a dancing saloon which had lost its licence.

In 1866 Squire was able to report that ten Church day schools and six Sunday schools were operating in the old parish of St Mary's. Six of the day schools were under the auspices of the National Society and had already provided education for 18,000 children who would otherwise have been left neglected. By the third quarter of the nineteenth century the Church was the most actively engaged of all the religious bodies in educating Swansea's children.

The Catholic Community

On 22 February 1646 Philip Powell was arrested on board a small vessel lying off Mumbles and charged with being a Catholic priest. After interrogation he was conveyed to London where a court sentenced him to be hanged, drawn, and quartered. He was executed at Tyburn on 30 June of the same year.

No event could have been better calculated to undermine the confidence and weaken the resolve of any Catholics who remained in the Swansea area at this time. Denied the ministrations of priests and without the protective umbrella which only a powerful Catholic landed family could provide, the Catholic community dwindled in numbers and eventually died out. In 1767 a return made of the number of papists in St David's diocese gave only seven for the Swansea area: a man aged forty, who acted as agent in one of the copper works, and a family of six (three male, three female) who were on the point of returning to France. As Swansea increased in industrial and commercial importance towards the end of the eighteenth century, however, a small Catholic community gradually formed and priests were occasionally sent down to minister to them by the Vicar Apostolic at Bristol. About 1797 the Jesuit Robert Plowden succeeded in making a temporary chapel at the Plas, and in 1799 the Catholic presence was strengthened by the arrival of five Frenchmen, refugees from the French Revolution. Three of them were priests, of whom one was the Abbé Albert Séjan, former chaplain to King Louis XVI. Séjan built the first Catholic chapel in Nelson Terrace, which opened in 1810 and catered for a congregation which rarely numbered more than twelve. With the restoration of the French monarchy in 1814 Séjan returned to France and the mission at Swansea languished, being served for short periods by a succession of priests, not all of them resident. The Catholic population was growing during these years, and when Father Charles Kavanagh was appointed in 1839 he was ministering to 135 souls in an area which covered Llanelli and Aberafan as well as Swansea. Most of his parishioners were Irish and had come to the area from the southern counties of Ireland even before the great famine of 1845-6.

Father Kavanagh was one of Swansea's memorable priests. He established the first purpose-built church of St David in 1847, built the Catholic school adjoining it in 1851, and another in Greenhill, where the majority of his parishioners lived in hastily-built, insanitary, and overcrowded dwellings. It was here in 1849 that the cholera claimed a large proportion of its victims. Kavanagh immediately offered his assistance to the doctor, William Harris Long, and performed the most menial services for the victims: washing them, combing their hair, making their beds, and offering them spiritual consolation whatever their faith. Between July and August he helped to bury 170 victims of the epidemic. He was joined by helpers from other denominations: the Rev. G. B. Brock, the High Street Unitarian minister, and Thomas Davies, part-time minister of Horeb Independent chapel, Morriston, who abandoned his job in the copper works to help the relief work.

Kavanagh's heroic conduct earned him a testimonial gift of fifty guineas from his fellow townsmen. Despite the backlash of anti-Catholic feeling which followed the restoration of the hierarchy in 1850 — there were petitions against papal aggression and public lectures on the errors of Rome — he rode out the storm and became an accepted member of many public bodies and improvement societies in the early 1850s. He was secretary of the Mechanics Institute, member of the Council of the Royal Institution in 1855, and an active supporter of the Swansea Infirmary. On his sudden death in 1856 he was honoured with what was virtually a civic funeral.

The Catholic population grew rapidly after 1850. St David's church was enlarged and a new presbytery built in 1864; but it now became urgent to provide a church in Greenhill. The first St Joseph's church (the present parish hall) was opened in 1866. In 1873 the Benedictines took over the Swansea mission and began an association with St David's which has lasted to this day. The mission was now divided into two districts. St David's took responsibility for the 1,200 Catholics in the area south of Croft and Thomas Streets, and St Joseph's for the 4,000 Catholics north of this line. In 1875 St Joseph's became an independent mission and a large new church, designed by the celebrated firm of Pugin and Pugin, was opened in 1888. The pastoral care exercised by the priests of St Joseph's was immeasurably strengthened by the work of the Ursuline nuns, whose convent had been established in Greenhill. They taught in the Catholic schools, visited the homes of the poor and needy, and rescued girls at moral risk, sending them to a home at the Good Shepherd Convent, Bartestree.

EDUCATION, 1870-1970
The Board Schools

'The working classes', wrote John Glasbrook in 1870, 'have too much knowledge already; it was much easier to manage them twenty years ago; the more education people get, the more difficult they are to manage.' Glasbrook was a colliery owner, tinplate manufacturer, and local alderman, and he was opposing the imposition of a special rate to establish a public library in Swansea. Fortunately, his sentiments were not widely shared. When Foster introduced his Education Bill into the Commons in 1870, members were aware of the need to educate the new electorate brought into being by the Reform Act of 1867. They were conscious, too, of the brittle nature of Britain's industrial prosperity in the face of growing foreign competition. In the General Exhibition of 1851 Britain had carried off nearly all the prizes. In the 1867 Paris Exhibition it barely managed to secure ten. It was no use urging an increase in technical education for artisans, when most of them lacked the basics of even an elementary education.

The object of the 1870 Education Act was to complete the provision of schools established under the voluntaryists, to fill up the gaps. In 1871 when the Swansea School Board had been set up in accordance with the 1870 Act, there was a deficiency of 4,035 school places in the borough alone. The Board now proceeded to take over the administration of a number of the existing schools and also set about building its own. Most of the schools taken over had been founded by the British Society and included Brynhyfryd, Cwm, Treboeth, Cadle, Morriston (Martin St.), and St Helen's and Goat Street, Swansea. Those newly erected by the Board were Tirdeunaw, Ynystawe, Llangyfelach, Penllergaer, Plasmarl, and Pentrepoeth. In 1881 the number of school places still wanting was 1,269 but this figure was for the whole School Board area. The deficiency was further reduced by the building of some very large schools. Terrace Road School was built in 1888, St Thomas in 1898 (to replace the outdated Kilvey Copperworks School), Manselton in 1900, and the new Hafod in 1905 (to replace the Hafod Copperworks School). These large, collegiate-style buildings still dominate the surburban landscape.

The Secondary Schools

The elementary schools concentrated attention on instilling into their pupils the 3 Rs. Other subjects were considered a luxury, particularly after the introduction of the Revised Code in 1861 with its emphasis on payment by results. As Swansea grew in industrial and commercial importance, however, middle and upper working class parents began to press for more advanced schools with a wider curriculum to fit their children for the clerical, educational, and technical careers they hoped to see them enter. Educational administrators, too, were now beginning to think in terms of an educational ladder which would enable the brighter pupils from the elementary schools to proceed by scholarship to a higher type of education. The early years of the College at Aberystwyth (opened in 1872) with its small number of inadequately prepared students demonstrated the need for higher grade and intermediate schools, a need which was further underlined by the recommendations of the 1881 Aberdare Report.

The Swansea School Board responded immediately to a circular issued by the Board of Education in 1882 suggesting the setting up of higher day schools and in 1883 established a Higher Grade School at Trinity Place. It admitted pupils who had reached standard four in the Board Schools and its curriculum included Chemistry and Physics as well as some French and Latin. Trinity Place had been a Board School, was ill-adapted to its new functions, and soon became overcrowded. A new site — Russell House in Dynevor Place — was obtained in 1891 but it was not until 1894 that the boys were able to enter the newly-erected premises. The girls remained at Trinity Place. The school's title changed to Higher Elementary School in 1896 and in 1908 both boys' and girls' schools assumed the status of Municipal Secondary Schools. A much-enlarged building on the Dynevor site to house what had now become known as the Dynevor Secondary School for Boys and De-la-Beche School for Girls was opened in 1929.

Meanwhile, as a result of the Welsh Intermediate Education Act of 1889, a Joint Education Authority was set up in Swansea which in 1895 converted the Swansea Grammar School into the Swansea Intermediate and Technical School for Boys. The High School for Girls (a private school founded in 1888) was also taken over by the new authority and became the Swansea Intermediate and Technical School for Girls. Neither title gained much currency except in official papers. The same year (1895) also saw a significant change of headmasters at the new Intermediate School for Boys. The long line of headmasters who had been ordained ministers of the Church of England came to an end. The new head was Dr George S. Turpin (former Principal of Huddersfield Technical College) whose post also included the principalship of a proposed new technical college at Swansea. In the

GYMNASIA   GIRLS' SCHOOL.   BOYS' SCHOOL

following years the role and curriculum of the old Grammar School were enlarged by the provision of day and evening classes in commercial and technical subjects. The technical school was eventually separated from the Grammar School with the appointment of Dr W. Mansergh Varley as Principal of an independent Technical College in 1910. By this date the control exercised independently by the School Board and by the Joint Education Authority came to an end, and responsibility for elementary, secondary and technical education was assumed by the new Local Education Authority created by the 1902 Education Act.

Swansea's structure of secondary education was completed by the setting up of Glanmor Boys and Girls Schools in 1922. Housed in the wooden buildings of a World War I American army camp, they began their existence as experimental schools with a status midway between secondary and elementary. Their secondary status was recognized in 1930. Wartime disruption brought the boys' school to an end in 1941 but the girls' school survived until 1972, when it was merged with the new Olchfa School.

Swansea Municipal Secondary School, c. 1930.

The University College.

At the beginning of this century what might be called the capstone of Swansea's educational pyramid was still not in place. Swansea did not have a civic university college. The desire for one was not merely a question of civic pride. Swansea had become in the nineteenth century a metallurgical centre of world importance and yet was forced to send its top technologists outside the area for training and research. Swansea's bid to be the site of the new college recommended for south Wales by the Aberdare Report in 1881 failed; but after the turn of the century, new hopes began to be centred on the newly-established technical college as the nucleus of a college which might be affiliated to the University of Wales. The Haldane Report on the University in 1918 viewed the proposal sympathetically and urged that the curriculum should not be confined to science and technology but should be liberalized by the inclusion of a faculty of arts. In 1919 the Privy Council consented to the admission of Swansea Technical College into the University as a constituent college. The newly-constituted college opened its doors to new students in October 1920 but the old Technical College retained its identity and site, and the new College eventually established itself in 1923 on a site in Singleton Park, with Singleton Abbey as its administrative headquarters. Both house and site were the generous gifts of the Corporation of Swansea.

The National Schools, Oxford Street, 1847.

The College grew steadily in the inter-war years, and student numbers rose from the original 89 to 488 in 1938-9. With the return of

ex-servicemen after the Second World War a period of more rapid expansion began. It was accelerated after the appearance of the Robbins Report in 1963 by government support and pressure for the expansion of higher education. Student numbers have grown to a record of over 4,500 students in 1987. The character and appearance of the College also changed. It began as a predominantly technological college with only a department of history as the nucleus of a faculty of arts and drew most of its students from a relatively small catchment area in south Wales. By 1970 it had a widely-spread apparatus of faculties and had long been part of Britain's national system of university education, drawing a much larger proportion of its students from other parts of Britain and from overseas. The 'temporary' pavilions erected in the twenties were slow to disappear but the new campus, begun under Principal John Fulton in 1957, was virtually complete by the early 1970s. By the mid 1970s the College was already being buffeted by a harsher economic climate and began devising schemes to generate new income, achieve lower costs, and still maintain student numbers. Swansea is not alone in facing these difficulties and a recent consultative document (1988) on the University of Wales considers that both the University as a whole and its constituent colleges could benefit if the University of Wales strengthened its federal structure to achieve optimum use of its resources and opportunities.

The Technical College, out of which the University College had grown, became the College of Technology in 1960 and in 1976 amalgamated with the College of Education (before 1965 the Swansea Training College) and the College of Art to form the West Glamorgan Institute of Higher Education.

The Comprehensive Ideal

Up to 1969 the educational lives of most Swansea children had been dominated by the prospect of the eleven-plus examination. This examination selected the academically able pupils for admission to the secondary grammar schools, relegating the remainder either to secondary modern or technical high schools. The Education Act of 1944 had made free secondary education available to all, but in the post-war years the selective process and the differentiated types of education which resulted came under increasing criticism. The selection made at 11-12 was more or less irrevocable and not always infallible. It took no account of late-developers and, it was claimed, perpetuated class divisions and social inequality. A lively debate followed. Those who defended the *status quo* maintained that the provision of 'comprehensive schools' — common schools for all within a given area — would debase educational standards.

The Labour-controlled Swansea Council was naturally sympathetic to the comprehensive ideal. It was adopted in principle in 1956 when Aneurin Bevan presided over the official opening of Penlan (then a multilateral). Gently, but with characteristic eloquence, he urged the Council to 'go comprehensive'. A long period of planning and building followed. Over the years a 'part-comprehensive' system operated, first at Penlan and Mynyddbach, and then at the new schoools at Bishop Vaughan, Cefn Hengoed, and Olchfa. A universal system of comprehensive education was first introduced into the city on 3 September 1970.

School Building

During the inter-war depression there was little money available for any major school building programme, but, apart from the timber structures at Cwmrhydyceirw, Cadle, Llansamlet, and Powys Avenue, the Swansea authority did succeed in building the large, traditional Townhill School (opened 1927), the imaginatively-designed, crescent-shaped Mayhill School with its breathtaking view (opened 1932), and new schools at Gors, where the provision of adequate play areas pointed to qualities which were to be considered essential in post-war school building.

After 1945 a major school building progamme began to replace schools destroyed during the war, to provide schools for the new housing estates and to implement the plan for comprehensive education. The new Bishop Gore school, planned before the war, opened in 1951. Among the major school buildings which followed were Penlan (1956), Mynyddbach (1959), Bishop Vaughan (1967), Cefn Hengoed (1968), Olchfa (1969), Morriston (1970), Pentre-Hafod (1976), and Dillwyn Llewellyn (1981). The contract for Pentre-Hafod was the last to be handled by the old Swansea City Local Education Authority before it handed over responsibility for education to the newly-constituted West Glamorgan County Authority in 1974. The new schools were built in the modern style; they were large, light and airy, and provided with ample playing field space and clearly distinguishable from the collegiate-looking board and secondary schools of an earlier period.

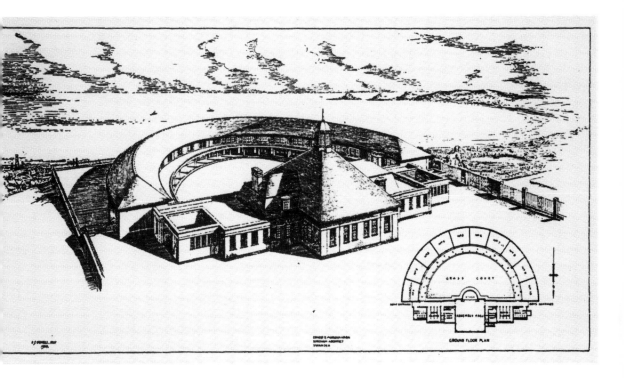

The Decline of Organized Religion

Mayhill School.

The present century has witnessed a marked decline in religious observance and practice. At the beginning of the century the churches and chapels of Swansea had large congregations and were powerful centres of worship and social life, as the evidence for 1905-6 presented to the Royal Commission on the Church of England and other Religious Bodies in Wales clearly demonstrated. The religious revival led by Evan Roberts in 1904-5 seemed to indicate that Wales was on the threshold of a new surge of religious activity. With hindsight, however, we now know that the decade marked the start of a prolonged decline in religious observance which has lasted to our own day. All denominations have been affected by the decline but the Nonconformists have perhaps suffered the most keenly. Prizing congregational autonomy and unrestrained by any strong centralized organization, they tended to over-build in the last century and many dwindling congregations are now finding it increasingly difficult to heat, light and keep in repair the large buildings they have inherited from the last century. Some have given up the task and allowed their chapels to be demolished or converted to secular uses. The Roman Catholic Church and the Church in Wales, with their more authoritarian organizations, have been able to exercise stricter control over the work of church extension and have also, through emphasis on the sacramental life of the Church, been able to impose stronger moral sanctions against non-attendance. But no-one will dispute the overall drop in membership and attendance for all denominations.

The underlying causes of the decline have frequently been debated. There was certainly a strong current of agnosticism flowing in the second half of the nineteenth century, partly set in motion by the discoveries of the new geology and the evolutionary theories of Darwin. These had weakened the literal authority of the Bible and unsettled the minds of fundamentalist believers. But it has been the rising tide of materialism and secularism rather than scientific argument that has had the most damaging effect on observance. Growing affluence has brought with it more leisure and new forms of entertainment — the cinema, television, and a variety of spectator sports which have made the churches less attractive centres of social life. Priests and ministers have been stripped, too, of some of their traditional roles as educators, counsellors, and social workers, functions which gave them status and prestige in previous centuries. State education has certainly advanced at the expense of religion. Vicar Squire spoke prophetically in 1874 when he stated that the School Boards were concerned with the maximum of secularity and the minimum of religion.

The decline in membership, attendance, and recruitment to the ministry proceeded slowly at first but with accelerated speed after World War II. Both World Wars with their policies of conscription had a socially disruptive effect on organized religion. Many who returned from the wars never returned to the churches and chapels in which they had previously worshipped. But World War II also caused disruption of a new kind. Aerial attack destroyed church members' homes and dispersed them away from their churches. It also destroyed many major places of worship: St Mary's, Holy Trinity, Capel Gomer, Wesley (College St.), Triniti (Park St.) and Pell St. Primitive Methodist chapel were among the church buildings destroyed in the blitz on the town centre. St Mary's was rebuilt and re-opened in 1959 and Capel Gomer in 1962; but most denominations now concentrated their energies on providing new centres of Christian witness and mission on the corporation estates which were rising on the town's periphery.

The 1950s formed a watershed conveniently dividing the period when the churches still enjoyed a measure of authority in influencing public policy from the period when this authority was being rapidly

eroded. Early in 1951, after a local poll, Swansea cinemas were opened for the first time on Sundays. In 1955 and 1957 Dr. Glyn Simon, bishop of Swansea and Brecon, conscious of the drift away from the churches, organized two acts of Christian witness in which Swansea churchmen processed through the streets to a service and address at the Guildhall. Late in 1961, after another poll, public houses in Swansea opened on Sunday for the first time since 1881. Not all churchmen were against the Sunday opening of cinemas and public houses but both events were significant pointers to the declining influence of the religious lobby which had secured the passing of the Sunday Closing Act in 1881.

For all the general indications of decline the period has not been one

Seilo Newydd Chapel, Landore.

of unrelieved gloom or institutional inertia for the churches. The Non-conformists have long abandoned the rivalries which embittered their relations a century or so ago. They have closed ranks, fostered schemes of inter-denominational cooperation, and played a major role in the ecumenical movement. The Wesleyan, Primitive, and United Methodists joined forces to form the Methodist Church of Great Britain in 1932 and most of the English Congregational churches in Swansea joined the United Reformed Church in 1972. For the Church in Wales, Disestablishment in 1920 was a blessing in disguise. The Church ceased to be an appendage of the Church of England and gradually developed its own identity within the Anglican communion. This new identity was reinforced in 1966 by the abandonment of the Book of Common Prayer and the introduction of new service books in English and Welsh. In 1923 a new diocese of Swansea and Brecon was formed but the cathedral centre, to the disappointment of many, was placed at Brecon. The Church was also enriched by the fruits of the Oxford Movement. The Church in Swansea had been a stronghold of evangelicalism but in the last quarter of the last century and the first half of this, Christ Church, St. Gabriel's and St. Paul's, Landore grew into noted centres of Anglo-Catholic churchmanship.

For the Roman Catholic community the present century has been one of great achievement and major change. The work of church extension proceeded cautiously and slowly but ten Roman Catholic churches now serve the town and its suburbs. The decrees of the second Vatican Council (1962-3) gradually altered traditional attitudes but also produced more noticeable changes. A vernacular Mass was introduced in the early 1970s and the altar areas of most churches were transformed to conform more closely with the practice of the primitive church. Altars have been brought forward and the priest now presides at Mass facing the people. The Catholic community have managed to retain their church schools and in 1967 acquired their first comprehensive school at Bishop Vaughan. In 1987 the church of St. Joseph was raised to cathedral status by papal bull and became the centre of a newly-organized diocese of Menevia.

ART AND ARCHITECTURE

Prys Morgan

ART IN SWANSEA

The Early Travellers and Tourists

Before the eighteenth century hardly any towns in Britain outside London had resident professional artists. Portraits of local gentry, such as those of the families of Aberpergwm or Penrice and Margam, were almost certainly executed by London artists or by the occasional itinerant venturing into the remote provinces. In the same period, few if any travellers had a notion of recording the landscape. The earliest surviving views of Swansea and Oystermouth date from 1678, drawn by Francis Place, an antiquarian and topographer from the north of England. In 1684 Thomas Dineley accompanied the duke of Beaufort, lord president of Wales and the Marches, around his satrapy, leaving us some thumbnail sketches of Swansea. An anonymous itinerant painter made some large bird's eye view paintings of Margam about 1700, and there is a crude sketch of Swansea from the harbour in the corner of a map dated 1729 by Emanuel Bowen. The first really well-known view of Swansea is a splendid one by the brothers Buck, engraved in 1741, showing the little town with its harbour, church and castle from the eastern bank of the Tawe estuary, on which, rather improbably, fashionably attired beaux and belles are disporting themselves. The brothers Buck also published engravings of local antiquities such as the Gower castles, part of a great series covering England and Wales, and part of a patriotic movement to encourage public interest in British history. Very different from them is the engraving by Thomas Lightfoot, dated 1744, of the White Rock works on the banks of the Tawe, two generations before such undertakings were to become such a threat to the beaux and belles shown in the Bucks' engraving.

Later in the century the fashion was for travellers and artists to seek out the wilder, mountainous parts of Wales, but for many, Swansea lay on the tourist route, moving as they did along the south Wales coastal roads, or travelling to Wales from Bristol by sea, and several artists drew Swansea while staying there. Paul Sandby's view of Swansea in 1775 shows the castle above a billow of smoke from rubbish being burnt on the quayside. Others such as William Payne (1791 and 1797) or Thomas Rowlandson (1799) drew the Mumbles, the town, and the harbour with its shipping, and some of the nearby coves. The young J. M. W. Turner stayed at the Mackworth Arms in 1795, but it seems that it was the Vale of Neath which inspired his brush and pen. The picturesque wooded inlet of Briton Ferry attracted many travellers and artists, such as Nicholas Pocock or Samuel Hieronymus Grimm. Others appear to have come at the behest of local landowners; for example, Hendrik de Cort and Sir Francis Bourgeois are known to have painted views of Clasemont House near Morriston. Other artist-travellers painting Swansea in this period included Samuel Austin, Samuel Prout, and Benjamin Barker, a native of Pontypool but generally known (as was also his brother, Thomas) as 'Barker of Bath'. Barker sketched around and about Swansea at the turn of the nine-teenth century, and worked some of his sketches into oil paintings. Others were fascinated by local colour: in 1799 John Nixon pictured the market at the top of Wind Street with colourful peasants bartering wares or grinning at rustic 'interludes' performed on a rough and ready stage. Some artists delineated Swansea antiquities, J. D. Buckler in 1815 describing with scholarly precision the elaborate late Gothic tomb of Sir Mathew Cradock in St Mary's, and Thomas Stockdale in 1826 drawing the Plas House (Sir Mathew's residence) in order to sell it as an engraving. The market for prints was considerable, and in 1832 James Wilcox sketched the 'house of Mr Vivian', Singleton Abbey, probably with an eye to its being engraved in a book of views.

Swansea was, of course, in this period becoming a large modern town with a bustling port and large-scale industry in the hinterland. One of the first painters to depict the incipient industrialization of the area in 1792 and 1795 was John Warwick Smith — the 'Warwick' in his name being a pseudonym adopted in honour of his patron, the earl of Warwick, one of the ultimate heirs of the Herberts of Swansea and a considerable landowner in and around the town. J. B. Pyne drew the harbour of Swansea about 1820, as did W. Bartlett about the year 1830, and a few years before (perhaps in 1825) the Merthyr artist, Penry Williams, drew a magnificent panorama of the town and the bay from a point high on Kilvey Hill. In his book, *The Rivers of Wales* (1811), J. G. Wood produced several views of the Tawe, describing clearly the transformation of its sylvan banks by the copper works.

Early Resident Artists and Craftsmen

The artists we have so far met were all travellers and visitors. But Swansea was being transformed by tourism and industry into a town of wealth and urbane culture, a consequence of which was that artists and craftsmen were drawn to live and work there. A sign of urbane civilization was the opening of a theatre, although this was in the teeth of the reactionary steward of the duke of Beaufort, Gabriel Powell. A cartoon of 1787, presumably produced by Powell's enemies in Swansea, shows the formidable 'King of Swansea' turning a blind eye to the existence of such a new-fangled thing as a theatre. Another cartoon shows him violently quarrelling with other Swansea burgesses at a town hall meeting. Both were drawn by an unknown artist called Moses Harris, and although we have no evidence that Harris lived in Swansea, this is a precocious instance of a cartoonist being involved in the politics of a Welsh town. The manager of the theatre (and possibly its architect) was the architect John Calvert. There is a tradition that one of the scene painters at the theatre in Swansea in the 1790s was the famous draughtsman and architect, Auguste de Pugin (an emigré from the French Revolution), and another artist who is said to have undertaken the same kind of drudgery in Swansea in that period is the artist David Cox, though in later years he came to be mainly associated with north Wales, and with Betws y Coed in particular.

In the early nineteenth century Swansea was known as a centre of heavy industry, but in the eighteenth century its best known industry was pottery (and for a while, porcelain). The pottery may have begun as early as 1764, was certainly active by 1768, and in 1790 was taken over by the entrepreneur George Haynes, who attracted to Swansea several artists, such as the engraver Thomas Rothwell and the painter Thomas Pardoe. Pardoe was always a pottery painter, but Rothwell produced in 1792 engraved views of Swansea, showing such features as the Bathing House and the potteries, apparently as part of a scheme to advertise Swansea's charms to the visitor, and he also painted some oil landscapes of Gower, such as his view of Oxwich (now at the Royal Institution of South Wales) showing the Reverend Collins driving along the beach.

The potteries expanded in the first years of the nineteenth century, especially under the dynamic management of Lewis Weston Dillwyn (1778-1855). He employed at his pottery a remarkably many-sided man, William Weston Young (1776-1847), similar to Dillwyn in his scientific and artistic tastes, but unlike his employer, an unsuccessful businessman. A mapmaker and artist, Young had been engaged by

Dillwyn to design the illustrations for his botanical study of the *Confervae*, and both he and Thomas Pardoe were obliged by Dillwyn to decorate Swansea wares with precise scientific diagrams of plants in all their botanical details. In 1835 W. W. Young also wrote and illustrated a guidebook to the beauties of the Vale of Neath. Young, Dillwyn, and their friends and kinsfolk in and around Swansea, linked the three worlds of industry, science, and the arts. Dillwyn was also a patron and collector of paintings: the Royal Institution has a painting of 1829 by the London artist, C. R. Leslie, showing the Dillwyn family standing tragically around the deathbed of Dillwyn's young daughter. L. W. Dillwyn attracted to the potteries other painters besides W. W. Young, painters who in turn gathered pupils and followers, often natives of Swansea.

It was by a series of accidents that the most celebrated porcelain painter of his day, William Billingsley (1758-1828), came to Swansea. He and his son-in-law, Samuel Walker, came to Nantgarw to perfect and market a new soft-paste porcelain of unsurpassed translucency, but the experiment was a commercial failure, and through the mediation of Dillwyn's friends, W. W. Young and Sir Joseph Banks, Billingsley and Walker were transferred for a while to Swansea, raising the standard of decoration to a high level, and creating a tradition carried on for many years by pupils such as Henry Morris and David Evans. Billingsley returned to Nantgarw in 1816 and in 1820 to the Midlands, but in 1816 a new artist had arrived at the pottery and porcelain works, namely Thomas Baxter (1782-1821), who had been a student at the Royal Academy and who had established an art school at Worcester. Baxter lived in Swansea from 1816 to 1819, painted water-colour landscapes there, and in 1818 made a series of engravings of Swansea and Gower for sale. In the same year he advertised himself as a portrait painter and a miniaturist, the first resident artist recorded in the town of Swansea, however shortlived.

The potteries were places of applied art, but they did attract to Swansea several able painters and engravers. The great wealth of the industrialists and merchants of the town in the first half of the nineteenth century created a public eager to encourage the arts and to record their enterprises themselves. The children of the rich were taught drawing and painting as a matter of course. For example, John Weir Padley, the son of one of the town's best-established trading dynasties, drew lively views of the harbour in the 1830s. A few portrait painters now lived in the town, such as William Watkeys, whose portrait of Julia Ann Hatton, 'Ann of Swansea', the poetess and sister of

Mrs Siddons, is preserved in the Royal Institution. Another kind of resident artist was the drawing master. One such was George Delamotte, who not only painted topographical landscapes of the town but also drew portraits and caricatures of local personalities: his album dated 1818, for example, has lively, humorous pictures of beggars, wastrels, itinerant musicians, shrimp boys, farm hands, and worthies such as 'Mr Howells the Methodist Minister', truly bringing late Georgian Swansea back to life. Other drawing masters appear to have been French emigrés to Swansea: Edgar Adolphe (active from about 1834 to 1839) taught calligraphy as well as the art of painting silhouettes and miniatures: and Alexander Butel worked in Swansea about 1840 as a drawing master. An 'Edmond Butel' and a 'Louis Butel' are also recorded at the same period (Louis being a founder member of the Royal Institution), and so it is possible that there was a whole family of artists at Swansea. What work was produced by the Butel studio is not known. Local public and private collections do, however, contain a good deal of the work of another drawing master, William Butler (who was active from 1843 to 1870, at which date he died aged forty six), who drew landscapes and especially buildings and townscapes in pencil and delicate watercolour. Butler assisted Fred Hosforth when the latter came to set up a school of art in the town in 1853, but he is said to have held drawing classes before that time at the Royal Institution.

One Englishman taking advantage of the wealth of the area was the Yorkshire landscapist, Thomas Hornor (1785-1844), who lived in Neath from 1814 to 1820, patronized by Lord Jersey at Briton Ferry, John Llewelyn at Ynysygerwn and Penllergaer, and by the Vaughans of Rheola, and who advertised in 1819 (one year after Thomas Baxter did the same thing) in the *Cambrian* and *Seren Gomer*, Swansea's two newspapers, offering his services as a painter of landscapes. Hornor soon returned to London, enjoying celebrity as a painter of panoramas, in which he was helped by his fellow-Yorkshireman, George Chambers (1803-40). It may have been Hornor's persuasion that induced Chambers to take on as an apprentice one James Harris (born in Exeter in 1810, but living in Swansea from early childhood onwards), and made Chambers visit Swansea to paint seascapes and some fine views of the town from 1836 to 1838. Chambers had been marine painter to King William IV, and his dramatic seascapes obviously shaped the style of the young James Harris.

James Harris (sometimes called 'Harris Senior' to differentiate him from his son and namesake) lived from 1810 to 1887, first in Swansea, then Oystermouth, and finally at Reynoldston, and had an intimate working knowledge of ships and seafaring. It appears that his early career and training were financed by one of the most remarkable members of Swansea's cultured upper class, the Reverend Calvert Richard Jones, the third of that name. Jones (1804-77) lived at Verandah at the northern edge of what is today Singleton Park, was a rich and talented amateur, a local rector and landowner — Calvert Terrace and Christina Street, for example, commemorate members of his family — and a painter and sketcher specializing in precise drawings of ships and seamen, though he also drew country houses. A friend of C. R. M. Talbot of Margam and of Talbot's cousin, Henry Fox Talbot of Lacock Abbey, and of Lewis Weston Dillwyn's son, John Dillwyn Llewelyn of Penllergaer, Jones was thus a member of a circle of pioneer photographers. Soon after Daguerre had invented the daguerreotype, Jones was experimenting with that method in Swansea and in March 1841 achieved what is probably the first example of photography in Wales, a beautiful daguerreotype of Talbot's house at Margam, which was purchased in 1988 for the National Library of Wales. Fox Talbot's photographic method was the calotype, and both Calvert Jones and John Dillwyn Llewelyn became in addition the pioneers of calotype photography, Llewelyn producing some remarkable early photographs of the sea, and Jones some early views of shipping.

The link between Calvert Jones, the rich patron of art, and James Harris, the budding professional artist, was of course the sea and sailing. Harris was able with great skill to combine a romantic feeling for the sea in all its perverse moods with a precise depiction of nautical details, such as rigging, both of which elements would appeal to his Swansea clientèle, who might be sea captains or ship owners. Harris came under the influence of his friend, Edward Duncan (1803-82), a landscape painter based in London who spent his summers with his family in the Gower peninsula, and who, from 1845 onwards, regularly showed some views of Gower at the Royal Academy. Duncan's style was less romantic or sublime than George Chambers's had been, and, probably under Duncan's influence, Harris's work became gradually more Victorian in feeling. Duncan painted seascapes of verve, animation, and technical virtuosity, as can clearly be judged by his watercolour of oyster dredgers in Swansea Bay (1874) now at the Glynn Vivian gallery, Swansea.

James Harris the younger (1847-1925) maintained his father's tradition into the twentieth century, although in a cautious style and

Dillwyn cup and saucer.

Seascape with Three Barques, by James Harris.

Swansea for Pleasure, by W. Grant Murray.

Temple Street, by Will Evans, 1941.

generally using water colours rather than oils. Would it be correct to say that there was a 'school of marine painters' here? Besides the Harrises and their friends, and Edward Duncan and his family, there were a few marine artists at work in Swansea, some such as William Burchall (recorded 1848-50), who may be the same man as J. W. Burchell (recorded in 1846) producing ships' portraits for sea captains or sailing companies. Some London marine artists, such as Adolphus Knell, would come from time to time to work in Swansea, and several Bristol painters would cross by sea to Swansea for painting holidays, such as E. F. D. Pritchard (1809-1905), who around 1850 painted a well-known view of Gower women crossing the sands to go to Swansea market, or such as John Syer (1815-85), who painted coastal landscapes or seascapes in and around Port Eynon in the 1860s, or Edwin Hayes (1820-1904), who was responsible for several seascapes around Swansea in the late 1870s. One little-known Bristol painter who settled with his family in Swansea in the mid-1860s was James Wall Langshaw (born in 1810 or 1811), who for many years lived near Oystermouth church, and whose clear topographical watercolours appear from time to time in local collections or salerooms. One of the few painters of the mid-nineteenth century actually recorded as having come from Swansea was Louis Garnaut Cawker (1834-1908), a man of partially French descent, who is known to have painted views in and around Swansea about 1860.

Art Societies and Collectors

The Royal Institution of South Wales founded in Swansea in 1835 gave the town a forum for discussing matters artistic and probably a studio for artistic tuition. Judging by the number of drawing masters already mentioned, it seems likely that there were several informal sketching groups, but the first group known to have left any record was the Swansea Sketching Club as late as 1882, which had a little-known professional artist from West Cross, W. H. Thomas, as its secretary. This club was abortive, but in May 1886 came the Swansea Art Society, which has lasted over a hundred years. The moving spirits in 1886 were John Squire, a banker from Liskeard in Cornwall, several members of the Birchall family (possibly this is an alternative spelling for Burchell, the name of a marine artist of the 1840s), William Terrill, a Cornish geologist and founder in 1877 of the Swansea Geological Society, Alfred Parkman, a professional painter active in Swansea from the 1880s to the 1920s, C. E. Schenk, an engineer at Swansea docks, and most distinguished, C. E. Hannaford, who left Swansea in

1902 to join Stanhope Forbes at the Newlyn school of painters, becoming a professional painter and dying at the age of 92 in 1955. With its art classes, sketching expeditions, and regular exhibitions, the Art Society created a climate of awareness of art, where amateur could encounter professional, and where producers and purchasers could meet.

During the nineteenth century, also, art collecting became markedly more popular. In the eighteenth century collecting had been largely confined to the aristocracy. Thomas Mansel Talbot went on the Grand Tour, bringing back with him to his new house at Penrice a great collection of statues and paintings, and his marble bust, carved at Rome by Hewetson, is still at Penrice. His son, C. R. M. Talbot, moved the antique marbles to his new house at Margam, where they remained until the collection was dispersed during the second World War. We know little about gentry collections, but Charles Morgan of Llanrhidian, farmer and barrister in the 1830s and '40s, and friend of the family of the watercolourist, Copley Fielding, and an amateur watercolourist himself, made a collection of the work of Benjamin West, which his descendants gradually dispersed, and they are now to some extent reassembled at the Kimbell Museum, Fort Worth, Texas. Lewis Weston Dillwyn amassed a considerable art collection, and J. H. Vivian, the industrialist, assembled a vast collection of curiosities and antiquities in the 1830s and '40s at his new house, Singleton Abbey. His son, Graham Vivian, devoted a greater proportion of his wealth to amassing *objets d'art*, *objets de vertu* and architectural items from France and Italy, and it was probably to house this collection that he bought Clyne Castle, Blackpill. His other son, Richard Glynn Vivian, purchased a collection of paintings, including several by Gustave Doré, for his home at Sketty Hall.

Little is known of collections made by Swansea townsmen in this period but one of the largest collections, it seems likely, was made by John Deffett Francis, the son of a Swansea coach-painter and brother of George Grant Francis, the historian, and himself a little-known portrait painter. From 1876 to his death in 1901, he assembled a huge collection of prints and engravings, as well as paintings by Wilson, Gainsborough, Cotman, and other British artists. This collection was donated to the town, displayed for some years in the old town library in Goat Street, and after 1887 transferred to the new library and art school built in Alexandra Road.

In 1905 the town was offered paintings and money to endow a municipal art gallery by Richard Glynn Vivian of Sketty Hall. By the time

the museum and gallery were actually founded in 1909 Glynn Vivian was dead. In 1908 a Scottish artist, W. Grant Murray, was appointed to head the Swansea School of Art and to direct the new gallery, though it should be noted that the Vivian family touch was kept by making T. H. Knibbs, personal servant of Graham Vivian, the gallery caretaker. The gallery, opened in 1911, was Swansea's second museum and the only one devoted entirely to the fine arts. The potteries had come to an end in the 1870s, but local interest in ceramics was such that the gallery acquired, in addition to paintings and sculptures, fine ceramic collections, such as the Herbert Eccles gift of 1919. A sidelight on Swansea's pre-war trade with northern France is cast by the gift to the gallery in 1911 made by François Depeaux, of impressionist works by painters of the Rouen school such as Delattre, Frechon, and Lebourge. Depeaux was the patron and friend of the French impressionist painter, Alfred Sisley (1839-99), whom he invited to south Wales in 1897, and after a short stay in Penarth, he was installed for a while at

Swansea Central Library, Alexandra Road, c. 1904.

the Osborne Hotel, Langland, painting views of the bay. Thirteen of these Langland views have been recorded, but none of them appears to be in any Welsh collection.

An Academy and its Students

An art school had existed in Swansea since 1853, but in 1887 it was moved into the premises above the public library in Alexandra Road which are still in use today. In 1908 with the appointment of W. Grant Murray (1877-1950) as its head, the school entered its period of greatest influence and vigour, for several decades becoming the leading art school in Wales. One striking result of a generation of art teaching and exhibiting in Swansea was that a significant number of artists began to emerge after 1900 from amongst the local people themselves, whereas in earlier generations most artists in Swansea were visitors or in-comers. Among the earliest generation of students (about 1910-3) were Will Evans (1888-1957), a landscapist who was for many years a commercial artist with the South Wales Canister Company in Swansea, but who set up the department of lithography at the School of Art; Bert Thomas, who became a well-known cartoonist on the London papers; and Evan Walters (1893-1951) from Mynyddbach near Swansea, who worked as a professional painter in Swansea and London, turning his hand to landscapes and society portraits (for example Admiral Walker-Heneage-Vivian of Clyne Castle) and, perhaps most characteristically, to portraits of Swansea 'characters', miners and cockle-women in the market.

More famous than these three was Ceri Richards (1903-71), the son of a steelworker from Dunvant near Swansea, who entered the School of Art in 1921, went on to the Royal College of Art, and held his first one-man show at the Glynn Vivian in 1930, becoming in the 1930s a leading British surrealist painter. He spent much of each summer at his cottage in Pennard and was deeply influenced by the poetry of Dylan Thomas and Vernon Watkins. His work is to be seen in many Swansea collections, public and private, and the art gallery at the Taliesin art centre at the University College is named the Ceri Richards Gallery in his honour.

Two natives of Swansea, students at the School, and friends of the poet Dylan Thomas, are Mervyn Levy and Alfred Janes, both painters and teachers. One can here, of course, only mention a handful of names of Swansea students who have become professional artists: the painter Hanlyn Davies has worked largely in America, Leo Solomon became principal of the Oldham School of Art, Peter Markey is a painter and maker of constructions, the late Jack Waldron was a sculptor, and Pickard Jenkins is a painter and designer (now living in Swansea). Other Swansea students have persisted in maintaining a studio in the neighbourhood of Swansea: Vera Bassett at Burry Port, William Powell Wilkins at Carreg Cennen near Llandeilo, Michael Freeman in Swansea itself, and Will Roberts in Neath.

The teaching staff at the School of Art (it was later called the College of Art) gave Swansea for the first time a permanent body of professional artists. Grant Murray himself depicted the Swansea scene in his paintings, and among the other teachers in the 1920s and '30s were the painter, Percy Gleaves (who painted the huge canvas of the royal opening of the University College, which is found reproduced in various books), the sculptor Harry Hall, and the watercolourist, the late Dorothy Kirkman. Grant Murray was succeeded as principal by the Swansea painter, Kenneth Hancock (1911-78), and he in turn was succeeded by the sculptor, the late Ronald Cour. Among the teachers (full time or part time) at the School are to be found the names of the etcher and printmaker Arthur Charlton, the etcher Alfred Lavender, the painters Glenys Cour, George Fairley, Griffith Edwards, George Little, William Price and Archie Williams. The late William Price, a native of Swansea, was the only Swansea student to win the coveted Prix de Rome. One unusual feature of the School is its teaching of the craft of stained glass. After an uncertain beginning in 1937, a real start was made after the second world war by the late Howard Martin and Hubert Thomas, with such success that the stained glass of Swansea became known far beyond the confines of Wales. The craft and tradition are maintained today by the artists John Edwards and Timothy Lewis.

The School or College was absorbed in 1963 into the West Glamorgan Institute of Higher Education. Clearly it has been over many decades the central artistic institution in Swansea, but by no means the only one. The painter and historian of Welsh art, David Bell, was for some years the curator of the Glynn Vivian Art Gallery, the watercolourist Irene Bache taught for many years at the Swansea College of Education, and continues to work in retirement in Swansea, and there are several painters in Swansea who have had no connexion with the School of Art, for example, the watercolourist the late Stanley Cooke, the painter John Uzzell Edwards, who has since 1972 worked as an artist and draughtsman near Swansea, and the landscape painter Gareth Thomas.

It is also true that there are several natives of Swansea who have trained and worked elsewhere, returning only occasionally to paint here: James Tarr the painter, a native of the Mumbles, was for many years the principal of the Cardiff College of Art; Maurice Barnes (1911-71), though born in Swansea, was a watercolourist based largely in Newport; and Jack Jones, though born in Swansea and a painter of the Swansea scene, for example its numerous chapels, has lived most of his life away from the area. Perhaps the most celebrated of Swansea expatriates was the late Sir Cedric Morris, born in 1889 in Sketty and the heir to the baronetcy of Morris of Clasemont, who trained as a painter in Paris, later setting up his own art school in Suffolk. His chief connexion with Wales occurred during the 1930s, when he worked in the settlements of the unemployed in Merthyr and Dowlais; very little of his work is connected with Swansea itself, although he painted some handsome views of Gower.

The Swansea Art Society began to hold regular exhibitions in 1887, there have been regular exhibitions at the Glynn Vivian Gallery since 1911, and since the 1960s Swansea has seen the establishment of several commercial art galleries, in addition to which the Association of Artists and Designers in Wales (AADW) holds regular exhibitions in the specially converted chapel of St Nicholas in Gloucester Place in the Maritime Quarter, and since 1984 the Ceri Richards Gallery in the Taliesin art centre on the University campus has regularly shown the work of Swansea artists.

In this section on artists we have been able to see three phases in the rise of art appreciation in Swansea: up to 1800 art was largely a matter for fleeting visitors; during the nineteenth century, with a few exceptions, artists and craftsmen came from elsewhere to settle and work in Swansea; in the twentieth century native artists have arisen to work alongside visitors and incomers, and natives of the area have in some cases, such as Sir Cedric Morris or Ceri Richards, gained an international reputation. The list of names mentioned above, craftsmen, artists, working or originating in Swansea, is a notable one, surprisingly large when one considers that Swansea is a small and not very wealthy British city. The Glynn Vivian Gallery and the Royal Institution have, over the past decades, effectively displayed the art of the visitors to Swansea and the craftsmen at the potteries. But the people of Swansea need to be shown what a remarkable flowering of artistic talent there has been here from about 1900 onwards, and it is imperative that there should be in the city a permanent display of the work of the artists of Swansea, so that this great achievement is recognized, and the impetus is not lost.

ARCHITECTURE IN SWANSEA

Building Before the Eighteenth Century

A famous Frenchman, asked what he had done during the Revolution, is said to have replied, 'Survived'. Ancient buildings which have managed to survive the changes wrought in Swansea by the coming of industry, the population explosion of the nineteenth century, and the bombs of the wartime Blitz, may be considered objects of wonder. It is little short of miraculous that the town has any ancient buildings at all. The fact remains that the town centre is dominated by the ruins of the castle of Swansea, which overlook the Castle Gardens to the west and the Strand to the east. It was sometimes called the 'New Castle' because an earlier castle had stood a little to the north in what is now Worcester Place. It was largely constructed in the fourteenth century, its most elegant feature being the white stone Gothic arcading along the roofline; arcading which is the distinctive hallmark of masons employed by Henry de Gower, bishop of St David's, both here and at his palaces at Lamphey and St. David's. A stone's throw away at the bottom of St Mary Street, is the Cross Keys Inn, now largely restored in a Tudor style by the architect Victor Ward, but incorporating at the back the remains of the Hospital of the Blessed David, founded in 1332 by Henry de Gower.

The Castle Gardens are laid out on the site of Swansea's biggest Victorian stores, Messrs. Ben Evans, built in 1893, and subsequently destroyed in the wartime Blitz. The stores were built on the site of the town's finest medieval house, the Plas or New Place, begun by the Horton family in 1383, extended, as a large hall house around an irregular courtyard, by their descendant, Sir Mathew Cradock, about 1500, and completed by his grandson, Sir George Herbert, in the 1550s. The Royal Institution has a cork model of the Plas and its surrounding streets as they were before the Plas was demolished in 1840. The stone mullions of its windows were taken by J. H. Vivian and may be seen today embellishing the picturesque Home Farm at the western edge of Singleton Park.

A few miles along the shore of the bay lies the parish of Oystermouth, its centre dominated by another medieval castle, a grey limestone keep on a prominent knoll overlooking the sea, a fortress partly built in the twelfth and thirteenth centuries, but largely completed in the fourteenth by Lady Aline de Mowbray. Its most striking feature is the south-eastern tower containing the chapel with a large window of Gothic tracery. Nearby is the ancient parish church of All Saints, now overshadowed by a Victorian Gothic nave, but behind which stands the small medieval nave and a medieval limestone tower. The medieval parish churches of Swansea, St Mary's, St John's (now St Matthew's), Llansamlet, and Llangyfelach, have been wholly or largely rebuilt in the nineteenth century — Llangyfelach's tower is a free standing building, the nave a short distance away being a re-used tithe barn. In order to see a church in a condition somewhat akin to its medieval self, the observer must go into peninsular Gower, and go to an ancient parish church such as St Teilo's, Bishopston.

The Eighteenth Century

Such was the cataclysmic force of industrial change in the eighteenth and nineteenth centuries that very little of the buildings of the Tudor and Stuart periods remains in Swansea. The recently published architectural study, *Glamorgan Farmhouses and Cottages*, gives details of over fifty ancient farmhouses of note standing (or fairly recently demolished) in West Glamorgan west of the river Neath, dating from the end of the middle ages up to the end of the eighteenth century. The public may gain a good idea of what a Swansea yeoman farmer's house of the mid-seventeenth century would have looked like from Kennextone, removed from Llangennith and rebuilt at the Welsh Folk Museum, St Fagan's. Most of the farmhouses remain in use as farms and private houses, and the experts of the Royal Commission on Ancient and Historic Monuments draw particular attention to the need to preserve some of these West Glamorgan farms of the seventeenth and early eighteenth centuries; Llysnini near Penllergaer, Overton House near Port Eynon, Pitt between Oxwich and Penrice, and Sanctuary between Penrice and Horton, all of them close to, or upon, public roads. The recent architectural survey, *Glamorgan: the Greater Houses*, notes very few examples in the early modern period in West Glamorgan: the recently demolished Llansamlet house of Gwernllwyn-chwith, which the Royal Commission on Ancient and Historic Monuments say was built by the industrial Smith family in the later eighteenth century, but with its red brick walls and its 'Queen Anne' features seems more likely to have been built by its owner around 1720, the countess of Leicester. Since it may have been Glamorgan's earliest brick-built house, its demolition was a tragedy. Nearby on the banks of the Tawe (close to Morriston) are the ruins of Upper Fforest, a late seventeenth-century house of the gentry Popkin family, one of several such houses engulfed by the Industrial Revolution. More fortunate to survive is Sketty Hall, in a fine park-

Sketty Hall, built c. 1758.

like setting west of Singleton Park, which although it is extended and covered with late eighteenth-century stucco, is probably at heart an early eighteenth-century three-storey sash-windowed house.

Thomas Lloyd, in his recent survey of houses demolished in Wales, notes the demolition over the years of a number of Georgian houses in and around Swansea, so that, apart from Sketty Hall, the observer has to go well beyond the confines of the town to see a good large Georgian house. Penrice Castle, in a magnificent setting above Oxwich bay, was designed in 1773 by Anthony Keck for Thomas Mansel Talbot, while the park surrounding the house was by a well-known landscape architect, William Emes. Kilvrough (near Parkmill), in origin an Elizabeth gentry house belonging to the Dawkins family, was rebuilt in a mock-castellated style for them in the 1780s, probably by William Jernegan. In contrast, Stouthall (Reynoldston) was built in an austere classical style by Jernegan for the Lucas family in 1787-90. Within the confines of the city of Swansea and surveying the city as it were from an eagle's nest, is the fine small gentry house of Glan Brân,

Birchgrove, built for the Jones family about 1775, approached from a steep lane above Birchgrove, Llansamlet.

The core of Singleton Abbey, now the administrative headquarters of the University College of Swansea, was built in 1783 as an octagonal villa, playfully called Marino, for the customs officer of Swansea, Edward King. This was designed by one of the first professional architects to be based in Swansea, William Jernegan, who designed Stouthall, possibly altered Kilvrough, and certainly extended Sketty Hall nearby, for its occupant at that time, the industrialist Ralph Sheldon. The original core, the southern section of Clyne Castle, Blackpill, was built as a classical residence by an otherwise unidentified architect called Wyatt for Richard Phillips, an industrialist and landowner, but it was castellated and greatly extended for a later owner, General Warde, by Jernegan. Tucked away in various corners of Swansea there are still one or two late eighteenth-century suburban 'villas'. Brynymor Road leads uphill to Eaton Crescent, running as a horseshoe around Bryn y Môr House, now an Ursuline Convent, but originally built for Robert Eaton, a banker, in the 1780s. Between Sketty and Cockett, and now a hospital beautifully sited above a valley, is Hill House, apparently built as a five-bay sash-windowed house by Iltid Thomas, who leased the buildings from 1768 to 1786, though the façade was extended slightly in 1920.

Late in the eighteenth century it became fashionable to take seaside holidays and to build villas along the sea shore, so that it is not surprising that a few late Georgian villas should survive along the coast west of the town, for example, Gwern Einon on Derwen Fawr Road, Blackpill, Llwyn Derw (near West Cross), which was elaborately redecorated around 1910 for the Folland family in a William-and-Mary style, or Danycoed (also near West Cross), a fine pilastered sash-windowed villa, somewhat marred by two Victorian additions at both ends. There are several good Georgian houses in Oystermouth itself, and perhaps the best of them (though now hidden from the sea by a row of modern houses) is the splendid neo-classical Norton Lodge, now an hotel, with its Grecian pillared portico and its verandah of cast-iron in a pattern of anthemions and Greek keys.

An Age of Improvements

At the end of the eighteenth century people were increasingly concerned with town planning, lighting and paving of streets, putting up public buildings such as town halls, theatres, hospitals, and prisons.

The new fashionable quarter of Swansea laid out between about 1800 amd 1830 was the Burrows, an area of former sand dunes, on which fine streets such as Somerset Place, Cambrian Place, and Gloucester Place (this to the designs of Jernegan), were laid out, and which, after a long period of blight and decay, have been recently refurbished as part of the Maritime Quarter. The northern side of Cambrian Place has tall brick houses, each with a large canopied balconied window on the first floor, the street being dominated by a good example of a Georgian public building, the Assembly Rooms. S. P. Cockerell's designs for them in 1804 were rejected, but Jernegan (who lived nearby) provided a new design and the rooms were built over many years, and opened in 1821, by which time Swansea's halcyon days as a resort were beginning to be besmirched and clouded by industry. The architect, John Calvert, was the theatre manager at Swansea from about 1778 to 1784, and was probably the designer of the theatre appearing in the background of Moses Harris's cartoon of Gabriel Powell.

Regency Houses in Cambrian Place.

The Public Assembly Rooms, Cambrian Place, opened 1821.

Wind Street follows the line of a medieval thoroughfare, but several of its buildings date from the late eighteenth century: Number 56, for example, the 'No-Sign Bar' existed before 1793 and with its simple sash-windowed façade, is a typical Georgian town house remarkably well preserved. A few Georgian houses survive scattered in various corners of the town, for example, Number 15 Mount Pleasant (now an hotel) was built as a villa late in the eighteenth century for one Edward Hughes. Despite the destruction of much of the High Street, the Bush Hotel retains many features of a late Georgian hostelry, and the backs of the High Street shops seen from the Strand reveal several late Georgian structures.

What of the remains of the early industrial activity? Most of the early copper and iron works have been demolished and cleared away in the last thirty years, but several portions of the early foundries of Upper Bank Works (1757) are incorporated into the modern factory of Messrs. Addis on the banks of the Tawe at Landore. This may once have been Swansea's largest building, and it is said that when the great preacher, Christmas Evans, came to Swansea early in the nineteenth century, this was the only structure large enough to accommodate the vast congregations avid to hear him. Above Landore, prominently sited on Craig Trewyddfa, are the gaunt ruins called 'Morris Castle', once a castellated block of flats for workers, probably designed by the Leicester architect, John Johnson, about 1775 for Sir John Morris. About the same time he also designed for Morris a country house at Clasemont on the hill above Morriston, to which the Morrises moved from their charming early eighteenth-century farm of Tredegar Fawr near Llangyfelach (which still exists). But because of the noxious fumes arising from all the foundries and copper works, the family decided in 1806 to demolish Clasemont and built a house at Sketty Park (designed by the ubiquitous Jernegan), a house itself demolished in 1975. Nothing now remains of Sketty Park save an unexpected Gothic

Hendrefoilan House, Sketty, built 1855.

octagonal belvedere, on a knoll at the side of Saunders Way, Sketty, which is said to have been built by the Morrises as a summer house.

The Morrises are, however, commemorated, by the town of Morriston, a rare and interesting example of industrial town planning, dating from the 1780s, a grid-iron pattern of streets with a church (rebuilt by R. K. Penson in 1857) at the intersection of the main streets. The plan was noted in its day for the neat houses and gardens of the workers.

A Battle of the Classical and Gothic Styles

Urban improvements meant the erection of public buildings, and two of Swansea's finest buildings, both in the Maritime Quarter, are late examples of the classical style which had dominated British architecture since the late seventeenth century. One is Swansea Museum, the Royal Institution of South Wales, designed in 1838 and completed in 1841 by a Liverpool architect, Frederick Long, a stone-porticoed, temple-like building with Grecian and even Egyptian features, echoing in its architecture the status of Egypt and Greece in the world of archaeology and learning. The other is the former Guildhall, Somerset Place. The ancient town hall of Swansea had been propped against the walls of the castle, its mainly seventeenth-century structure being rebuilt about 1820. Soon afterwards, a new site was chosen on the Burrows, and in 1825 the local builder, Thomas Bowen, built a Guildhall in a Doric style to the design of John Collingwood of Gloucester. The reform of local government in 1835 and the population growth made such a small building obsolete, and the 1825 building was effectively extended from 1848 to 1852 by the local architect, William Richards, under the supervision of the London architect, Thomas Taylor. It remained in use until 1934 as a Guildhall. A most impressive edifice of fine golden stone, with a giant order of eight Corinthian columns across the front, with tall, arch-headed sash windows, and fine balustrading all round, it is now in a part of the city which is developing rapidly and it is imperative that a worthy use should be made of it.

Classical styles were all very well for grand public buildings such as museums or town halls, but by the 1840s Gothic and Tudor styles — sometimes in eclectic mixtures called Jacobethan or Tudorbethan — predominated in other fields. Even before 1818 General Warde crenellated Clyne Castle so that it looked something like a castle, and when in 1860 Graham Vivian bought the building he added extensions in a Tudorbethan gabled style. Marino was in 1816 bought by J. H. Vivian, who extended it with two short wings in the original classical style of the house. Then in 1823 he had the London architect, P. F. Robinson, transform the place into an imitation of an ancestral seat. Robinson's design was in an eclectic Gothic and Tudor style with an ornately high-chimneyed, turretted skyline, dominated at one end by a pencil-thin tower, crowned by a circle of spirelets. The design was turned into reality from 1827 to 1837, although it is sad to relate that the tower has been recently demolished. In 1829 Vivian bought Singletons Farm nearby and renamed Marino Singleton Abbey. Robinson was famous for his designs of lodges and estate cottages, which he published in a series of books. Singleton Abbey itself was illustrated in *Domestic Architecture in the Tudor Style* (1837). Dr Nigel Temple has identified several other buildings at Singleton from Robinson's other books: the Swiss Cottage in the park appears as an 'Entrance Lodge' design in *Designs for Ornamental Villas* (1836, first edition 1827), the Sketty Lane Thatched Lodge (behind the Hospital) closely resembles a lodge in *Designs for Lodges and Park Entrances* (1833), while the Boating Lake Lodge at the bottom of Sketty Lane closely resembles another in the same book. His lodge which he says in *Rural Architecture* (fourth edition 1836) was built for J. H. Vivian, Esq., M.P., near Swansea 'for a Bailiff having a family', has probably been demolished, but its design must have been copied by the neighbouring Clyne estate, for Clyne Lodge, which stands at the entrance to the gardens, just behind the Woodman Inn, is all but identical to this design, according to Dr Temple. It is possible that the other ornamental and ancillary buildings at Singleton, such as the once-delightful (and retrievable) Home Farm, originated as designs by P. F. Robinson.

Across Brynmill lane from Singleton Park is the large Gothic house of Parc Wern (now Parc Beck, the nurses' home), bought and rebuilt as a dower house by the Vivian family in the 1840s and similar to Singleton although in a more rugged style, with a massive tower and more jagged gables. A little to the north of Singleton is Sketty and beyond that is the estate of Hendrefoilan, which was bought about 1840 by the son of Lewis Weston Dillwyn, the industrialist Lewis Ll. Dillwyn, M.P., and rebuilt for him by an architect, William B. Colling, in whose obituary in *The Builder* (23 January 1886) it was said that Hendrefoilan was one of only two buildings he built under his own name. William Richards was the local architect supervising the work on the ground. Hendrefoilan is a large, square, symmetrically-gabled and bay-windowed house in the Tudorbethan style, and now houses the Extra-mural department of the University College of Swansea. The Richards family were eminent local builders and architects responsible for many mid-nineteenth century buildings in Swansea, such as the Music Hall (1864), renamed the Albert Hall when extended in 1881, the Mansion House (the mayoral residence) formerly Brooklands House at Ffynonne, built from 1859 to 1863 in a weak, asymmetrical, vaguely Gothic style, with an octagonal roofed corner turret and a variety of differently shaped windows, for Evan Matthew Richards by his brother William. It became the mayoral residence in 1922.

Swansea has a large number of houses in various Romantic or Gothic styles. One of the most extreme examples of the High Gothic revival at its most pointed is Langland Bay House, built in the mid-nineteenth century for a member of the Crawshay dynasty of iron-masters of Cyfarthfa, Merthyr, which has been used partly as an hotel and partly as a convalescent home for many years.

Townscape of Victorian Swansea

Although the town centre was destroyed by the Blitz and although its outer suburbs are largely twentieth-century development, Swansea remains a profoundly Victorian town, reflecting its industrial heyday from about 1830 to 1890. Many of the inner suburbs, the terraces of St Thomas hanging above the harbour and docks, old industrial districts such as Greenhill, Hafod, Manselton, Landore, Plas-marl, and many others, remain deeply Victorian in character, with terraces of brown stone houses with slate roofs or with brightly-painted stucco fronts, the roofline broken only by the larger bulk of taverns or chapels. Land-owners such as the earl of Jersey appear to have had a policy of standard designs for any houses built on their sprawling industrialized estates, such as the rigid uniformity of design of houses, for example, found in Llansamlet, with a central pedimented and consoled doorway surrounded by five sash windows.

The Victorian middle-class suburbs are found mainly to the west of the old town centre, St Helen's, Ffynonne, Heathfield, Uplands, Glanmôr, Rhyddings, Brynmill, Sketty, all being excellent examples. The large houses in St Helen's Road, dating from the 1840s, with pillared porches and pilastered stucco façades, or the terraced villas of Richmond Terrace in the Uplands, set back behind gardens, retain the character of Georgian architecture, while the terrace of stucco villas

'And Death Shall Have no Dominion', by Ceri Richards.

Hafod Copperworks, by James Harris.

The Plas House, c.1835.

Swansea Bay, Colts Hill, and Underhill, c. 1800, by Benjamin Barber of Bath.

Ann of Swansea by W. J. Watkeys.

set behind long tree-shaded lawns in Belgrave Gardens, Uplands, epitomizes the early Victorian ideal of *rus in urbe* ('country inside the town'). Walter Road, leading from the town centre to the Uplands, commemorates the Walters family, who were amongst the most enterprising of urban developers, and although now shorn of most of the trees which gave it the air of a boulevard, its houses still retain the true character of Victorian urban design, with rows of three or four-storeyed stuccoed houses, gabled, bargeboarded, bay-windowed, with pedimented and consoled doorways, chimneys of yellow and blue-grey bricks, and elaborate cast-iron railings. To take one more example out of many dozens which could be cited, Bryn Road, in Brynmill, is a single terrace running the whole length of this long street which looks over the sea, its architectural rhythm depending on row upon row of two-storeyed bay windows, the sashes having elliptical arches. It is of the very essence of the Victorian 'Marine Terrace'. The observer standing on the seashore, looking landwards at

Walter Road, c. 1910.

Swansea, sees row upon row of these long terraces, glistening with paint, rising up Townhill, from Heathfield in the east to Glanmôr in the west. At the moment such terraces do not appear in any way extraordinary to people in Swansea, but the time may well come when people will come from afar to study and admire such splendid examples of mid-Victorian town planning, assuming, that is, that Swansea's citizens and planners have treated them with care and taste.

Victorian Churches

In reaction to the growth of nonconformity many churches were built in Swansea in the nineteenth century. The medieval parish church of St Mary, rebuilt once in 1739, was again rebuilt on a large scale (save for one chapel) by Sir Arthur Blomfield from 1895 to 1899, using a tame Gothic style, a rebuilding which in turn was destroyed in the Blitz. The church was rebuilt, still in Blomfield's style, by L. T. Moore and Sir Percy Thomas from 1954 to 1959. At the top of High Street stood Swansea's smaller medieval parish church of St John, much rebuilt by Jernegan in 1823-4, then rebuilt in an amalgam of Romanesque and classical styles in 1886 by the Swansea firm of Bucknall and Jennings, the dedication being changed to St Matthew, because the Vivian family had in 1878-80 built a new church at the Hafod (designed by Henry Woodyer of Guildford) which they insisted was to be dedicated to St John, and which would serve Vivian employees. Woodyer had in 1850 already built a much finer church near Singleton Abbey, St Paul's, Sketty, its tall broach spire rivalled by the splendid church of St Thomas, Kilvey, erected by the Grenfell family in 1886.

The diocesan architect of St David's in the 1850s and '60s was Richard Kyrke Penson, who designed several churches in the area, one of them being St Peter's, Cockett, in 1857. The mariners' chapel, St Nicholas, at the end of Gloucester Place, was designed by Bucknall in 1868, Christ Church, Oystermouth Road, designed by J. T. Nicholson of Hereford in 1871-2, and later churches were designed by the Cardiff architect, Colonel E. M. Bruce Vaughan, such as St Luke's, Cwmbwrla (1889) and St Michael's, Manselton (1904-5).

Swansea had a small Catholic community from the time of the French Revolution onwards, a small pool transformed into a torrent by the influx of Irish immigrants in the 1840s. The shopping centre by St Mary's parish church is today called St David's centre, standing as it does just north of the Catholic church of St David, designed by the

Bristol architect, Charles Hansom, in 1847. Irish immigrants tended to cluster in the suburb of Greenhill, Hafod, and it was the firm of Pugin and Pugin which designed in 1886 the tall, soaring Gothic Catholic church of St Joseph at Greenhill, which was opened in 1888 and recently designated St Joseph's Cathedral.

Victorian Chapels

There are so many nonconformist chapels in and around Swansea that one can only draw attention to one or two here and there. In the centre of the town, York Place (Baptist) was built in 1830 as a neat, square, preaching box with a fine classical doorway. The Unitarian chapel (on the site of the dissenting meeting house of 1689) was rebuilt in 1840 in High Street in an early Tudor Perpendicular Gothic style. Near High Street station stands Bethesda (Baptist) a large classically-styled chapel, with a florid baroque porch, probably dating from about 1870. Nearby in Ebenezer Street is Ebenezer (Baptist, formerly Independent), first erected in 1803, altered in 1826, and given its present form in 1862 — by the minister-architect, Thomas Thomas or 'Tomos Glan-dŵr' of Landore, an architect with an extensive chapel-building practice even stretching as far as Stoke Newington. It is in the typical, pedimented, classical Welsh style of the period. Thomas of Landore was also responsible for the design of Siloam, Llangyfelach Road (built 1864, enlarged 1914), and, together with Thomas Freeman, for the immense Siloh Newydd (Independent) at Landore in 1874. Freeman was a prominent Independent layman and mayor of Swansea, who designed Hermon (Independent) Plas-marl in 1878. Ebenezer's façade of 1862 is typical of mid-nineteenth century Swansea chapels, with its pediment rising over a late-Roman glorification arch, which in turn arches over a Palladian 'Venetian' window above a central door-way. Siloh Newydd, on the other hand, shows the eclecticism of Swansea chapels of the later nineteenth century, mixing as it does all kinds of Romanesque and Lombardic details with a basically classical structure, and, to crown it all, a large crucifix atop the pediment.

One of the best-known chapel architects was George Morgan of Carmarthen (1834-1915), designer of the most conspicuous chapel in the centre of Swansea, Mount Pleasant (Baptist) in the Kingsway, a chapel originally built in 1825-6, but elaborately extended by Morgan in 1875-6 with a handsome golden sandstone portico having four Corinthian columns. Morgan was also responsible for another chapel in an utterly different style, Dinas Noddfa (Baptist) above Landore and

Plas-marl, a well-built edifice in a Lombardic or Romanesque style, its façade dominated by a huge rose window. The whole of the Morriston area has, or had before the demolition or adaptation of several such buildings, an enormous number of chapels, one of the most elegant being the classical Seion (Baptist) built in 1845, with an extremely broad pediment. All these places of worship are dwarfed by the 'Cathedral of Welsh Nonconformity', the immense Tabernacl (Independent) designed in 1870 by the Morriston architect, John Humphreys, and built from 1870-2 by Daniel Edwards of Morriston. Edwards, Humphreys, and the minister, Emlyn Jones, are said to have toured the British Isles in search of the perfect chapel style, and the Tabernacl is an idiosyncratic mixture of late Roman styles, with a giant order of eight Corinthian columns grouped in pairs, from the capitals of which spring directly a linking trio of rounded arches, the centre being slightly wider, and above which rises a heavily dentilled pediment, and from one corner rises that rarest feature of non-conformist architecture, a clock tower with a spire, the feature which gives the building its ecclesiastical sobriquet.

In the mid-nineteenth century, Welsh-language congregations stuck to classical styles in their chapels, while English-language congregations were attracted more and more to Gothic. But there were many exceptions to that rule. Alfred Bucknell of Sketty designed Argyle Presbyterian Church of Wales on St Helen's Road in 1873 in a classical style, the chapel resembling an immense Roman temple with a portico of pilasters and columns in a giant composite order. Nearby, John Dickson in 1862-4 designed St Andrew's (Presbyterian, now United Reformed) in St Helen's Road in a light and airy Gothic style, the façade culminating in two high octagonal corner pinnacles. In the Mumbles, the architect A. Totten designed the Victoria Chapel (Methodist) in 1877 in a Romanesque style. W. W. Williams in 1896 designed an elaborate and pinnacled Gothic chapel for the Welsh-language congregation of Independents in Henrietta Street (now called Ebeneser Newydd). Some of the chapels built at the turn of the century are in a remarkably flamboyant style: Pantygwydr (Baptist) was designed by C. T. Ruthen in 1906 in the Uplands with nave, transepts and a Gothic tower and spire which might have come from medieval Spain.

As with Swansea's Victorian churches, the Victorian and Edwardian chapels offer a rich contrast to simple and often austere terraces of houses; they punctuate each corner of the town with their colourful medley of styles, and as they are converted, vandalized and demolished, so the essential character of central Swansea is destroyed.

Victorian Public Buildings

We have already mentioned the work of Thomas Taylor re-designing the Guildhall in 1848: he was commissioned in 1850 by a group of citizens led by George Grant Francis to build a new home for the Grammar School (founded originally by Bishop Gore) on Mount Pleasant hill. This school, which Taylor modelled on a mullioned one-storey Elizabethan schoolroom, was destroyed in the Blitz. The school was moved to a new site in Sketty after 1945. The Swansea architect, J. H. Bayliss, designed in 1858 the town post office in a towered and curvy-gabled Tudor style, a building used before its recent demolition as the offices of the *South Wales Evening Post*. A second post office, again in a Tudor style but with a fine classical cupola, was built in Wind Street from 1898 to 1901.

Swansea's ancient market had been a one-storeyed, pillared construction in the middle of Wind Street, and in 1828 a new site was given for a market in what is now Oxford Street. By the 1880s the market buildings of the 1830s were quite inadequate, and in 1887 the Swansea architects, James Buckley Wilson and Glendinning Moxham, designed a new market, which was the pride and joy of Swansea. It was one of the most deeply lamented victims of the Blitz, and a new

Swansea Workingmen's Institute, built 1885.

market was built on the same site in 1959-60 by the Percy Thomas partnership, the bustling stalls to-day being covered by one gigantic arched roof.

Many of Swansea's schools date from the Victorian period, though several of them by now have been converted to other uses. Early or mid-nineteenth century schools were often built in a Gothic or Tudor Gothic style, for instance, the school opposite St Paul's, Sketty, or Oxford Street Schools at the corner of Union Street and Oxford Street. Terrace Road School was built in 1888 on a typical late Victorian central-hall school plan, one of a large number of schools built in the wake of compulsory state education after 1870. One of the most unusual school buildings, built by an unknown architect, is Manselton School, designed in 1900, with its careful design to separate boys and girls and its large stair towers in a kind of Scottish Jacobean style.

Most often the names of the designers of these schools are not known. Private papers have recently revealed, for example, that Bishopston school, a picturesque Gothic building next to St Teilo's, now a private house, was designed by a Swansea architect called Woolcott in 1848. The rest of his work in the area has not been identified. Unknown also is the builder of one of Swansea's most prominent landmarks, the Cambrian Institute for the Deaf and Dumb, transferred from Aberystwyth to Swansea in 1850, and whose buildings form a very long, two-storeyed gabled range, hanging, as it were, in the trees above Heathfield and Mount Pleasant, and visible from everywhere in the town centre. A fine monument to Victorian civic spirit and resourcefulness, it has long been a school for children with special problems.

Another monument to the Victorian civic spirit is the block in Alexandra Road containing the Central Library and School of Art designed by Henry Holtom of Dewsbury in 1886-7, having a tall façade with mansard roofs in a French Empire style, its windows with T-shaped glazing bars giving the building a curiously central European air. Besides the Glynn Vivian gallery, in the same street are to be found the Working Men's Club (1885) and the former municipal Board of Guardians building, now the headquarters of the B.B.C. in Swansea, a neo-Jacobean building of pink brick with good carved freestone detailing.

Two of Swansea's theatres date from the end of the last century: the Palace, designed by Bucknall and Jennings in 1888, another mansard-roofed building on a difficult, three-cornered site north of High Street

Head Post Office, Wind Street, opened 1901.

Swansea Harbour Trust Offices, opened 1903.

Station, now looking rather forlorn, but in many ways a most handsome building; and the other is the Grand Theatre, recently restored and extended, designed by William Hope in Singleton Street in 1897 (again in a classical mansard-roofed style) and opened by the famous soprano, Adelina Patti (whose home was at Craig y Nos Castle in the Swansea valley). The Grand's gilt and plush interior wonderfully recalls the tone of Victorian Swansea. Adelina Patti loved Swansea and the Tawe valley, and after her death left to the citizens a large Victorian cast-iron and glass Winter Garden pavilion from the gardens of Craig y Nos. This was re-erected as an entertainment pavilion in 1920 in Victoria Park, one of the parks created by the zeal of William Thomas of Lan, 'Pioneer of Open Spaces', in 1887. This curious curved-roofed building is called the Patti Pavilion and, most appropriately, Thomas of Lan's statue stands in front of it.

Swansea had been overtaken commercially and industrially by Cardiff at the end of the nineteenth century, and Swansea's Edwardian buildings do not compare in grandeur with those of Cardiff. Perhaps it is symbolic that it was a Cardiff architect, Edwin Seward, who designed the offices of the Swansea Harbour Trust in 1902-3, these being a florid baroque pile in red brick and white stone, surmounted by a weather-vaned cupola encrusted with statuary. Now that the gloomy railway embankment at the bottom of Wind Street has been demolished, and with Quay Parade as the main artery of traffic through the city, this building, which is now the offices of Associated British Ports, has been thrust into prominence. Swansea's own architects were, of course, active in the period leading to the First World War: the borough architect, Ernest Morgan, designed in 1912-3 the baroque revival Police Station on a narrow site between Alexandra Road and Orchard Street, and Sir Charles T. Ruthen (then living in Swansea) designed several impressive blocks in the same period; such, for example, as the white stone baroque revival Exchange Buildings (1913-4), the Mond Buildings in Union Street (1911), and the Carlton Cinema in Oxford Street (1913-4). Ruthen also made alterations to the Morriston Tabernacl in 1922. More extensive than the practice of Ernest Morgan or Charles Ruthen was that of Glendinning Moxham, designer of a large number of private houses from the 1880s to the 1920s in suburbs such as Sketty, Langland, and Caswell. Moxham designed in 1895, for example, Gors Cottage in Caswell Bay. The Moxham style was picturesque and irregular, with red tiled roofs, tile hung and close-studded half-timbered walls, oriels, high-roofed corner turrets, and small-paned windows, all of which are illustrated in his book *Country*

Swansea Central Police Station, Alexandra Road, erected 1912-13.

The Exchange Buildings, built 1913-15.

Houses and Cottages (1914). Moxham designed the Market buildings but his best-known work is the Glynn Vivian Gallery, built from 1909 to 1911 with its colourful façade of brick and stone, its florid baroque windows and porch and its elegant, galleried interior.

Swansea had had some form of public hospitals since the early nineteenth century, but the chief hospital of the town, the Swansea General and Eye Hospital was designed by a London architect, Alexander Graham from 1865 to 1878 (and subsequently extended by Moxham), with the approval of Florence Nightingale. Most of the buildings have recently been demolished, but the main administrative block with its slim clock cupola still stands at the junction of Brynymor Road and St Helens Road. A mental hospital was long discussed in Swansea, but was not designed until 1912, and then by the London architect, T. G. Hine, a specialist in this particular field, the building not being completed until 1928. This hospital on the hill of Cefn Coed above Cockett, with its tall brick tower, is visible for miles around.

There was an enormous amount of industrial building in Swansea during the reigns of Victoria and Edward VII, much of it now demolished. One remarkable monument which cannot be allowed to pass without mention is the huge Victoria Flour Mills — Weaver's Building in popular parlance — designed by the pioneering French

firm of Hennebique from 1895 to 1898, and one of the earliest reinforced concrete buildings in Europe, if not the earliest. Having become
redundant, the building was recently demolished, its site being now
occupied by the carpark of J. Sainsbury PLC.

One aspect of Swansea's rapid industrialization was the slum
problem. From 1876 to 1883 the town corporation began a programme
of slum clearance, but overcrowding remained a terrible problem, and
it was only in the first years of the twentieth century that serious steps
were taken to build council houses. One of the earliest of these municipal schemes was on the Baptist Well estate near Greenhill; Byron
and Shelley Crescents being designed in 1907-8, and these, being such
notably early examples of municipal housing, were restored soon after
1977. Many environmental reform groups were active in Swansea
about 1905 to 1907, and in the wake of their agitation, Mayhill became
the venue for the South Wales Cottage Exhibition in 1910. As a result
of a competition, judged by such Garden City pioneers as (Sir)
Raymond Unwin, James Crossland drew up a garden city design for
Mayhill, and several architects planned the working-class housing in
the picturesque vernacular styles in favour at that time. In 1912 the
corporation decided to develop the whole mountain top site of
Townhill (to the west of Mayhill) as a garden city, and this was laid out
by the borough surveyor, George Bell, and Unwin himself. Unwin's

*Council housing at Mayhill,
1936.*

layout of roads was kept when the main part of the scheme went ahead
from 1922 to 1929, the delay being caused by the First World War. An
outlying suburb, still called 'Garden Village', is to be found between
Gorseinion and Fforestfach, north-west of the city, designed in 1909 by
the Garden City architects, George Pepler and Ernest Allen, who had
set up an office in Swansea. The war again frustrated the full development of the project which seems to have been largely abortive. It is
clear that in Swansea there was great public interest in workers'
housing, and that strenuous efforts were made by environmental
groups in conjunction with the municipality in the opening years of
this century to solve the housing crisis in most imaginative ways.

Building Since the First World War

The historian devotes such a lot of attention to the architecture of
the past that he leaves little time to deal with the present, and here we
can only devote a brief word to the main architectural trends of this
century as they are reflected in Swansea's buildings. Swansea, like most
of south Wales, was severely hit by the depression soon after the end of
the First World War, so that it is somewhat surprising to find that its
largest twentieth-century edifice dates from 1930 to 1934. This is the
whole complex of municipal buildings, the new Guildhall, the
Brangwyn Hall, and the Law Courts placed at the eastern end of
Victoria Park, and designed by the Cardiff architect, Sir Percy
Thomas. It is important in an architectural survey because it was
Swansea's first real taste of the Modern Movement in architecture,
designed in an austere monumental 'stripped classical' style, where
almost all external ornament has been banished, an assemblage of
subtly designed cubes from which rises an immense plain clock tower,
like a lighthouse over-looking the bay, with its smooth white stone
exterior and its travertine marble within, it is highly reminiscent of
large public buildings built by Mussolini's régime in Italy in the same
period. The interior is much more lavishly decorated than the exterior:
the Council Chamber is in a Grecian neo-classical style, its columns
contrasting with a frieze showing the Gorsedd of Bards processing at
the Eisteddfod, and the Law Courts have classical interiors decorated
with details from the medieval Welsh Law Book of Chirk (*Llyfr Du'r
Waun*), while the huge Brangwyn Hall is decorated with the teemingly
colourful panels by Sir Frank Brangwyn, originally planned for the
House of Lords as a memorial to the dead of the First World War, but
thought to be more appropriate for Swansea. The architecture of the

1930s is still too close to the present-day to be properly evaluated, but it may well be in the not too distant future that Swansea Guildhall will come to be seen as a splendid text-book example.

Rather similar in style was the Plaza Cinema, designed by the Cardiff architect, Howard Williams, immediately before the Second World War on what later came to be the Kingsway, its fine foyer and restaurant decorated with Welsh insignia and symbols. Its demolition was all the more ironic, in that it had withstood the Blitz unscathed, while there were acres of bleak devastation all around it. The Blitz gave encouragement to the urges to redesign and develop the whole of the old town centre; hence so much of central Swansea appears to consist of blocks of three or four storeys in the modern styles of the 1950s and 1960s, a good example being the tall plain brick tower block of the Dragon Hotel at the junction of the Kingsway and Bellevue Street, and dating from the late 1950s. The only exception to that period of austere plate-glass and concrete modernism was the gabled, half-timbered Beau Nash House, a row of shops on the southern side of Caer Street and Castle Gardens, the target for the protests of the

Interior of the Brangwyn Hall, opened 1934.

'Anti-Ugly Brigade', the squads of demonstrators on behalf of the buildings of the Modern Movement.

The University Campus at Singleton Park, developed largely between the late 1950s and the mid-1970s, has a large number of buildings in the steel-framed, plate-glass or concrete office-block styles of the Modern Movement, buildings which are all flat-roofed, as is the Singleton Hospital, immediately to the west of the Campus in Singleton Park, a large edifice of the same period. When the huge area of central Swansea just south of St Mary's church came to be cleared for redevelopment, the first new buildings to be put up, such as the Leisure Centre or the stores of Messrs. C. and A. Modes, were all in the unadorned, flat-roofed no-nonsense style of the 1960s and '70s, but by the time the new West Glamorgan County Hall was built, from 1981 to 1984, designed by the Architects' department of the County

Aerial view of the post-war reconstruction of the City Centre.

Council, on a wonderful site along the shore at Oystermouth Road, a perfect example of the international Modern Movement style with its long low white concrete wings and its dark windows designed as sleekly unbroken strips, the style was already being overtaken by the Post-Modernist movement.

Already during the late 1970s many of the shops of the St David's Shopping Centre, gabled and picturesque, and grouped around a domestic red-brick courtyard, harking back almost to a medieval market-place, had gone beyond the Modern Movement. The Maritime Quarter, with its refurbished quayside, its bollards and capstans, sculpted archways, self-consciously artistic gables and 'toytown' towers, all reflected in the waters of a harbour dotted with colourful pleasure craft, seems to be a perfect example of the 1980s Post-Modern Movement in architecture, playful, picturesque, traditionalist, and even frivolous. Above all, it seems a world away from the puritanical architectural asceticism of the 1960s. This infectious playfulness has spread even to such a sober and dignified edifice as the Crown Court (1988) newly built opposite the Guildhall, its white stone façade broken and enlivened with high roofs, gateway, pinnacles, bay windows, oriels and sidelong windows. The wheel of fashion has turned once again, and this time there has been no whimper of protest from the 'Anti-Ugly Brigades'.

ACKNOWLEDGEMENTS

A draft of this chapter was read and corrected by my friends, Thomas Lloyd of Cresselly, Pembrokeshire, and Paul Joyner of the National Library of Wales, and to both I am grateful for saving me from many errors. I am also indebted for material on Swansea architecture and town planning to my colleague, Mr Michael Simpson, University College of Swansea, and to my friend, Mr David McLees, of Cadw, Cardiff. I am also grateful to my friends, Mr and Mrs Howard Fry of Horton, Gower, for showing me their collection of works by Edward Duncan, his family and friends . Over the past year I have profited also from conversations with Mr Donald Moore and Dr Roderick Howell. I also have to thank Dr Nigel Temple of Cheltenham for allowing me to make use of his current research into the architecture of P. F. Robinson.

'UNDER A RAINBOW': LITERARY HISTORY

Chapter 8

James A. Davies

When George Borrow visited Swansea in 1854 before writing *Wild Wales* (1862) he was told by a man in a grimy suburb, 'You have taken your last farewell of Wales, sir; it's no use speaking Welsh farther on'. Though this, at any time, would have been exaggeration it is a reminder that, for whatever reason — persisting Norman influence, perhaps, strong links with a cosmopolitan maritime world, or because writing in Welsh flourished in more rural places — Swansea's literary history is mainly in English. That said, the town-become-city has still made a substantial contribution to Welsh-language literature.

During the late middle ages it edged into that great tradition when Dafydd y Coed, a 'poet of the gentry', came to Kilvey, the area on the east bank of the Tawe, and praised the fine library of Hopcyn ap Tomas; Lewys Glyn Cothi (*c.* 1420-89) also stayed at Kilvey and wrote lyrically about Gower. Two centuries later, in 1661, Stephen Hughes (1622-88), the Puritan translator and editor, came from Carmarthen to Swansea and, in 1668, was one of the co-translators into Welsh of *The Pilgrim's Progress*.

These were marginal moments. More importantly, in 1801 Joseph Harris ('Gomer') (1773-1825), from Pembrokeshire, became a minister in Swansea. He also became owner of a printing works producing religious material. In 1814 he launched and edited *Seren Gomer*, the first weekly newspaper in Welsh. Its circulation was reasonable, it attracted much attention, and had national ambitions, but it lasted less than two years. Revivals followed and it survived, mainly as a Baptist quarterly, until 1983.

In the nineteenth century Swansea was prominent in the tragic life of William Thomas ('Islwyn') (1832-78). His fiancée, Anne Bowen, who died suddenly, and his wife, Martha Davies, were both from the town. Love for the former dominated marriage to the latter, the resultant tension fuelling his greatest poetry. In the 1890s Daniel James

('Gwyrosydd') (1847-1920), the Treboeth poet, wrote words to music by John Hughes (1872-1914) of Landore. The result was 'Calon Lân', famous hymn and rugby anthem, arguably Swansea's greatest contribution to Welsh popular culture.

During modern times there have been further highlights, including, in schools and chapels, the sustaining of a fine tradition of eisteddfodau with their literary competitions, and the publishing and bookselling activities of Tŷ John Penry. William Crwys Williams ('Crwys') (1875-1968), of Craig-cefn-parc, for many years a minister in Swansea's Brynmill, dominated eisteddfod competitions and became Archdruid of Wales. David Myrddin Lloyd (1909-81), the Swansea born and educated scholar and editor, had a distinguished career in the National Libraries of Wales and Scotland. Following the founding of University College of Swansea in 1920 much of importance in Welsh writing has come from its academics. They include the essayist T. J. Morgan (1907-88), the scholar Stephen J. Williams (b. 1896), whose son Urien (b. 1929) is a well-known novelist and dramatist, J. Gwyn Griffiths (b. 1911), poet and scholar, and his wife Kate Bosse-Griffiths (b. 1910), the German-born Welsh-language novelist, the philosopher J. R. Jones (1911-70), and the historian (in English as well as Welsh) Glanmor Williams (b. 1920). Elsewhere in the city, at the Swansea Memorial College, of which he was principal, Pennar Davies (b. 1911), who sometimes wrote as 'Davies Aberpennar' because of his Mountain Ash upbringing, furthered a distinguished career in poetry and prose, occasionally in English.

Pre-eminent was Saunders Lewis (1893-1985), one of the foremost Welsh-speaking Welshmen of his age and a poet, dramatist and literary critic of high quality. Cheshire-born, he lectured in the College's Department of Welsh from 1922 until 1937, when he was dismissed following imprisonment for setting fire to the R.A.F. bombing school at Penyberth in Caernarvonshire as a nationalist protest, and left the area.

All the while, in parallel, Swansea developed a literary history in English which also began quietly and briefly in the books of early visitors. Gerald of Wales (*c.* 1146-1223) came recruiting in 1188 and commented in much-translated Latin, prophetically though wearily, on the locals' insistence on singing in parts; John Leland (1506-52), in his famous *Itinerary*, confined himself to basic facts; Daniel Defoe (1660-1731) was impressed, though sceptical, about claims made for local mineral waters, and said as much in his *Tour Through the Whole Island of Great Britain* (1724-6). Richard 'Beau' Nash (1674-1761),

Swansea-born, is its first figure of literary importance, though indirectly and in another place. In Bath from 1705 he reorganized the city as the elegant pleasure-garden so vividly described and re-imagined in English literature from Smollett to Sheridan, Jane Austen and Dickens.

In 1739, the poet Richard Savage (*c.* 1697-1743), harassed by debts and enemies, left London to live in Swansea on an allowance of £50 a year subscribed by friends who included Alexander Pope. Savage lingered in Bristol before sailing reluctantly to Swansea and took lodgings in Barber Court, off Orchard Street, the site, now, of the Kingsway roundabout. Despite his lack of means he mixed in good local society, publishing verses praising the Swansea barrister, John Powell, in the *Gentleman's Magazine*. Unfortunately for civic pride, Savage took up with Bridget Jones, a wealthy widow and well-known beauty from Llanelli. He wrote poems to her, and an epitaph on her grandmother, again in the *Gentleman's Magazine*. Bridget Jones was 'Llannelly's fair' and, when she refused his proposal of marriage and the relationship ended, he told the world

> my *Chloe's* charms no more
> Invite my steps along *Llannelley's* shore

Swansea's western rival had gained the textual points, but revenge came in 1744 when Johnson, in his classic *Life of Mr Richard Savage*, describing the Swansea excursion mentioned Llanelli not at all.

During his stay in what was then a small and probably quiet provincial town Savage also completed *The Tragedy of Sir Thomas Overbury*, but he left Swansea after less than two years, dying in Bristol on his way back to London. A strong but unsubstantiated belief persisted that Savage wrote 'On Hafod, Swansea', a long, mainly accomplished but conventional poem of the period celebrating what was then a beauty spot and favourite walk. It opens:

> Delightful Hafod, most serene abode!
> Thou sweet retreat, fair mansion for a god!
> Dame Nature, lavish of her gifts we see,
> And Paradise restored in thee.
> Unrivall'd thou beneath the radiant sun;
> Sketty and Forest own themselves undone . . .

Savage left Swansea as the town's expansion and a new interest in sea-bathing encouraged civic ambitions to become a seaside resort. These developed too slowly for the next refugee. William Combe (1741-1823), later to find fame and fortune as the author of *Dr Syntax* (1809), was, like Savage, forced to leave London when debts and scandals pursued him. He spent the period 1769-73 wandering the provinces doing what he could and was sighted in Swansea 'as a waiter at an inn', the old Mackworth in Wind Street.

For almost fifty years after Combe's departure, Swansea tried to become 'the Brighton of Wales'. It had 'every accommodation for using the marine fluid with effect': to the Bathing House, with its bathing-machines and facilities for eating and dancing, it quickly added a theatre and circulating libraries. By 1802 there were two of the latter, both in 'handsome and well-paved' Wind Street, near the Burrows, the area between Wind Street and the sea favoured for fashionable loitering. Both libraries offered profitable quarterly rates for the summer season and stock aimed at visitors seeking diversion. More followed, and others closed, up to 1830. A more serious rival appeared in 1804, when the Glamorgan Library was founded as a proprietary subscription library owned by thirty local notables, including Lewis Weston Dillwyn and Thomas Mansel Talbot, and with rules that excluded the buying of novels. The library had gone by 1822.

The Cambrian newspaper began in 1804. Six years later, Elijah Waring (*c.*1788-1857) settled in Neath. In 1813 he founded and edited *The Cambrian Visitor*, a monthly journal with literary pretensions, 'written', in the editor's own words, 'in the lively manner of the Spectator, the Rambler, and other papers of the same class'. This grand ambition was never achieved and a mixture of local intelligence, derivative verse, scholarly pieces, and some scissors-and-paste culling from other journals, sustained the monthly for only seven issues. The overall tone was moralistic, the poetry, in particular, too often lurching into a lugubriousness best illustrated by one far-from-snappy title:

A Thought

On covering a Snow-drop, which broke off while planting its root.
By a Lady who had lost a lovely and favourite Daughter.

The journal's failure notwithstanding, Swansea was developing a cultural infra-structure amenable to the arts. Into this developing seaside town came Walter Savage Landor (1775-1864). From 1793 he spent his summers in Tenby and the following year was in Gower, to judge from his poem, 'Voyage to St Ives, Cornwall, from Port-Einon, Glamorgan, 1794'. In 1796 he was in Swansea, his brother Robert noting, years later, that Landor had 'seduced a Girl at Tinby the year before, with whom he lived at Swansea till the birth of a child'. The 'Girl' was Nancy Jones but nothing is known of her fate or that of the child. Certainly, neither appears to have cramped Landor's style. He

Walter Savage Landor in 1804, from a portrait by George Dance.

was friendly with Howell Price of Laugharne and during 1796 he met Price's step-daughter, Rose Aylmer, 'walking on the burrows at Swansea'. She was then sixteen, Landor twenty-one. There is no evidence that they were more than friends; certainly both were members of a lively group of young people. We know she lent him books; one of them, Clara Reeve's *Progress of Romance* (1785), borrowed by Rose from one of those early circulating libraries, become a source for *Gebir* (1798), the epic poem that first made Landor's name. One of their seaside meetings is described in 'Abertawy', which opens lyrically:

> It was no dull tho' lonely strand
> Where thyme ran o'er the solid sand,
> Where snap-dragons with yellow eyes
> Lookt down on crowds that could not rise . . .

But the poem ends:

> Where Ganges rolls his widest wave
> She dropt her blossom in the grave;
> Her noble name she never changed,
> Nor was her noble heart estranged.

For in 1799 Rose Aylmer went with an aunt to India and six months later was dead of the cholera. News of her death inspired Landor's most famous lyric:

> Ah what avails the sceptred race,
> Ah what the form divine!
> What every virtue, every grace!
> Rose Aylmer, all were thine.
> Rose Aylmer, whom these wakeful eyes
> May weep, but never see,
> A night of memories and of sighs
> I consecrate to thee,

The lines triumphantly survive Landor's unromantic observation that they were composed 'when I was cleaning my teeth before going to bed'. Dylan Thomas described the poem as 'great poetry in every sense of the word; not a phrase, not a word, could be altered to its advantage; it is . . . full of . . . dignity and chastened splendour'. Here, as in

'Abertawy', we feel the tension between elegant form and emotional pressure that distinguishes Landor's best work.

In 1797 he was back in London and did not return to Swansea until 1813. He was then in a desperate financial plight, following grave problems with his estates and neighbours at Llanthony in Monmouthshire. In Swansea he raised high-interest loans from local bankers and looked to the settling of his business affairs. He also wrote the 'Calvus' letters attacking Bonaparte and surprisingly, given his shortage of cash, published them as a pamphlet at his own expense. Seven months later he left Swansea for ever and lived abroad, mainly in Italy, until 1835.

Writing to his mother from Italy in 1826 Landor recalled his time in Swansea with nostalgic longing:

> How beautiful was the sea shore covered with low roses, yellow snapdragons, and thousands of other plants. That streak of black along the most beautiful coast in the universe will never succeed in rendering me indifferent to Swansea . . . The Gulf of Salerno, I hear, is much finer than Naples; but give me Swansea for scenery and climate. I prefer good apples to bad peaches.

If ever he returned to England, he continued, he would wish to live out his life 'in the neighbourhood of Swansea — between that place and the Mumbles'.

The celebrated comparison between Swansea Bay and Naples is not as clear-cut as later enthusiasts would have us believe. What is implicit, however, here as in 'Abertawy', is Landor's strong affection and nostalgic longing for Swansea as a place where, once upon a time, he found beauty, romantic adventures, and much-needed sanctuary. Landor is important in Swansea's literary history for two reasons. He is the first writer of real quality to use Swansea as a literary setting and, secondly, in recalling Swansea as a lost golden place, he is the first to offer what becomes a typical and important reaction.

In 1799, when Rose Aylmer went fatally to India, Ann Julia Hatton ('Ann of Swansea') (1764-1838) and her husband leased Swansea's Bathing House. She was born in Worcester into a theatrical family, her elder sister being Sarah Siddons, the famous tragic actress. In her scandalous life she had had a bigamous marriage, a deserting husband, a career as an artist's model, and a suicide attempt in Westminster Abbey. After the latter her famous sister paid her twenty pounds a year on condition (it was rumoured) that she lived at least 150 miles from London, and her brother another £70. She married William Hatton in 1792 and came to Swansea after a period in North America.

She was already a published poet in *Poems on Miscellaneous Subjects* (1783). The Bathing House didn't pay and, after her husband's death in 1806 and a short time running a dancing school in Kidwelly, she returned to Swansea to a period of awful prolificity. She wrote a number of long novels, amounting to over fifty volumes of slackly-written, substandard Mrs Radcliffe 'plus a dash of social scandal', including *Cambrian Pictures* (3 volumes, 1810) and *Chronicles of an Illustrious House* (5 volumes, 1814), this last full of references to Swansea people. In 1810 her play, *Zaffine or the Knight of the Bloody Cross*, was performed in Swansea starring Edmund Kean. The following year saw her second volume of verse, the aptly named *Poetic Trifles*.

This volume is dedicated 'to the Officers of the Royal Western Regiment of Local Militia', some of the poems' titles — such as 'Sonnet to the Virginian Hyacinth' and the inevitable 'Lovers' Vows' — contributing further to the socially elegant, Austenish ambience she so obviously tried to cultivate and which is so much at odds with her past life and recent occupations. Too often her style is pseudo-Spenserian, pseudo-Shakespearian, but genuinely derivative, over-written and tinkling. When she adds preciousness the results are not inspiring, as in 'Invitation to a Robin':

> Come, little flutt'rer, freely come,
> No fraud, no guile inhabits here;
> Dost thou not see the scatt'red crumb?
> Dispel, sweet bird, thy *causeless* fear.

Dickens had the measure of writers like her: Ann of Swansea would have been a welcome guest at the public breakfast given by Mrs Leo Hunter, author of 'Ode to an Expiring Frog', in Chapter 15 of *The Pickwick Papers*.

Occasionally, despite the hackneyed language, she demonstrates some rhythmic strength, as in 'To the cuckoo':

> But not, as o'er my native hills,
> With pure delight I stray,
> Thy well-known voice my bosom thrills,
> Gay harbinger of May.

Dylan Thomas, a Drawing by Alfred Janes.

and in her best-known poem, 'Swansea Bay':

> The restless waves that lave the shore
> Joining the tide's tumultuous roar;
> In hollow murmurs seem to say —
> Peace is not found at Swansea Bay.

Here the correspondence between the sea and the feelings creates a
dirge-like effect that is simple enough but does reveal some pressure of
felt emotion. Usually, as Dylan Thomas observed, 'she managed . . to
keep her verses on a nice drab level of mediocrity'.

Perhaps because of her scandalous beginnings, in her Swansea
writings her moral heart is always in the right place. Because of this
she might well have appealed to Thomas Bowdler (1754-1825), the
Edinburgh doctor who, in 1811, 'fixed his residence at the Rhyddings,
near Swansea, in a small house situated on the rising ground immediately above the sea, and commanding a view of that beautiful bay'.
Bowdler had given up medicine following severe illness. He became
prominent in London literary and scientific circles and came to
Swansea, via Malta and the Isle of Wight, because his health required
sea-bathing and a mild climate and he knew the town from a previous
visit as a prison commissioner. Each summer he travelled extensively,
each winter he spent at the Rhyddings, separated from his wife and
without children. He was probably back in Swansea in October 1816
and doubtless read the *The Cambrian's* account of the suicide of
Shelley's step-daughter, Fanny Imlay, in the Bush Hotel in Wind
Street. Shelley came the following day, read her pathetic note, and
wrote lines that ended,

> Misery — O Misery,
> This world is all too wide for thee!

At the Rhyddings Bowdler worked first on a memoir of his friend,
the late General Villettes. Then, as winter storms struck the windows
of that isolated house still standing at the corner of St. Alban's Road
and Bernard Street, he turned to the work that would make him
famous and give his name to the language. He had 'an hereditary desire
to be doing good', coming from a pious family with a special interest in
mangling Shakespeare. The great expurgator was influenced by
memories of his father reading the plays to the family, skilfully and un-
obtrusively deleting all unsuitable words, and by the example of his
sister Harriet who, in 1807, had published a little-noticed expurgated
edition of selected plays. In 1818 his *Family Shakspeare* appeared in ten

volumes, 'in which nothing is added to the original text, but those words and expressions are omitted, which cannot with propriety be read aloud in a family'.

Bowdler deleted even the mildest profanity ('God' is always replaced by 'Heaven') and was ruthless on 'indecency or suspected indecency', thus revealing, as the *Monthly Review* noted, 'the truth of the old saw, that the *nicest* person has the *nastiest* ideas'. A good example of Bowdler in action is in *Henry IV, Part One*, Act I, Scene ii, when Hal speaks to Falstaff:

> Thou art so fat-witted with drinking of old sack, and unbuttoning thee after supper, and sleeping upon benches after noon, that thou hast forgotten to demand that truly which thou wouldst truly know. What a devil hast thou to do with the time of the day? Unless hours were cups of sack, and minutes capons, and clocks the tongues of bawds, and dials the signs of leaping-houses, and the blessed sun himself a fair hot wench in flame-coloured taffeta, I see no reason why thou shouldst be so superfluous to demand the time of the day.

Bowdler's version is:

> Thou art so fat-witted, with drinking of old sack, and sleeping upon benches after noon, that thou hast forgotten to demand that truly which thou wouldst truly know. What hast thou to do with the time of the day? Unless hours were cups of sack, and minutes capons, I see no reason, why thou shouldst be so superfluous to demand the time of the day.

This may be 'Shakspeare' but isn't 'Shakespeare'; the text is emasculated, drained of life and character. But, whether because of fears about the effect of the printed word on the young and the newly literate, or reaction against Regency licence, or evangelical influence, Bowdler's work was a best-seller. Even when *Blackwood's Magazine* attacked the edition as 'that piece of prudery in pasteboard' it worked to his advantage: *Blackwood's* great rival, the *Edinburgh Review*, was then obliged to praise it. *The Family Shakspeare* ran quickly through four editions; others appeared regularly into the 1860s. Immortality followed when 'to bowdlerize', meaning 'to expurgate', entered the language.

A buoyant Bowdler began expurgating Gibbon's *Decline and Fall*. He edited a selection from the *Old Testament* for use in Swansea Sunday Schools, and was generally philanthropic. In February 1825, only a few months after completing his Gibbon, he died from a chill and was buried in Oystermouth Church. 'The sigh of regret was universal', observed his memoirist. Among numerous bequests he left to St Mary's church in Swansea a painting of the Madonna and Child by the sixteenth-century Italian artist, Sassoferato, a work described by Bowdler as 'invaluable'. Following destruction by enemy action in World War Two and claims for compensation it turned out to be worth little. The same might be said of *The Family Shakspeare*.

Thirteen years after Bowdler's death Ann Hatton died at her home in Park Street. Her work had not always been admired and at least one local writer had attacked her 'after a most dastardly fashion'. He was Joe (or Jos) Jones, a Swansea surgeon, in *Ambition: a Poetical Essay* (1819), published under the pseudonym of 'Cambrienze Beppo'. Yet this poem, like Jones's *Lorin; or, the Wanderer in Wales* (1821) was strongly influenced by Ann Hatton's brand of banal romanticism. Both were long narrative poems in rhyming couplets, the latter about a misanthrope redeemed by love, that in such lines as

> The limpid current, in whose lucid wave
> The chastest nymph her fairest form might lave

is poetry-by-the-yard influenced by all the poetry-by-the-yard that had escaped the good effects of the romantic revival.

Such an attack as Joe Jones's was unusual for, in general, Swansea people were proud of their Ann. She was 'their novelist and poet'. In 1834 Henry Watkeys was commissioned by the town to paint her portrait; a glass tankard inscribed 'Ann of Swansea' is still extant. But as she aged towards death her health broke down, her means were now meagre, she was lonely and without friends. The sad pressures of her circumstances on occasion enabled the poems of her last years to touch more directly more affecting notes:

> Let us not mourn because we die,
> And in the grave forgotten lie,
> But rather joy because we know
> Death brings release at once from woe . . .

She died on 29 December 1838 and was buried in the churchyard of St. John's (now St. Matthew's) Church in High Street on the last day of the year. With her went what little now remained of Swansea's ambitions to be a genteel seaside resort. Her death was a small reminder that for the briefest of moments Swansea was not only the Brighton of Wales but, in the literary sense, had a fleeting resemblance to a small-scale Bath-on-sea.

Having deserted 'fashion', Swansea was becoming the 'metallurgical capital of the world' and the main energies of the town flowed into works and foundries. Possibly because of this, the Victorian age is the drab period of its literary history. Yet there were still some notable visitors: George Borrow, of course, and Francis Kilvert (1840-79), who stayed with clergyman friends and noted in his famous diary that 'the lurid copper smoke hung in a dense cloud' over the town. In 1878 Frances Ridley Havergal (1836-79), the poet and hymn-writer ('Take my silver and my gold'; 'I give my life for thee') came to live at Caswell for her health's sake, spent much of her time enrolling bemused locals in the temperance movement, and died from a chill the following year. T. J. Llewelyn Prichard (1790-1862), author of *Twm Shon Catti* (1828), the first Welsh novel, lengthened the list of those forced to Swansea by unfortunate circumstances. Prichard was an actor whose career ended when he lost his nose in a fencing-accident. He lived his last, unhappy, poverty-stricken years as a deformed drunkard in Thomas Street, where he completed his un-successful *Heroines of Welsh History* (1854) and died of burns after falling into his own fire.

All the while, under the copper smoke, the town developed institutions of literacy and culture. The circulating libraries persisted throughout the century: as late as 1875 a new one, owned by Stephen Hatchard, opened in Wind Street. Even on the Burrows, no longer the rendezvous of fashionable visitors, a reading-room functioned during the 1820s, a 'Club News Room' at the Assembly Rooms during the next decade, and the Swansea Burrows Reading Club from 1840. In the town other ventures fostered literacy and the reading habit: a National Schools Book Club from 1851, a reading society attached to the British and Foreign Seaman's Society, also from 1851, a library at the Mechanics' Institute in Goat Street, and, from 1868, a reading room for working men in Back Street.

Most importantly, in 1835 the Swansea Philosophical and Literary Institution was founded, renamed the Royal Institution of South Wales in 1838 and soon installed in the imposing building now known as the Museum. George Grant Francis (1814-82), brother of John Deffett Francis (1815-1901), whose fine book collection was given to the town later in the century, was its librarian for almost fifty years. He built up the town's first good general library, accumulating 10,000 volumes by 1876. Many came from the Royal Institution Book Club, whose purchases, after two years' use by the members, were presented to the main Institution library. Book Club rules excluded the purchase of novels, thus influencing the composition of the Royal Institution Library which, in 1876, was strong in the sciences, history, geography, and jurisprudence, but less so in what the catalogue described as 'Polite Literature'.

Subscriptions were social sifters; the Royal Institution was mainly for the toffs. Not until 1870 were the Public Libraries Acts adopted in Swansea, thus allowing a rate to be levied to establish a Free Library. An early gift was the Rowland Williams collection, chiefly of religious books, and, after initial problems, mainly caused by lack of funds, a thriving public library service emerged. In the present century that development has been paralleled by the sad decline of the Royal Institution and the disbanding of its fine collection.

The 'practical' strain, the bias against imaginative literature, was detected in the constitution of the old Glamorgan Library, and is characteristic of antiquarianism, an example being George Grant Francis's books, tracts, and pamphlets on local matters, and of amateur science, such as Lewis Weston Dillwyn's contributions to botany and conchology, and the Swansea physician William Turton's interest in natural history. Another may have been the lack of any outstanding literary figure during most of the nineteenth century.

But many published, with varying success. They included the Reverend C. W. Ireland Jones, of Verandah, who wrote pious, florid poems much possessed by death. His great year was 1840, with *Lines on Miss Vivian's Marriage* and *Poems* and *Various Subjects*. The opening of 'On My Birthday — 1839' —

> O Lord, another year is past,
> And I am spared still.

— demonstrates his ready gift for platitude and uneasy grasp of metre.

E. Darby, *Nothings*, also in 1840, has poems on local themes. The length of one title, 'Written on the Sands at Swansea, near to where a Lady had written, with the end of her parasol, some good wishes in favour of a friend' would, in itself, have ensured publication in Waring's long-gone *Cambrian Visitor*. The poem, not surprisingly, is moralistic and predictable.

Samuel Palmer Chapman, who came to Swansea from Waddington, is much the same kind of poet. Neither *The Poet's Almanack: A Didactic Poem* (1866) nor *Stolen Minutes with the Muses* (1877) rise much above the banal. H. A. W. Rott worked in Swansea as a lithographer from 1862. His *Fugitive Pieces* (1883), as Dylan Thomas recognized, has its simple, charming moments:

> The Summer comes,
> With days so warm and bright,
> When the bee hums,
> And the hawthorn blossoms
> And the butterfly roams,
> And new mown hay the air around perfumes.

Clement Scott (1841-1904), a better-known literary figure of the period, makes only a brief appearance in this literary history as author of *The Women of Mumbles Head* (1883), a vigorous ballad with great popular appeal that celebrates the heroic exploits of the Mumbles lighthouse keeper's two daughters, who rescued a lifeboatman from drowning:

> Up to the arms in water, fighting it breast to breast,
> They caught and saved a brother alive! God bless us we know
>   the rest'.

John Chapman Woods is a more substantial figure, his literary career lasting for more than half a century, from *A Child of the People* (1879) to *A Pageant of Poets* (1931). Woods is essentially a late-Victorian who can write good, if derivative lines.

> We rode to Camelot, I and he
> It was the time of Spring turned lover.
> A wind, caught in the greenery,
> Shredded with glancing shafts the cover.

William Morris is the strong influence and would not have despised these lines with their affecting cadences. These last are found elsewhere, as in the line, 'This year I have not heard the cuckoo call', where the conversational rhythm intensifies the sadness.

In 1887 Woods published *In Foreign Byeways: A Rhapsody of Travel*, a prose account of a holiday in Belgium and Germany with a friend

called Gallio. For the most part its sequence of descriptions and obser-
vations is conventional Victorian material. But it ends:

> . . . Gallio and I are slaves of the Ring; to-morrow we fall again
> beneath the spell of the tyrant whose name is Toil, and his twin
> whose name is Commonplace; and must fit ourselves to their
> measure, or look for ostracism and penury. Yet deep in our hearts
> we hide the diminished flame, and brood above it with memories
> of forest and mere; and, when again the summer grows and the
> spell relaxes, if we live so long, I know that the self-same ardour
> will drive us forth together into foreign byeways amid new
> scenes, —
>
> *"Strange faces, other minds."*

Despite the bookish allusions and the unexceptionable sentiments, the
plangent cadences and taut syntax movingly convey the sad pressure of
circumstances. In such a moment Woods is far more than just another
local writer succumbing to print.

Vivian A. Webber of Sketty also has such moments. His *Journal of a
Voyage Round Cape Horn* (1859), 'Printed for Private Circulation', is the
diary of a passenger sailing from Swansea:

> The magnificence of the "ocean billow" — the real, genuine
> "seas", can never be appreciated but by those who have seen
> them. No description and no painting can convey an idea of their
> enormous sweep. There is something peculiarly fresh, pure, and
> grand in their nature — very different to the tumultuous
> "waves" that are met with in arms of the sea. Each undulation
> obeys that first impulsive force of radiation which it has received
> from the wind.
>
> As to their inspiring us with awe, no doubt they do, but I must
> confess I do not feel humbled at sea. A ship is such a triumph of
> "mind over matter" — such a wondrous and exquisite piece of
> mechanism, so admirably adapted to man's use, that human
> nature appears to me to be dignified when I contemplate man,
> making the very elements subservient to him! And then again the
> infinity of space, harmonizing as it were, so gloriously with the
> unfathomable blue below us, the unknown depths of the one
> being "echoed" as it were by the unseen mysteries of the other —

the harmony of all, undisturbed by the inroads of man — surely these, and things like these, tend to spiritualize and elevate us.

The passage is typical of its time in its confidence in the self and in technological achievement, excited involvement in new experience, pre-Darwinian response to nature, and firm religious faith, expressed in clear, vigorous and occasionally poetic prose. Webber's account can stand for all the lost or forgotten diaries and jottings made in swinging hammocks or at shifting tables by sea-sick passengers or seamen struggling with their pens, and for the countless unexpressed feelings of inarticulate, often illiterate Cape Horners who sailed from Swansea through seas that drove them to the limits of skill and endurance and sometimes beyond. Webber's *Journal* reminds us of the irrecoverable part of Swansea's history.

So much local writing during the Victorian period is no more than escapist reaction, often privately printed and never widely read, to a grimier, smokier place. In the later part of the century, Woods apart, two writers, in particular, achieved slightly more.

The first is Samuel Clearstone Gamwell, the son of poor Hafod parents who became editor of *The Cambrian* newspaper. There he published most of his many verses, usually under the pseudonym of 'Pierre Claire', a witty use of his middle name. Gamwell is the local poet *par excellence*, writing prolifically on Swansea scenes, characters and events. Typical are 'At Singleton':

> The leafy park of sea-side Singleton
> Lay in the sunlight of as fair a sky
> As ever wooed the unreluctant earth
> And won her answering smile. Below, the beach —
> A semi-circle of some twenty miles
> Of yellow sand dunes and grey limestone rocks,
> Rugged and bold — with outstretched arms embraced
> That beauteous Bay which not unfitly claims
> To share the palm that favoured Naples holds.
> Behind, the shelt'ring ridge of Sketty Hills . . .

and 'St Gabriel's':

> Where Swansea widens to the west,
> And o'er the Rhyddings sweeps and swells,
> The gables of St. Gabriel's
> The people's piety attest . . .

The conventionally 'poetic' language is an obvious limitation. Another is a weakness for philosophizing: 'St. Gabriel's' becomes a debate about ways of worshipping and ends with a moral:

> "Dogmas breed doubt; 'the letter kills;'
> Hot zealotry can only ban;
> But love — true love of God and man,
> The world with light and beauty fills."

But Gamwell is more than a typical 'local bard' for two reasons. One is his humour, as in ' "Don't, Joe; Don't" ', where the activities of a courting couple in Cwmdonkin Park are described with Gilbertian vigour and a developing refrain:

> But I've sometimes heard an odder bird
> Sing: "No — I — won't!"
> (Then after a rustle, as if of a tussle):
> "Don't, Joe; don't!"

Secondly, from his best lines we can recapture the atmosphere of vanished Victorian Swansea, whether viewed from Sketty —

> White lie the roads in dust; the distant Town
> Looms on the backward vision like a hill
> Mantled in mist, now white, now grey, now brown

— or at night, when it lay ' 'neath a haze of sombre brown,/Lamp-dotted'.

E.A. ('Amy') Dillwyn (1845-1935) had a very different upbringing from Gamwell's in the Hafod. As the grand-daughter of Lewis Weston Dillwyn she grew up at Parkwern and Hendrefoilan as an eccentric, intelligent, independent, cigar-smoking spinster. Her novels were published by Macmillan; for ten years she reviewed for *The Spectator*, though it has to be said that her father, owner of Llansamlet's Spelter Works, was friendly both with Daniel Macmillan and Richard Holt Hutton, *The Spectator's* editor. Most of her novels have 'society' themes but her first, *The Rebecca Rioter* (1880), is an exciting tale centred on the attacks on the Pontarddulais tollgates in the early 1840s. Though marred by an alarming use of coincidence the novel has a strong narrative line and some vigorous dialogue; it also remains of interest because of Amy Dillwyn's use of the local *milieu* — the Bay is lyrically

Amy Dillwyn in 1904.

described, the villain dies in a bell-pit in Clyne Valley — and the evidence it supplies of the period's social attitudes. The working-class is treated paternalistically, to say the least, and as stage-Welshmen, whose 'look yous' and 'indeed to goodnesses' are accompanied by little correct grammar. A second novel apparently with a local setting, *Nant Olchfa* (1886), was serialized in the *Red Dragon,* but this rather bland, country-house tale could have taken place anywhere.

As for her reviewing, this was done with commonsense. Its highlight was a favourable notice of *Treasure Island* in 1884; as her biographer notes, 'she immediately recognized its classic quality'. So, of course, did other reviewers.

Gamwell was dead by the end of the century; Amy Dillwyn preoccupied with managing the Spelter Works after her father's death. During the first decade of the twentieth century there was a brief scholarly flurry when David Salmon, Principal of Swansea Training College, edited Bacon's essays and More's *Utopia.* Distinguished visitors came and went. W. H. Davies (1871-1940), in *The Autobiography of a Supertramp* (1908), set a record for the briefest reference to Swansea: 'I . . . tramped over the Welsh hills, day after day, ultimately finding my way to Swansea. I did not remain long in that town, but began other rambles . . .'. Edward Thomas (1878-1917) had stronger links, often staying with John Williams, headmaster of Waun Wen school. In 1914, in the *English Review,* he published an essay entitled 'Swansea Village', an early instance of the 'ugly-lovely' approach to the town. To Thomas, Swansea was 'a dirty witch. You must hate or love her, and I both hate and love her . . .'. It was a town of abrupt contrasts, of fascinating and 'sublime' industrial townscapes:

> They take you up on Townhill at night to see the furnaces in the pit of the town blazing scarlet, and the parallel crossing lines of lamps . . If it is always a city of dreadful day, it is for the moment at that distance a city of wondrous night.

Because of Thomas's later stature as a poet, even this minor essay helps re-establish Swansea as a distinct literary presence.

But through the first third of the twentieth century the spluttering torch was mainly carried by Woods, his wife, who wrote novels as 'Daniel Woodruffe', and the poet E. Howard Harris (1876-1961). The latter's titles tell all: *An Exile's Lute* (1919), *The Harp of Hiraeth* (1922), *Songs in Shot-silk* (1924). He is a late and overblown romantic who.

through a lifetime mainly spent away from Swansea, wrote nostalgically of his upbringing. His capacity for romantic transformation — the smoke stacks of Landore, for instance, transformed into the 'domes and minarets of Ispahan', surprised the young Dylan Thomas. Harris is an interesting example of a well-travelled and cultured man — he translated Finnish and Estonian poetry — who wrote as if the modern movement (and much else) had never been.

The 'golden age' of Swansea's literary history was from the 1930s into the 1960s. It began in 1906 in Maesteg with the birth of Vernon Watkins (1906-67). His father was a bank manager who moved to Swansea's Uplands when Watkins was aged seven. Four years later the boy left for boarding school, Cambridge for a year, and digs in Cardiff when a bank-clerk. A nervous breakdown returned him to the family home at Caswell, then at Pennard, where he also lived after his marrriage, and to a post in Lloyds Bank, St Helen's Road, which he left only on retirement. After 1913 he never lived permanently in the city; after 1927 at the end of every working day he withdrew to poetry and seascapes.

Those four happy childhood years in the Uplands, plus the fact that in his troubled young manhood the city served as refuge and strength,

At the Old B.B.C. Studio, The Grove, Swansea, October 1949. Standing: John Griffiths (Producer), Seated: (L. to R.) Vernon Watkins, John Prichard, Alfred Janes, Daniel Jones, Dylan Thomas.

help explain why Watkins's poetry idealizes Swansea. The key poem on that Uplands period is 'Elegy on the Heroine of Childhood: in memory of Pearl White', centred on watching films in the Uplands Cinema, to which Dylan Thomas went later:

> From school's spiked railings, glass-topped, cat-walked walls,
> From albums strewn, the streets' strange funerals,
> We run to join the queue's coiled peel
> Tapering, storming the Bastille,
> Tumbling, with collars torn and scattered ties,
> To thumbscrewed terror and the sea of eyes.

Of crucial importance in his developing concept of 'Swansea' was his friendship with Dylan Thomas, celebrated in 'A True Picture Restored: Memories of Dylan Thomas':

> I see the house where we would meet;
> I see my steps return,
> Kicking the sparks of the Swansea street,
> And still those windows burn . . .

Through Dylan Thomas, Watkins joined the Kardomah Café circle of writers and artists that met during the 'thirties. All memories and impressions combined in the superb *'Ode to Swansea'* to present the city, almost, as a latter-day Renaissance Florence:

> Prouder cities rise through the haze of time,
> Yet, unenvious, all men have found is here.
> Here is the loitering marvel
> Feeding artists with all they know.
>
> . . . the town . . .
> Nurtured under a rainbow,
> Pitched at last on Mount Pleasant hill

Such feelings made loss almost unbearable. The destruction of old Swansea in the air-raids of 1941 inspired some of his finest writing in 'The Broken Sea':

> Here, like Andersen's tailor, I weave the invisible thread.
> The burnt-out clock of St. Mary's has come to a stop,

And the hand still points to the figure that beckons the
  house-stoned dead.

Child Shades of my ignorant darkness, I mourn that moment alive
Near the glow-lamped Eumenides' house, overlooking the ships
  in flight,
Where Pearl White focussed our childhood, near the foot of
  Cwmdonkin Drive,
To a figment of crime stampeding in the posters' wind-blown
  blight.

I regret the broken Past, its prompt and punctilious cares,
All the villainies of the fire-and-brimstone-visited town.
I miss the painter of limbo at the top of the fragrant stairs,
The extravagant hero of night, his iconoclastic frown.

'Eumenides' house' is the Uplands cinema, a further reminder of the
abiding importance to Watkins of those four childhood years, the
painter Alfred Janes, whose studio was over a flower-shop in College
Street, the 'hero of night' Dylan Thomas. Swansea is recreated as a
vibrant cityscape of the imagination. For Watkins, who when he died
had an international reputation that has never been wholly lost and
will again increase, and who was a favourite for the Poet Laureateship
that went to Day-Lewis, was a modern metaphysical whose work
explored the conquest of time by memory or by the Christian belief in
immortality. Swansea becomes a powerful symbol of loss and of
inspiring memory.

Wynford Vaughan Thomas (1908-88) deserves a brief mention as a
fine war correspondent who later wrote lively topographical,
historical and autobiographical volumes. So does John Griffiths (1907-
80) of Treharris and then Uplands, a B.B.C. producer and writer,
whose *Griff and Tommy* (1956) and its sequel, delighted children.
Necessarily, they are both overshadowed by Dylan Thomas (1914-53),
who dominates Swansea's literary history through the stature of his
own work, its influence on contemporaries and successors, and
because he wrote his own version of part of this history in his articles
on 'The Poets of Swansea' in *The Herald of Wales*.

The details of his life are well-known. He was born at 5,
Cwmdonkin Drive; his mother was from St. Thomas, his father, born
in Johnstown, Carmarthen, was English master at Swansea Grammar
School. Thomas was brought up in the Uplands, educated privately in

At Rhosili, June 1940. Dylan Thomas, Swansea friends Wyn Lewis, Vernon Watkins.

Mirador Crescent, then at the Grammar School. In the 1930s he worked briefly as a journalist for the *South Wales Evening Post* and was the centre of the Kardomah Café circle that included, at various times, the artists Alfred Janes and Mervyn Levy, the composer Daniel Jones, Vernon Watkins, John Prichard, and Charles Fisher, the last two publishing poetry and prose during the 1930s that was much influenced by Dylan Thomas, before their early promise faded. In 1914 he left for London but soon returned. Thereafter he was frequently in the town.

As, away from Swansea, his life began to dissolve into chaos, Dylan Thomas came more and more to value his roots and to idealize Swansea with a desperate affection. In rebellious 1934 Swansea was 'this blowsy town . . . a dingy hell' and 'an overpeopled breeding box'; it soon became 'the best place', 'marble-town, city of laughter, little Dublin', a 'stained and royal town' and, famously, 'an ugly, lovely town . . . crawling, sprawling, slummed, unplanned, jerry-villa'd, and smug-suburbed by the side of a long and splendidly-curving shore'. A similar nostalgia is present in his 'Cwmdonkin' poem:

Once it was the colour of saying
Soaked my table the uglier side of a hill
With a capsized field where a school sat still
And a black and white patch of girls grew playing;
The gentle seaslides of saying I must undo
That all the charmingly drowned arise to cockcrow and kill.
When I whistled with mitching boys in a reservoir park . . .

The poem is permeated with the exact topography of Thomas's up-bringing, viewed from the window of 5 Cwmdonkin Drive. The 'uglier side' was the urban side of Townhill, where the Drive had been recently built; the school with its sloping field was Clevedon College; the park, of course, was Cwmdonkin, part of which was once a reservoir. These were the known, ordered surroundings of a happy, carefree childhood and of easier, more fluent composing of what he now regarded as 'gentle seaslides of saying', the image, suggesting boys bathing, stressing the spontaneous integration of poetry and life that he had once enjoyed.

Again, in 'The Hunchback in the Park', compassion for the hunch-back's plight is shot through with happy memories of Cwmdonkin days when

> the boys among willows
> Made the tigers jump out of their eyes
> To roar on the rockery stones
> And the groves were blue with sailors

The resemblance to Watkins is very marked: for both the town is at once a haven and a symbol of loss. In one of his greatest achievements, *Portrait of the Artist as a Young Dog* (1940), Thomas increases that symbol's complexity. Throughout his sequence of short stories Swansea is a strong presence and Thomas endows the topography of the pre-war town with thematic force. For his own Swansea was the town-centre and the bourgeois enclaves of the western suburbs; of the rest, such as Swansea East, he knew very little but imagined as a place of odd behaviour and sexual suggestiveness. In particular, he seized on the startling juxtaposition of the sordid and the respectable typified, in 'Old Garbo', by the proximity of the solid commercial heart of High Street, Wind Street and Temple Street, and the old Strand area of slums, sleazy pubs, and the sexual promise of a busy port. One moment the characters are in the 'Three Lamps' in Temple Street, 'in a prosperous house, out of the way of the rain and the unsettling streets', the next they 'crawled down Strand alleys by the side of the mortuary' on their way to the 'Fishguard Arms' in lower Wind Street. In 'One Warm Saturday' the young man and his pick-up drive from Swansea West to Swansea East and 'saw the town in a daze spin by them . . . the lightning lines of the poor streets growing longer . . . [as they] . . . tore past black houses and bridges'. In both stories the journeys are from order to chaos, marking the repeated sudden loss of an understood and controllable world, a recurring theme in many of his stories and poems and the tragic theme of his own life.

Since that life had few points of orderly reference Thomas treasured them. One was his once-despised middle-class, suburban upbringing. Thus, as with Vernon Watkins, when the bombs fell on Swansea in 1941 the experience was traumatic. His friend, Bert Trick, met him in the still-smoking ruins the day after the raids. 'Our Swansea is dead', said Thomas, and wept. *Return Journey*, broadcast in 1947 and later filmed, is an attempt to come to terms with that sudden destruction. It is an unavailing search for Kardomah-ed Swansea and earlier happiness that ends in Cwmdonkin Park with recollections of lost idyllic childhood and a despairing insistence on death.

Through his great fame and sustained literary reputation Dylan Thomas's Swansea is now part of a literary tradition that includes Dickens's London, Hardy's 'Wessex', and Joyce's Dublin. He has made it virtually impossible to separate the city from literary connotations.

In this he has been helped by John Ormond (b. 1923), a Dunvant man educated and later employed in the city. In 'City of Fire and Snow', Ormond also responds poetically to the 1941 bombing:

> Here buildings flowered red upon the air
> And here a street, inaccurate and pale,
> Lit but unconquered by the flame

and uses this Swansea as a powerful symbol of urban ruin in a poem more generally concerned with the effects of atomic warfare.

Also of Ormond's generation are three writers born and bred in the city. Harri Webb (b. 1920), only occasionally writes poetry about his Swansea upbringing, 'Cox's Farm', or Swansea jail, being one example. He has for long been more concerned with nationalist issues and the valley communities where he has spent his working life. Peter Hellings (b. 1921) has also spent most of his life-time away from his birthplace but, unlike Webb, has been drawn, more and more, to the poetic exploration of his own past, as in *A Swansea Sketchbook* (1983). Paul Ferris (b. 1929), well-known as an investigative reporter and as author of the standard biography of Dylan Thomas, is an accomplished novelist who, in *A Distant Country* (1983), presents Swansea as 'Vivianstown', a slightly distanced reaction to Welsh nationalist issues and the city of his youth.

The most important Swansea writer since the era of Vernon Watkins and Dylan Thomas is Kingsley Amis (b. 1922), a Londoner who lectured at University College of Swansea for a decade from 1949. Amis's second novel, *That Uncertain Feeling* (1955), charts the adventures of a librarian in a Swansea thinly disguised as 'Aberdarcy'. A year later came poems in *A Case of Samples* and, in 1967, in *A Look Around the Estate*, a sequence of poems called 'Evans Country'.

Amis's Swansea is mainly that of moneyed professional people, immoral, pretentious, vulgar and provincial, described from a superior,

Kingsley Amis.

ironically-mocking, metropolitan point of view. Thus, in *That Uncertain Feeling* he lists the patrons of a pub:

> an occasional grocer or butcher in his Yacht Club blazer and lavender trousers, a publican or two in subfusc accompanied by an ignorant doctor or two in sportive checks, the odd golfing-jacketed cinema-manager, café-owner or fish-shop proprietor . . .

As for Landor's Bay:

> an almost smooth sheet of yellowish rock running from the line of roof-tops hiding the beach to the docks over on the right, to the power-station at Tai-mawr, and, beyond the estuary, to the blast furnace at the Abertwit strip-mill, a fat red cylinder rising, so it seemed at this distance, from the surface of the water . . the narrow-waisted tanks of the Cambrio-Sudanese people, full, among other things, of the wherewithal for more dry Martinis, garden statuary and black cigarettes with gold tips.

Much of his attitude to Swansea is summed up in 'Aberdarcy: the Main Square', the first poem of 'Evans Country', which describes the Castle Gardens area of central Swansea:

> The journal of some bunch of architects
> Named this the worst town centre they could find;
> But how disparage what so well reflects
> Permanent tendencies of heart and mind?

Amis returned to a Swansea subject in *The Old Devils* (1986), his best-selling Booker Prize winner. Weather apart, Swansea has become a version of 'Costa Geriatrica' in a powerful and bleak study of old age. And yet, surprisingly, the book is strongly nostalgic, as Amis mocks many aspects of modern Swansea, the results of a thoughtless social and cultural vandalism. The supreme example is the Uplands Hotel, once beloved of Dylan Thomas, now turned into a garish and incoherent 'theme-pub', in which the customers sit under beach umbrellas on canvas chairs, surrounded by an old telephone kiosk, park railings, and painted shop-fronts. Yet, implicit in such satire is affectionate longing for, in Amis's case, the Swansea of the 1950s, when pubs were pubs, county halls county halls, and churches not yet arts centres or pornographic cinemas. He has become, perhaps despite himself, yet another writer whose lost Swansea was the golden one.

Amis apart, Swansea's modern literary history has three main aspects. A body of popular fiction has developed to which Alun Richards (b. 1929) has contributed. Richards's serious work is a considerable achievement but pays attention to his south Wales valley upbringing. His more 'commercial' work on the Mumbles boating world in *Ennal's Point* (1977), which acquired brief fame as the basis of a television series, was followed by a historical novel, *Barque Whisper* (1979), set in maritime Swansea in the nineteenth century. Iris Gower has also created a popular image of Swansea by using the history of coppermaking in Swansea as well-researched background for romantic historical fiction in the tradition of Richard Llewellyn and Alexander Cordell. Immense sales have been the result. On a smaller scale Edith Courtney has written popular, humorous, anecdotal books about life on Swansea's east side.

Courtney's stress on working-class Swansea is an unusual element in a literary history that has invariably reflected middle-class sensibilities (and has continued to do so in the poetry of J. P. Ward (b. 1937) and Peter Thomas (b. 1939) and the Swansea campus novel by Moira Dearnley (b. 1942)). The *serious* manifestation of changing social interests begins with Bryn Griffiths (b. 1933), whose poetry made its main mark in the 1960s. He was fascinated by the nightmarish landscape of the copper-making areas before reclamation:

> They are trying
> to erase the stain of the past,
> to seed earth soured by a century
> of slag and sulphur fumes,
> to heal the cankered sore that
> is today Landore.

and, reflecting his experiences as a merchant seaman. by the sea and sailors, principally in *The Dark Convoys* (1974). In this he is the heir to Vivian Webber in celebrating, at times over-romantically, the old Cape Horners and the lost days of sail, where as now

> the timbers of the dead ships
> grope like rotting fingers upwards, up,
> up and up through the river's scum

Graham Allen (b. 1938), Alan Perry (1942), John Beynon (b. 1943), and Peter Thabit Jones (b. 1951) are among those who have followed Griffiths in attending to the old East-side world and the problems of personal and community change. Of these Perry is a prize-winning writer who, particularly in *Live Wires* (1970), draws on his own experience of casual jobs to offer a city of cranes, dredgers, ship painters, scaffolders, welders, hospitals, that is alive, dynamic and sometimes beautiful:

> sparks fly
> in the night sky
> cold sparks that spin
> and waterfall
>
> torches shine
> rods burn between
> the night's thin backcloth

Lastly come the supporting players: the historians, scholars, literary critics, and philosophers at the University College, the publisher Christopher Davies, now permanently based in the city, the newspapers and occasional magazines, the Association of Bookmen that flourished for some years after World War II, extra-mural classes, workshops and writers' circles, and the library service augmented by a fine university collection at Singleton.

All Swansea's literary roads lead to Dylan Thomas and his work articulates most powerfully the main concerns of this history. For Swansea-born writers rarely desert the place even if they have to leave it. Many others have settled in the town-become-city, or retreated to it, as did Savage, Combe, Landor, Prichard and Watkins, or re-imagined it as Landor also did, and Watkins, Thomas, and Amis after him. Few who actually came failed to find either happiness, contentment, or sufficient inspiration. Those who returned via the creative imagination have invariably recreated, for us as for themselves, a rain-bowed world, a 'golden clime', of potent artistic persuasiveness and 'Swansea' as a dynamic literary symbol. This has been achieved, to return to Dylan Thomas, with the affection verging on love that came to dominate *his* famous writings on his birth-place. The result is a literary history of which many larger cities would be proud: rich, varied, studded with fine achievements and, best of all, unfinished.

Chapter 9

THE ENTERTAINMENT OF THE PEOPLE

Peter Stead

The city of Swansea encircles Townhill, a feature that elsewhere would almost certainly be topped by a major fortification or even a religious statue, but which here just offers modest houses and a magnificent view in all directions. It is always the horizon which first takes the eye. To the north and east there is the distant splendour of the Welsh hills: the Black Mountains, the Brecon Beacons and the Glamorgan moorlands; only slowly and reluctantly is one's attention drawn to the foreground and to an undulating landscape, obviously much faulted, folded and altered, and covered with what are unmistakably the homes of working people. There are some signs of industry but rather it is the freshly grassed sites of former activity and the general aspect of abuse which suggest that this was once a great industrial and metallurgical centre. To the south it is the huge saucer of enclosed sea that dominates, quite eclipsing the immediate foreground of the harbour, of the city centre squeezed between the hill and the beach, and the leafier suburbs stretching westward to Gower. The temptation is always to think of the desecration of the landscape but then one begins to note the details: the places of worship with their spires, the presence of theatres and parks, numerous playing fields, yachting in the bay, and, most spectacularly of all when viewed from that Townhill vantage-point, the centrality of what the accompanying stands would suggest are two major sports grounds. All in all it would seem that this hilly seaside town had once been an important place of manufacture but one developed by a population that had tried to make something of their lives. Certainly the historian needs to emphasize the importance of Swansea in the development of metals, visitors will recall their surprise in discovering one of the most scenically dramatic of Britain's industrial towns, but perhaps what local people would choose to remember and celebrate most was the way in which they had been entertained.

During the second half of the eighteenth century the population of Swansea doubled as the old medieval town became increasingly important as a centre for the manufacture of metals and as a port. In 1800, the small town with its population of 6000 was still in the early stages of an even greater transformation that would make it internationally famous, but already the local pattern of social interaction had determined what were to be distinctive and enduring traits. Those very decades in which Swansea was first realizing its industrial potential were a crucial period in determining the nature of the social and economic élite that would dominate nineteenth-century Britain and, already, the town was benefiting from the emergence of a distinctive pattern of local leadership and from the way in which those leaders had cultivated certain notions of how their community should develop. It was a period which saw the emergence of a gentry that existed in two worlds, an 'amphibious' class in Michael Thompson's phrase, that earned much of its money in industry and yet which at home chose to live like traditional aristocrats. That domestic lifestyle, however, now tended to include a cultivation of the arts that might have greatly surprised earlier generations of bucolic squires. In the late eighteenth century many landed families and many of the newer industrial gentry had begun a pursuit of literary, artistic, and athletic excellence and, in particular, began to associate these pursuits with seasons spent at small urban spas and resorts where facilities could be centralized. These organized opportunities for recreation and pleasure became all the more important during the thirty years or so after 1790 when the playground of Europe was cut off by war and revolution. What was remarkable about Swansea was that the juxtaposition of traditional estates, new industry, and magnificent scenery helped to create a talented local gentry whose interests were more than usually urban and from their essentially suburban big houses they were well able to appreciate the adjacent town's potential as a spa. And so it happened that at the very moment industrial lift-off was taking place a group of local leaders was pressing ahead with its plans to make Swansea into what one newspaper described as 'the Brighton of Wales'. That was an apt term, although it is perhaps rather more useful and accurate to think of Swansea as having been specifically planned as the next centre of civilization beyond Bath, Gloucester and Bristol. Prompted and sponsored by the local gentry, municipal leaders decided to make Swansea fashionable and to a remarkable extent the subsequently larger and more democratic town was always to retain in its cultural life a flavour of that original eighteenth-century impulse.

The Theatre Royal, Temple Street, c. 1891.

It is not difficult to see that people would want to live in style and to play well around the delightful Swansea Bay; what is somewhat surprising is that from the very beginning it was the existence of live theatre that became the hallmark of Swansea's fashionability. Throughout the period there were theatrical evenings at the homes of local gentry but as early as 1785 their patronage had led to the opening of Swansea's first theatre. For almost a generation thereafter, that theatre in Wind Street and then the New Theatre in Temple Street, which had opened in 1807, allowed both residents and visitors alike to enjoy performances of quality as good as any to be seen in the land. Managers and actors trained in London, Bath and Bristol had come to accept Swansea as a vital link in the national theatrical network. The greatest and most charismatic actor of the day, Edmund Kean, gave Swansea a Hamlet and a Richard III to remember and in so doing inaugurated what was to be a remarkable tradition in which many of the finest nineteenth-century actors forged strong artistic and emotional links with the town. Throughout its modern history Swansea has been able to recall theatrical triumphs, and later that would help to inspire those who had to struggle to keep things going in more difficult days. From the outset the theatre, like so many other urban pastimes, was always to be effectively managed and presented by a class of professional showmen. The audiences that they attracted tended to be mixed, for there were always some shopkeepers, sailors and even workers who welcomed entertainment, but in the years before 1830 it was always the patronage of the gentry that guaranteed continued success. What was true of the theatre was to be equally true of all those facilities and activities that made the town into a resort, whether it was dancing, sea-bathing, or the use of the assembly rooms, the circulating libraries, the pleasure gardens and walkways. Through their tutelage, the local 'quality' had created a new urban alliance which often stood in opposition to older Dissenting and conservative traditions and which now emphasized that a town could be a place of enjoyment and recreation. Throughout decades of changes and upheaval that patrician notion of urban pleasure was always there as a model.

Certainly at their balls, but even when at the theatre or sitting in sea water, the gentry would expect to be largely in the company of their own kind, but there were aspects of the new urban culture in which the traditional role of the squire was more obviously put on display for a larger audience. The hunt had always been the perfect rural entertainment as it functioned on so many levels: it had a specific and necessary object, it ensured the retention of equestrian skills, it provided exercise, and it allowed the leaders of society both to lay claim to their feudal rights and to display openly their social power, even as they insisted on either the participation or acquiescence of the peasants. In some areas the hunt was already becoming an anachronistic flourish but in so many ways it set the tone of the newer forms of recreation that were now being taken up by the more urban gentry of the post-industrial revolution period. The pattern was still one in which utility, and open displays of skill, power, and prestige could be accompanied by a carefully controlled participation of the lower orders within some kind of festival format. At the height of its fashionability it was the races that saw Swansea at its most festive and which allowed the pleasure of the rich and the recreation of the crowd to coincide most successfully. Later attempts to hold races in Swansea always seemed rather sad affairs; but those who remembered the great meetings that were held at Crymlyn Burrows in the early nineteenth century stressed their splendour and the way in which crowds of fashionable visitors intermixed with the locals who had used the ford or the ferry to cross from the town. It was inconceivable that Swansea could have held these race meetings without the sponsorship of the gentry; but perhaps it was a little more surprising that it took those same families to indicate the pleasures that could be developed on Swansea Bay itself. At race meetings and regattas alike, as David Boorman has shown, local athleticism could be encouraged by the offer of cash prizes and yet at the same time the whole occasion would be one in which the indispensability of the gentry's role within the culture would be advertised. The races were to die away but the rowing and yachting traditions were to survive, and it is no accident that almost two centuries later the town's most prestigious gentlemen's club was a yacht club and that its commodore should be the duke of Beaufort, whose local landholdings had always been extensive and whose ancestors, after some initial reluctance, had been patrons of nearly all recreational endeavour in the town from the reign of George III onwards.

Archery was another pastime in which leading families like the Vivians would combine their own recreation with festive embellishments such as dinners, balls, and military bands. There were always to be what the local press would invariably describe as toxophilites in Swansea; but not surprisingly, theirs was not to become a mass sport and neither did its later rival, rifle-shooting, at which activity a latterday Lord Swansea was to represent his country. There was one sport, however, which once made fashionable by the gentry was never to lose its place in the affections of the people and that was cricket. This ageold game of the common people was taken up nationally by the gentry in those vital decades of the 1770s and 1780s, as it was increasingly appreciated that the sport was one in which a gentleman could display power and style in hitting a ball at the same time as he developed leadership skills in co-ordinating the more robust efforts of local lads who could bowl, chase, catch, and throw. The earliest cricket in the area was probably played at Crymlyn Burrows, but it is appropriate that locally the game was to find its real and permanent home on sandy ground at St Helen's near the beach, on one of the most desirable of the local estates. Since the early years of the nineteenth century it was teams selected and led by various local gentlemen, or from amongst the military and yeomanry, that had kept cricket going in Swansea, and now in the 1840s it was the preparation of a wicket on Colonel Llewellyn Morgan's land in the St Helen's area of the town that marked the moment when the game was on its way to becoming a local passion. The passion for golf came later and, perhaps from the very beginning, was associated more with local industrialists and businessmen seeking diversion from affairs at the metal exchange but, as local clubs were formed, it was always to the gentry that committees turned for leadership and support. The Langland Bay Golf Club was formed in 1904 with Sir John Jones Jenkins (later to be Lord Glantawe) as President; the Clyne Golf Club came later in 1920 but could boast of the patronage and support of the duke of Beaufort. In sport as in the arts the people of Swansea were always aware of the aristocratic and gentry lead that had first stimulated recreation in the locality and on many occasions they seemed eager to retain it. In the town's fashionable era its leading families had channelled energies into specific organized activities and in so doing had shaped an agenda for an expanding industrial town. Without knowing all the details of the history, later generations of play-goers, concert-attenders, and sportsmen seemed to look back to an earlier age as they drew up their lists of patrons and even more perhaps in the ways in which they assumed that their very participation in these activities gave them something of the distinction that had once belonged exclusively to the wealthy. Echoes of that eighteenth-century fashionability continued to sound in a late twentieth-century Swansea, where the prevailing notion of urban style still owed a little to an earlier gentry.

The age of fashionable urban pastimes and seasonal resorts had to a certain extent withered away in the 1820s and 1830s as so many aristocrats and landowners now felt safe to return to the European playground. In any case the first decades of peace had made it clear that within Britain itself there were massive new problems involving the control and discipline of greatly increased urban and rural populations. Inevitably, the day-to-day question of ordering life within communities passed to a wider group of industrialists and managers and began to necessitate social planning on an altogether unprecedented scale. Towns were now 'the barracks of industry', and the greatest urban imperatives seemed those of maximizing work and minimizing disorder. In every aspect of life, routine discipline was the order of the day and in almost every respect urban culture began to reflect the strict sense of utility and personal preferences of businessmen, their commercial and clerical assistants, and their foremen and skilled workers. Even at the height of its fashionability Swansea had offered visitors quite close glimpses of industry but now industry and its needs had entirely taken over both in the vicinity of the harbour and in the valley that formed its hinterland. Priority now had to be given to manufacture and transportation and, of course, to housing the new crowds of industrial workers. Recreation was no longer the hallmark of distinction, it could only be a peripheral diversion.

The old traditions of entertainment were never entirely to be eclipsed, for gentlemen were still able to sustain their own chosen recreations and there were always aspiring families eager to participate. In cultural matters, however, the initiative passed to that class of showmen who had sprung up at the gentry's behest and who now had to struggle to detect those pleasure-loving families that had lived on into a bleaker age. The pattern in Swansea was one in which travelling showmen and actor-managers would come to the town to experience mixed fortunes, as the trade cycle and the fluctuating tone of local industrial relations and religious life interfered with audiences who had thus become notoriously unreliable. In any one year Swansea patrons would be offered Shakespeare and the latest melodramas as well as the very best exponents of Italian opera, but it was undeniable now that the arts had become a mere sub-culture and a somewhat dubious one at that. Once again, theatre had become associated with drink and promiscuity; and to many it appeared that the showmen who offered *Hamlet* and *La Sonnambula* were not much better than those who put up booths and tents in order to present exotic wild animals, magicians, acrobats, and human freaks. The authorities appreciated that there would always have to be entertainments for what we can think of as 'the down-town set' and that there would need to be occasions when a certain degree of popular carnival could be tolerated, as prize-fights, race-meetings, circuses, and even public executions were organized, but there was no mistaking the prevailing attitudes that all these matters were now regarded as essentially worthless and ephemeral. The Victorians did not need a popular culture for they had replaced it with religion.

To Marx and Engels and their disciples the chief and obvious characteristic of nineteenth-century Christianity was the way in which the discipline, regularity, seriousness, and fellowship it encouraged so precisely coincided with the qualities which most suited and benefited employers. From this viewpoint, faith and devotion allowed exploitation, even as they contributed to a new cultural bleakness that was the very essence of industrial civilization. The notion that the good Christian was the best worker is one which needs to be contemplated, but the trouble with the Marxist generalization is that it misses so much of the fluid and dynamic process of change that was going on in early and mid nineteenth-century society. Quite apart from the danger of doubting the validity of religious experience, Marxists tend to avoid the point that, in any case, life in factories and crowded towns was always going to need effective new constraints, and what was so gratifying was that Christianity provided a discipline in which matters of class and relative wealth could be by-passed, in which there were elements of self-developed democracy, in which family values were stressed, and in which there was as much emphasis on both contemplation and self-expression as on inhibition. Organized religion had many positive aspects, and it should always be remembered that, whatever the advantage to employers of a virtuous workforce, one of the great social and historic values of the denominations was the way in which they kept people, and especially young people, away from the drink and sex that flourished in towns. 'Swansea is a very wicked place', claimed one magistrate in mid-century, and the historian, W. C. Rogers, has documented the extent to which he was right. The citizens of Swansea were not the first to discover that manual labour and sea voyages created appetites, and in this instance it seems as if over 300 public houses and 300 prostitutes were needed to satisfy the demand. As social and religious leaders looked in detail at how sections of the labour force lived their lives they found much that they could condemn, from both the moral and physical standpoint. We should never underestimate the extent to which religious fervour was rooted in a desire to save young people from a hell that was all too real in the slums and on the waterfront of the Victorian town. Religion was indispensable in establishing a very necessary respectability and responsibility in the wicked city. It had done that first by emphasizing submission, then by stressing self-discipline, and finally by encouraging a balanced mix of activities in which the recreational and cultural took their place alongside the devotional. More recently, revisionist historians like Joyce and Hargreaves have conceded that the hegemony of religious organizations did not preclude entertainment. Inevitably, the churches had to cater for the variety of energies and talent that had been delivered into them.

Music, in particular, had become the hand-maiden of popular

Victorian religion. In the era of fashionability the gentry had valued musical accomplishment, and whilst in the new Victorian dispensation dance and musical theatre needed to be relegated to the showmen's world, the acceptability of individual musical skills had not entirely faded and found an honoured place within the home and increasingly within the church and chapel as well. From the gentry, the middle class took the notion that the piano was an essential object within any respectable home. At the same time, the enthusiasm that went into hymn-singing could be developed into a choral tradition that started within individual churches and then burst out into a more popular pattern, in which festivals and the performance of oratorios quite eclipsed anything the showmen had to offer. To read about the mid-Victorians is to sense the way in which, within the conventions of respectability, the enthusiasms, energies and skills of the population were always bursting through. It was this which encouraged the leaders of the business world and sections of the gentry to become increasingly patrons of quasi-religious festivals, in which the emphasis on serious matters and self-improvement did not rule out entertainment. The National Eisteddfod of Wales came to Swansea in 1863 and as an event it was to illustrate very neatly the ways in which, after a period of fragmentation, a new social alliance in which the leaders of local society and commerce worked with denominational officers and scholars in promoting activities that both entertained and added lustre to the image of the town.

Many commercial leaders had hitherto been antagonistic to the National Eisteddfod, which they thought of as being too narrowly and provincially concerned with archaic Welsh-language modes; but in 1863 nobody doubted that there had been what *The Cambrian* described as a 'rapprochement of the two languages'. Furthermore, there was ample evidence that the festival was showing enormous potential as a meeting place for all the most admired and influential groups within the urban and rural society. Patronage came from the top, but much of the organization and adjudication came from the rapidly developing class of educated and self-taught clergymen and scholars. More crucially, the event was popular. Press advertisements announced that excursion trains would bring the crowds and that in the huge pavilion, which had seats for 7,000, admission prices would run from 3s. 6d. down to one shilling. That the four days of activity belonged to the populace was a matter of great pride. It was emphasized that the 400-strong choir was indeed 'a real people's chorus made up of workers in the mine, in the forge, on the farm' and one participant commented on how there had been a coming together of 'the brawny puddler, the swarthy collier, the gentle lady ever lapped in luxury, the finished parliamentary orator and mitred prelate'. There was more than a little rhetoric and hyperbole of this kind but we need not doubt the popularity of the occasion, for the recruiting of the choir and the filling of the pavilion proved that point decisively. A useful note of prosaic reality, however, was sounded in a letter to the press from a grocer's assistant who served as a representative of the 'Tradesman's Assistants of Swansea': few members of this particular body would attend, it was argued, unless a general holiday was declared for one of the four days.

On each of those four days the Eisteddfod's programme of competitions was followed by public concerts in which distinguished soloists joined with the choir of 400 and 'a band of harps' to perform both old melodies of Wales and more recently composed cantatas. A local critic writing as *Athenaeum* regretted that heavy reliance 'on so few tunes' that was to become the bane of Welsh musical culture, but that did not prevent him from seeing that the Eisteddfod was in the process of becoming really worthwhile musically. One wonders how he responded some six weeks later when the local Eisteddfod Committee arranged for the pavilion to be used for a concert performance of that most popular of all nineteenth-century operas, Gounod's *Faust*, followed inevitably by a programme of miscellaneous pieces, all performed by a company from Her Majesty's Theatre, London. Clearly there was an audience for some good music and obviously there were some civic leaders who welcomed that, but nevertheless, later historians can only feel frustrated by the tendency for Victorian prejudice and restrictions to prevent a more total and sustained commitment to the organization of musical and theatrical events along the lines organized by the Eisteddfod. In that very same week of the Eisteddfod the popular tragedian, Charles Pitt, had been offering Hamlet, Othello and Macbeth to satisfactorily sized audiences at the Theatre, although the company manager, Wybert Reeve, ended his generally successful season by reflecting on how expenses had prevented the fulfilment of his 'pecuniary expectations'. The drama, he reminded his faithful supporters, 'is a great instrument of either good or evil in the education of a people' and it remained his intention to make Swansea's Theatre 'a fitting home for the drama — a place where a husband could bring his wife, or a father his daughter'. As Reeve's company departed, the Theatre prepared itself for the visit of the Lyric Opera Company from Covent Garden with its productions of *La Traviata* and *The Quaker*. An earlier age had bequeathed Swansea an actual theatre, and at a time when there were very few places either in London or the provinces where opera could legally or technically be staged, the two or three London companies were still prepared to take their chance in a prosperous industrial town where a degree of refinement had lingered on. It cost only 6*d.* to sit in the gallery to listen to Verdi but obviously there would not be 7,000 queuing up for that opportunity as there had been earlier for the band of harps. What entertainment the churches had sanctioned was now on its way to becoming a mass culture, whereas the older pattern of secular entertainment remained a sub-culture for those who adhered to a more cosmopolitan urban style. In a later age there would be those historians who would have chosen to take their place not at the Eisteddfod or at the opera but rather with those more ordinary people who would have gone during that hectic Swansea August to see that internationally acclaimed illusionist, Herr Horace Henri, 'the Greatest Wizard of the Age', or Jem Mace's Circus. Those who feel nostalgic for more democratic forms of popular culture, however, should note that the reporter who opted for the circus found 'a real paucity of horses', 'wretched riding', 'unworthy clowns' and in general entertainment of 'the most indifferent description'. Mid-Victorian citizens of Swansea were indeed paying their money and taking their choice.

If Swansea citizens of the late twentieth century could be magically taken back to that mid-Victorian town that had welcomed the National Eisteddfod they would find much that was familiar in the way that people were entertained, but as yet the community was only slowly moving towards what were perhaps to be the two most crucial developments in the shaping of a truly modern popular culture. The first of these decisive innovations came in the way in which the often struggling and frustrated theatrical showmen realized that an increasingly working-class audience required that the programme of often quite exaggerated classical acting and opera be filled out not only with the by-now standard fare of melodrama but also with that burlesque and variety that had hitherto been associated with booths. This popularization of the theatre was a bowing to the inevitable but it also reflected a greater indulgence on the part of Parliament as to what could be allowed to be performed in legitimate theatres. Nationally there was a brief mushrooming of what were now called music rooms or halls before the stricter regulations re-introduced in 1878 forced these halls to become truly theatres rather than drinking saloons. Swansea benefited as much as any town from the encouragement now being given to showmen, and musical and variety acts became increas-

The Albert Hall, 1929.

ingly the staple fare of the Music Hall opened in 1864 (renamed the Albert Hall in 1881), the Star Amphitheatre of 1869, and the Pavilion Music Hall, which opened in December 1888 with entertainment of 'a decidedly high-class character'. The opportunities and the difficulties now confronting showmen can perhaps be best appreciated by the remarks of the Pavilion's manager who, on opening night, stressed that his actors, jugglers, acrobats, and comedians, both Irish and negro, were of the highest standard and that 'nothing would appear which would offend the most fastidious'. The local reporter came to his help by casually noting that the opening had been attended by 'some of the best known local families'. As always, entertainment had to been seen to be arbitrated and sanctioned by the local social élite.

Of these new developments by far the most genuinely popular was undoubtedly the opening and then gradual transformation of the Star in Wind Street. At first it was merely a competitor to the old Theatre, in that it offered high tragedy and great acting, but then after 1871, when both halls were in the same hands, the Theatre was effectively closed, a fate that was temporarily to befall the Music Hall and for the same reason. The father and son team of George and Andrew Melville (the latter invariably referred to as 'Emm') were concentrating on making the Star into a venue really beloved by local audiences, with programmes of musical acts and cut-throat melodrama performed by the 'Landore Linnets' and 'Cwmbwrla Cuckoos'. Emm's legacy was to live on into the first years of the twentieth century in the hands of Billy Coutts, remembered by George Long as 'the doyen of Swansea showmen', who retained the format of variety, melodrama, and touring opera companies at the Star, even as he pioneered the bioscope and film in four other local halls. The demand for down-town entertainment was now so great that Swansea was to be given two further theatres, both of which survived to be venues which offered much that was best in the twentieth-century town. The Grand opened in 1897 and was to experience what were undoubtedly its finest moments as early as 1903 and 1905, when Sir Henry Irving, the greatest actor of the day and the man who more than anybody else had persuaded the middle class that theatre could be respectable, gave performances that elicited quite remarkably emotional responses from capacity audiences. The 1905 tour had been announced as his last, and as the final curtain fell at the Grand, the entire audience followed the lead of a man in the gallery and rose to sing 'Lead Kindly Light'. At the time of Sir Henry's visits there were still clergymen like the Rev. Talbot Rice fulminating against the stage, but it mattered little now, and there was widespread pleasure that the 1903 company's leading lady, Miss Mabel Hackney, was indeed a Swansea girl and that the local appreciation of fine acting which had been created by Edmund Kean in the eighteenth century, and which was sustained by Sheridan Knowles, W. C. Macready and George Melville, had now been carried into a new century by Sir Henry himself and by the much respected Mr and Mrs Kendal, who in 1903 had followed the great knight into the Grand.

Some 90 years later the Grand was still going strong, but in all honesty it must be admitted that as a theatre it was never loved by the people of Swansea in the way that the Empire had been. The Empire was opened in 1900 by that great showman, Sir Oswald Stoll, who,

starting from a base in Cardiff, went on to develop the Moss Empire
Company with halls in London and the provinces. The Empire was
meant to be a showpiece and a money-spinner. The crowds paid their
money to see top variety acts and on admission they found themselves
in an Italian Renaissance world of red plush, electric lights and
polished brass. Popular musical theatre and variety had come of age in
Swansea and, on opening night, Lady Morris of Sketty Hall and many
other prominent townspeople were there in the boxes and circle
dressed in their silk skirts and satin bodices. Significantly, it was once
again stressed that there was nothing here to which 'prudish women
could possibly take exception'. That could well have been so, but not
infrequently there were bizarre happenings at the Empire: for
example in 1914 when Fred Dyer, the Welsh baritone-boxer, gave a
'Selection of Songs and Ballads from an Extensive and Exclusive
Repertoire' and then proceeded to fight exhibition bouts with
specially selected opponents and volunteers. Come what may, there
was always the promise of 'top-notch entertainment' and, con-

The Grand Theatre, opened 1899.

The Palace Theatre (later The People's Bioscope Palace), c. 1906.

Oxford Street, showing the Empire Theatre and Carlton Cinema, c. 1930.

sequently, in Swansea variety had found a home that allowed it to compete with the new force of the cinema. The Empire survived until the 1950s, by which time it had inspired the career of Sir Harry Secombe, one of Swansea's most popular sons. The St Thomas lad had loved the Empire and the very title of his later autobiographical novel, *Twice Brightly*, evoked the guarantee that the old theatre had striven to fulfil.

In the last decades of the nineteenth century it was the showmen who had been responsible for the first act of transformation towards a fuller and more popular round of organized entertainment, but the second and more significant transformation was essentially inspired by a handful of the nation's great public schools. In a development that was eventually to change the nature of modern industrial society these public schools had begun to play the games that had for centuries been played solely and largely spontaneously by peasant youth. Cricket led the way as it had already been fashionable for a generation or so, but from the 1840s, the two kinds of football, soccer and rugby, were added and were now organized according to newly codified rules and entirely associated with the kinds of athletic prowess and energy, team loyalty and co-operation, initiative and risk-taking, elegance and style that defined those true Christian gentlemen who were being trained to be the rulers of the world. In the decades that followed, public schools *alumni* took this new version of chivalry into the towns and villages of the land, and indeed of the Empire. There, they found a more open-minded generation of employers and clergymen eager to encourage physical recreation amongst workers who had been trained into group activity by urban life and were now looking for things to do in their leisure hours. Cricket, rugby and soccer teams came into being wherever there was an enthusiastic landowner, vicar, headmaster, solicitor, or industrialist. At first, villages, or cathedral or school towns were as likely to have teams as the larger cities where working-

The Plaza Cinema, Kingsway, opened 1931.

The Regatta at Mumbles,
1929.

class housing predominated, but it was inevitable that urban sport would develop, especially in places like Swansea where there was a tradition of following the gentry lead. The town had a cricket team by 1850 and a soccer team by 1872, both of them playing at Colonel Morgan's sandy field at St Helens. Within a few dramatic years, the Football Club switched from the association to the fifteen-man rugby code, Colonel Morgan's field was bought and an amalgamated Swansea Cricket and Football Club came into existence. The take-off into sustained and well-organized activity had only been made possible by the degree of class cooperation. As Andrew Hignell has shown, the sportsmen were only able to block the development of the whole St Helens area for commercial housing projects through the financial support of Lewis Llewellyn Dillwyn MP and, as the whole sporting facility developed, the donations from Sir J. T. D. Llewellyn, the squire of Penllergaer, were absolutely vital. The players, of course, came from every kind of background, but organization, administration, and leadership, both on and off the field, were nearly always in the hands of educated professional gentlemen; those clergymen, solicitors, teachers, and aspiring businessmen, who modelled themselves on the gentry and who made up what John Hargreaves has described as 'a subaltern class'.

There was something delightful about the social mix and, throughout the decades, it was to remain the essence of both games played at St Helens. The public-school types, with those accents that seemed to carry so well, recruited the grammar-school boys in their blazers and also the talented working youths from the mill and the mine. Nowhere did the professional and clerical classes of the Uplands, Sketty, and Mumbles so clearly display their refined emotionalism as on that sun-drenched terrace that faced the cricket-square and the sea. Years later, the journalist, Alan Watkins, was to comment on how, as a boy, he was always struck by the predominance of smart caps, overcoats, and gloves in the St Helens rugby stand, as compared to other west Wales venues. It was mostly workers, though, who provided the entertainment. In particular, there were the James Brothers, those Welsh-Jewish copper workers from St Thomas, who in the 1890s 'played like squirrels' behind their pack and who, in the brilliant evocation of David Smith and Gareth Williams, performed like clowns, 'jackanapes', as they set out to win matches and to enchant increasingly larger crowds. Perhaps the most symbolic figure of the age was the man who was to become the first of the town's sporting legends: W. J. (Billy) Bancroft, born into a family that had long shown its skills at playing cricket for and against the gentry. His grandfather had become the groundsman at St Helens, and it was the cottage that went with the position which provided the base for the young star whose career so fully reflected the transformation that was affecting organized sport. It was later claimed that the diminutive full-back could kick conversions from anywhere, including the corner flag, with his eyes open or closed. Whatever the truth he was clearly respected, for he captained his club and held a secure position in the Welsh national team. Meanwhile, his cricketing skills enabled him in 1895 to become the Glamorgan County Cricket Club's first professional, the recipient of a salary that was almost entirely paid by the gentry. The prowess of Billy Bancroft was recognized as an essential component of sporting success in Swansea and in Wales generally, and officials were delighted that the groundsman's job and cottage at St Helens gave the star player a guarantee of security at a time when competition was very definitely hotting up.

What was remarkable about these popular sports was the rapidity

Victoria Park and St Helen's Rugby and Cricket Ground.

with which the formation of a club took officials and players into a larger world, for soon, fixture lists were standardized and bureaucracy swollen, as committees and boards of control and regulation were formed. The initial strength of both cricket and rugby in the Swansea area was that they had become village games and thus allowed rivalry between communities such as Gowerton and Briton Ferry, Bonymaen and Waunarlwydd; but very soon, what caught the attention of the press and potential spectators was a wider pattern of rivalry, first between the south Wales towns and then between the nations of the United Kingdom and the Empire. Within a remarkably short period of time, organized sport had taken the town out of a mid-Victorian anonymity, that all its economic and industrial significance had never really overcome, and given it a new and honoured place within the context of the region, the nation, and the Empire. The official historians of rugby in Wales emphasize the honourable role that

Swansea played in the emergence of the Welsh rugby union and they thought it not inappropriate that the first rugby international match ever played in Wales saw the English team travel to St Helens in December 1882. In 1888 the New Zealand touring team came to St Helens to play both Wales and the Swansea club, and in the years before 1914 the national sides of England, Scotland, Ireland, France, New Zealand, and South Africa all appeared before the Swansea public and there were also several club fixtures against touring sides. The Swansea cricket team was usually engaged in fierce competition against neighbouring teams, like Gowerton and Neath; but one senses the enormous pleasure that local enthusiasts like Sir J. T. D. Llewellyn of Penllergaer must have taken in the formation of a County Cricket Club in 1888, in that first game against Warwickshire played at St Helens in that same summer, and in the club's subsequent minor county fixtures. In all of these developments there was a sense of the town

Crowd Scene at St Helen's Ground, early 1950s.

taking an honoured place in a universally appreciated Anglo-Saxon culture and, as individual athletes were acclaimed, so local officials and administrations began to bask in the kind of cosmopolitan distinction that had previously been reserved exclusively for the gentry. The sense was always that of opportunities opening up and of the town taking its place on a genuinely international stage, though these new horizons did not preclude the nourishing of already existing provincial and parochial jealousies. The deep determination to defeat the English and the New Zealanders could never rival the hostility felt towards the players, and more especially the supporters, from Llanelli. The All Whites and the Scarlets first met at Felinfoel in 1876 and, at the time of writing, the records indicate that of the total of 328 games now played the Scarlets have won 145 and the All Whites 143, although it is more pleasurable to reflect on those early years before 1914 when Llanelli only managed to win 28 out of 117 games. It might surprise the partisan to know that almost nothing has changed in the relationship between the towns since those earliest rugby and cricket fixtures. In a 1903 cricket match the Swansea Second XI beat Llanelli but only after the Swansea umpire had no-balled the Llanelli captain for throwing. The local reporter appealed for fresh umpires to be found for this fixture and hoped for 'peace and good fellowship' in place of 'the old smouldering fire'. That of course was never to be. The rivalry was always largely a question of size and function. The small-towners from Llanelli always resented what they thought of as social pretension at St Helens, just as in turn the talent of Swansea players and the justifiable pride of Swansea officials somehow always seemed to be somewhat inhibited when confronted by the confidence of Cardiff, even in those years before 1914.

Until the mid-Victorian years soccer and rugby had shown very similar histories but thereafter they took root as popular games in slightly different patterns, so that one game remained an amateur one administered by that 'subaltern class' of professional gentlemen eager for respectability within the Empire, whilst the other became a professional sport controlled in the main by industrial employers, businessmen and their clerks. The one great variation and complication in that pattern came in the way in which the industrial circumstances in northern industrial towns led to a rugby break-away and the emergence of a new professional form of that sport. As we have seen, the initial impulse at St Helens was to play football according to the association code but the switch was soon made to rugby. In their official history, David Smith and Gareth Williams stress that what really accounted for the popularity of rugby in south Wales was the proximity of schools and communities to the border English counties of Gloucestershire and Worcestershire, where rugby had gained a stronghold. What was equally crucial was that sense of a south Wales regional identity which made the 'subaltern' class very eager to enhance the social, educational and cultural prestige of an area that had far too often been dismissed as backward and indeed dangerous. Certainly that was the case in Swansea, where there was an inclination to emulate a sophisticated gentry which had never forgotten how its ancestors had made the town fashionable. Social aspiration, the need once again to feel on a par with Gloucester and Bristol, had prescribed rugby and so, in that last quarter of the nineteenth century, soccer was, as far as Wales was concerned, almost entirely a game belonging to the north. In his history of the game in Wales Peter Corrigan has described how in 1882 J. R. Morgan of Swansea became the first south Walian to play for the national side and how in 1884 some 7,000 turned up at St Helens to see Wales play Ireland. Certainly there was soccer in the town: there were exhibition games, there was a succession of teams bearing the town's name, including a Swansea Villa, that played its games on the Vetch Field which belonged to the adjacent gas company, and by 1900 some publicans and school teachers had even organized a local league for those former schoolboys who wanted to go on playing. In Swansea, however, as in south Wales generally, the crucial breakthrough only came in those few years after 1906, when English, north Walian and Irish migrants were flooding into the rapidly expanding mining and harbour towns. It was in 1912 that a group of local businessmen met to form a 'First Class soccer club', a professional team officially to be named the Swansea Town Association Football Club Ltd. but which was immediately identified in colloquial parlance as 'the Swans'. Appropriately and perhaps ominously, the first competitive fixture was that against Cardiff on 7 September when a crowd of 8,000 was present to see the dawn of a new era of athletic skill and crowd rivalry. The Swans were indeed latecomers and it was not until 1920 that they entered an English league that had been in competition since 1888, but from that first game it was evident that the board of directors had created an institution that would occupy a central role in the affections and popular culture of the town.

Edwardian towns and cities oozed pride from every pore of their being. They loved to refer to all the things that their citizens could do and to the undoubted quality of the entertainment that was laid on for them. It was widely appreciated that industrialization had been about the creation of national and local wealth, and the civic leaders and press of every town saw it as entirely appropriate and patriotic to boast openly about the degree of leisure activity and cultural participation that had been made possible by commercial success. The novelist, Gwyn Thomas, was to reflect on how in the Rhondda of his childhood 'every day was a jamboree' and very much the same thing could be said of Edwardian Swansea. People worked long hours for their money, and groups such as the railwaymen felt very bitter about the ways in which they were exploited, but nevertheless there was such a cascade of popular activity and intensity of enjoyment that one can only talk in terms of leisure hours as allowing a celebration of the town. These were heady days for showmen and organizing committees, who were now well aware of the great enthusiastic audience that was there to be entertained, although that guaranteed support of the masses for concerts, shows, and sport can only really be understood if examined alongside the tremendous degree to which so many people were themselves prepared to participate in clubs and societies of all sorts. Organizers and professional entertainers alike were always feeding off that same basic energy which made people of all classes want to be involved in activity publicly, collectively, and for almost every minute of their leisure time. By 1913 Swansea had its own sports paper, *The World of Sport,* which reported that the Swans already had a Supporters Club, whose 550 members were organizing prize draws, smokers, and trips to away matches, as well as singing their own 'War Song'! The editor of this journal recognized that there was a need to cover 'every branch of local sport': there would be lots of information on the Swans and their rugby equivalent, the All Whites, on both the rugby and association junior leagues, and he also gave an assurance that he would not be forgetting 'the doggy world' of canine fanciers, the cage bird breeders, the trotting and galloway horse owners, the cyclists, and the bowlers. Here clearly was a man who knew his Swansea.

Meanwhile, in the world of popular entertainment, local boasting concentrated on activities at those 'eighteen places of amusement' that one local newspaper listed in 1914. These were the theatres, music halls, and picture houses that were always making claims about their unique features as they competed for audiences: they always promised 'de luxe' entertainment, 'the last word' in pleasure for 'refined' tastes, prizes were on offer, and new technological advances, such as 'kinema-color' or 'the vivaphone', were announced with pride as they took their place in 'the full swing' of the local scene. On occasions, the showmen would bring quality entertainment to the town and, undoubtedly, the visits of companies like Quinlan Grand Opera remained as highlights of the musical calendar, but although always less heralded and boosted the best things on offer were those events in the staging of which local people played a part. When the National Eisteddfod came to Swansea in 1907 the 68-strong orchestra and choir of 350 voices were recruited locally; and, primarily through the efforts of a local composer, David Vaughan Thomas, new levels of musical distinction were achieved, not least in the performance of Berlioz's *Damnation of Faust*. There was now a full round of musical and choral events, and perhaps not surprisingly in the Victorian town where Swansea Valley resident, Dame Adelina Patti, had given occasional recitals, the favourite format was always that in which 'celebrated artistes' would join with local musicians and one or other of the local choral societies for an irresistible 'Grand Concert'. Perhaps that pre-1914 Swansea experienced its quintessential moment in November 1908, when John McCormack, Penfro Rowlands, and other soloists came to the Albert Hall, to be accompanied by local harpist Megan Glantawe and the Swansea and District Male Voice Society, for an evening during which Llew Bowen, the choir's conductor, was crowned with the Gold Crown that he had won at the Tonypandy National Eisteddfod earlier that year. Many strands came together during an evening in which the audience heard a Mozart minuet and other violin solos, and John McCormack sang Beethoven with the choir, as well as 'I Hear You Calling Me'. All this took place under 'distinguished patronage': not everybody could be listed but there, at the head, were His Grace the duke of Beaufort, the Rt. Hon. the earl of Jersey, the Rt. Hon. Lord Glantawe, Sir J. T. Dillwyn-Llewellyn, and the Hon. Odo R. Vivian, who was actually President of the Male Voice Society. The programme requested 'carriages at 10.10 p.m.', but also promised that there would be 'special trams to Cwmbwrla, Brynhyfryd, and Morriston' as well as 'late trains to Llanelly, Llansamlet, and Neath'.

Those Edwardian years saw Victorian participation achieve a crescendo and, in so doing, determine a full calendar of events to which the citizens of a new century would contrive to adhere. To a quite remarkable extent, the latter-day citizens of Swansea were to relax, play, and exercise according to a timetable that had been established when the town was in its heyday as a port and a manufacturing centre. In general, the popular culture of the Edwardian era was to remain at a plateau for a generation and, in terms of sheer participation, was to peak in the 1940s; but looking at the twentieth century as a whole one can see how the crowded pre-1914 years had established a pattern that was to last well beyond that decade. Those who were to enjoy Swansea did so within a popular culture whose standards and expectations had been established in an earlier era, when the town had instinctively sensed its distinction. The new century brought new levels of prosperity, new opportunities, and new achievements, but it also brought fresh problems and the story became one in which leaders, showmen and organizers were now far more aware of having to compete for audiences and indeed for funding and sponsorship. Swansea's varied economy and proximity to an anthracite coalfield ensured that the town was never brought to a complete standstill, as were so many industrial towns in the Great Depression of the 1930s, but, nevertheless industrial decline in that decade and again in the 1950s was to cause considerable local frustration. What was most troublesome as far as popular culture was concerned was the way in which the post-1918 era saw the gradual disappearance of that highly distinctive local economy that had once occasioned so much pride. As local industry and transport became part of wider regional and national undertakings, so there was a diminution of the size and role of that distinguished, distinctive and highly self-conscious class of gentry and entrepreneurs which had moulded the town for almost a century and a half. A town whose affairs had been conducted by wealthy and talented gentlemen and their ladies was now passing into the hands of small businessmen, managers and councillors, who were by the very nature of things less wealthy, socially of a lower profile, and often associated with sectional or partisan interests. All the while, education, a national press and broadcasting stations and an American cinema were creating a population with new appetites and standards. Far more frequently than in the past there were to be debates about priorities, so that it was not always easy for local leaders to keep up with the changing tastes and energies of a far less homogeneous citizenry.

In terms of the culture that had been made possible by Nonconformity a real highlight came in 1926 when the National Eisteddfod returned to Swansea. This great festival of the arts was attended by massive crowds, many of them released by the great coal dispute that was effectively bringing to an end the classical period of Welsh industrial prosperity. Once again Swansea basked in glory as the duke and duchess of York, Lloyd George, and other notables graced the Eisteddfod field, but what really electrified the town and proved once again that things Welsh were not parochial was the standard of musical performance. Above all, the week was to provide yet another highspot in the career of David Vaughan Thomas who, as musical director, had been given 'almost autocratic powers'. Thomas had already secured his reputation with a memorable performance of the Brahms *Requiem*, during the build-up to which it had been noted that his own Mount Pleasant Choral Society had become 'obsessed with the work'. Now at the Eisteddfod he turned his attention to Beethoven's Ninth and he proceeded to 'stagger' the audience both with the music and his own inspired conducting. According to J. D. Williams there had 'never been such enthusiasm at a concert in Wales', and undoubtedly Dr Thomas had proved 'that Beethoven was for the ordinary man as well as for the musical scholars'. Once again the Eisteddfod had performed its feat of harnessing local talent to provide quality music for the masses, but these headline-making festivals were only possible because the tradition of good choral music lived on in innumerable choral societies and individual chapels. One did not have to wait for the big festival or even to travel to the centre of town, for throughout the region there was a steady routine of choral concerts and oratorios, with both choirs and chapels in Morriston and Dunvant providing the real centres of excellence. In terms of sheer pleasure and emotional gratification it was perhaps the Morriston Orpheus Choir of the 1940s and 1950s and the Swansea Philharmonic choir of the 1960s that made the most lasting impact, but even as standards improved and a bolder selection of music was performed, audience appreciation was always tinged now with a nostalgia for that earlier period when concerts had been so much part of a fuller Welsh-language and chapel culture.

For his 1926 performance of the Choral Symphony Thomas had used the London Symphony Orchestra and that was an indication that in Swansea, as in Wales as a whole, it was always easier to raise a choir than an orchestra. In the last decades of the Victorian era and the first decades of the new century the Swansea experience was one in which able local conductors would bring together amateur musicians in orchestras that would accompany both choirs and amateur opera productions as well as live concerts in which it was not unusual for original compositions to be played. Perhaps the outstanding figure in this respect was W. F. Hulley, the organist at St David's church, who conducted a Swansea Orchestral Society in the 1880s. In the 1930s orchestral playing was given a great boost by the opening of a concert hall at the new Guildhall, and at that time there was much talk of developing either the small Brangwyn Hall Orchestra, or the newly-formed Swansea Festival Orchestra under Morgan Lloyd, into a fully-fledged municipal orchestra. But those plans never really worked out and the old pattern of the nineteenth century was to continue as far as local musicians were concerned. What the Brangwyn Hall had provided, though, was a real opportunity to attract the best orchestras to the town. When Adrian Boult brought the BBC Symphony Orchestra to Swansea in October 1935 he was really inaugurating a whole new area as far as the lovers of good music were concerned. Without a local music school and with so many talented students leaving the town there was no hope of sustaining a professional orchestra, but from 1935 on the town was to play host to many of the world's leading orchestras, conductors and soloists.

In many respects this triumph of the professional over the amateur was reversed in the story of local theatre. The 1930s were a bad decade for the theatre in general and in Swansea there were far fewer visits by touring companies; the Grand was occasionally dark and more often than not bowed to the inevitable and showed films. The future seemed to belong to the movies and perhaps the event which more than any other indicated that a new era of popular culture had begun was the opening in 1931 of the magnificent new Plaza cinema, the flagship of the town's new pattern of entertainment. What the public wanted now was the dazzle and style of Hollywood, and when those things were presented in a picture house with a 'cathedral-like organ' and with 'Renaissance style' teak and walnut panels bearing Celtic motifs, then even respectable middle-class and chapel-going families could join with the workers and youngsters who had already discovered the joys of film. One such youngster who was made into a life-long film-fan by local cinema was Dylan Thomas and, accordingly, the Plaza was to figure prominently in that memorable celebration of urban Swansea that he called *Portrait of the Artist as a Young Dog*. Professional theatre was struggling, but perhaps surprisingly this was not to be the experience of amateur theatre, and during the Depression the people of Swansea were to share with the inhabitants of the mining valleys a new passion for drama. The Swansea Amateur Operatic Society put on productions every year, but now they were joined by local amateur dramatic societies who in 1935 came together to stage the first Swansea Drama Festival. Throughout the town every hall and vestry was now taken over by drama clubs and societies, and one-act plays had become a popular craze. It was a craze that did no harm to the cause of Welsh-language drama, and new life was given to a tradition of short seasons of Welsh drama that had begun before 1914 and been sustained by the 1926 Eisteddfod, which had actually used the Grand Theatre. Meanwhile, in 1928 a Swansea Little Theatre had been formed, and from the outset it offered a guarantee that every winter there would at least be some quality dramatic entertainment in the town. At its Southend base the Little Theatre would offer Shakespeare, Shaw, Ibsen, Congreve, and more recent plays, but perhaps equally crucial was the way in which its activities brought together local intellectuals, writers, actors, university teachers, and in so doing allowed the formation of a new arts sub-culture. This highly distinctive west Swansea arts group was later to be somewhat bitterly satirized by the writer, Kingsley Amis, especially in his novel *That Uncertain Feeling*, but over the years it was to nurture many local talents, not least that of Dylan Thomas, and in a very real sense its members were to replace the gentry as the leaders in the fight to bring culture to the town. Certainly they ensured that theatre in Swansea did not become entirely a matter of low-grade amateur dramatics and tired music hall. If it was the wider popular passion for the drama that was eventually to bring a repertory company to the Grand, it was perhaps the work of the Little Theatre that was to prompt that company into introducing controversial contemporary drama into its regular diet of farce and Agatha Christie.

If cinema-going and amateur dramatics were passions of the 1930s, it was even truer of sport. In every village and suburb, young people played soccer, rugby, and cricket, and eyes were always fixed on the major events held in the centre of town. Undoubtedly, in that decade before the War, it was St Helens that seemed to stage the fixtures that gave Swansea most opportunity to celebrate. Glamorgan had been playing county cricket since 1921, and at St Helens the team would attract good crowds to see such heroes as Turnbull, Clay, Mercer, and Emrys Davies. There were large crowds, too, for local league games, and there were many who argued that the play against sides such as Neath and Gowerton was easily of county standard. The Welsh rugby team came regularly to the ground to play championship games as well as one against South Africa in 1931, but it was the All Whites who were to provide the sporting highlight of the whole inter-war period when, in September 1935, they were inspired by Haydn Tanner and Willy Davies, cousins from Penclawdd and Gowerton Grammar School, into defeating the mighty All Blacks. This victory, the first by a club side against New Zealand, together with the subsequent victory by a national side which relied heavily on Swansea talent, eclipsed so many of the frustrations of those years and served as an inspiration in almost every big game that was to be played in the next generation. Elsewhere in the town there were crowds to see boxing at the Mannesmann Hall, the Drill Hall and the Vetch Field, and at a time when whole committees tended to be closely associated with individual fighters it often seemed as if Len Beynon and Ronnie James were carrying the hopes of the town. Normally, of course, the Vetch was the home of the Swans, who had won the Division Three (South) Championship in 1925 and who thereafter played mostly in the Second Division.

All of this constituted a full, regular and diverting sporting calendar, but it was one that was not as richly rewarding as it should have been. Throughout the decade there was a sense that earlier promise and excitement had not been fulfilled and that circumstances were preventing the full potential of local teams and stars from being developed. Playing at St Helens in the 1930s Wales were to lose as many games as they won. The All Whites were undoubtedly the local pride and joy, but they already had a reputation for inconsistency, both from season to season and against particular Welsh rivals. Glamorgan had not yet fully convinced their supporters that they could bring together the right blend of talented gentlemen and hired professionals to move away from the lower depths of the championship. The boxing tournaments held at the Vetch in 1934 and 1935 were part of a fundraising appeal to help a soccer team that was struggling. A sporting culture that had been programmed in an age of full employment and local economic control and management was far from flourishing in a new era in which there were no longer rich patrons or well-paid working men. The hunger for quality entertainment and the thirst for victory were there but not the local means of support. More than anything it was confidence that was lacking, and the clue to this new uncertainty was provided by the way in which Swansea went on worrying about the way in which Cardiff Arms Park seemed to be emerging as the show-piece of Welsh sport. The status of St Helens had been marked in 1927 by the opening of a new cricket pavilion, but that was nothing really compared to the new double-decker rugby stand built in Cardiff in 1933. From that time on Swansea was convinced that it was about to lose its internationals, and a sustained campaign was mounted against 'Eastern propagandists': nothing, it was claimed, could rival the 'magnificence' of St Helens and surely everyone could see that the main advantage of the ground was the way in which it served as 'the hub of Welsh rugby': it was a natural home for

Welsh people, whereas 'Cardiff is near the borders of England and most of its population is English in sympathy'. The rhetoric that went into the defence of St Helens was a reflection of the new sensitivity that the Depression had induced. It would be a mistake to concentrate facilities in one town, a Swansea newspaper editor quite rightly warned the BBC in 1936, for 'Swansea is the natural centre for a great proportion of the characteristically Welsh items that it proposed to broadcast'.

People who enjoyed Swansea were making the most of a town that reflected the wealth and confidence of a successful Victorian economy. They lived in a town whose churches and chapels, theatres, and stores spoke volumes for what had been an era of prosperity and style. The frustrations of the 1930s had in part grown out of a sense that there was not quite the degree of success that the town's history required, or its physical heritage suggested. It was at this point that aerial bombardment during the Second World War intervened to destroy the very structures that had witnessed earlier successes. The Luftwaffe killed 387 Swansea citizens, but it also did its best to kill off a popular culture, for it was the down-town area that was devastated. Basically, the Germans removed the biggest stores, the oldest churches, the grandest chapels, the synagogue, the market, and that very Theatre of which the old town had been so proud. The local economy had already lost its identity and confidence, and now the town lost much of its architectural distinction as well as those comfortable, familiar, and atmospheric hotels, restaurants, bars, and haunts that had sustained the conviviality, nostalgia, and myths that turned a popular culture into a sense of community. Physically, it took Swansea years to recover from Hitler's War, and there were many who agreed with poet Kingsley Amis that the new physical mediocrity of the town reflected a general condition:

> The journal of some bunch of architects
> Named this the worst town centre they could find;
> But how disparage what so well reflects
> Permanent tendencies of heart and mind?

Mercifully, however, St Helens and the Vetch had survived, and it was here that the real beauty of the town was to be found. A sporting tradition that had grown over two or three generations now provided a magnificent coda as, inspired by old legends, brought together by the collective experience of both a war and better schools, and given sustenance by full employment and a welfare state, local sportsmen took to competition with more fervour and flair than ever before, and, in decades that in so many respects were indeed dull and austere, Swansea was entertained as never before.

Sadly but inevitably, St Helens staged its last rugby international in 1954, but at least in those post-war years a steady stream of talent made the All Whites into a formidable and stylish team. There were larger than ever crowds now to see sides in which public school and varsity men like R.C.C. (Clem) Thomas would play alongside ex-grammar school boys and miners and steel-workers recruited by the club from the outlying villages where the rugby fervour always seemed to be strongest. The All Whites were always at their best when driven forward by a creative and foraging back row and even in seasons of inconsistency they would pull out something extra on the big occasion. In December 1953, inspired by the tackling of the young centre John Faull, the All Whites held the All Blacks of New Zealand to a 6-6 draw and so ensured that the reputation of St Helens as a ground where touring teams could be matched lived on. It was cricket, though,

The All Blacks versus a West Wales XV at St Helen's, 1967.

which really ensured the international reputation of St Helens. Glamorgan had won the County Championship in 1948 and was now a highly competitive county, especially in the field. They had attracted something of a national following, and those English commentators such as E. W. Swanton and John Arlott who had taken up the county liked nothing better than to come to St Helens where they could sit on the balcony or in the turrets of a splendidly eccentric pavilion, which one writer was to describe as 'an architectural shambles'. There, they could write their copy and their poems as they turned away from the cricket to watch channel shipping, the farmers of Exmoor, and the comings and goings of the equally eccentric Mumbles Train. They especially enjoyed the good humour of what were now quite vast and very Welsh crowds who reacted to incident with an emotional spontaneity that was unique on the county circuit. It was often remarked that this was in essence a rugby crowd but nevertheless one that followed every nuance of the summer game that had become a passion

Glamorgan celebrates victory at St Helen's.

in their west Wales villages. There were regularly Bank Holiday crowds of 25,000 to see the tourists and some quite remarkable games were served up for them. A 1948 match against the Australians and then an astonishing 1951 defeat of the South Africans, which ended with the singing of the national anthem, marked the opening of an era in which St Helens was to witness some of the most wonderful cricket played in the county. The cricket had a truly local flavour, for there was always the elegance of Gilbert Parkhouse, the maiden overs of Don Shepherd, and the rescue operations of Jim Pressdee, but there was a more fully Welsh flavour, too, and there was more singing of the national anthem following victories over the Australians in 1964 and 1968. The real hallmark of the ground, though, was its internationalism and in particular the warmth of the welcome always given to great stars who usually responded by playing at their very best. The shortness of the boundary, the sureness of the track and the immediacy of the crowd seemed to invite greatness, and Gary Sobers, Clive Lloyd, Ian Botham, Majid Khan and Javed Miandad were not slow to respond. Why is it, pondered Henry Blofeld, that the best innings were always played at Swansea?

Meanwhile, just over a mile away the Vetch Field was home for a football team that seemed to be a permanent fixture in the Second Division. The bare statistics do not look too impressive, for the Swans were at best a mid-table team and it was only in 1955-56, a season that was ruined by Tom Kiley's injury, that promotion had suggested itself as a possibility. Usually, the crowds packed into the intimate but again very eccentric ground, with its open bank cowering under Townhill, a doll's house central stand and a double-decker which looked as if it had been borrowed to keep out a westerly wind. Most supporters seemed resigned to second-division football, but that was acceptable because there was a very real sense that the town had a sure place within the national soccer scene, which had been earned by a tradition of ball-playing skills that had permeated every level of the local game. Soccer was the game of Swansea's down-town working class, that cosmo-politan labour force of mixed Welsh, English, Irish and foreign extraction that lived in terraced streets fairly adjacent to the main tram and bus routes that fed into the town centre. It was an urban rather than a village game and it sustained local leagues that brimmed over with talent in these years. This was talent that excited the world for the big one had got away. John Charles, whose giant physique and gentle skills made him into one of the all-time greats, had never played for the Swans, but some other stars had at least been glimpsed at the

Tom Kiley playing before the uncovered North Bank at the Vetch Field, 1952.

Vetch before moving on: Trevor Ford to stun the nation by the way in which he put both goalkeeper and ball in the back of the net, and Cliff Jones to bring something of the rugby player's speed and swerve to first-division wing play. Above all, though, there was 'the Golden Boy', Ivor Allchurch, who season after season delighted the Vetch crowd and gave them the crucial satisfaction of knowing that they were supporting a team that was genuinely local and which could boast of one player who was regularly included in most experts' British XI. Ivor's rather refined blondness, his seeming inability to commit a foul, his elegant turn on the ball and then the pin-point pass to an eternally grateful winger as he accelerated forward seemed to most fans to add up to what was best in their town. Throughout a significant strand of 1950s British working-class culture, the name of Swansea had become synonymous with the sheer class of Allchurch.

There were amazing days yet to come at the Vetch: the great cup run of 1964 and then a sensational Toshack era, which took the club from the bottom of the Fourth to almost the top of a First Division that most fans had never thought they would live to see. Yet even as new heights were climbed and a new generation of support recruited, there were always those who would retain their strongest affection for the team of the 1950s. At that time that team seemed very much at one with the personality of the region. Allchurch had been the classic hero of a club and of a culture that was so appropriately designated as Swansea Town. His only subsequent rival was the stylish boxer, Brian Curvis, who failed to win a world championship but who, as undefeated British and Empire welter-weight champion between 1959 and 1966, gave Swansea and it citizens a secure place within the much publicized and televised world of international boxing. Cricket and rugby were important within the Imperial sub-culture, but a respected fighter like Curvis performed on a truly world stage and allowed Swansea to bask momentarily in a greater glory. At the same time what was probably the town's oldest sport was given a boost that allowed a new generation of youngsters to be enticed into the gyms.

Swansea, it seemed, still wanted to be entertained and still needed its heroes. Yet very suddenly, in the 1960s, social changes that had been accumulating in the previous decade came to a head and induced a real sense of crisis in almost every aspect of the local culture. The final collapse of the small old tinplate and steel mills had further punctured the confidence and identity of many local communities, and now television was keeping supporters away from Victorian and Edwardian facilities that in truth had hardly been improved for decades. Suddenly it became apparent that what was thought of as a genuinely popular local culture was being sustained by just a small number of people. In the heady days of success the crowds had just assumed that their theatres and their sports teams had belonged to them, belonged as it were to the community of Swansea. Now, as attendances and revenues dwindled, it became more apparent that it was showmen, boards of directors, and councillors who effectively ran, financed, and controlled local culture, and quite simply they no longer had the resources to sustain the quality of entertainment that a tradition-ridden town expected. Increasingly fickle audiences demanded the quality that they saw on television without realizing that in the past there had not only been significantly higher box-office and gate receipts but also the quite decisive sponsorship of wealthy patrons and the risky investment of speculative showmen. It was time

Ivor Allchurch, 'The Golden Boy'.

for organizers to cut through the rhetoric and sentiment and to confront the stark facts, although fans and audiences refused to join them in this and so were essentially unable to comprehend that the local culture that they thought of as theirs needed to be sponsored in new ways or it would die. From activity to activity the details varied but in general now the Borough Council was forced to play a vital role in sustaining what passed as popular culture. John Chilvers struggled admirably to give Swansea good local rep., but the Grand Theatre would have closed permanently if it had not been for guarantees and assistance from the Borough Council, which eventually took over the premises in 1969. The Swans, of course, had never belonged to the people of Swansea but rather to a Board of Directors who had usually been much abused for selling stars and refusing to buy when the need was generally apparent. The old tradition of Swansea directors had been to retain a second-division equilibrium that was suited to the resources available, but almost inevitably things went dreadfully awry in an era when the team yo-yo'ed through the divisions, attendances slumped and yet wages escalated. With hindsight it can be so clearly seen that in 1974 a heavily overdrawn club should have been allowed to sell parts of its ground for commercial development. As it was, it sold its ground for a pittance to the local council and so it was that in the 1980s a vastly over-ambitious club went bankrupt and found that it had no real security to fall back on. To the horror of the town and disbelief of many fans who had not been near the ground for years, the club was closed down by a high-court action. A proud old soccer team had been killed by sheer bad management, and yet in what was undoubtedly the greatest miracle in the history of Swansea the team was immediately revived and lived on to win new battles. It was revived above all through the efforts of one local businessman, and Doug Sharpe's fight to save the team he loved proved perhaps the most dramatic of all reminders that what the public had for so long taken for granted essentially relied on the wealth, the passion, and the showmanship of a few. It is also worth noting that the Council, which had so dramatically intervened in the affairs of the Grand and the Vetch, had actually owned St Helens since 1939 and so had always cushioned rugby and cricket against temporary decline. Both the All Whites and Glamorgan, however, were well aware of how gates plummeted when there were no home team stars and massive efforts were made to ensure that there were personalities on show and that standards were maintained. All the while there were nagging thoughts about whether the safety of municipal control had really prevented the full development of the ground's potential. Again a resource that supporters thought of as belonging to the community as a whole was really effectively under the control of small committees.

Each generation will have its own cultural memories and sporting heroes, and perhaps nostalgia will tend always to be an enemy of objective assessment. The organizers and councillors of today will join with their supporters and patrons in acclaiming a continuing pattern of success. In the last decade of the twentieth century the city of Swansea finds itself with two very notable achievements to its credit. Most spectacularly the city now imports the very best music and it is very much the sponsorship of the Council and of the Welsh Arts Council which makes that possible. The story of the Swansea Festival which was launched in 1948 has been a remarkable one and it has seen some of the world's finest performers coming to do justice to a concert hall that the town had the foresight to build in an earlier difficult decade. Similarly, the survival of the Grand has allowed the increasingly internationally acclaimed Welsh National Opera to build up support in a community that did much in the early years to ensure the quality of that company's acclaimed chorus. Meanwhile, local jazz enthusiasts, who had quite astonishingly sustained an organization throughout the lean years of the 1960s and 1970s, celebrated the revival of interest by bringing top American stars to a city where 'live' music became a new feature of pubs and clubs. The second achievement is that which allows and encourages local people actually to play as many sports as possible, and again in this respect the local council has played a key role in providing facilities. Perhaps more than ever before people take exercise, but they do so now in a far greater number of sports. The world champions that the town produces are likely to be bowlers, wrestlers, gymnasts, weightlifters, or perhaps even swimmers and atheletes, for certainly they have been given superb new facilities. The community is as active as ever and even in terms of theatre and dance there are stages and rehearsal rooms available as never before. It is an era which invites participation and which encourages national and international success as obviously and decisively as any in the past. Which leaves us really with those homes of ghosts, St Helens and the Vetch, venues which on their day can offer large crowds entertainment as brilliant and dramatic as any in the past, but which play host to sports which have never fully adjusted to the changed habits and standards of the television and suburban age. It is not just a local problem, but it does manifest itself in Swansea in a particularly dramatic fashion because the two old grounds are so central to the city's history. The challenge that faces cricket, rugby, and soccer officials is whether their sports can nurture the talent and whether their grounds can be made comfortable enough to attract the family crowd of the suburban area. As in contemporary Britain as a whole, the indications of future promise can be so easily eclipsed by the physical settings and by a nostalgia for a community culture whose logic was determined in a previous era.

Chapter 10

Municipal Administration and Politics from the 1830s to 1974

J. R. Alban

The 1830s were a decade of great reform in England and Wales. Several acts of parliament marked significant changes between the old and new systems of local government, while the parliamentary franchise was revised and extended. Each of these acts, in turn, was hailed by contemporaries as a revolution, and they are still regarded as such today. The year 1832 saw the first attempt at parliamentary reform and this was followed by significant changes in the Poor Law in 1834. Indeed, the Poor Law Amendment Act, 1834 (4 and 5 William IV, *cap.* 76), which created elected authorities with paid officials, has been regarded by many as the first piece of legislation to deal with local government along modern lines. However, its importance was soon eclipsed by legislation of the following year. The Municipal Corporations Act, 1835 (5 and 6 William IV, *cap.* 76), in reforming the 'chartered hogsties' of the unreformed boroughs, truly laid the foundations of modern local government. Nationally, it marked a significant watershed, and one town where its effects were felt was Swansea.

The Municipal Corporation after 1835

The Industrial Revolution brought with it many changes, not least of which was the unplanned growth of towns under the pressures of increasing population. By the third decade of the nineteenth century it had become obvious that local government in the towns had not kept in step with those changes and that there were numerous anomalies and inconsistencies which urgently needed attention. In Swansea's case, the population doubled between 1800 and 1830, yet at the latter date the town was still governed by a corporation which had come into existence many centuries before, and whose self-nominated members ruled the borough almost exclusively for their own profit. This corporation, even by the eighteenth century, did not represent the interests of the majority of residents: for instance, out of a population of over 13,000 in 1833 there were only 104 burgesses.

The situation in Swansea was mirrored in numerous other boroughs throughout the country. Reform was desperately needed. Thus, in 1833, a royal commission to look into the state of municipal corporations was established. A number of energetic young investigators — mainly up and coming barristers — were appointed, and by 1835, they had produced a series of reports on 246 towns, of which Swansea was one. These reports, which were published as appendices to the *Report of the Commissioners on Municipal Corporations* (London, 1835), are excellent starting points for any study of borough history before 1835, and the conditions which they describe clearly show why reform of some kind was necessary. As a consequence of the *Report*, the Municipal Corporations Act was passed in the same year. The act applied to 179 named corporations and swept away the old system in each. As a result of this legislation, Swansea's oligarchy of burgesses, which was described in chapter 4, was abolished and replaced by a municipal corporation which was to be elected by ratepayers of at least three years' standing. The Portreeve was replaced by a Mayor, an office which previously had existed only briefly in Swansea under Cromwell's Protectorate, in the 1650s.

The new municipal borough was given the same boundaries as the parliamentary borough, which had been established three years earlier, an area of approximately 5,000 acres. Thus, for the first time the powers of the local municipal corporation extended far beyond the boundaries of the ancient franchise of the borough which had been established in the middle ages. The new borough was divided into a North Ward and a South Ward, and representation was by twenty-four elected councillors, who themselves elected six aldermen.

This first step towards democracy in Swansea was not as far-reaching as may appear at first sight. For instance, out of a population of more than 13,000, only 747 persons were entitled to vote in local elections. Moreover, the act laid down substantial property qualifications for candidates and thereby ensured an essentially middle-class character for the council. In boroughs with fewer than four wards, intending candidates had to possess £500 in real estate or pay £15 a year in rates.

If the franchise for local elections in Swansea was narrow after 1835, so too were the powers of the new corporation. In some respects, the activities of the unreformed corporation were continued. For example, the extensive corporate estate passed into the control of the new body, one of whose main roles was its effective administration. The estate included many properties in the town centre, large tracts of land on Townhill and the Burrows, which had been enclosed in the 1760s, together with the market and other trading activities. Unlike the situation before 1835, however, the new corporation was no longer permitted to use this property for the benefit of its own members, either corporately or individually. All revenues received from rents (and, indeed, from other sources such as fines imposed by courts) were to go into a borough fund, which was to be used to pay for the running of the authority. The average annual receipts of about £4,600 were more than sufficient to cover the corporation's outgoings for many years, and, in consequence, the borough council had no need to levy rates until 1872. This was also facilitated by the fact that very little was actually undertaken by the corporation during the first few decades of its existence. The narrowness of its responsibilities and a strict adherence to the stifling principle of *ultra vires* bred a timidity which limited the authority in its actions for many years. The townsfolk of Swansea did not, however, avoid paying rates during this period. Rates were levied for Poor Law purposes, and certain other authorities such as the Paving Commissioners and, after 1850, the Local Board of Health also made a rates precept.

The new corporation was a governmental institution and, as such, could make byelaws for the better administration of the town. It could also, if it so wished, undertake responsibility for street lighting, and, indeed, under this provision the powers of the Paving Commission were taken over in 1836. Through its Watch and Ward committee, established in the same year, the corporation undertook responsibility for a new borough police force. The act of 1835 also permitted the corporation to petition the Privy Council for a court of Quarter Sessions separate from that of the county; thus in 1836, Swansea received its first Borough Commission of the Peace, it having already been made an Assize town in the previous year, in respect of its new municipal status. In 1847, under the provisions of the County Courts Act, 1846, it also became a County Court town, and, although entitled to apply to the Home Secretary, under the terms of the Municipal Corporations Act, 1835, for the appointment of a stipendiary magistrate, Swansea did not do so until 1872. Subsequently, the use of this privilege was always intermittent. Quarter Sessions and Assizes continued to be held in Swansea until the establishment of the Crown Courts in 1972.

The municipal corporation did not, however, have the powers to deal with pressing problems of the age, such as public health and poverty. These areas were the responsibilities of other authorities. If one drawback of the new corporation was the narrowness of its powers, another was the fact that the act of 1835, having established new authorities on a universal pattern, did not provide for a central, overseeing body to monitor the workings of the act in the provinces. This was a surprising omission, since the Poor Law Amendment Act of the previous year had provided for such central control by establishing the Poor Law Commission, while later legislation in the sphere of public health also set up similar supervisory bodies. One element of control, however, was the stipulation that a yearly public audit of the corporation's accounts should be carried out, with the Borough Treasurer preparing an annual abstract of accounts for public inspection by the ratepayers.

The picture was not one of total inactivity, however. Admittedly, the new authority was bridled by the principle of *ultra vires* and handicapped by financial limitations and a series of expensive lawsuits in the first few years of its existence. Nevertheless, it is clear, if only from the increased volume of paperwork, that the work of local government in Swansea after 1835 was far greater than it had been before that date. For example, by the early 1840s, there were frequent complaints that there was insufficient storage space for documents in the Guildhall. By 1848, it was clear that the Guildhall — which had only opened in 1829 — had insufficient office space and facilities, and, consequently, an elaborate programme of extension on a grand scale was put in hand, and was completed by 1850.

The meetings of the local authority also became more frequent after 1835. The Council met once a month, with its annual meeting, at which the Mayor and committees were appointed, taking place in November. (The municipal year ran from November to November until 1949, when its beginning was changed to May). The reform of 1835 also witnessed the adoption of the modern committee system, whereby certain aspects of the corporation's responsibilities were delegated to specific committees, which normally also met monthly. Resolutions passed by each committee were then submitted to the monthly Council meeting for consideration and ratification. By the beginning of the 1840s, the corporation had established committees for

The Old Guildhall at Somerset Place, extended 1848.

Finance, Markets, and Property, as well as the Watch Committee. As time went by, other committees were added to these, while sub-committees and special committees were established as the need arose. After 1835 also, salaried officials, such as a Town Clerk and Treasurer, were appointed.

While the sphere of operation of the corporation was limited, it did achieve some notable success in the enactment of byelaws and the establishment of a police force, whose strength by 1867 stood at forty-seven officers. A more professional approach was also taken with regard to the management of the corporation estate. A series of regular surveys began in 1847 and these were followed by published estate reports and estate maps, the first edition of which appeared in 1851.

Narrow though the corporation's powers may have been, other aspects of local administration were not neglected, but instead became the responsibility of separate bodies. Haphazard urban growth and population increase in the first half of the nineteenth century brought many problems which, strictly speaking, lay outside the corporation's remit. Between 1801 and 1851, the population increased from 6,099 to 16,993. This almost three-fold growth resulted from the pull of the town's industry, which drew in people from rural Wales, from England, Ireland, the Continent, and even North America. By 1891, the population stood at 90,349. Many of these people found work for themselves, but inevitably there were those who, through sickness or poverty, became a burden on the community.

To accommodate this rising population, an unplanned, urban expansion of mainly jerry-built houses occurred in the years before 1830, although after 1858 there were stricter controls on building. Development took the form of expansion northwards, to Greenhill, and westwards, along the Sandfields, but, in the main, the building programme in the first few decades of the nineteenth century concentrated on the original area of settlement, and resulted in a housing density hitherto unequalled. Spacious back gardens were turned into a warren of squalid courts and alleys, erected without any concern for the necessary, accompanying sanitary arrangements. Inevitably, drainage, sewerage, and water supply were thus woefully inadequate by 1850, and illness and epidemics were the natural result, worsened by the atmospheric pollution from the nearby industries. Swansea's nineteenth-century growth was therefore attended by the twin problems of poor relief and public health, the two main concerns of most industrial towns in Britain in that century.

Poor Relief

Since the sixteenth century, the relief of the poor in England and Wales had been the obligation of the parish, and administered by the vestry meeting and the Overseers of the Poor, who raised a rate and doled out poor relief from the revenues obtained. In the eighteenth century, the 'select' vestry of St Mary's parish was dominated by the corporation, which enjoyed a two-thirds majority of representation on it. In addition, the corporation itself often acted charitably towards the poor, as, for example in 1816, a year of exceptional poverty and hardship, when the annual Michaelmas dinner was cancelled and its cost donated to the Overseers for the care of the poor in the town.

The rising tide of pauperism in the country as a whole necessitated reform in the system of poor relief by the third decade of the nineteenth century. The Poor Law Amendment Act, 1834 (4 and 5 William IV, *cap.* 76), by which this was effected, established poor law unions,

Slum Clearance at Cross Street, 1879.

comprising several amalgamated parishes, under the control of Guardians of the Poor. Thus, in Swansea, from 1834 to 1930, the administration of poor relief was in the hands of an elected body other than the corporation. Indeed, the Swansea Union was responsible for an area far more extensive than the administrative borough of Swansea. The union comprised the parishes of Clase, Llandeilo Talybont, Llansamlet, Penderry, St John-juxta-Swansea, and Swansea (St Mary's) itself.

The management of the Swansea Union was in the hands of the Board of Guardians, each constituent parish contributing members. Like the borough council, the Board of Guardians was an elected body, but while borough elections were based on a simple household

franchise, voting for the Guardians was on a graded property basis.
The electorate consisted of ratepayers and property owners, who
received one vote for every £50 worth of property, up to a maximum
of six votes. A person who was an owner-occupier could therefore, in
theory, receive up to twelve votes. Candidates for election had to
satisfy the requirement of possessing £40 in land, while the local magistrates were also *ex officio* members of the Board. Plural voting was
abolished in 1894, by the Local Government Act of that year, which
also stipulated twelve months' residence in the Union district as the
only qualification for election. This opened up the way for greater
working-class representation on the Board. Indeed, it was in elections
to the Board of Guardians after this date that Labour candidates
achieved some of their earliest successes in local government in
Swansea. Under the act of 1834, elections to the Board were annual,
but from 1894, members were elected for three years, with one-third
of their number standing for re-election each year.

The main duty of the Guardians was to administer poor relief.
Anyone who genuinely needed relief was not refused it, but it was
usually offered on condition that the applicant should accept 'indoor
relief' within the workhouse. By the early twentieth century, however, most of the relief granted in Swansea was to people who were
not in the workhouse. A workhouse had been established in Swansea in
the eighteenth century, the earliest one being within the confines of
the castle. In 1817, the parish took over part of the former bathing
house on the Burrows for use as a workhouse, the other part of the
building becoming the Swansea Infirmary. The Board of Guardians
took over the running of the workhouse in 1834, and the building
served as a workhouse until 1861, when a new one, built at a cost of
£15,750, opened at Mount Pleasant. This subsequently became known
as Tawe Lodge, and was enlarged several times, so that by 1926, it had
accommodation for 584 inmates. Part of Tawe Lodge was used as an
ill-equipped workhouse infirmary, and after 1929, in common with
many other former workhouses, the whole of the building became a
hospital, known today as Mount Pleasant Hospital.

In 1877, the Guardians availed themselves of the gift of land at
Cockett, granted to them under the terms of a trust by John Dillwyn
Llewelyn and his son, Sir John Talbot Dillwyn Llewelyn, to build six
'Industrial Cottage Homes for pauper children'. The running of these
homes was taken over by the Children's Committee of the County
Borough of Swansea in 1930, and in 1974, they were transferred to
West Glamorgan County Council's Social Services Department.

In addition to their main task of relieving the poor, the Swansea Guardians acquired a number of additional responsibilities. For example, between 1837 and 1930, they were responsible for the registration of births, marriages, and deaths under the act of 1836 (6 and 7 William IV, *cap*. 86), a function for which the County Borough of Swansea, and then West Glamorgan County Council, subsequently became responsible. The Guardians also had some involvement in matters of public health under the Nuisances Removal and Disease Prevention Act, 1846 (9 and 10 Victoria, *cap*. 96), and an administrative involvement under the Vaccination Acts from 1841 onwards.

To carry out their functions, the Guardians came to employ a substantial body of officials, ranging from their clerk and treasurer to relieving officers, clerical staff, workhouse staff, and medical officers. The Board itself, which comprised thirty-nine Guardians and fourteen Justices of the Peace resident within the Union, met every Thursday, first at the workhouse, but from 1899 they had purpose-built offices at Alexandra Road, in the building which is now occupied by the BBC.

Swansea Infirmary and Workhouse on the Burrows, originally built as the Bathing House.

During its lifetime, the Board of Guardians, being always supervised by a central government department, had the accountability and guidance which the reformed corporation lacked. From 1834, the responsible supervisory body was the Poor Law Commission, which was replaced in 1847 by the Poor Law Board. This in turn was taken over in 1871 by the newly-established Local Government Board, a department with responsibility for both poor relief and public health.

From the 1870s, the administration of the poor law in Swansea remained fairly static, although, in common with the rest of the country, it was beginning to be eroded by changes made in the first years of the twentieth century. As early as 1886, central government had been encouraging municipal corporations to provide relief work schemes for the unemployed as an alternative to their becoming dependent on the parish, and it appears that certain works in Swansea were carried out by such labour in the 1880s and 1890s. The momentum of relief work was kept going by the County Borough's Distress Committee, and many significant schemes, such as the Townhill Housing Estate, the Main Drainage Scheme, and the Guildhall at Victoria Park were achieved through the use of unemployment relief labour. The introduction of old-age pensions in 1908 and the establishment of health and unemployment insurance in 1911, which was administered the Swansea Local Insurance Committee, further eroded the scope of the Guardians. The financial tensions which followed the First World War placed an added strain on the Poor Law system, both locally and nationally, and the government took steps to counter this. Thus, the Rating and Valuation Act, 1925 (15 and 16 George V, *cap.* 90) removed the function of rating valuations from the Guardians and gave it to a newly appointed Local Assessment Committee, while by the Local Government Act, 1929 (19 and 20 George V, *cap.* 17), the responsibility for poor relief in Swansea was transferred to the Public Assistance Committee of the County Borough of Swansea, and on 1 April 1930, the Swansea Board of Guardians ceased to exit. The advent of the Welfare State after 1946 hived off a substantial proportion of that committee's functions to central government departments, while the 'Social Welfare' role was continued by the County Borough of Swansea until 1974, and thereafter by the Social Services Department of West Glamorgan County Council.

Public Health

Along with the relief of the poor, the other urgent problem caused by rapid urban growth in the nineteenth century was that of public

The Reservoir at Brynmill Park.

Cockle Woman by Evan Walters.

Swansea Marina from Dylan Thomas Square, 1989.

health. It has been noted above that the first half of the century had seen a massive increase in housing density in the town centre of Swansea, and expansion of the town towards the north and west. In general, the houses which were thrown up were devoid of many of the basic rudiments, such as piped water and sanitation. Here and there, among the sprawl of alleyways and courts, were back-to-back houses, although these were fewer than in many industrial towns in the north of England. Of course, there were many good areas within the town: for instance, the area known as the Burrows, on the western side of the river mouth, had developed as a pleasant, middle-class suburb since the early 1800s (although, after the opening of the South Dock in 1859, it quickly declined into a tough, seedy dockland area). Indeed, there were also some working-class areas which were pleasant and relatively healthy. For example, the philanthropy of the Vivians, the proprietors of the Hafod Copperworks, had led to the building of what many considered to be an almost model housing estate at Trevivian, where the houses had spacious gardens, separate lavatories, and a standpipe in each backyard. But elsewhere, the picture was certainly different. At 'Little Ireland' in Greenhill, an area into which countless Irish immigrants poured to escape the potato famines of the 1840s, one commentator reported that 'a new workingmen's district [was] in the process of formation, . . . a bleak and bare hillside where roads and streets had yet to be made, undrained and unlighted'.

Even by the 1850s, Swansea's water supply was inadequate; only a small area of the town took its water from the reservoirs at Brynmill and Cwmdonkin. Most people had their water from watersellers or from the natural springs and wells of the area, whose existence is recalled in placenames such as Baptist Well, Ffynonne, and Ffynnon y Graig. In many parts the water supply was unwholesome and polluted. Both G. T. Clark and Sir T. H. de la Beche, who reported on the sanitary conditions of Swansea in the 1840s, cited numerous examples of wells into which percolated the contents of adjacent privies. The most poignant example, however, is still to be seen on the Local Board of Health plan of 1852, which shows a water-drawing place on the Nant y Glasdwr (the stream which supplied water for most of Green-hill) situated 20 feet downstream from a privy which spanned the stream and ejected its ordure into it!

To add to the problems, refuse collection, as we have seen in chapter 4, was sporadic, and was usually farmed out to private contractors who neglected to do the job properly. The suburbs on the eastern side of the town also had to contend with noxious fumes from the copperworks and other manufactories in the Lower Swansea Valley. Small wonder, then, that the mortality rate in Swansea in 1849 stood at 23.6 per 1,000, while in nearby rural Gower it was 15 per 1,000. Life expectancy varied from twenty-two years for labourers to thirty-nine years for the better-off. In addition to the constant squalor, there were all-too-frequent epidemics, notably of cholera in 1832, 1849, and 1866, while in 1865, Swansea had the dubious distinction of being the only British town to have a positively certified outbreak of tropical yellow fever. Typhus and dysentery also made frequent visits, while bronchitis and catarrh were — and still are — a regular fact of life for many Swansea folk.

Against this, before 1850, there were few doctors in the town. Personal health services for the public at large were given only by voluntary bodies. A Dispensary for the treatment of out-patients had been established in Nelson Street in 1808, while a Dorcas Society had been set up in the same year. In 1817, an Infirmary for the treatment of in-patients was opened in the old bathing house on the Burrows, but, as

Swansea General Hospital, opened 1864.

the town's population grew, this became inadequate, although it was not until 1869 that a new General Hospital was opened at St Helens.

While there was clearly much need for action, the reformed corporation did nothing in the sphere of public health. What little was done before 1850 was left to private enterprise, as in the case of water supply and the Infirmary, or else to the Paving Commissioners, the statutory body responsible since 1809, whose activities have been discussed in chapter 4. As we have seen, the Commission's track record was not a great success.

The sanitary conditions of Swansea paralleled those in many other British towns. By the 1830s, this decline in standards of health had given the government cause for concern, but nothing was achieved until the passing of Edwin Chadwick's Public Health Act of 1848 (11 and 12 Victoria, *cap.* 63), the first of several positive measures taken by the Victorians to improve the health of towns. The act laid down that a General Board of Health should be established for five years to oversee the implementation of the proposed measures, an echo of the Poor Law Board set up in 1834. It also provided that Local Boards of Health should be set up in towns of over 10,000 inhabitants. The act was adoptive, thus a local board could be established in those towns where a majority of the ratepayers requested one. Moreover, in towns where the death rate exceeded 23 per 1,000, the General Board of Health could impose a local board. Swansea's death rate, as we have seen was 23.6 per 1,000, but the townsfolk actually petitioned for the establishment of a Local Board of Health. This was not without some bitter opposition, mainly on the grounds of expense and fear of massive rates. Nevertheless, a petition was eventually submitted under the leadership of W. H. Smith, the erstwhile champion of the local waterworks, and, as a result, the eminent engineer and surveyor, G. T. Clark, was dispatched to inspect the town and prepare a report on its sanitary condition. Some years earlier, in 1845, Sir H. T. de la Beche had prepared a report on Swansea. Clark's report echoed the worst findings of the de la Beche report, and as a result of his investigations, a Local Board of Health was established in Swansea in 1850.

The powers of the new local board were vested, from the outset, in the corporation, although, in strict legal terms, the board was an entirely separate body, whose decisions were not binding on the corporation or *vice versa*. It was not always automatic that a local board's powers should be given to a municipal corporation, but there were obviously many sound reasons for uniting the two bodies. The establishment of the Local Board of Health removed the *raison d'être* of the Swansea Paving Commissioners, who went out of existence shortly afterwards.

Under the terms of the act of 1848, the Local Board of Health in Swansea had wide powers, including the control of sewerage and water supply, the regulation of offensive trades, street maintenance, and the making of byelaws, particularly with regard to building regulations. There was a host of minor responsibilities, including the inspection and licensing of common lodging houses and the inspection of nuisances, while the board also functioned as the Burial Board for the town. Nevertheless, there were still some limitations to their powers: for instance, the right to remove slums for redevelopment was not acquired until 1876.

The Local Board of Health displayed the structure of a modern local authority, with departments under chief officers and a formalized committee system. The Public Health Act laid down that salaried officials were to include a Clerk (who, in Swansea's case, also held office as the Town Clerk, in distinction to the Clerk of the Paving Commissioners, who had been a separate official), and a Treasurer (again, the Borough Treasurer acted in this capacity). Then there were specialist officers, the principal of whom were the Surveyor, the Inspector of Nuisances, and the Sanitary Inspector. The act also sanctioned the post of Medical Officer of Health, but in Swansea this was not filled until 1853, when Dr W. H. Michael was appointed. Dr Michael had been a town councillor, who had resigned his seat to take this office, at an annual salary of £150. His appointment was not without opposition from some quarters, since it necessitated a 2s. rate to support its functions. However, Michael resigned after a year, realizing that he could achieve more by becoming an elected member of the Borough Council and Local Board of Health once again. Thereafter, the post of Medical Officer of Health remained unfilled until 1865, when Dr Ebenezer Davies was appointed, at a reduced salary of £100.

From its inception, the Local Board of Health operated a committee system along modern lines. The Board itself met once a month, but it delegated specific aspects of its responsibilities to committees. The principal of these were the Sanitary Committee, the Water and Sewers Committee, the Works Committee, and the Finance Committee. The Fire Brigade Committee exercised a function formerly carried out by the municipal corporation's Watch Committee, while there was a host of sub-committees and special committees convened for specific purposes.

The act of 1848 has been hailed as a great step forward, yet to many contemporaries it was unpopular. The General Board of Health was widely regarded as autocratic and tactless, and, while its life was extended to 1858, by that date it had ceased to exercise an effective controlling influence. In Swansea, the local Board underwent criticism from many quarters, particularly from those members of the public who resented the extra burden of rates levied to cover the costs of the new services.

Despite local opposition and the fact that the local board did not exceed the pace set by the General Board of Health, great improvements were achieved in Swansea after 1850. One of the first steps taken by the new board in that year was to conduct a detailed survey of the town, the results of which were embodied in the large-scale Public Health Plan of 1852 and the water map published in 1854. Both showed building problems and dealt with water supply; this latter problem being one which the board tackled with great zeal. As early as 1852, the board had bought out the Swansea Waterworks Company for £25,000, thus beginning a direct municipal involvement with water supply which was to last until the formation, in 1966, of the West Glamorgan Water Board, whose functions, in turn, were taken over by the Welsh Water Authority in 1973.

A series of loans made possible improvements at the existing reservoirs at Brynmill and Cwmdonkin in the 1850s, while in the same decade, consideration was given to the construction of additional reservoirs. The first site selected was at Cwmgelli, near Treboeth, but opposition from local coal owners, whose workings ran under the proposed location, caused the Local Board to look elsewhere. Thus, from the 1860s onwards, a series of reservoirs were built in the upland area to the north of Swansea, and these still ensure an excellent water supply to the town. The first reservoir was constructed at Lower Lliw between 1861-7, at a cost of £160,000, to be followed by Blaennant Ddu (1874-8), Upper Lliw (1886-94), and Cray (1898-1904), each of which cost well in excess of £100,000. The building programme continued into the twentieth century, with Usk, opened in 1955, and Llyn Brianne (which had originally been conceived by the County Borough of Swansea's Water Department, but opened by the Welsh Water Authority) in 1973.

In 1872, the Local Board of Health was reconstituted as an Urban Sanitary Authority under the Public Health Act of that year. Like the Local Board of Health before it, this new authority was the borough council statutorily delegated to that task. It was responsible to the

Local Government Board, which monitored its activities. Although still subject to the principle of *ultra vires*, the new authority practised a more liberal interpretation of its powers than had been the case hitherto in Swansea, and increased the momentum of works begun by the Local Board of Health. Thus, the second half of the nineteenth century witnessed improvements in many aspects of public health. Cemeteries provide a notable example. In the year in which the Local Board of Health was established, there were ten denominational graveyards in Swansea, most of which were almost full. Indeed, the need for additional burial space had been felt as early as the 1830s when the parish of St Mary was obliged to find an 'overspill' burial ground in the neighbouring parish of St John's. By 1856, the Local Board of Health, as the Burial Board, had applied itself to the problem, with the opening of a new municipal cemetery at Danygraig and the framing of strict regulations for burials. As needs increased, further burial grounds were established at Cwmgelli (1896) and Morriston (1915), while Oystermouth cemetery, opened in 1883, was taken over by Swansea in 1918 with the demise of the Oystermouth Urban District.

By the end of the nineteenth century, many miles of sewers had been laid, with most of the central area connected to them. However, in outlying districts, such as Morriston and Treboeth, many houses still relied on cesspits and were to continue to do so until the Main Drainage Scheme of the 1930s. The extensions of the borough and a rapid building programme meant that for much of the nineteenth century sewerage did not keep pace with urban development.

Both the Local Board of Health and its successor also concerned themselves with the improvement of housing conditions, although the provision of council housing by the local authority did not arrive in Swansea until the first years of the twentieth century. For instance, in 1859, the Local Board instituted byelaws for the stringent regulation of building, and these were modified and extended on several occasions, notably in 1869 and 1884. In the 1870s, moreover, the Urban Sanitary Authority took advantage of powers under the Artisans' and Labourers' Dwellings Improvement Act, 1875 (38 and 39 Victoria, *cap.* 49) to obtain an order for the removal of slums and the redevelopment of five of the worst areas in the town. In so doing, Swansea was one of only a small number of towns to avail itself of powers under the act and actually to carry out works, although part of the scheme was abandoned. The order was obtained in 1876, but because of financial and labour problems, work did not begin until 1879, and eventually only two areas were completely cleared, those around St Mary's church and the notorious Back Street. However, instead of then leasing out the cleared land to private developers for the building of workers' houses, the Urban Sanitary Authority used the powers of the order cosmetically, to improve the town centre: for instance, Alexandra Road was constructed as a 'grand boulevard', and within the thirty years after 1880, some imposing new public buildings were erected along it.

The public health authorities in Swansea, particularly after 1872, did much to improve the quality of life in the town. There had been a long tradition of public open spaces which dated back to the eighteenth century: in 1789, for example, the unreformed corporation had erected pleasure gardens on the Burrows and had maintained them until the building of the South Dock in the 1850s. The construction of reservoirs had also provided the townsfolk with wooded, open spaces, which were enjoyed from at least 1849. Indeed, in 1854, the Local Board of Health (not without some heavy criticism) expended £100 on land-scaping a public area around Cwmdonkin reservoir. By the 1870s, the energies of William Thomas of Lan had inspired an 'Open Spaces Movement', which gained momentum in 1876 through the gift by John Dillwyn Llewelyn of Cnap Llwyd Farm, which subsequently became

Election card in support of Sir John Talbot Dillwyn Llewelyn, 1892.

June 25th, 1892.

Sir,

I respectfully request the honour of your Vote and Interest at the coming Parliamentary Election, and I promise that if elected I will at all times pay especial attention to the interests of our ancient Borough.

Your obedient Servant,

JOHN T. D. LLEWELYN.

Parc Llewelyn. Thomas of Lan himself was directly responsible for saving a large area at St Helens from the developer, and this was opened as Victoria Park in 1887, the year of that queen's jubilee. Numerous other parks followed, so that today Swansea possesses fifty-two public parks.

One area where the authorities dragged their heels, however, was the provision of libraries and museums. The first museum in Swansea was founded by private initiative. A Literary and Philosophical Society, founded in 1835, was renamed the Royal Institution of South Wales in 1838, and in 1845 opened its museum, which was the first museum in Wales. From 1876 onwards, John Deffett Francis made a series of gifts of art works to the town, but the real development of art galleries and museums did not occur until the twentieth century,

The Central Library, opened 1887, within its townscape.

beginning with the Glynn Vivian Art Gallery, which was opened in 1911.

With regard to public libraries, there was more direct local authority involvement. Several privately-owned circulating libraries had been established at Swansea by the end of the eighteenth century, but the provision of a public library came late. The Public Libraries Act, 1850 (13 and 14 Victoria, *cap*.65) empowered boroughs with a population of over 10,000 to levy a halfpenny rate for the upkeep of a public library, with the consent of two-thirds of their electorate. In 1866, further legislation changed this to a simple majority and a penny rate. In Swansea, however, nothing positive was done until the 1870s. Earlier attempts at establishing a library — such as that of 1868 — met with hostile opposition from the ratepayers, which was not assuaged

until 1871, when the first public library opened in Goat Street. Hope-
lessly inadequate, this was replaced in 1887 by a purpose-built central
library at Alexandra Road, which still serves as Swansea's main
library, although its resources are today inadequate for a city of
Swansea's size.

By the end of the nineteenth century, great advances had been made
in the field of public health in Swansea, although much still remained
to be done. If a declining death rate can be regarded as a measure of
success, then clearly the Local Board of Health and Urban Sanitary
Authority were successful: from 23.6 per 1,000 in 1849, the rate had
fallen to 17.35 per 1,000 in 1900. However, that success had to be paid
for, and increasing expenditure was a prominent feature of local
government in Swansea after 1850. In the year in which the Local
Board of Health was formed, the borough council had been able to live
of its own without levying a rate, while the Paving Commission's total
annual revenues amounted to about £2,000. The increased activity of
the public health authorities had to be paid for, and the money came
from two main sources: rates and loans. By 1872, Swansea's loan debt
stood at £220,000, of which £200,000 was committed to public health.
By 1900, the revenues amounted to £167,142, while the loan debt was
£1,092,968, a far cry from the situation in 1832, when the unreformed
corporation had a revenue of £1,803 from rents of houses and lands, an
expenditure of £1,637, and a loan debt of £23,000.

By the 1870s, the separate identities of the town council and the
Urban Sanitary Authority were becoming blurred. Although they
were still legally separate bodies, they were, in many instances,
serviced by the same officials, who did not always respect the
difference. For example, minutes of the Urban Sanitary Authority
began to refer to 'the Mayor in the chair' rather than the chairman.
Gradually, Urban Sanitary Authority minutes came to be written up in
pro forma volumes with the corporation's insignia on the cover. By the
1880s, many townsfolk regarded all the functions of local government
as stemming from the corporation, and the process of *de facto*
amalgamation speeded up after 1889, when Swansea became a County
Borough. By the beginning of the twentieth century, the separate identities of both authorities had been lost.

Politics

The pattern of politics in Swansea before the 1830s has been discussed in chapter 4. However, the Reform Act, 1832 and the Municipal

Corporations Act, 1835 substantially changed the system and altered the pattern of politics in the town.

Under the terms of the first Reform Act, 1832 (2 and 3 William IV, *cap.* 45), the franchise in Swansea, in common with other boroughs, was extended to all male householders who paid a minimum annual rental of £10, while those persons who were burgesses also retained their right to vote. However, no new voting rights could be created through the admission of new burgesses. The majority of the new voters were lower middle class, such as victuallers and tradesmen. Within the wider county of Glamorgan, the representation was extended: the 'body of the shire' received an extra member, Swansea and Merthyr Tydfil were each given a member, while Cardiff, as the county town, retained the borough member. Each of the borough seats was supported by contributory boroughs, Merthyr being linked with Aberdare, and Cardiff with Cowbridge and Llantrisant. Swansea's contributory boroughs were Aberavon, Kenfig, Loughor, and Neath, the joint electorate of the whole amounting to 1,307 out of a total combined population of 18,833 in 1832. Within the immediate vicinity of Swansea, the area of the borough was increased from the 1,918 acres of the ancient franchise to 5,000 acres, taking in the hamlet of St Thomas and parish of St John's, and parts of the parishes of Llangyfelach and Llansamlet. The area of the municipal borough was extended in 1835 so as to be co-terminous with the parliamentary borough.

While the Reform Act had extended the franchise, it had not reduced the property qualification for parliamentary candidates. Under the Qualification Act, 1710 (9 Anne, *cap.* 5), a borough member had to possess £300 worth of annual income from land, and this qualification was not repealed until 1858. Moreover, members were not paid until 1911, so until that date prospective candidates had to be men of some substance. In the eighteenth century, the majority of members for the borough seat had come from the ranks of the country gentry, but one of the consequences of parliamentary reform in the borough was the rise and dominance in politics of up-and-coming, wealthy local industrialists. This change in the character of the personnel concerned also resulted in a change of members' political inclinations. Before 1832, most borough members had been Tories, while from that date, until the 1920s, Swansea became a stronghold of Liberalism.

The new, extended electorate, however, had few opportunities to exercise its right to vote for many years after the passing of the Reform Act. No election in Swansea borough was contested before 1874, an echo of the usual state of affairs before 1832. Between 1832 and 1874, Liberal members were elected unopposed, the first being John Henry Vivian, the prominent industrialist and proprietor of the Hafod copperworks, who held the seat until his death in 1855. At the ensuing by-election in February of that year, he was succeeded by Lewis Llewelyn Dillwyn, an extremely radical Liberal and, like Vivian, an ardent free trader. Another prominent local industrialist, with metal-lurgical interests in the Lower Swansea Valley, he held the seat (which became Swansea Town in 1885) until his death in 1892, being re-elected without contest on two occasions and defeating opposition on three.

The second Reform Act of 1867 extended the borough franchise to all ratepaying, male householders and to lodgers paying £10 a year in rent. This swelled the electorate in the Swansea borough constituency to just over 7,500. While Merthyr Tydfil received a second member in this year, Swansea did not. However, as a result of the act, there was a boundary extension in 1868, taking in land at Caebricks, Cwmbwrla, Graig Trewyddfa, Cwmbath, and Pentrepoeth, which extended the borough to 5,363 acres, with a population of 56,995 by 1871.

The next great change occurred in 1885, when the Reform Act of that year gave Swansea two members. The former constituency was divided into the two new seats: Swansea Town (the southern and western portions, of the old constituency) and Swansea District (the northern portions, which also included the four contributory boroughs). Thus, for the first time, people living in central Swansea were exclusively represented by a single M.P. The act of 1885 also split up the body of the shire into five parliamentary divisions, one of which was the Gower Division. This area included the peninsula and the hinterland of the former marcher lordship up to the county boundary with Carmarthenshire and Breconshire, and took in settlements such as Loughor and Pontardawe. Many parts of this area have since been incorporated into the municipal area of Swansea, thus nowadays, Swansea is always regarded as being represented by three M.P.s. The act extended the lower borough franchise to county areas, thereby removing many anomalies which had previously existed, and giving voters in Gower the same rights as their counterparts in the Town and District constituencies.

The two new Swansea seats were first contested in the general election of November 1885. The Town seat was won by L. L. Dillwyn, the Gladstonian Liberal member for the old Swansea seat, who defeated a Conservative opponent, W. H. Meredyth. He regained the seat in the general election of the following July against the challenge of a Liberal Unionist opponent. The new Swansea District seat was first represented by Sir Henry Hussey Vivian, a Gladstonian Liberal, who was elected unopposed in 1885 and 1886. Vivian remained the member for Swansea District until his elevation to the Lords as the first Baron Swansea in 1893, having contested only one election for the seat, in 1892, when he defeated the Conservative, H. Monger Vivian.

On Sir Henry Hussey Vivian's vacating the District seat, it was won in an unopposed by-election by William Williams of Maesygwernen, near Morriston, a tinplate proprietor who had been prominent in local politics for many years, on both the borough and county councils, and who sat in Parliament as a Gladstonian Liberal.

In 1892, the Swansea Town seat was won by Robert John Dixon Burnie, a Gladstonian Liberal 'of very advanced views', who defeated a Conservative opponent, Sir John Talbot Dillwyn Llewelyn, with strong support from the Swansea Trades Council. However, Burnie was to lose his seat to Llewelyn in the General Election of 1895, a result reflecting the flagging Liberal fortunes nationally in that year. This result was the first victory for a Conservative in a Swansea seat. At the same election, Swansea Town was held for the Gladstonian Liberals by · David Brynmor Jones, a prominent barrister. This election in the Town constituency was the first time a Swansea seat had been contested by a Labour candidate, E. H. Hedley, who came second in the poll, beating the Conservative candidate into third place. Labour were not to contest either of the two Swansea seats again until 1910, when Ben Tillett stood unsuccessfully for Swansea Town. However, in the Gower Division there was a different story. The Independent Labour Party's candidate, John Williams, a miners' agent, won the seat from the Liberals in 1906, and remained its member until 1922.

This win for the socialists in Gower was an indication of changes which were to come. But these changes were not to occur in the two Swansea seats until the third decade of the twentieth century. It is clear, then, that by the end of the nineteenth century, the kind of member representing the Swansea constituencies was basically the same as in the 1830s: usually a Liberal and drawn from the ranks of wealthy industrialists. One difference, however, was that elections were contested more frequently than they had been before 1874. Indeed, the last uncontested General Election in a Swansea seat was in 1910 in Swansea District, when Sir David Brynmor Jones was returned unopposed (although in by-elections, T. J. Williams was returned unopposed for the District in 1915 and D. L. Mort, for Swansea East in 1940).

The Liberals continued to hold the two Swansea seats until the 1920s. From 1900 to 1910, the Town was represented by Sir George Newnes, baronet, a publisher and newspaper magnate, and he was succeeded by the local industrialist, Sir Alfred Mond, baronet, who sat in parliament until 1923. In the District, Sir David Brynmor Jones, K.C. held the seat until his appointment as a Master in Lunacy in 1915, when he was replaced by Thomas Jeremiah Williams of Maesygwernen, a prominent local industrialist.

In 1918, the Representation of the People Act altered the Parliamentary representation of Swansea. The two former constituencies of Swansea Town and Swansea District were replaced by Swansea West and Swansea East, while the former contributory boroughs were removed, Loughor being added to the Gower Division. The act also extended the franchise to all males over twenty-one and women over thirty, thereby more than doubling the local electorate:

1910		1918	
Swansea Town	12,935	Swansea West	31,884
Swansea District	12,983	Swansea East	27,185
Gower	14,712	Gower	29,667

Labour candidates had been contesting elections in the two Swansea constituencies since 1910, but not on every occasion, although from 1918 this situation changed. The extension of the franchise was accompanied by widespread gains for Labour over the country as a whole. However, the Liberals continued to hold on to the two Swansea seats for a few years more. Swansea East was held from 1919 to 1922 by David Matthews, a Coalition Liberal who was a leading light on the borough council and a wealthy tinplate owner from Morriston. He was defeated in the General Election of 1922 by David Williams, a boiler-maker, who, in 1898, had been the first Labour member of the borough council and, in 1912-13, had been the town's first Labour mayor. Swansea East has been held by Labour ever since. David Williams was succeeded in 1940 by David Llewelyn Mort, a steelworker from Briton Ferry, who represented Swansea East until his death in 1963. At the ensuing by-election Neil McBride, a Scot and a shop steward in the shipbuilding industry, was victorious. McBride died in 1974, and his successor, Donald Anderson, a barrister and former lecturer at the University College of Swansea, continues to hold the seat today.

The Liberals held on to Swansea West until December 1925, when Sir Alfred Mond was defeated by Howell Walter Samuel, by a slender majority. Samuel, who had begun his working life as a miner, had qualified as a barrister by 1915. His tenure of the seat was short-lived, however, because at the General Election of the following October, the seat was regained for the Liberals by Sir Walter Runciman, baronet, a shipping owner. Since that election, the Swansea West seat has often been considered to be a marginal one. In 1929, Walter Samuel regained it for Labour, but in 1931 it reverted to the Liberals. Their candidate, Lewis Jones (later, Sir Lewis), who had been a schoolmaster and was later involved with the South Wales Siemens Steel Assoc-iation, retained the seat until 1945, when it was won for Labour by Percy Morris, the leader of the council, who had unsuccessfully contested it once before, in 1935. Morris held the seat until 1959, when he himself was defeated by a Conservative candidate, Hugh Rees, a local chartered surveyor. In 1964, the seat was regained for Labour by Alan Williams, a lecturer in Economics, who has held it ever since.

Thus, while Swansea East and Gower had a long history as safe Labour seats, the pattern in the Swansea West constituency was one of fluctuation. The seat was often described as marginal, and this was certainly the case as late as the 1979 General Election, when Labour's majority over the Conservatives was only 401, although in subsequent elections that majority has substantially increased. Indeed, since 1983, boundary changes have affected the three local constituencies, but these fall outside the chronological scope of this chapter.

The pattern of politics in the parliamentary sphere in Swansea since the 1830s has, to an extent, been reflected in the politics of the council chamber. With the passing of the Municipal Corporations Act, 1835, the majority of elected councillors were industrialists, businessmen, or others of high standing in the community, and men drawn from these ranks in society dominated the council until the 1890s. Many of these members were 'of Liberal persuasion', but they often classed them-selves as independent members or as representatives of the interests of the ratepayers rather than followers of a party line. Indeed, it was not until the end of the nineteenth century that party politics in the modern sense began in earnest.

The composition and the workings of the council began to change in the 1890s. Although the Reform Act of 1867 had extended the franchise to ratepayers and £10 lodgers, no working-class councillor was elected in Swansea until 1890, when David Jones, a 'working man candidate', was returned for Victoria Ward and John Hopkin John, a 'Lib-Lab' candidate, won Morriston Ward. The Labour movement began in earnest in Swansea in 1880, with the establishment of the Swansea Trades Council, on the original initiative of the Carpenters' Society. For the first ten years of its life, the Trades Council was mainly concerned with industrial matters, although it gradually turned its attention to gaining representation on local government bodies such as the corporation, the Board of Guardians, and the School Board. In 1890, a branch of the Labour Electoral Association was founded in Swansea, under the aegis of the Trades Council (which, in the previous year, had changed its name to the Swansea Trades and Labour Council). Candidates for local elections began to be put up regularly, and by 1900 there were five Labour members on the borough council, two on the Board of Guardians, and one on the School Board. In 1906, the Swansea Labour Association was formed, and from that date, the impetus increased. Thus, by 1914, nineteen Labour members had sat on the council, and indeed, in 1912 Swansea had its first Labour Mayor, David Williams, who had originally been elected a councillor in 1898 and who was to become the first Labour M.P. for Swansea East in 1922.

After the First World War, Labour began to make big inroads into the council chamber, so much so that by 1933, the representation had narrowed down to thirty-two ratepayer and independent members against twenty-eight Labour members. In the municipal elections of November 1933, however, control of the council passed for the first time to the Labour Party, whose majority of thirty-one to twenty-nine was a slim one. From 1933 to 1974, Labour kept control of the council, with an ever-increasing majority; thus, by 1974, the year of the demise of the County Borough of Swansea, Labour held forty-one seats while the opposition groups held only nineteen. Since the reorganization of local government in that year, the pattern of Labour domination, on both Swansea City Council and West Glamorgan County Council, has remained unbroken, except for the period 1976-9, when the City Council was controlled by the Ratepayers' Group.

The County Borough of Swansea

By the 1880s, Swansea was at the height of its industrial prosperity and was a thriving centre of commerce with a population, at the 1881 census, of 76,430. In respect of its size and status, Swansea became a County Borough in 1889, under the terms of the Local Government Act of the previous year (51 and 52 Victoria, *cap.* 41). The act of 1888 established county councils on the pattern of those councils set up in

Hancocks Brewery, Little Wind Street, c. 1969.

The Grand Theatre after modernisation, 1989.

boroughs after 1835, and abolished Quarter Sessions as an administrative organ of county government. In towns with a population of 50,000 or more, 'County Boroughs' were created. Completely autonomous from the counties in which they were situated, they were endowed with all the functions necessary for local government, including that of the Urban Sanitary Authorities. In the eyes of some commentators, they have been regarded as the most perfect form of local authority ever devised. In 1889, also, the area of the new authority was extended under the Swansea Corporation Act (52 and 53 Victoria, *cap*. 199) to 6,229 acres, and included parts of the parishes of Penderry and Swansea Higher, and of the hamlets of Clase Urban and Rural. By 1891, the population of this area stood at 90,349. The new County Borough was divided into ten wards, represented by thirty councillors and ten aldermen.

The County Borough continued the momentum of the Borough Council and the Urban Sanitary Authority, and in the course of its existence took on additional powers and responsibilities. This increase in scope was evident even before 1900. For example, in 1889, a provisional Order under the terms of the Electricity Acts of 1882 and 1888 was obtained to enable the establishment of a Municipal Electricity Undertaking, which was in operation by the end of the century. This continued to be managed successfully by the County Borough until the nationalization of electricity in 1947, when its assets were transferred to the South Wales Electricity Board.

After 1900, the scope of the activities of the County Borough increased enormously, to embrace almost all matters pertaining to the town. Such was the complexity of the authority's activities, that only the most basic summary of them can be given here. The existing responsibilities, such as public health, were widened enormously in scope, while others were added, and expenditure rose accordingly. In some cases, additional duties were grafted on to existing departments; in others, new departments were created. The first decade of the twentieth century thus witnessed the creation of a Housing Department in 1901, an Education Department in 1902, and an Estates Department in 1904, while in 1911, a Borough Architect's Department was established. In 1914, in addition to these, the County Borough's business was executed by the following departments: Town Clerk, Borough Treasurer, Borough and Water Engineer, Borough Surveyor, Electrical Engineer, Health and Schools Medical Department, Weights and Measures, Parks and Cemeteries, Police, Public Libraries, Art Gallery, and Meat and Veterinary Inspection. Thus, a

The Swansea Corporation Electricity Power Station at The Strand, built 1899-1901.

high degree of specialization had been reached by that date. Some of these departments had been created for administrative convenience as the work of local government became more complex. The Estates Department, for example, had grown out of the Town Clerk's office, as the increasing needs of estate management necessitated specialist treatment: the annual estate rental rose from £6,039 in 1871 to £12,000 in 1901, while by 1931 it stood at £33,000. 'Direct administration' in council house building from 1902 and increased involvement in urban development made the appointment of the first Borough Architect in 1911, a wise decision.

Other departments came into being because of statutory provisions. For instance, the Education Act, 1902 constituted the County Borough of Swansea as the Local Education Authority, and so created an Education Department, to take this important function into the direct control of the local authority for the first time. For most of the nineteenth century, the direction of education had lain with other bodies, although the corporation had had a share in the appointment of governors of the Grammar School, which had been refounded in 1853. Other schools were either private, or, like the Vivians' school in the Hafod, endowed by local industrialists, or else established and run by religious charities: the Anglican Church's National Society for the Promotion of Church Schools built schools at Oxford Street and Christchurch, the nonconformist British and Foreign School Society built at Brynhyfryd, Morriston, and elsewhere, while Roman Catholic schools were built at Greenhill and St Thomas. After the Education Act of 1870, the Swansea United District School Board erected numerous schools in the town, but the act of 1902 enabled the County Borough to take them over. From that date until the transfer of this function to West Glamorgan County Council in 1974, the Education

Works for the construction of Main Drainage Scheme at the corner of Bryn-y-Mor Road and King Edward Road, 1934.

Department of the County Borough provided a service ranging from elementary schools to higher education, and also had responsibility for the school health service and the work of the Children's Committee.

The Housing Department, also established as a result of legislation, was slow in coming. As has been seen, the bodies responsible for public health in nineteenth-century Swansea had shown some concern for housing, but had not been empowered actually to build houses themselves. The Housing of the Working Classes Act, 1890 (53′ and 54 Victoria, *cap.* 70) confirmed local authorities' powers to demolish unfit premises and also permitted them to build new houses to let to working-class tenants. However, in Swansea nothing was done until 1901, with the establishment of the new department. The Swansea Corporation Act of 1902 made some provision for council housing, and in the same year the first four houses were built by 'direct administration' at Well Street, Brynmelyn. In 1906-7, thirty-three more were built at Colbourne Terrace, and by 1914, 315 had been erected in areas such as Brynmelyn, Cwm Road, Mayhill, Baptist Well, Plasmarl, and Trewyddfa Common. Real expansion came after the First World War, when the 'Addison' Housing Act of 1919 gave great impetus to council house building. After 1919, an extensive estate was laid out at Townhill to the plans of Raymond Unwin, the exponent of the 'garden suburb', while from the late 1920s, other estates were developed at Birchgrove, Fforestfach, Llanerch, Morriston, and St Thomas. The Second World War brought a halt to the construction programme, but it continued with renewed vigour after hostilities ended, and by 1974, over 15,000 council houses had been built on estates in all parts of the borough. Housing was one of the functions retained by Swansea City Council after 1974.

The responsibilities which devolved upon the County Borough of Swansea in the course of the present century were legion and included town planning, social welfare, vehicle licensing and taxation, local land charges, mental health, and numerous public trading enterprises such as electricity, water, and telephones. To discuss these adequately would require far more space than is available here. Even the area of the County Borough increased. In 1918, an extension of boundaries took in the Oystermouth Urban District, the parishes of Brynau, Cockett, Llansamlet, and parts of the parishes of Clase Rural and Penderry in the Swansea Rural District. The population was thus increased from 131,476 to 160,810, while the area of the County Borough jumped from 6,229 to 24,241 acres. In 1835, the borough had been divided into two wards, and these had been increased to four in

The Guildhall, opened 1934.

1875. By the extension of 1918, the County Borough was divided into eighteen wards, represented by forty-five councillors and fifteen aldermen, although in 1952, the number of wards was reduced to fifteen so that each could have an alderman.

As early as the 1890s it was apparent that the increased scope of local government had rendered the Guildhall at Somerset Place inadequate to house all the departments of the County Borough. To combat over-crowding, houses in the adjoining streets of Cambrian Place and Prospect Place were taken over for departmental use. In 1907, the corporation resolved to build a new Guildhall, but the advent of war in 1914 delayed construction, and nothing was done until 1929, when an architectural competition was announced. Work on the building at Victoria Park began in 1932, and the new Guildhall opened in October 1934, at a cost of £420,000. However, government grants amounting to £90,000 in part offset this total, the price thus being kept low by utilizing unemployed manpower. Indeed, the Guildhall was only one of a number of important capital projects embarked upon by the County Borough in the 1930s which made use of unemployment relief schemes. The others were Cefn Coed Mental Hospital, opened in 1932, Tir John North power station, 1935, and the Main Drainage Scheme, 1936.

If the Depression and the decline of local industry brought with them problems of unemployment, the two world wars brought even greater difficulties. In both wars, the corporation involved itself in the welfare of troops and the succour of refugees, while the requirements of the Air Raid Precautions Act, 1938 led to the establishment of a new department with an enormous need for manpower and resources. The air raids of the Second World War, particularly those of the 'Three Nights' Blitz' of February 1941, brought problems on a gigantic scale. The damage caused by the raids led to immediate problems of dealing with casualties, housing and feeding the homeless, and removing ruined buildings in the short term. In the long term, it necessitated the almost complete rebuilding of the central commercial area, a task which fell upon the shoulders of the County Borough of Swansea. In 1943, preliminary plans were drawn up, a Compulsory Purchase Order was obtained in 1946, and the work of reconstruction began in 1947, a task which took over thirty years to accomplish.

Redevelopment of an area damaged by enemy action was paralleled from the 1960s onwards by reclamation of land devastated by industrialists. The decline of traditional industries by the end of the Second World War had left the Lower Swansea Valley scarred with the

detritus of 200 years of industrial activity. In 1961, the University
College of Swansea began the Lower Swansea Valley Project, to
investigate this derelict area, and from 1967 onwards, the County
Borough of Swansea became involved in direct executive action to
reclaim the valley, a huge task which has been continued by the present
City Council since 1974, with undeniable success.

*Post-war Town Centre
reconstruction at the
Kingsway, 1950.*

    Although the scope of local government was widening in Swansea
after 1900, several of the functions of the County Borough were transferred to other bodies from the 1940s onwards. In fact, as early as 1907,
the town's municipal telephone service, which had been established in
1901, was taken over by the GPO. In 1947, the corporation's electricity
undertaking was nationalized, while in the following year, many of
the County Borough's responsibilities in the realms of poor relief and
health care were transferred to other bodies on the establishment of
the welfare state. The organization of Civil Defence, for which the

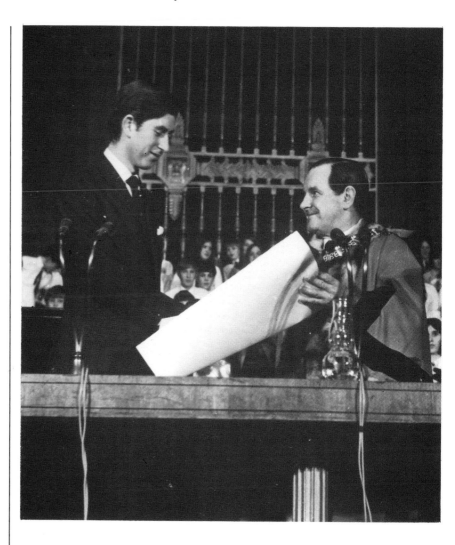

H.R.H. The Prince of Wales presenting the Charter of City Status at the Brangwyn Hall, 15 December 1969.

County Borough had been responsible since 1938, was wound up in 1963, while in 1966, the council handed its water undertaking to the West Glamorgan Water Board. Other transfers included the control of the police force going to the South Wales Police Authority in 1968, while the Courts Act, 1971 amalgamated Swansea's courts of Quarter Sessions and Assizes under the direction of a new Crown Court Service from 1972.

The loss of these functions actually benefited the corporation since it relieved pressure on overcrowded office space. Even without them, the County Borough of Swansea was a massive authority, and its importance was recognized by the granting of city status in 1969. Swansea had, in fact, first petitioned for such status in 1911, the year of the Investiture of a Prince of Wales. The town had to wait until the

Investiture of a later Prince before receiving city status, which in practical terms was an honour which did not alter the administrative role of the County Borough. City status was regranted to Swansea after local government reorganization in 1974, while the further honour of having a Lord Mayor was granted in 1982.

Thus, by 1974, the City of Swansea, with its population of 173,413, the second city in Wales, was successfully administered by a County Borough Council which was the heir to a long tradition of municipal government. On 1 April 1974, that heritage was split between two new authorities, as the Local Government Act, 1972 came into force. Henceforth, the citizens of Swansea would have to rely on West Glamorgan County Council for services such as Education, the Fire Brigade, Highways and Transportation, Libraries, Consumer Protection, and Social Services. Council Housing, Cemeteries, Parks, Museums, Environmental Health, and Rating would be the responsibilities of the City of Swansea, as a District Council, while the County and the City were both to share Planning powers until 1981. Under the terms of reorganization, the area of the former County Borough was amalgamated with that of the Gower Rural District, to make a new administrative District of 60,509 acres, with a population of 187,000. For this greatly extended City of Swansea, a new era in local government was about to begin.

TWENTIETH-CENTURY CHANGE

Chapter 11

Graham Humphrys

Introduction

In the first decade of the twentieth century, Swansea was a place in which the developments of the previous two hundred years were evident and familiar. It was rooted in heat and flames, in the metal smelting and metalworking industries, in the coal mines supplying coal for steam raising, in the steam-engined ships and railways which moved materials to and from and in the docks serving to link Swansea and its hinterland with the world. The landscape had been moulded by this economic matrix and so had its people. In the next two decades Swansea continued to grow in population and the built-up areas expanded to keep pace. But then, economic depression followed by war caused stagnation. Industries shrank, and the population first stopped growing and then began to decline. As a result, by 1950 the basic patterns of Swansea remained little changed. The same industries as had founded the prosperity of the city in the previous century were still prominent. Metal making and working were still dominant, coal was still being mined and the railways and docks were still major employers. Although the industries were being modernized, many of the old buildings were still in use. Much of the private housing was that built in the nineteenth century, with most of the new houses having been added by the corporation in the 1920s and 1930s. A familiar picture survived. The role of Swansea was that of a centre of heavy industry in its own right and a trade and transport centre for western industrial south Wales and rural areas to the west.

But in the second half of the twentienth century all that changed. By 1970 a reshaping of Swansea was well under way and by 1989 it was virtually complete. A new Swansea had arisen from the ashes of the old, literally in some places like the Lower Swansea Valley, and had assumed a softer, gentler form. Within the city the traditional industries had all but disappeared, trade through the docks was a shadow of its former self, and the railways employed few local people. Colliery

Old Swansea slums: Rosser Court, York Street, 1929.

tips had been levelled and metal works demolished to make way for new factories or shopping complexes, railways were turned into country paths and docks into marinas. The majority of the workforce was now employed in Services, which dominated not only the local economy and scene but much of the society of the area as well. Population growth had been resumed and outstripped that of the surrounding areas. By 1989 nearly half the people of western industrial south Wales lived within the administrative boundaries of the city. Extensive new housing had filled in many open spaces, and the urban areas of Swansea had themselves enlarged to merge with neighbouring settlements which spread. The whole had now coalesced to create the new conurbation of Swansea Bay City, reaching from Port Talbot in the east to Llanelli in the west, with Swansea at its heart. The city no longer depended upon the railways and docks for its main links with the outside world. It was much more oriented to serving domestic British markets to which it sent goods by road. In the reverse direction came tourists and holidaymakers, and the people that served them locally far outnumbered the remaining dock and railway workers. The role of the city now was that of a major service centre and a dormitory for those who lived locally and worked elsewhere, with increasingly important functions as a retirement and resort town as well. For the city the twentieth century was a time of metamorphosis.

Old patterns persist: 1900-1945

The heyday of heavy industry in Swansea was the Edwardian era, which the First World War extended in effect to the mid 1920's. In this period, outside the Gower peninsula there were few places that did not have at least one colliery, quarry, metalworks, or factory. Even those without, did not miss out on the industrial scene, having to live with the tramroads, railways, and steam engines constantly busy with train-loads of coal, ores, or metal. The distribution of the main industries and railways in 1908 is shown on figure 1 (*page 349*).

Coal had earlier been the anchor of industrial prosperity, but by 1900 it had been mined intensively in Swansea for decades and the best reserves were worked out. In the non-ferrous metal industries only four copper refineries remained, but the seven local spelter works meant that Swansea was still the centre of zinc smelting in Britain. There was a new addition in 1902 when the Mond Nickel Company opened the largest nickel refinery in the world at the time, at Clydach just outside the later northern administrative boundary of the city.

Chemical works had grown up, often using by-products from the smelters as feedstock, and there were a surprising number of local Patent Fuel works. The latter used small coal to manufacture briquettes using pitch as a binder. While the making of non-ferrous metals was still important in the Swansea economy it was the steel-sheet and tinplate industry which had now come to dominate. By 1903 tinplate production had recovered from the restriction of imports to the U.S.A. ten years earlier and the local industry was once more booming. It was concentrated in the middle Swansea Valley from Morriston northwards, though there were also works at Cwmbwrla and at the King's Dock.

Most of the heavy industries produced waste, some of it poisonous, which was tipped in mounds wherever convenient near the works. Since most of the latter were in the Lower Swansea Valley it was there that the most devastated landscapes were created. There were also fumes, sometimes sulphurous, which poured out of works chimneys with the smoke. Living down-wind of these was not a pleasant experience, but not all the waste was harmful and some of the slag was

Advertising the importance of Swansea for Coal Exporting and Patent Fuel Making, 1915.

cast into building blocks still to be seen at the end of the twentieth century as coping stones on walls in older housing areas. All these industries were largely concerned with sending their output to other parts of the world. But brickworks and stone quarries were also to be found locally, supplying builders with materials needed to expand the urban area to meet the needs of the rapidly growing population.

The jobs of Swansea people in 1911, shown in table 1 (*pages 349–50*), reveal what the town was engaged in during these first years of the new century. For men, iron and steel and tinplate and non-ferrous metal making provided most of the employment in the manufacturing industries. The machine making and general engineering industries were engaged in making and repairing machinery for the heavy industries of Swansea and the surrounding areas. The importance of the food, drink and tobacco industries reflects the way in which far more food was made locally at that time. There was a large flour mill near the entrance to the North Dock using imported wheat to make flour. This was distributed to the many small bakers found in every locality who, in total, employed a large number of people. The Swansea Brewery near the bottom of the Strand is another example of local food production, and locally-made carbonated mineral drinks known as 'pop' were also in great demand. The surge in housebuilding, in particular, at this time is reflected in the large number of building and construction workers. Housebuilding was very labour-intensive, with few machines to help with the physical work and much more of the construction done on site. There were four different railway companies with links to Swansea which together employed over 2,000 men; but even more men were needed at the docks to handle the expanding port trade. There had been so much growth of exports in particular that the King's Dock had been built, opening for traffic only two years earlier in 1909.

For women, the picture was very different, with nearly 40 per cent of all their jobs being in domestic service. The great majority worked as indoor domestic servants though there were also 295 laundry and washerwomen. The making of clothes was the second most important employment for women, with half of them classified as dressmakers and another 320 as tailoresses. Almost all of these were employed in shops where dresses and other clothes were made to order. Similarly, those shown in the food and drink group mostly worked in shops. The tinplate works had traditionally employed women as packers and it was the tinplate works that employed all 472 women shown in the table as having jobs in the iron, steel and tinplate industry. Working

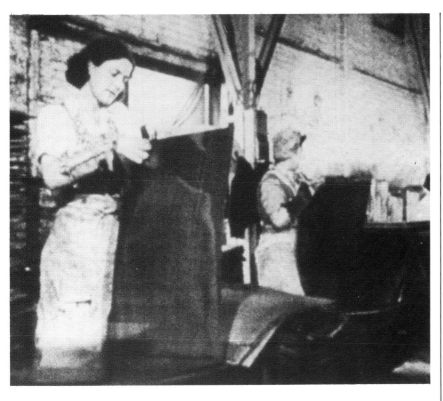

Women at work in a Swansea Tinplate Works in the 1920s.

outside the home was something that was almost entirely confined to unmarried women or widows. The 1911 census records that, of the 10,659 women engaged in occupations, only 99 were married.

The typical industrialist in the Swansea area at this time was a small-scale entrepreneur living in the locality where the works or pit he owned was situated and heavily involved in local life and the community. Almost all businesses were also locally owned, including the large shops in the town centre such as Ben Evans, and the small bakers and the milk and coal delivery merchants. There were also small numbers of major proprietors and owners, like Alfred Mond of the nickel works, who made important contributions to local government.

Patterns of people

The prosperity and economic expansion of Swansea in the first part of the twentieth century were reflected in rapid growth of the population. From around 134,250 in 1901 the population rose to 152,619 in 1911 and 164,225 in 1921. There was in-migration, but the birth rate was also high, so that in 1901 three-quarters of the population were born in Swansea, a further 10 per cent were born in other parts of Wales, and less than 15 per cent had been born elsewhere. By 1921 this was unchanged. Swansea throughout this period was a very Welsh city, with the great majority of the population born in Wales and with over 45,000 people recorded as being able to speak Welsh in 1921. This was twenty-nine per cent of the population and, although most of the Welsh speakers lived in the north and west, in the Morriston area and in north Gower, the language was commonplace in the centre of the city and in the tinplate, copper and zinc works.

The added numbers of people led to overcrowding and growing concern about inadequate housing. The commercial and industrial activity of Swansea was concentrated in the Lower Swansea Valley and around the mouth of the Tawe, where it was squeezed in between Townhill and Kilvey Hill and the sea. With much of the flat land here taken for industry, railways and the docks and with competition from shops and offices, a lot of housing had been squeezed up onto the steep hillslopes. Much of the working-class housing was substandard and, being in short supply, was overcrowded. Many of these houses were very small, no more than two rooms and a scullery, and in the centre of the town they often had two or more families living in them. The fact that there were eighty applicants for four Corporation cottages built in 1901, shows how much demand there was for good cheap housing.

The corporation took further action to help and in 1906 began to build 210 houses and flats on the Baptist Well estate at the eastern end of Townhill, for which they received 2,000 applications. These early starts on providing local authority housing soon blossomed and in 1906 the possibility of developing housing on the top of Townhill was mooted. This idea was taken further in 1910 when the corporation sponsored a competition to find the best layout for a housing estate to be built on Mayhill and for the design of cheap houses for rent. The competition required the design houses to be built before being judged, to give a practical demonstration of what was possible. The result was twenty-nine houses around Llewellyn Circle and Nicander Parade on Townhill, which were still occupied in 1989. They remained as monuments to the farsightedness of the Corporation of the time, demonstrating that Swansea was in the vanguard in town planning and council house design. In 1912 the Corporation continued to pursue their intentions and had plans drawn up by George Bell, the Borough Surveyor, in cooperation with Raymond Unwin, for the development of housing on Townhill. Raymond Unwin had a distinguished reputation as the designer of Letchworth Garden City and Hampstead

Garden suburb. The First World War delayed implementation of these plans but the estate was completed between 1922 and 1929.

The First World War from 1914 to 1918 only temporarily disrupted local industrial activity and by the 1920s the earlier pattern of economic development had been resumed. Copper refining had declined further but in 1924 a greater tonnage of trade passed through the port than ever before. Part of the reason for this was the opening of the Queen's Dock on the east side of the river Tawe in 1920, completing the development of the dock system. The new dock was designed to handle the import of crude oil for the Llandarcy oil refinery built in the same year two miles to the north-east and the export of refined products. The prosperity was not to last. Before 1930 strikes in the coal industry were followed by the Stock Market crash, and an economic depression set in. By the mid 1930s all the local industries had contracted. The coal mines in the Morriston and Llansamlet areas had closed and only six continued to work in Swansea; five in the area from Dunvant west and one at Felin Fran near Clydach. In the steel and tinplate industries the orders available were shared between works to try to keep them open. As a result by 1939 only two works had closed in Swansea, while 12 survived, though most of the people employed in them worked only part-time. In the non-ferrous industries only three works remained open, a copper refinery and a zinc smelter in the Lower Swansea Valley, and the nickel refinery at Clydach. Trade through the docks fell from nearly 9 million tons in the peak year of 1930 to around 5 million tons in 1936. It was exports of metal products, especially tinplate and galvanized sheets, which declined most. Coal exports were maintained because of the continued overseas demand for anthracite from the coalfield north and west of Swansea. Changes in methods of working, the increased size of ships, and reduced trade led to changes in the port. The North Dock was closed and the South Dock reduced to handling mostly sand and gravel dredged up from the Severn Estuary. Employment on the railways fell, too, as the economic depression caused fewer goods and materials to be moved around.

Though local economic activity was drastically reduced as a result of the economic depression, the basic economic structure remained almost unchanged. The dominant industries were still steel and tinplate making, non-ferrous metal production, and coal mining, with large numbers still employed in rail and port activities serving these industries. There was substantial employment in services in Swansea, meeting the needs of a wide area covering the western south Wales coalfield where the same heavy industries were dominant. Thus not

Aerial view of the main entrance to the University College, Swansea.

only did the economic pattern established in the nineteenth century remain dominant but most of the works and coal mines were still those first developed in the nineteenth century with little modernization. There were other developments, however, which anticipated greater change in the future. By the end of the 1930s, the use of electricity, which began at the turn of the century, was widespread. Lorries and buses were making substantial progress in local goods and passenger transport, and cars were now familiar. In industry, most of the works were now owned by large companies with headquarters elsewhere, replacing the traditional structure of local entrepreneurship and ownership in the control of local operations.

Towards the end of the 1920s the rate of population growth slowed, affected by the economic depression. Even so there were still over 7,000 more people in Swansea in 1931 than in 1921. The number of individual houses and flats had increased by over 6,000, with half of them having been built by the Corporation. This had reduced overcrowding but not eliminated it. In the central wards of Swansea, people were still living in houses with an average of more than one person per room and the 1931 census recorded fifteen per cent more private families than there were separate houses and flats.

By 1931 unemployment was rising rapidly, with a rate of male unemployment of just under twenty-five per cent. A slow economic recovery began in 1935 but even in 1936 there were still 8,980 men aged between 18 and 64 unemployed in Swansea, nearly half of them in the 18-34 age group. Not surprisingly, the population now ceased to grow, staying at around 174,000 until 1935 and then falling in the next four years to around 171,500. As there were far more births than deaths during this period the loss was caused by people moving away, with around 500 more people moving out each year than moved in. There were also shifts in the locations where people lived. The fall in population was entirely within the boundary of Swansea County Borough area, while Gower Rural District continued to gain population through in-migration. Even within Swansea County Borough there were people moving from the central areas to the new council houses. Most of these were built on Townhill, but with some also added east of the river Tawe in St. Thomas and Bonymaen. Between 1931 and the outbreak of the Second World War in 1939 the Corporation had provided a further 2,399 new houses and flats. At the same time more than 2,000 new private houses were built, the latter mainly in the Sketty area. Swansea Corporation continued its active policy of slum clearance in the 1930s, demolishing 1,245 houses in which 6,034 people lived. The areas most affected were in Alexandra Ward, north and north-west of High Street Station, where there was a concentration of old houses, some built around inner courtyards. Other municipal developments were also reaching fruition at this time. A main drainage scheme was completed, including great storage tanks under Mumbles Hill, which stored sewage until a suitable state of the tide and then released it through a large sea outfall off Mumbles Head. A new Guildhall was built as unemployment relief work and opened in 1934. A year later the Tir John electricity generating station was opened on the east side of Kilvey Hill, with a major generating capacity for the time of 40 megawatts.

The Second World War brought about several further changes in Swansea which were to become more important in the post-war period. The coal industry was put under central government control

Industrial dereliction in the Lower Swansea Valley, 1960s.

and output was increased to meet wartime demands. Lack of men and supplies meant that maintenance was reduced to a minimum, and since this followed a period of depression when investment had already been low, by the end of the war most of the coal mines were in a poor state and in desperate need of modernization. Subsequent changes in the tinplate industry were foreshadowed when many of the tinplate works were taken out of production on being requisitioned for wartime storage and packaging. Increased wartime demand for non-ferrous metals, however, ensured that their output was maintained or increased. There were some new factories built in the Lower Swansea Valley and an aluminium plant set up at Waunarlwydd, again to produce materials for the war effort. With men recruited for the armed forces male unemployment disappeared, but an even greater change occurred in the kinds of jobs that women did. Before 1939 the place of a woman in Swansea, as in the rest of south Wales, was in the home, either as a housewife or in domestic or personal service. During the war, far more women took paid jobs as they replaced men conscripted for the armed forces.

Other major changes during the war were the development of a fighter aerodrome on Fairwood Common and the construction of a hospital at Morriston to take war wounded. In the post-war period the aerodrome was taken over by the Corporation and turned into Swansea airport, and Morriston Hospital was retained for civilian use. In 1940 and 1941 the city centre was destroyed by bombing, allowing it to be comprehensively redesigned and rebuilt in the post-war period.

Modernization and additions, 1945-1966

Three major changes occurred in the underlying economic structure during the twenty years after the end of the Second World War. There was the modernization of the inherited industries, the addition of new economic activities, and the growing importance of services.

The modernization of the older industries involved investment to upgrade operations that were going to survive and the closure of those

Kitchen in a Council House at Cwmrhydyceirw, 1944.

not worth saving. In addition there was change of ownership, which in most cases made modernization possible. In the coal industry the need for investment in modernization had become desperate by 1945. Far less mechanization had been introduced than in other countries, the methods used were outdated, and the facilities for the men were in most cases primitive. At the same time, increased output was needed to meet the deferred industrial demands of the war years. It is unlikely that the private owners of the industry would have been able or willing to make the necessary investment and the industry was taken into public ownership in 1947. Only one coal mine survived in Swansea by this time, a drift mine at Felin Fran just south of Clydach. Investment here enabled production to continue until the late 1960s.

There was a similar situation in the steel and tinplate industry. The need for modernization of the industry in the Swansea region had been recognized in the 1930s but had been deferred as a result of the outbreak of the Second World War. In 1945 the government accepted a tinplate redundancy scheme for permanent closure of some works. Rationalization of ownership had already got underway when two companies which owned a substantial proportion of tinplate making capacity in the Swansea region amalgamated to form Richard Thomas and Baldwins Limited early in 1945. In 1946 the government announced a plan to replace all the steel, steel-sheet, and tinplate making works in the Swansea region with three new plants using the latest technology. Iron and steel making and steel-sheet production were to be concentrated at Port Talbot, with tinplate works at Velindre north of Swansea and Trostre at Llanelli. In 1951 Richard Thomas and Baldwins Limited became part of the British Steel Corporation when the industry was taken into public ownership. Under the modernization plans all the Swansea works were to close when the new capacity became available. The Trostre Works opened in 1953 and Velindre in 1956. In practice, demand for tinplate remained high into the late 1950s, so that even in 1960 the King's Dock tinplate works and the Upper Forest and Duffryn Steelworks in Morriston were still working. But their days were numbered and by 1966 they had closed. The Landore steelworks survived as a small operation, making ingot moulds for use in other steelworks. Tinplate making had now ceased in Swansea after more than a hundred years. Many Swansea men continued to be employed in the industry at the Velindre works located just beyond the city boundary to the north and in the Bryngwyn coated sheet works at Gorseinon just to the north-west. Swansea also supplied workers to the Port Talbot Steelworks complex, where they had been transferred by agreement when their local works had been closed down.

The non-ferrous metals industry fared less badly. Copper working became confined to a small factory at Landore, making boilers from copper sheets; but the zinc smelter at Llansamlet continued to flourish throughout this period. More important for employment were two aluminium works which were established. At Waunarlwydd the major aluminium works built during the Second World War was taken over by the Aluminium Company of America to produce aluminium sheet and extrusions. On an adjacent site Imperial Metal Industries established a works to roll titanium into tubes and sheets in 1957. At Port Tennant near the Docks the Aluminium Wire and Cable Company built a works in 1946 and added an extension just outside the city boundary at Jersey Marine to the east in 1965.

While these changes were taking place in the older industries, new manufacturing was being added. At the southern end of the Lower Swansea Valley, a government wartime factory was taken over by the Addis Company to produce plastic brushes and containers. To the north near Morriston, the Morganite Carbon Company built a new works in 1961 to make carbon brushes for electric motors, transferring their whole operation there from Battersea in London. But the major new industrial development was the establishment of the Fforestfach Industrial Estate in north-west Swansea immediately after the end of the Second World War. This attracted industries making a range of goods from toys and clothing to food products and bakery equipment. By 1965 three-quarters of all manufacturing jobs in the Swansea Labour Exchange area, other than in the metals group, were located on the Fforestfach Industrial Estate.

Road and rail transport during this period was also modernized, though the dock system remained little altered. Trade through the port remained constant after 1950 at around 8 million tons a year. There was a shift, though, in that coal and coke exports which had been as much as 3 million tons a year in 1938 now fell to between 1 and 1.8 million tons a year. More important was the trade in crude oil imports and refined petroleum product exports. These remained at around 5 million tons a year in total until the late 1980s, when the Llandarcy oil refinery contracted to become a small specialist lubricating oil producer only. Rail transport was modernized following nationalization in 1947, with diesel locomotives replacing steam engines in the 1950s and improvements in signalling and goods depots. The effect of this modernization programme was to reduce the workforce needed.

In 1965 radical restructuring of rail transport began, following adoption of the Beeching Plan in 1963. But the effects were only just beginning to be felt by 1966. Road transport increased, especially after 1950 when petrol and diesel fuel became more readily available. Road freight increased markedly after 1954 when more competition was allowed. A major factor affecting public service passenger transport was the rapid and continuing increase in private car ownership. In 1956 10,000 private cars were registered in Swansea for the first time. This reduced demand for bus and rail passenger services. The Mumbles railway, which had provided the first passenger service on rails in the world at the beginning of the nineteenth century, was closed in 1960, being replaced by a bus service.

The major economic change, however, was in the growth of other Services in Swansea. The city benefited in particular from national-ization, which was accompanied by rationalization and centralization, though the last two were not confined to public sector services. Nationalization of the gas, electricity and health services in the late 1940s led to modernization and reorganization. In most cases this led to Swansea gaining new jobs as the centre serving the surrounding area. Electricity is a good example. After nationalization in 1948 the South Wales Electricity Board divided south Wales into three regions, one of which was centred on Swansea. The Swansea area was divided into six districts with the headquarters of the region located in Swansea, which also had the main maintenance and supply depot. By 1964 the six

Electric Tramcar at Pentre Estyll, c. 1903.

districts had been merged to become just three, and some of the administration relocated to the south Wales headquarters east of Cardiff. Local government and national government administration employment increased markedly. Swansea again gained in being a County Borough, with County and District level functions needing to be administered, and housed the main offices of national government services such as the Inland Revenue serving the wider Swansea region. Similar developments were occurring in the private sector through the rationalization of such things as bread and confectionery production and the spread of multiple store ownership. During the 1950s, in particular, the number of small local bakers rapidly decreased in face of competition from large companies, and most bread and confectionery came to be manufactured in factories. As well as all these essentially regional services, there were other services which catered for national needs and which also grew. The most obvious examples were the University College and the Swansea College of Education, both located in west Swansea. In 1945 they had 800 and 200 students, respectively , whereas in 1976 these figures had risen to 2,000 and 800, with employment rising accordingly.

Two other changes deserve special mention. It was during this period that the number of women going out to work increased markedly and the proportion of women employed rose accordingly. The kinds of jobs they did changed dramatically. No longer was the personal service category the largest employer of women as it had been before the Second World War. A substantial number worked in the new factories which had been built, where there were more women than men making clothing and toys. Shops and warehouses were now the largest employers of women in Swansea; but women had also come greatly to outnumber men in such professional services as education and health. The dramatic increase in car ownership had coincided with the increasing separation of production industry jobs, in particular, from the areas where people lived. People had to travel further to work at a time when the ability to travel further was increased. The result was a growth in the average distance travelled to work. By 1966, 30 per cent of the workers who had jobs and lived in Swansea travelled beyond the city boundaries every day to work. Most of these were men. One of the main reasons for this was that within Swansea it was services which employed mostly women that were growing rapidly, while older industries which employed mostly men were closing down and many of the new industries and the replacements for the old were locating beyond the city boundaries.

The main economic changes during this period, then, were modernization of the older industries, the addition of some new manufacturing, and the modernization and growth of services. As late as 1966, however, the old economic structure and patterns of Swansea persisted. They had been modified but were still evident. A greater change had taken place in the growth of commuting, but even in 1966 the local patterns had not adapted very much to the increasing affluence and growth in mobility allowed by widespread car ownership.

In the immediate post-war period, recognition of the need to ensure orderly urban development, and concern about the environment and land use led to the passing of the Town and Country Planning Act of 1947. This required all County Authorities to prepare plans for the development of their areas and required planning permission to be obtained for all new buildings. The Corporation acquired the freehold of the centre of Swansea, which had been devastated by bomb damage during the Second World War. In 1946 a plan was adopted for reconstruction of the city centre with a different street pattern from the old. At the same time the city resumed its programme of house building, setting itself a target of 6,000 new houses to house people removed by clearance of the worst of the remaining slums. By 1954 they were halfway to their target, with over 3,000 new houses and flats completed. The majority of these had been built at Penlan in the north of the city, on an extensive area of common land at about 600 feet above sea level west of the Tawe Valley.

The disruption of the Second World War and the subsequent post-war adjustments resulted in the Swansea population in 1951, at 172,731, being very little different from what it was in 1939. Comparison of the more accurate figures from the 1931 and 1951 censuses shows that over this twenty-year period the population of Swansea declined by about one per cent. Since more people were born than died in the intervening period, the loss was caused by about 17,000 more people moving away than migrated into Swansea and Gower. The conditions in which people lived improved dramatically. For example, whereas there were 90 people for every hundred rooms in 1931, by 1951 there were only 76 persons per hundred rooms. This was brought about mainly by the fall of about 8,000 in the number of people living in private families, while the number of houses and flats had increased by about 8,000. By 1951 fifty per cent of households had exclusive use of all five main household facilities, that is, a cooking stove, a kitchen sink, piped water, a W.C., and a fixed bath. These average figures conceal quite wide variations within Swansea. The central areas of the city came out worst, with

Alexandra Ward, between High Street Station and Mount Pleasant, still having over five per cent of people living at more than two to a room, and other older areas, such as Landore, Victoria, and Llansamlet, having over two per cent of their population living at two or more to a room.

An important cultural change in Swansea between 1931 and 1951 was in the numbers of those speaking Welsh. In 1931 the census reported that of the 156,679 people aged 3 or over in Swansea County Borough, 42,862 or twenty seven per cent spoke Welsh. By 1951, of the smaller number of 153,372 who were aged 3 or over, only 30,735 or only twenty per cent were recorded as being able to speak Welsh.

The modernization of Swansea's economy, which continued in the 1950s, was accompanied by a number of social changes. Between 1951 and 1961 the population grew by 7,247, mostly by natural increase but with a small amount of net in-migration. At least sixty per cent of the immigrants to Swansea County Borough came from outside industrial south Wales. Swansea Corporation maintained its programme of building council houses and clearing older, poorer housing, most of which was in the Dyfatty-Greenhill-Waun Wen-Hafod district north of High Street railway station. By 1961 most of the worst housing had disappeared and over seventy per cent of all households had exclusive use of cold and hot running water, a fixed bath and a W.C. Until the mid 1950s, shortage of men and materials and the demands made by reconstruction in post-war Britain, meant that private house building was restricted. Between 1945 and 1954 the local authority built eighty six per cent of the 3,547 new houses in the Swansea County Borough area. Most of the council houses continued to be added in the Penlan and Clase areas, but a substantial new council housing estate was added at Sketty Park, and additions were made to the estate at West Cross which had been begun earlier. From then on, however, private building proceeded apace. Infilling with individual new private houses occurred throughout Swansea and large new estates of private houses were built in the Killay and Dunvant areas. In Gower there had been demand for new private housing since the 1930s, especially in south Gower. This had increased as bus services improved and car ownership began to grow. Following the easing of building restrictions in the early 1950s new private housing soon began to appear once again. Shortly afterwards, the Gower peninsula was designated by the Government as the first Area of Outstanding Natural Beauty in Britain under the National Parks Act and Access to the Countryside Act of 1949. This led to the establishment of a special committee with planning powers responsible for ensuring that the beauty of Gower was maintained and that development would be in keeping with that aim and channelled in the right directions. The new planning controls allowed the urban growth to be concentrated in the area from Bishopston out to Pennard. Most of the new residents moving here worked in Swansea and so this became a dormitory suburban extension of the city.

Because most of the new private and council housing in Swansea was built at the relatively low densities of not more than eight houses to the acre, the effect of this growth was to expand the urbanized area and fill in new areas with housing associated services. Schools which were needed in these areas to cater for the large number of children, also required large areas of land for their modern buildings and extensive playing fields, adding to the urbanization process. Typical examples were the all-through secondary schools, opened at Penlan in 1956 and Mynyddbach in 1959, for boys and girls respectively, which soon grew to take over a thousand pupils each. In 1952 Bishop Gore, a secondary school, made its own contribution, when it moved from the city centre to a new site on the northern edge of Singleton Park.

1966-1988, the restructured economy

In many ways the period from 1945 to 1966 can be seen as a time of adjustment and renewal following a major economic depression and the disruption of war. The next period was utterly different. Not only did the old economic structure of the city finally disappear but many of its remains in the landscape were cleared away, leaving little evidence that it had ever existed. In its place a new economic structure appeared, much more in keeping with what was happening elsewhere in Britain at the end of the twentieth century.

Coal mining in Swansea finally ceased when the Felin Fran mine was closed in 1968. Coal mines in the hinterland of Swansea were gradually closed, until by 1989 only two survived, employing in total less than 2,000 men. The industry was no longer of importance to Swansea. The last link with the copper industry disappeared when the Landore copper works was closed; and 1973 saw the last activity at the Llansamlet zinc smelter site. The old smelting industries had been lost and the remaining non-ferrous industries were concerned with working metal shipped in from elsewhere. Aluminium working was now dominant, with the Alcoa sheet and extrusion plant at Waunarlwydd, and the aluminium wire and cable making works taken over by the Aluminium Company of Canada near the docks. The works owned by the IMI Company making titanium and zirconium alloy rolled and sheet products next to the Alcoa plant was also still in production .

The last link with the steel and tinplate industry within the city was lost when the Landore steelworks was converted to a small engineering factory in 1980. Steel and tinplate jobs for Swansea people disappeared in large numbers as the industry in the local region was decimated. Employment at the Port Talbot steelworks dropped from 18,500 in 1967 to 4,500 in 1989, and the Velindre tinplate works just beyond the northern boundary of the city was closed in 1989 with the loss of 800 jobs. Steel and tinplate making thus also became minor local employers of Swansea labour.

With the loss of the old heavy industries, modern manufacturing came to dominate local production. Most of these industries, other than the metal works mentioned earlier, were located on industrial estates and in the redeveloped Lower Swansea Valley. On Fforestfach Industrial Estate, operated by the Welsh Development Agency, many factories came to the end of their useful life in the 1970s and their sites were redeveloped. Over 5,000 people were employed there by 1989, many of them women making clothes, food, and toys, and assembling products such as computers. A second industrial estate, at Cwmdu between the town centre and Fforestfach, was developed by the city council in the late 1960s. It housed much smaller factories and had more service activities than manufacturing but it provided jobs for 1,000 people. The Lower Swansea Valley is the other major centre of manufacturing. Three earlier post-war industrial developments — the Gasworks Estate, the Addis moulded plastic products plant, and Morganite Carbon — continued to operate there. More new manufacturing was attracted following the redevelopment of the derelict areas after 1966 and the designation by the government of a large part of the Lower Swansea Valley as the first Enterprise Zone in Britain in 1981. A new industrial estate was established at Waun Wen on the east side of the Valley, with a mixture of services and manufacturing operations. On the floor of the valley, retailing and services predominated but small industrial units added there in the 1980s proved to be very popular and were fully occupied.

About 73,000 people worked in Swansea in 1989. Of these, some 13,000 or 17 per cent had jobs in manufacturing, and nearly 60,000, more than 80 per cent, were employed in Services. By then, in terms of the jobs people did, Swansea was predominantly a service centre with some manufacturing taking place as well. The increased dominance of services had come about in two ways. The loss of jobs in the older inherited industries had not been matched by the growth of new manufacturing, so that the proportion of employment in production industries had shrunk. At the same time many service employments had grown to meet the demands of an increasingly affluent society, causing them further to increase in importance.

Several important changes after 1966 led to the further growth of local service employment. The first was the decision to build the Driver Vehicle Licensing Centre, to serve the whole of the United Kingdom, at Clase near the northern boundary of the city west of Morriston. It was located there as part of Government policy to disperse Civil Service employment away from south-east England. With a workforce of 4,000, the DVLC is by far the largest single employer in Swansea other than the County Council. In addition, Post Office facilities had to be expanded to cope with the increased demand placed on the postal service by the centre. The second major boost to local service employment came with the reorganization of local government in Britain in 1974. Swansea was demoted from County Borough status to being a District within a new County of West Glamorgan, but the latter decided to build its new headquarters in Swansea. The city now had two local government administrations to house — the District Council with headquarters in the Guildhall, and the new County Council with a headquarters on the seashore near the city centre. Between them they employed over 9,000 people. Other changes added further service growth. Singleton Hospital was built in the mid 1960s and subsequently expanded, and the Morriston Hospital complex was substantially rebuilt in the late 1980s. These two came to provide jobs for nearly 2,000 people. The University College of Swansea continued to expand and the former Swansea College of Education was combined with other institutions to create the West Glamorgan Institute of Higher Education. The total number of jobs in higher education in the city increased to over 3,000 as a result.

In addition to this growth, directly financed by or within the public sector, there were also important changes taking place in private sector services. The most obvious were the developments in shopping. The rebuilding of the town centre was completed according to the original plan in the late 1960s. In the 1970s and 1980s large additions extended the shopping area, first south and west, and then east onto the former site of the North Dock. Major out-of-town shopping complexes were built, mostly on the north side of the city. Particularly prominent was the growth of large retail outlets on the northern edge of the redeveloped Lower Swansea Valley from the late 1970s. By 1989 over one-third of all the retail shopping space in the Swansea region was located there, south of the main road between Morriston and Llansamlet. Swansea had always drawn holiday-makers and tourists because of its many attractions. Being in the south of Britain on a south-facing coast was one. More important was the superb coastal scenery of the Gower peninsula close to a major city providing a range of alternative attractions to visit in bad weather. With growing affluence in Britain and western Europe, the number of visitors expanded in the 1980s, as did provision for them. Two major new hotels were built, the International Hilton and the Holiday Inn, and the number of hotel and bed-and-breakfast rooms expanded. There was also growth of other leisure services, particularly restaurants, discos, and cinemas. The City Council added to these when it took a decision in the mid 1970s to convert the abandoned South Dock in Swansea into a marina. It had already built a leisure centre complex on the site of the old Victoria railway station nearby. All this, too, added further service employment in the heart of the city.

Not all services expanded. Transport was one area which declined. Continual contraction of demand for rail services contributed and especially the loss of heavy rail-using industries in Swansea and its hinterland. Other factors were the modernization of operations and the drive towards increased efficiency, which generally meant fewer people to achieve more work. The freightliner terminal and the diesel servicing depôt were closed with loss of jobs. Bus passenger services were reduced, as use of private cars increased, and some private-hire bus companies were closed. Decline of trade through the docks occurred after 1970 when imports of crude oil for the Llandarcy oil refinery were transferred to Milford Haven, with a pipeline linking the two. Coal exports were maintained until 1980 but then fell, and in 1987 the coal loading hoists, symbols of a past era when coal was king, were finally removed. The docks were sold to Associated British Ports Plc in 1987 and by 1989 barely a hundred dock workers remained employed.

Throughout this period the number of women working in Swansea continued to increase, rising from about 25,000 in 1966 to 35,000 in the late 1980s. By then they accounted for 48 per cent of the total number of employees in work, though a substantial number had only part-time jobs. There were more women than men employed in all the services other than construction, gas, electricity, water, and transport. Car ownership had risen to the point where over 60 per cent of households had a car and a majority of workers travelled to work by car.

By 1989 the transformation of Swansea was almost complete. In the first half of the twentieth century the people of Swansea had continued to depend on the inherited industries of coal, non-ferrous metal working, steel and tinplate, and on the railways and docks to provide most of the jobs. As late as 1966 these continued to be locally important. But by 1989 they had either disappeared or shrunk to minor importance. The economy of the city had been reshaped. Far more important now in bringing money into the city were the modern services meeting national needs, including higher education, leisure and tourist provision, and the Driver and Vehicle Licensing Centre. Swansea was also benefiting from providing such services for its hinterland as hospital provision, shopping, and county level administration. Fewer than one in six jobs in the city were in manufacturing, so that many of those who lived locally and wanted to work in industry had to travel to neighbouring areas to find a job. Many of the places where people worked in Swansea had been built in the previous twenty-five years. Little evidence remained of the earlier economic base and that little was rapidly being removed.

There were two important changes in local government by 1975. In 1969 the Queen granted Swansea the status of a City, which it clearly now deserved. More significant for local development was the reorganization of local government in Britain in 1974. Swansea lost the County Borough status and functions it had been given in 1889, though it remained a city, and was joined with the former Gower Rural District to create a new Swansea District. At the same time the new County of West Glamorgan was created, within which there were four Districts: Swansea, Lliw Valley, Neath, and Afan. Swansea was by far the largest of these, with almost half the population of the new county. As a District the enlarged City retained many of the responsibilities it had before, but the County was given responsibility for such things as transport planning and education services. The fifteen years from then to 1989 saw the completion of the transformation of Swansea into its new form. Where this could be seen best was in the area extending from the northern end of the Lower Swansea Valley south to the city centre and the mouth of the Tawe and then west to the Guildhall. The biggest change was in the Lower Swansea Valley. By the early 1980s all the preparation work of the previous twenty years undertaken by the City and latterly helped by the West Glamorgan County Council, came to fruition. The dereliction had been cleared away. In its place, new commercial and industrial buildings had appeared in places, the central area had been smoothed, and landscaping around a new lake had begun. Trees planted in the 1960s had matured, adding a green swathe to the scene, and a new sports complex had been built just south of the Landore railway viaduct. People around the valley sides now looked into it rather than turning away as they had done in the past; and the major shopping developments in the north-east had begun to attract large numbers from elsewhere in the City and beyond. In 1981 the redevelopment received a further boost when most of the Lower Swansea Valley was declared the first Enterprise Zone in Britain, with incentives such as a five-year rate-free period for new businesses, attracting more investment. By 1989 more shops, offices and small 'starter unit' factories had taken the redevelopment further, and a new International Hilton Hotel was opened on the edge of the lake.

In 1975 the City planners produced a new plan, which envisaged part of the Lower Swansea Valley as a park area leading south by landscaped riverside walkways to the shores of Swansea Bay. As part of this plan it was a courageous and inspired decision to redevelop the run-down and derelict areas around the South Dock, between the city centre and the sea, and the North Dock area east of the city centre. By 1989 the South Dock had been turned into a commercially successful leisure boat marina. Around it a thousand people had moved in to occupy a range of newly constructed houses and flats. The City Council had taken over an old warehouse and converted it into a maritime and industrial museum and had helped to provide a theatre. Leisure craft soon occupied most of the berths in the marina, and restaurants and shops developed. The high quality of design won architectural and design awards and attracted visitors to the new promenade backing the sandy beach. A new hotel had been built at the western end of the Marina. Beyond it on the shore, the West Glamorgan County Council had already completed an imposing headquarters building in 1978. By 1989 the long filled-in North Dock Site had also been redeveloped, with new major shopping installed, including a Sainsburys supermarket and a Toys 'R Us store, together with a leisure complex of cinemas and a bowling alley. Plans were already afoot to extend this redevelopment across to the east bank of the river Tawe, where new housing was to be built.

In the city centre, the Quadrant, a covered shopping centre with associated bus station had extended the shopping area south-west in the late 1970s, and in the early 1980s the St. David's shopping centre was also opened on the south side. Almost all the new shops in both developments were branches of large companies, some of them like Boots and C and A's being multinational companies. Locally owned shops were now located in older premises extending west along Oxford Street. The growth of financial and legal services such as building societies and estate agents had been accommodated by conversion of post-war premises along the Kingsway and of older, larger houses along the north side of St. Helen's Road and Walter Road, built by the more affluent people of Swansea a hundred years previously. The growth of leisure services and tourism was marked by the spread and upgrading of bed and breakfast hotels along Oystermouth Road, facing the sea just west of the town centre, and of restaurants along the south side of St. Helen's Road. Similar development was occurring in the Newton and Langland Bay areas. There, conflicts arose because of the demand for holiday and retirement accommodation in an established highly desirable residential area. In addition to the upgrading of hotels, holiday flats and residences for the elderly were built, and, in places, larger older houses with ample gardens were torn down and replaced with higher density accommodation. With proximity to attractive bays in an already urbanized area this was the sensible location to provide for the growing demand for accommodation from visitors. Local residents saw this as a threat to their community.

The changes in the Lower Swansea Valley and city centre areas were the most comprehensive in the city. Many other changes were occurring at the same time. After 1975, the emphasis shifted from demolishing poorer housing to that of housing improvement. Government housing improvement grants of up to 90 per cent of the cost for older properties, resulted in many homeowners extending their houses to add bathrooms and kitchens, and installing hot water and central heating systems. Particularly obvious in older parts of the city was the replacement of slates on roofs with tiles, which were more colourful. New housing was still being built. In the 1970s the layout and design of council houses changed, with higher densities per acre and distinctive styles being adopted. Council house building almost came to an end in the 1980s and occupiers of council housing, encouraged by government policy, began to buy their properties. Even so, about 30 per cent of households in Swansea still rented their accommodation from the City Council. More housing was now being built by housing associations which received financial help from the government and let property to tenants. Between 1971 and 1981 the number of households in private

A City Mini-bus at Penygraig Road, Mayhill, 1989.

rented accommodation declined by a massive 36 per cent. The availability of rented accommodation had declined dramatically since the 1960s, mainly as a result of legislation controlling the rents which could be charged and security of tenancy. Much of what survived was rented mainly to the large number of students, most of whom wanted short-term lets of less than a year at a time.

Major changes in the population structure were being reflected in the Swansea scene by the end of the 1980s. These can be readily identified in the 1981 census figures. The usually resident population of Swansea fell between 1971 and 1981 by 2,505, or 1.3 per cent, from 185,989 to 183,484. By then over thirty-three thousand people were of pensionable age in Swansea and of these over nine thousand were living alone. One in eighteen of the retired population was aged 75 or over.

Despite the population decline, the number of households continued to increase as the average number of persons per household fell. The rise in the number of people of pensionable age, in particular, encouraged an increase in the number of blocks of private flats being built. Many of these were inserted within the existing urban areas, either on land on which there had been previous buildings or on land previously unbuilt upon. They were particularly prominent in the areas south of Townhill and west of the city centre. Older people here were able to benefit from proximity to shops and other services without the problems of maintaining larger gardens, usually found with detached or semi-detached houses in the suburbs.

Only 10.6 per cent of the population were now able to speak Welsh, a far cry from the 30 per cent at the turn of the century. The percentage owning cars had increased by 20 per cent over the 1971-1981 period. By 1981 60 per cent of all households had at least one car and there were 14 per cent of households with two cars or more. Nearly 75 per cent of residents who travelled to work either went by car, or walked, and only 18 per cent went by bus. The increase in car use, both by residents of Swansea and those travelling into the city to work or for services or leisure, had necessitated continual upgrading of the road system and the building of five large multi-storey car parks in the city centre. The largest traffic flows continued to be along the south side of the city centre. There, further reconstruction in the late 1980s added a second bridge over the river Tawe and provided dual carriageways north to the Hafod and west to the St. Helen's rugby and cricket ground. From the Hafod junction, most of the road west to the city boundary was now dual carriageway. Along the Tawe valley a new dual carriageway from Landore bypassed Plasmarl and, with a few single carriageway stretches, extended north to the M4 motorway. From there, the dual carriageway road extended north up the Tawe Valley, bypassing Clydach, and on to Pontardawe. All these road schemes made travel to and from and within Swansea much easier. The major provider of local bus services, the South Wales Transport Company, was sold into private ownership in the mid 1980s. Many of the double-decker buses and large single-decker fifty-seat buses used on the local routes had been running almost empty outside peak travel hours and were expensive. The new owners soon replaced most of these with short wheelbase twenty-seat buses providing more flexible city services.

For two-thirds of the twentieth century Swansea had been essentially a set of individual urban villages, each of them separated physically from the others by open areas. They had a large degree of functional independence as well, in that many people lived within walking distance of their work and there were more local shops and services. Until 1920, places like Oystermouth and Morriston had been in different local government areas, and Gower had remained a separate Rural District until 1974. As the century wore on, however, the urban areas grew and the open spaces were either filled in with houses or converted to other urban uses, such as school playing fields or hospital grounds. The close proximity of home and work was broken, too, as old industries closed down and the new works were a travelling distance away. As early as 1966 this process had welded the urban areas of Swansea much more closely together physically and integrated them functionally. Over the next quarter of a century this development continued. More housing was added around the edges and more open spaces were urbanized in other ways, as in the conversion of the lower Clyne Valley into a country park and the building and widening of roads. The functional integration was extended when new shopping, aimed specifically at car-borne shoppers, was added, and more people were travelling more often and further for leisure pursuits. The result of this was to integrate the Swansea City urban area much more closely with the adjacent urban areas, which had themselves been developing in the same way. The physically continuous and functionally integrated Swansea Bay City, with Swansea City at its core, extending from Port Talbot in the east to Llanelli and Burry Port in the west, was now obvious for all to see. In this century Swansea was transformed from a nineteenth-century city to become the core of a twentieth-century conurbation. It is as the core part of this new conurbation that any future history of the city will be written.

Figures And Tables

Figure 1. The distribution of major industries in Swansea in 1908.

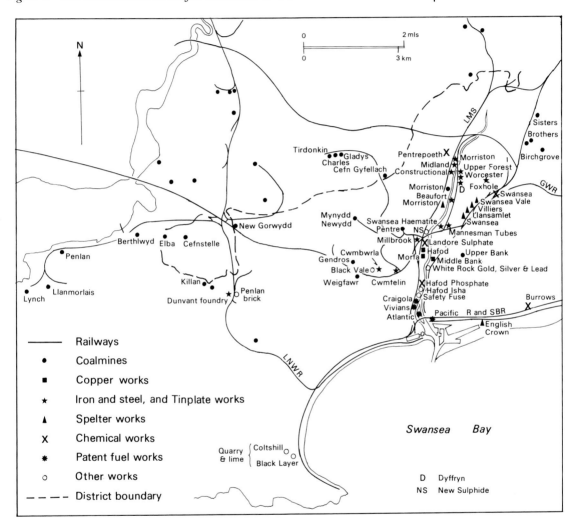

TABLE 1. Occupations of workers aged 10 or over in Swansea County Borough in 1911.

Grouped Occupations	Males	Females
Mines, Quarries, Brickmaking etc.	1477	—
Food, Drink etc. Making and Rtlng.	2532	1739
Chemicals	355	105
Iron, Steel and Tinplate	5573	472

Copper and Zinc	2175	—
Engineering, Vehicles, etc.	3585	33
Clothes etc. Making and Rtlng.	1447	2523
Timber, Furniture, etc.	818	65
Building and Construction	3293	—
Railways	2029	—
Docks	2095	—
Other Transport	4397	—
Commercial and Financial	2647	192
Professional	1196	931
Government, Defence and Admin.	737	249
Domestic Service	328	3897
General Labourers	2501	—
Others	2501	380
TOTAL	38967	10659

Source: Census 1911

TABLE 2. Population, Housing and Welsh Speaking in Swansea, 1931-1951.

Year	District	Population	Private Families	Dwell-ings	Persons/ Room	Welsh Speaking
1931	Swansea CB	164,797	40,951	34,850	0.90	42,862
	Gower RD	9,676				
1951	Swansea CB	160,988	46,916	41,938	0.76	30,735
	Gower RD	11,743	3,504	3,258	0.68	2,792
1961	Swansea CB	167,322	51,119	49,392	0.67	27,947
	Gower RD	12,656	3,866	3,841	0.60	2,760
1981	Swansea District	186,589	66,266	65,048	0.52	18,465

Figure 2. The employment structure of Swansea in 1911 and 1931 as shown by the Population Censuses. The occupations shown in 1911 are: 1. Mines, Quarries, Brickmaking etc., 2. The Making and Retailing of Food, Drink etc., 3. Chemical Industry, 4. Iron, Steel and Tinplate Industries, 5. Copper and Zinc Industries, 6. Engineering and Vehicles, 7. The Making and Retailing of Clothes etc., 8. Timber and Furniture Industries, 9. Building and Construction, 10. Railways, 11. Docks, 12. Other Transport, 13. Commercial and Financial Services, 14. Professional Services, 15. Government, Defence and Administration Services, 16. Domestic Service, 17. General Labourers, 18. Other Occupations. The Industrial employments shown in 1931 are 1. Agriculture and Fishing, 2. Mining and Quarrying, 3. Bricks, Pottery and Glas, 4. Food, Drink and Tobacco Making, 5. Chemical Industries, 6. Iron and Steel Smelting and Rolling, 7. Tinplate and Foundry Work, 8. Non-Ferrous Metals Making, 9. Engineering, 10. Textiles, Leather and Clothing, 11. Timber and Furniture, 12. Paper and Printing Industries, 13. Other Manufacturing, 14. Construction,

15. Gas, Electricity and Water, 16. Railways, 17. Docks, 18. Other Transport,
19. Commerce and Finance, 20. Professional Services, 21. Public Administration and
Defence, 22. Entertainments and Sport, 23. Other Employments.

Figure 2. Employment Structure, 1911 and 1931.

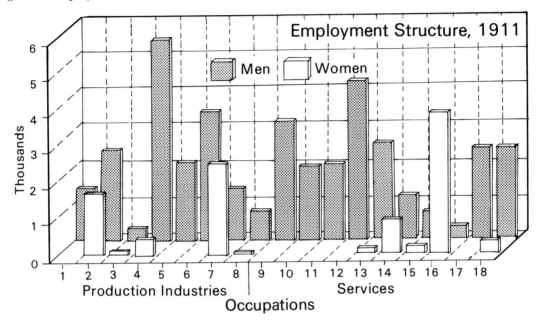

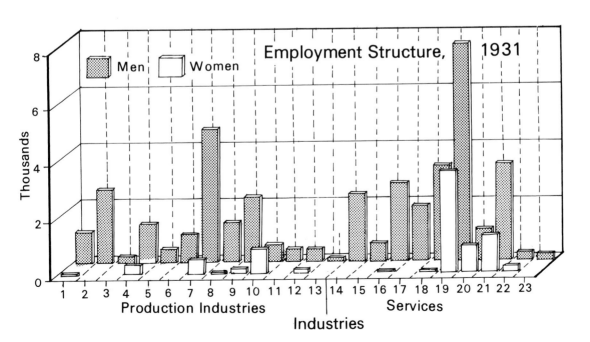

TABLE 3.   Employment in Industry in Swansea County Borough in 1931.

Industries	Males	Females
Agriculture and Fishing	1106	53
Mining and Quarrying	2590	37
Bricks, Pottery, Glass	210	24
Food, Drink, Tobacco	1370	347
Chemicals	456	14
Iron and Steel Smelting and Rolling	989	6
Tinplate and Foundry Work	1715	504
Non-ferrous Metals	1409	41
Engineering	2305	164
Textiles, Leather, Clothing	605	872
Timber and Furniture	442	32
Paper and Printing	430	138
Other Manufacturing	122	28
Construction	2397	30
Gas, Electricity, Water	631	9
Railways	2772	64
Docks	1970	12
Other Transport	3374	61
Commerce and Finance	7696	3607
Professions	1109	958
Public Aministration and Defence	3416	1316
Entertainments and Sport	282	202
Other	218	13
TOTAL	41902	13795

Source: Census 1931

Figure 3. Employment Structure, 1961 and 1981.

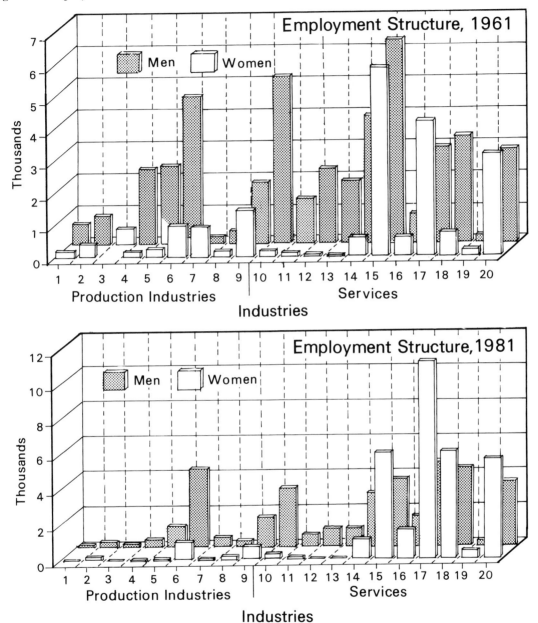

Figure 3. The employment structure of Swansea in 1961 as shown by the Census of Population and in 1981 as shown by the Census of Employment. The industrial employments shown on both charts are: 1. Mining and Quarrying, 2. Food, Drink and Tobacco, 3. Chemicals, 4. Iron and Steel Making, 5. Non-Ferrous Metals, 6. Engineering, 7. Textiles, Leather and Clothing, 8. Paper and Printing, 9. Other Industries, 10. Construction, 11. Gas, Electricity and Water, 12. Railways, 13. Docks, 14. Other transport, 15. Retail and Wholesale Distribution, 16. Insurance, Banking and Finance, 17. Professional Services, 18. Public Administration and Defence, 19. Entertainments and Sport, 20. Other Employments.

354 *Swansea — An Illustrated History*

Figure 4. The growth of housing in Swansea from 1915 to 1989.

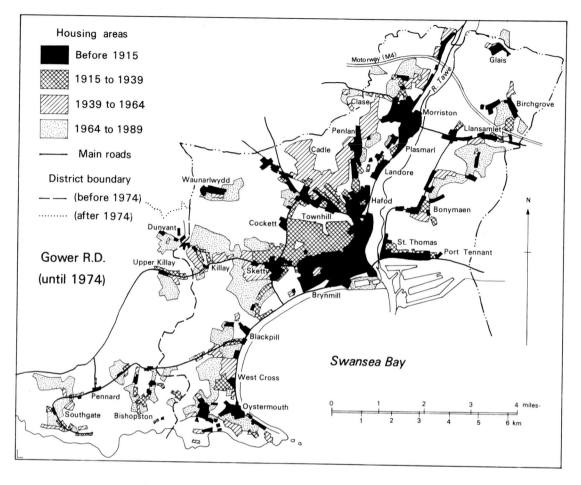

TABLE 4. Employment in Industry in Swansea County Borough in 1961.

Industries	Males	Females
Agriculture and Fishing*	90	—
Mining and Quarrying	640	180
Bricks, Pottery, Glass	460	40
Food, Drink, Tobacco	890	430
Chemicals	500	40
Iron and Steel	2350	180
Non-ferrous Metals	2460	270
Engineering	4650	1010
Textiles, Leather, Clothing	210	950
Timber and Furniture*	360	30
Paper and Printing	420	200
Other Manufacturing	1010	1400
Construction	5250	170

Gas, Electricity, Water	1400	120
Railways	2350	80
Docks	1950	50
Other Transport	3990	600
Distribution	6390	5940
Insurance, Banking, and Finance	910	620
Professions	2990	4240
Public Administration and Defence	3340	760
Entertainments and Sport	210	210
Other	2930	3210
TOTAL	45750	20730

* Note that these figures are included with the category Other Manufacturing in the chart.

Source: Census 1961

Figure 5. The urbanized area of Swansea Bay City in 1989.

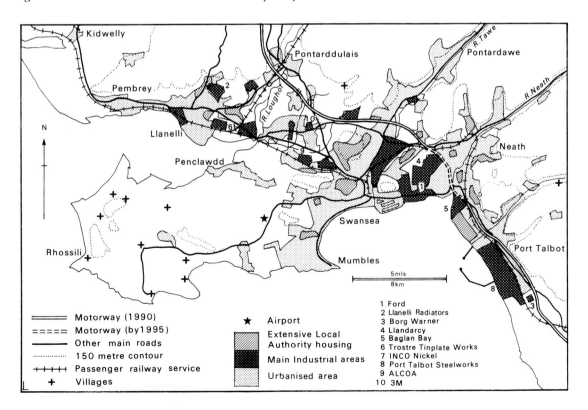

TABLE 5. Employment in Industry in Swansea and Morriston Employment Exchange Areas + in 1981.

Industries	Males	Females
Agriculture and Fishing*	265	71
Mining and Quarrying	122	20
Bricks, Pottery, Glass	630	232
Food, Drink, Tobacco	309	149
Chemicals	166	36
Iron and Steel	411	74
Non-ferrous Metals	1190	93
Engineering	4474	981
Textiles, Leather, Clothing	54	72
Timber and Furniture*	201	77
Paper and Printing	316	226
Other Manufacturing	679	352
Construction	3331	252
Gas, Electricity, Water	668	133
Railways	1028	31
Docks	1029	39
Other Transport	3051	1102
Distribution	3838	6054
Insurance, Banking, and Finance	1724	164
Professions	4666	11282
Public Administration and Defence	4400	6114
Entertainments and Sport	269	425
Other	3667	5657
TOTAL	36488	35115

+ Note that adjustments have been made to exclude the employment at the Mond Nickel Works and at the Velindre Tinplate Works.

* Note that these figures are included with the category Other Manufacturing in the chart.

Source: Employment Census 1981

BIBLIOGRAPHY

Alban, J. R., 'The Activities of the Swansea Belgian Refugees Committee, 1914-16', *Gower*, xxvi (1975), 80-4; *Calendar of Swansea Freemen's Records from 1760* (Swansea, 1982); 'The Formation of the Swansea Battalion, 1914-15', *Gower*, xxv (1974), 28-32; (ed.), *The Guildhall, Swansea* (Swansea, 1984); *The Mansion House* (Swansea, 1979); *Portreeves and Mayors of Swansea* (Swansea, 1982); 'Preparations for Air Raid Precautions in Swansea, 1935-9', *Morgannwg*, xxviii (1974), 55-73; *Swansea, 1184-1984* (Swansea, 1984); *Swansea in Old Picture Postcards (Zaltbommel, 1985);* 'The Visit of the Swansea Harbour Trustees to France in 1910', *Gower*, xxxvii (1986), 51-6.

Amis, Kingsley, *That Uncertain Feeling* (London, 1955); *A Look around the Estate* (London, 1967).

Ancient and Historical Monuments in Wales, Royal Commission on, *Inventory of Ancient Monuments in Glamorgan. IV. Domestic Architecture from the Reformation to the Industrial Revolution. 1. The Greater Houses* (HMSO, 1981); *2. Farmhouses and Cottages* (HMSO, 1988).

Art in Wales (Exhibition Catalogue, Swansea, 1964).

Awbery, Stanley, *Labour's Early Struggles in Swansea* (Swansea, 1949).

Balchin, W. G. V. (ed.), *Swansea and its Region* (Swansea, 1971).

Ball, Enid, 'Glamorgan Members during the Reform Bill Period', *Morgannwg*, x (1966), 5-20.

Barker, Felix, *The House that Stoll Built* (London, 1957).

Bassett, T. M., *The Welsh Baptists* (Swansea, 1977).

Bell, David, *The Artist in Wales* (London, 1957); *Catalogue of the Glynn Vivian Art Gallery* (Swansea, 1959).

Beynon, John, 'Warning Lights: A Critical Appreciation of Alan Perry, Painter-Writer', *Poetry Wales*, xxiv (1988), 6-13.

Boorman, David, *The Brighton of Wales. Swansea as a Fashionable Resort, c. 1780-c. 1830* (Swansea, 1986).

The Borough of Swansea, Local Historical Records. Catalogue of an Exhibition Held at the Library, University College of Swansea, 21 June-16 July 1969 (Swansea, 1969).

Bowdler, Thomas (1782-1856), *Memoir of the Late John Bowdler, Esq., to which is Added Some Account of the Late Thomas Bowdler, Esq., Editor of the Family Shakspeare* (London, 1825).

Brennan, T., Cooney, E. W., and Pollins, H., *Social Change in South West Wales* (London, 1954).

Bromham, I. J., *Through Changing Scenes* (Swansea, 1965).

Bromley, R. D. F. and Humphrys, Graham (eds.), *Dealing with Dereliction: the Redevelopment of the Lower Swansea Valley* (Swansea, 1979).

Bromley, R. D. F. and Thomas, C. J., *Retail Parks, Enterprise Zone Policy and Retail Planning – a Case Study of the Swansea Enterprise Zone Retail Park* (Swansea, 1987).

Brook, Donald, *A Pageant of English Actors* (London, 1950).

Brooke, E. H., *A Chronology of the Tinplate Works of Great Britain* (Cardiff, 1944).

Burgum, John, *Swansea City Football Club* (Manchester, 1988).

CADW, *Buildings of Special Architectural or Historic Interest: City of Swansea* (Cardiff, n.d., c. 1986).

Carter, Harold, *The Towns of Wales: A Study of Urban Geography* (Cardiff, 1966); (ed.), *Urban Essays: Studies in the Geography of Wales* (London, 1970).

Cedric Morris. A Retrospective Exhibition Catalogue (Cardiff, 1968).

A Century of Municipal Progress. The Last 100 Years, ed. H. J. Laski, W. I. Jennings and W. W. Robson (London, 1935).

Charles, Rollo, 'Some Penrice Pictures', *Glamorgan Historian*, v (1968), 213-9.

Claybrooke, Frank, 'Swansea Houses: the First Building By-laws', *Gower*, xxix (1978), 46-51.

Clegg, H. A. *et al.*, *A History of British Trade Unionism* (London, 1962).

Coleman, W., *Yellow Fever in the North: The Methods of Early Epidemiology* (Madison, Wisconsin, 1987).

Colvin, H. M., *Biographical Dictionary of British Architects, 1660-1840* (London, 1981).

Corrigan, Peter, *A Hundred Years of Welsh Soccer* (Cardiff, 1976).

County Borough of Swansea. Opening of the Main Drainage Works on Thursday, 30 July 1936 . . . (Swansea, 1936).

Craig, R. S., 'The Copper Ore Trade' in D. Alexander and R. Ommer (eds.), *Volumes not Values: Canadian Sailing Ships and World Trade* (St John's, Newfoundland, 1979).

Darlington, W. A., *The Actor and His Audience* (London, 1949).

Davies, J. A., 'A Picnic in the Orchard: Dylan Thomas's Wales' in Tony Curtis (ed.), *Wales: the Imagined Nation* (Bridgend, 1986).

Davies, H. M., 'The Place of the Royal Institution of South Wales in the History of Scientific and General Education in the Nineteenth Century' (M.A. Thesis, Wales, 1940).

Davies, H. W. E., 'The Development of the Industrial Landscape of Western South Wales in the Nineteenth and Twentieth Centuries' (M.A. Thesis, London, 1955).

Davies, T. G., *Deeds Not Words: A History of the Swansea General and Eye Hospital* (Cardiff, 1988); 'Dau Iachawr o Abertawe: y Baron Spolasco a James Rogers', *National Library of Wales Journal: Cylchgrawn Llyfrgell Genedlaethol Cymru*, xxv (1987), 98-113.

Dictionary of Welsh Biography down to 1951 (London, 1959).

Dillwyn, L. W., *Contributions towards a History of Swansea* (Swansea, 1840).

Drabble, Margaret (ed.), *The Oxford Companion to English Literature* (5th ed., Oxford, 1985).

Dunthorne, K. B., *Artists Exhibited in Wales, 1945-74* (Cardiff, 1976).

Dykes, D. W., 'The University College of Swansea: Its Background and Development' (Ph.D. Thesis, Wales, 1982).

Evans, D. G., 'The Growth and Development of Organized Religion in the Swansea Valley, 1820-1890' (Ph.D. Thesis, Wales, 1977).

Evans, Edith, *Swansea Castle and the Medieval Town* (Swansea, 1983).

Evans, T. Ll., *Y Cathedral Anghydffurfiol Cymraeg* (Abertawe, 1972).

Evans, T. S., 'The History of Nonconformity in Swansea', *National Council of Evangelical Free Churches, Swansea Meeting* (Swansea, 1909).

Farington, Joseph, *The Farington Diary*, ed. James Greig (London, n.d.).

Farmer, David, *Swansea City, 1912-82* (Swansea, 1982).

Fawks, Richard, *Welsh National Opera* (London, 1986).

Ferris, Paul, *Dylan Thomas* (Penguin, 1978).

Forster, John, *Walter Savage Landor* (2 vols. London, 1869).

Francis, G. G., *Charters Granted to Swansea, The Chief Borough of the Seignory of Gower* (London, 1867 [1871]); *Notes on a Gold Chain of Office Presented to the Corporation of Swansea in the Year 1875* (Swansea, 1876).

Gaudie, Enid, *Cruel Habitations. A History of Working Class Housing, 1870-1918* (London, 1974).

Glamorgan County History. III. *Medieval Glamorgan*, ed. T. B. Pugh (Cardiff, 1971); IV. *Early Modern Glamorgan*, ed. Glanmor Wiliams (Cardiff, 1974); V. *Industrial Glamorgan*, ed. A. H. John and Glanmor Williams (Cardiff, 1981); VI. *Glamorgan Society, 1780-1980*, ed. P. T. J. Morgan (Cardiff, 1988).

Grant, R. K. J. *On the Parish. An Illustrated Source Book on the Care of the Poor under the Old Poor Law* (Cardiff, 1988); *The Parliamentary History of Glamorgan, 1542-1976* (Swansea, 1978).

Grenfell, Harold and Morris, Bernard, 'Castles of Gower', *Gower*, xx (1969), 39-51.

Griffiths, R. A. (ed.), *Boroughs of Medieval Wales* (Cardiff, 1975); *Clyne Castle, Swansea* (Swansea, 1977); *Singleton Abbey and the Vivians of Swansea* (Llandysul, 1988).

The Guildhall, Swansea. Essays to Commemorate the Fiftieth Anniversary of its Opening, ed. J. R. Alban (Swansea, 1984).

Hamilton, H. W., *Doctor Syntax* (London, 1969).

Hargreaves, John, *Sport, Power and Culture* (Cambridge, 1986).

Harris, Edward, *Swansea. Its Port and Trade and their Development* (Cardiff, 1935).

Heald, Tim, *The Character of Cricket* (London, 1986).

Hignall, Andrew, *The History of Glamorgan County Cricket Club* (London, 1988).

Hilling, J. B., *Historical Architecture of Wales* (Cardiff, 1976); *Plans and Prospectus: Architecture in Wales, 1780-1914* (Cardiff, 1975).

Hilton, K. J. (ed.), *The Lower Swansea Valley Project* (London, 1967).

Howe, G. R., 'Swansea's Early Water Supply', *Gower*, xxix (1978), 54-60.

Howell, R. G., *Under Sail. Swansea's Cutters, Tallships and Seascapes, 1830-1880* (Swansea, 1987).

Hughes, Gareth, *One Hundred Years of Scarlet* (Llanelli, 1983).

Hughes, J. V., 'Thomas Mansel Talbot of Margam and Penrice, 1747-1813', *Gower*, xxvi (1979), 71-9.

Hughes, Peter and Keen, Richard, *Industrial Wales in Art* (Cardiff, 1975).

Hughes, S. R., 'The Industrial Archaeology of Wales and Associated Rail Transport in the Swansea Valley Area' (M.Phil. Thesis, Birmingham, 1984).

Humphrys, Graham, *Geographical Excursions from Swansea. II. Human Landscapes* (University College of Swansea, 1983).

Hunt, W. W., '*To Guard My People*'. *An Account of the Origin and History of the Swansea Police* (Swansea, 1957).

Inglis, Simon, *The Football Grounds of England and Wales* (London, 1983).

James, A. J. and Thomas, J. E., *Wales at Westminster. A History of the Parliamentary Representation of Wales, 1800-1979* (Llandysul, 1981).

Jenkins, Elis, 'Thomas Baxter's 1818 Drawings', *Gower*, xix (1968), 50-5; 'The Return of the Natives — a Postscript on Thomas Baxter', *Gower*, xxiii (1972), 34-9; 'J. M. W. Turner in Glamorgan', *Glamorgan Historian*, xi (1975), 53-70; 'William Weston Young', *Glamorgan Historian*, v (1968), 61-101.

Jenkins, Elis and Rogers, W. C., 'Some Old Photographs of Swansea', *Glamorgan Historian*, ii (1965), 115-20.

Jenkins, G. H. and Smith, J. B. (eds.), *Politics and Society in Wales. Essays in Honour of Ieuan Gwynedd Jones* (Cardiff, 1988).

Jenkins, Randal, 'The Poetry of John Ormond', *Poetry Wales*, viii (1972), 17-28.

John, A. H., *The Industrial Development of South Wales* (Cardiff, 1950); 'Iron and Coal on a Glamorgan Estate, 1700-40', *Economic History Review*, new ser., xiii (1943), 93-103.

Johnson, Samuel, *Life of Savage*, ed. C. Tracey (Oxford, 1971).

Jones, Alan, *The Story of the Grand* (Llandybïe, 1983).

Jones, Aneurin, 'Rhai o Artistiaid Abertawe', *Taliesin*, liv (1985), 44-51.

Jones, Anthony, *Welsh Chapels* (Cardiff, 1984).

Jones, Daniel, *My Friend Dylan Thomas* (London, 1977).

Jones, I. G., *Communities* (Llandysul, 1987); *Explorations and Explanations. Essays in the Social History of Wales* (Llandysul, 1981); 'Denominationalism in Swansea and District', *Morgannwg*, xii (1968), 67-96; 'Franchise Reform and Glamorgan Politics in the Mid Nineteenth Century', *Morgannwg*, ii (1958), 47-64.

Jones, Ifano, *A History of Printing and Printers in Wales to 1923* (Cardiff, 1925).

Jones R. and Reeve, C. G., *A History of Gas Production in Wales* (Cardiff, 1978).

Jones, Vivian, (ed.), *The Church in a Mobile Society. A Survey of the Zone of Industrial South-west Wales* (Swansea, 1969).

Jones, W. H., *The History of Swansea and the Lordship of Gower* (Carmarthen, 1920); *The Port of Swansea* (Carmarthen, 1922).

Jones, W. T., *The Rise and Progress of Religious Free Thought in Swansea* (Swansea, 1900).

Joyce, Patrick, *Work, Society and Politics* (London, 1980).

Knight, Roy, *The History of the Swansea Art Society, 1886-1986* (Swansea, 1987).

Leger Galleries. Catalogue of English Watercolours (London, 1985).

Lee, C. E., *The Swansea and Mumbles Railway* (3rd ed., South Godstone, 1970).

Lewis, J. M., 'The History of Calvinistic Methodism in the Swansea and Cwmtawe Area between 1859 and 1979' (M.Th. Thesis, Wales, 1984).

Literary Swansea. Catalogue of an Exhibition of Books about Swansea and by Swansea Authors (Swansea, 1951).

Lloyd, Bernard, 'Richard Savage in Swansea', *Anglo-Welsh Review*, 27 (1978), 98-104.

Lloyd, Thomas, *The Lost Houses of Wales* (London, 1986).

Lloyd, W. Ll., *Trade and Transport* (Swansea, 1940).

Lovell, John, *Stevedores and Dockers* (London, 1969).

Lowe, J. B., *Welsh Industrial Workers' Housing, 1775-1875* (Cardiff, 1977).

Martin, R. M., *T.U.C. The Growth of a Pressure Group* (London, 1980).

Mathias, Roland, *Vernon Watkins* (Cardiff, 1974).

Matthews, B. E., *The Swansea City Story* (Swansea, 1968); *The Swans: Seventy-five Years. Swansea City Football Club, 1912-1987* (Swansea, 1987).

McCarry, T. J., 'Labour and Society in Swansea, 1887-1918' (Ph.D. Thesis, Wales, 1986).

Meager, K. S., 'Swansea and Nantgarw Porcelain', *Glamorgan Historian*, ii (1965), 104-14.

Minchinton, W. E., *The British Tinplate Industry. A History* (Oxford, 1957).

Moore, Donald, *The Earliest Views of Glamorgan* (Glamorgan, 1987); *Artists' Views of Glamorgan: the Nineteenth Century* (Cardiff, 1988); 'Yr Arlunydd yng Ngorllewin Morgannwg', in I. M. Williams (gol.), *Abertawe a'r Cylch* (Abertawe, 1982).

Moore, Donald, and Moore, Patricia M., 'Bucks' Engravings of Glamorgan Antiquities', *Glamorgan Historian*, v (1968), 133-51.

Morgan, J. H., *Glamorgan County Cricket* (London, 1952).

Morgan, K. O., *Wales in British Politics* (3rd ed., Cardiff, 1980); 'Democratic Politics in Glamorgan, 1884-1914', *Morgannwg*, iv (1960), 5-27.

Morgan, T. J., *Peasant Culture* (Swansea, 1962); 'Peasant Culture of the Swansea Valley', *Glamorgan Historian*, ix (1973), 105-22.

Morgan, W. Ll., *The Castle of Swansea* (Devizes, 1914); *The Town and Manor of Swansea* (Carmarthen, 1924).

Morris, Bernard, 'Swansea Houses: Working-class Houses, 1800-50', *Gower*, xxvi (1975), 53-61; 'The Earliest Views of Swansea, 1678', *Gower*, xxxiii (1982), 6-12.

Morris, Richard, *John Dillwyn Llewelyn: Pioneer of Welsh Photography* (Cardiff, 1980).

Morris, J. H. and Williams, L. J., *The South Wales Coal Industry* (Cardiff, 1958).

Nance, E. M., *The Pottery and Porcelain of Swansea and Nantgarw* (London, 1943).

National Museum of Wales. Catalogue of Oil Paintings (Cardiff, 1955).

Orrin, G. R., *The Gower Churches* (Swansea, 1979); *The History of Bishopston* (Llandysul, 1982).

Painting, David, *Swansea's Contribution to the History of Photography* (Swansea, 1982); *Amy Dillwyn* (Cardiff, 1987).

Pearsall, Ronald, *Victorian Popular Music* (Newton Abbot, 1973).

Perrin, Noel, *Dr Bowdler's Legacy* (London, 1970).

Portraits of Welsh People. A Catalogue (Cardiff, 1967).

Portsmouth O. S., 'The Cross Keys Inn', *Gower*, xx (1969), 25-34.

A Postal History of Swansea and District, ed. D. R. Gwynn, P. R. Reynolds and H. R. Warren (Swansea, 1984).

Powell, Glan, *Dynevor, 1883-1958. Dynevor School Magazine, Anniversary Number* (1958).

Price, C. J. L., *The English Theatre in Wales* (Cardiff, 1948); *The Professional Theatre in Wales* (Swansea, 1984).

Proceedings of the Subscribers to the Fund for Obviating the Inconvenience arising from Smoke Caused by the Smelting of Copper (Swansea, 1823).

Pryce, P. D. and Williams, S. H., *Swansea Blue and White Pottery* (n.p., n.d.).

Raban, Jonathan, *Soft City* (London, 1974).

Recording Wales. vol. 2. Chapels (Cardiff, 1969).

Redlich, Josef and Hirst, F. W., *The History of Local Government in England*, ed. B. Keith-Lucas (2nd. ed., London, 1970).

Rees, Eiluned and Walters, G., 'Swansea Libraries in the Nineteenth Century', *Journal Welsh Bibliographical Society*, x (1966-71), 43-57.

Report of the Royal Commission on Municipal Corporations in England and Wales (London, 1835).

Reports of the Commissioners of Inquiry into the State of Education in Wales (3 vols. London, 1847).

Rhys, W. J., *Hanes Eglwys y Ddinas Noddfa, Glandŵr* (Caerdydd, 1934); *Hanes Seion, Treforus* (Abertawe, 1946).

Ridd, Tom, 'The Development of Municipal Government in Swansea in the Nineteenth Century' (M.A. Thesis, Wales, 1955); 'Gabriel Powell, the Uncrowned King of Swansea', *Glamorgan Historian*, v (1968), 152-60.

Roberts, Glyn, *The Municipal Development of the Borough of Swansea to 1900* (Swansea, 1940).

Roberts, R. O., 'The Development and Decline of the Non-ferrous Metal Smelting Industry in South Wales', *Transactions Hon. Soc. of Cymmrodorion*, 1956, 78-115; Reprinted in W.E. Minchinton (ed.), *Industrial South Wales, 1750-1914* (London, 1969).

Roberts, R. P., 'The History of Coal Mining in Gower from 1700 to 1832' (M.A. Thesis, Wales, 1953).

Rogers, W. C., 'The Swansea and Glamorgan Calendar' (Unpublished MS., Swansea Central Library); *A Pictorial History of Swansea* (Llandysul, 1981).

Ross, J. E., *Letters from Swansea* (Llandybïe, 1969).

Rosser, Colin and Harris, C. C., *The Family and Social Change. A Study of Family and Kinship in a South Wales Town* (London, 1965).

Rowan, Eric (ed.), *Art in Wales, 20,000 B.C.-A.D. 1850* (Cardiff, 1986).

Royal Commission on Trade Unions. Fifth Report, Parliamentary Papers, 1867-8, xxxix (3980).

Royal Commission on Friendly and Benefit Building Societies. Fourth Report, 1874, and *Reports of Assistant Commissioners, Parliamentary Papers*, 1874, xxxiii.

Savage, Richard, *Poetical Works*, ed. Clarence Tracey (Cambridge, 1962).

Secombe, Harry, *Twice Brightly* (London, 1974).

Shannon, R. T., *Mr Gladstone and Swansea* (Swansea, 1982).

Smith, Carl, *A History of Swansea Grammar School* (Swansea, 1982).

Smith, C. E. G. and Gibson, M. E., 'Yellow Fever in South Wales, 1865', *Medical History*, xxx (1986), 322-40.

Smith, David and Williams, Gareth, *Fields of Praise* (Cardiff, 1980).

South Wales Evening Post Guildhall Supplement, 23 October 1934.

Spencer, Gerard, *Catholic Life in Swansea, 1847-1947* (Cardiff, 1947).

Stead, P. P., 'The Welsh Working Class', *Llafur*, i (1973), 44-52.

Steegman, John, *Catalogue of Portraits in Welsh Houses. 2. South Wales* (Cardiff, 1962).

Stephens, Meic (ed.), 'John Ormond', *Artists in Wales*, ii (1973), 155-64; *The Oxford Companion to the Literature of Wales* (Oxford, 1986).

St Joseph's Church and Greenhill: A Centenary Exhibition. Catalogue of an Exhibition held in the Guildhall, Swansea. (Swansea, 1988).

Super, R. H., *Walter Savage Landor* (New York, 1954).

Swansea's Municipal Electricity Undertaking, 1889-1948. Catalogue of an Archives Exhibition held in the Guildhall, Swansea (Swansea, 1988).

Swansea Pottery. A Bi-centenary Catalogue (Swansea, 1968).

Ten Marine Artists. A Catalogue (Swansea, n.d., *c.* 1983).

Thomas, Dylan, *The Collected Letters*, ed. Paul Ferris (London, 1985); *Early Prose Writings*, ed. Walford Davies (London, 1971); *Portrait of the Artist as a Young Dog* (London, 1940).

Thomas, J. E., 'The Poor Law in West Glamorgan, 1831-1930', *Morgannwg*, xviii (1970), 45-69.

Thomas, N. L., *The Story of Swansea's Districts and Villages* (2 vols. Neath, 1964; Swansea, 1969); *Education in Swansea, 1870-1970* (Swansea, 1970); *Of Swansea West: The Mumbles: Past and Present* (Swansea, 1978); *The Story of Swansea's Markets* (Swansea, 1966).

Thomas P. D. G., 'Glamorgan Politics, 1700-50', *Morgannwg*, vi (1962), 52-77.

Thomas, P. S., *Industrial Relations* (Swansea, 1940).

Thomas, R. G., *Edward Thomas: A Portrait* (Oxford, 1985).

Thomas, W. S. K., 'The History of Swansea from the Accession of the Tudors to the Restoration Settlement' (Ph.D. Thesis, Wales, 1958); 'Tudor and Jacobean Swansea: The Social Scene', *Morgannwg*, v (1961), 23-48.

Thomas, Wynford Vaughan, *Madly in All Directions* (London, 1967).

Toomey, R. R., 'Vivian and Sons, 1809-1924' (Ph.D. Thesis, Wales, 1979); subsequently published (London, 1985).

Trott, A. L., 'A History of Church Schools in Swansea, 1800-1870' (M.A. Thesis, Wales, 1941).

Treble, J. H., *Urban Poverty in Britain* (London, 1979).

Tyler, Froom, 'Bowdler, Censor of Shakespeare', *Glamorgan Historian*, vii (1972), 194-202; 'Lucien Pissarro in Gower', *Gower*, xx (1969), 23-5.

Walker, D. G., *St. Mary's, Swansea* (3rd. ed., Swansea, 1967).

Walters, E., 'The Development of the Walters Road Area of Swansea', *Gower*, xxx (1979), 45-51.

Watkins, Gwen, *Portrait of a Friend* (Llandysul, 1983).

Weaver, J. A., 'The Development of Education in Swansea, 1846-1902' (M.A. Thesis, Wales, 1959).

Webster, J. R., 'The Place of Secondary Education in Welsh Society, 1800-1918' (Ph.D. Thesis, Wales, 1959).

Williams, D. T., *The Economic Development of Swansea and the Swansea District to 1921* (Swansea, 1940).

Williams, Gareth, 'The Longest, Most Stormy Meeting that Swansea Ever Had', *Gower*, xxx (1979), 18-21.

Williams, Glanmor, 'Henry de Gower (?1278-1347): Bishop and Builder', *Archaeologia Cambrensis*, cxxx (1981), 1-18; 'The Herberts of Swansea and Sir John Herbert', *Glamorgan Historian*, xii (1981), 46-58.

Williams, I. M. (gol.), *Abertawe a'r Cylch* (Llandybïe, 1982).

Williams, John, *Hanes Eglwysi Annibynnol Abertawe a'r Cylch, 1860-1915* (Abertawe, 1915).

Williams, L. J., 'The New Unionism in South Wales', *Welsh History Review*, i (1963), 413-30.

Williams, M. F., 'Glamorgan Quakers, 1654-1900', *Morgannwg*, v (1961), 49-75.

Williams, W. R., *A Parliamentary History of Wales* (Brecon, 1895).

Wohl, A. S., *Endangered Lives. Public Health in Victorian Britain* (London, 1983).

Wooller, Wilfred, *A History of County Cricket: Glamorgan* (London, 1971).

Young, David, *The Origin and History of Methodism in Wales* (London, 1933).

INDEX

A

Abraham, William ('Mabon'), 138.
Acts of Union, 1536-43, 12, 14, 18, 103.
Addis Works, 333, 339.
Air raids, 80, 275, 316, 336.
Albert Hall, 132, 142, 198, 256, 269.
Aldermen, 89, 91, 96.
Allchurch, Ivor, 279-81.
'All Whites', 266-7, 273-4, 276, 282; see also rugby.
Aluminium industry, 330, 333, 338-9.
Amis, Kingsley, 241-3, 273, 275.
Anglicans, Anglican Church, 26, 129-30, 133, 145-6, 154, 161-5, 176.
Anglo-Persian Oil Company, 75, 78.
'Ann of Swansea'; see Hatton, Julia Ann.
Archery, 249.
Architecture, 189-213.
Argyle Chapel, 202.
Art, 177-88.
Art School, 186-8, 204.
Art Societies, 183-5, 188.
Assembly Rooms, 117, 193, 227.
Associated British Ports, 108, 341.
Aylmer, Rose, 220.

B

Bancroft, W. J. ('Billy'), 263.
Baptists, 130, 146, 153, 154.
Baxter, Thomas, 180, 181.
Beaufort, dukes of, 5, 48, 59, 61, 65, 89, 104, 105, 107, 109, 126, 177, 249, 250, 269.
Beau Nash House, 211-2.
Bell, David, 187.
Bell, George, 209, 326.
Ben Evans Store, 189, 325.
Bethesda Chapel, 153, 155, 201.
Billingsley, William, 180.
Bishop Vaughan School, 172.
Blackpill, 7.
Blomfield, Sir Arthur, 164, 200.
Bonymaen, 117, 264, 329.
Borough Charters, 7.
Borough Council, 282.
Borough, medieval, 4, 7.
Borough officials, 13.
Borrow, George, 215, 227.
Bowdler, Thomas, 224-6.
Brangwyn Hall, 210-1, 272.

Braose family, 5, 7, 87.
'Brighton of Wales', 110, 246-7.
Bristol Channel, 1, 8, 17, 23, 34, 57, 63, 115, 125.
British and Foreign Schools Society, 158-9, 313.
British Steel Corporation, 332.
British Transport Docks Board, 80-2, 108.
Brynhyfryd, 117.
Brynmill, 112, 295, 299.
Brynymor, 118.
Brynymor House, 192.
Buck brothers, 177.
Burgesses, 7, 13, 14, 20, 26, 29, 60, 61, 89, 90, 91, 96, 98, 99, 101, 102, 103, 105, 109, 139, 286, 305.
Burials, 300.
Burnie, R. J. D., 307.
Burrows, 64, 96, 109, 117, 193, 227, 287, 295, 296, 301.

C

Calvert, John, 193.
Cambrian newspaper, 63, 65, 66, 70, 110, 218, 224, 253.
Caput, 3, 4, 5, 12.
Cefn Coed Hospital, 208, 316.
Cefn Hengoed School, 172.
Central Library, 204, 304.
Chapels, 133, 136-8, 154-7, 174, 201-3.
Chapman, Samuel Palmer, 229.
Cholera, 113, 129, 220.
Christ Church, 163, 176.
Circulating Schools, 151-2.
Circus, 255.
City status, 319, 342.
Civil defence, 317-8.
Civil Wars, 1642-8, 21-2.
Clark, George T., 111, 122, 135, 295, 297.
Clasemont, 178, 188, 195.
Clyne Castle, 192, 196.
  Golf Club, 250.
  Valley, 7, 234, 347.
Cnap Llwyd, 152, 301.
Cockett, 50, 51, 124, 292.
Coal industry, coalmining, 16-7, 23-4, 30, 31, 33, 35, 39, 41, 47-52, 55, 88-9, 124, 321, 322, 327, 329-30, 332, 338.
  trade, 77-9, 82-4.

Collins, Charles, 59-60.
Combe, William, 218.
Commissioners on Municipal Corporations, 87.
Common Attorneys, 89, 91.
Common Hall, 90, 96, 100, 101, 102, 106.
Conservatives, 307, 309.
Constables, 108, 113.
Copper industry, smelting, 24, 29, 31-7, 52, 53, 58, 72-3, 89, 322, 327, 333, 338.
Copperworkers, 36, 37, 49, 124-5.
County Borough, 85-6, 304, 310-9, 329, 335, 340, 342.
Court Leet, 90, 100, 102, 107, 108.
Courtney, Edith, 243.
Coutts, Billy, 257.
Cradock, Sir Matthew, 19, 178, 189.
Cricket, 249-50, 261-3, 264-5, 277-8, 281.
Cromwell, Oliver, 16, 21, 26, 87, 102, 104.
Cross Keys public house, 9, 189.
Crown Court, 213.
Crug-glas, 148, 150, 153.
Curvis, Brian, 281.
Cwmbwrla, 7, 127, 130, 269, 323.
Cwmdonkin, 232, 238-9, 295, 299, 301.

D

Davies, Christopher, 244.
Davies, W.H., 234.
Defoe, Daniel, 3, 23, 57, 88, 216.
De la Beche, Sir Henry T., 122, 295, 297.
De la Beche School, 168.
Delamotte, George, 181.
Depression, economic, 1930s, 270, 275, 316, 327-8.
Dillwyn, Amy, 232-3.
  Lewis Llewelyn, 38, 40, 131, 197, 262, 306.
  Lewis Weston, 126, 130, 161, 179-80, 184, 197, 218, 228, 232.
Dineley, Thomas, 177.
Dissent, Dissenters, 25-6, 146-7, 152-7; see also Nonconformists.
District Council, 85, 319, 340, 342.
Doctors, 296-7.
Dragon Hotel, 211.

Driver Vehicle Licensing Centre, 340, 342.
Duncan, Edward, 182.
Dunvant, 271, 327, 337.
Dyfatty, 113, 119, 337.
Dynevor School, 168.

E

Ebenezer Chapel, 154, 155, 201, 202.
Education, 157-61, 167-72.
Education Department, 313-4.
Edwards, Daniel, 44, 46, 202.
Electorate, 139-40.
Electricity, 328, 334-5.
Empire Theatre, 257-9.
Employment, 324-5, 327-31, 339-40, 341, 349-50, 351, 352-3, 354-6.
of women, 324-5, 330-1, 335, 341-2, 349-50, 351, 352-3, 354-6.
Enterprise Zone, 339, 341.
Entertainment, 247-84.
Epidemics, 19, 113.
Estates Department, 312.
Exports, 8, 16, 23, 42, 58, 73-4, 77-9, 83-4, 327, 333, 341.

F

Fabian's Bay, 92, 105, 120.
Fairs, 5, 8.
Fairwood Common, 331.
Fashionable resort, 110, 119, 218, 246-8, 249-50.
Felin Frân, 55, 327, 332.
Ferris, Paul, 241.
Ferryport, 81-2.
Fforestfach, 50, 115, 124.
Industrial Estate, 333, 339.
Fishing, 76.
Foxhole, 122.
Foxwist, William, 104.
Franchise, 305, 308.
Francis, George Grant, 126, 160, 161, 184, 203, 227-8.
John Deffett, 184, 227-8, 302.
Friendly Societies, 135-6.
Fulton, John, 171.

G

Gamwell, Samuel Clearstone, 231-2.
Garngoch, 52.
Gas supply, 113.
General Hospital, 208, 297.
Gentry, 246, 247-9, 251, 253, 270.
Georgian Houses, 192, 194.
Glamorgan County Cricket Club, 263, 265, 273-4, 277, 282.

Glanmor School, 169.
Glasbrook, John, 51, 52, 167.
Glyndŵr Rebellion, 6, 11.
Glynn Vivian Art Gallery, 185, 186, 187, 188, 208, 303.
Gore, Bishop Hugh, 26.
Gower, Gŵyr, 1, 3, 4, 5, 143, 152, 296, 337-8, 341, 347.
lordship of, 3, 10, 11, 12, 86-7, 88, 145.
parliamentary division, 306, 307, 308, 309.
Gower, Bishop Henry de, 6, 9, 145, 189.
Gower, Iris, 243.
Grammar School, 26, 159-60, 168-9, 172, 203, 313.
Bishop Gore Grammar School, 338.
Grand Theatre, 206, 257, 272, 282, 283.
Great Western Railway Port, 75-80, 108.
Greenhill, 119, 166, 201, 290, 295, 337.
Grenfell, family, 34, 37, 121, 126.
Grenfelltown, 36.
Griffiths, Bryn, 243.
Guildhall, old, 100, 107, 117, 196, 203, 288, 316.
new, 175, 210-1, 271-2, 294, 316, 329, 340.
Gwernllwyn-chwith, 190.

H

Hafod, 117, 122, 127, 128, 130, 217, 337.
Hancock, Kenneth, 187.
Harbour Trust, Trustees, 61-8, 105-8, 118, 207.
Harris, E. Howard, 234-5.
Harris, Howell, 148-9, 150-1.
Harris, James, 181-2.
James, the Younger, 182-3.
Harris, Joseph, ('Gomer'), 130, 133, 153, 215.
Harris, Moses, 106, 110, 179.
Hatton, Julia Ann ('Ann of Swansea'), 180, 221-4, 226-7.
Havergal, Frances Ridley, 227.
Hellings, Peter, 240-1.
Hendrefoilan, 197-8.
Herbert, Sir George, 13, 14, 19, 145, 189.
High School, 168.
Hill House, 192.
Holiday-makers, 341, 343.
Hornor, Thomas, 181.
Hospital of the Blessed David, 9, 19, 145, 189.

Hospitals, 208, 292, 296-7.
Housing, 18-9, 119, 120-2, 209-10, 290, 295-6, 300-1, 314, 321, 322, 326-7, 336-8, 344-6, 354.
Housing Department, 314, 326-7, 329, 344-5.
Hughes, Stephen, 26-7, 215.
Humphreys, John, 202.

I

Immigrants, 127-8, 153, 201, 295.
Imports, 8, 16, 23, 58, 73-5, 77-9, 83-4, 333, 341.
Independents, 130, 146, 149, 153, 154, 157.
Industrial development, 29-55, 126-7, 139, 349.
Industrial Revolution, 29, 285, 321.
Infirmary, 292, 296.
Investiture, royal, 318-9.
Irish, 127, 165-6, 295.
Iron industry, 35.
Irving, Sir Henry, 257.

J

James II, 87, 102.
James brothers, 263.
James, Daniel ('Gwyrosydd'), 215-6.
Janes, Alfred, 237, 238.
Jenkins, John Jones, Lord Glantawe, 139, 250, 269.
Jernegan, William, 191, 192, 193, 195, 200.
Jews, 154.
Jones, David, M.P., 137-8, 309.
Jones, Sir David Brynmor, M.P., 307, 308.
Jones, Joe, Jos., 226.
Jones, Sir Lewis, M.P., 309.
Jones, Col. Philip, 21.
Jones, Richard Calvert, 49, 182.

K

Kardomah Café, 236, 240.
Kavanagh, Charles, 165-6.
Kean, Edmund, 248, 257.
Kilvert, Francis, 227.
Kilvey Hill, 37, 326, 329.
King's Dock, 67, 76, 80, 81, 82-3, 323, 324.

L

Labourers, 125-6.
Labour Party, 140, 141-3, 155, 307-10.
Landor, Walter Savage, 219-21.

Landore, 58, 117, 122, 127, 128, 130, 152, 333, 346.
Lane, Dr John, 24, 29, 30, 31, 32, 33, 40.
Langland Bay Golf Club, 250.
  House, 198.
Layer Keeper, 92, 93, 107.
Lead industry, 29, 40.
Lewis, Saunders, 216.
Lewis, William ('Lewys Afan'), 137.
Liberal, -ism, 142-3, 155, 305-9.
Libraries, 227-8, 302-4.
Literary Associations, 215-44.
Llandarcy, 77, 78, 327, 333.
Llangyfelach, 128, 145, 146, 152, 162, 190, 195, 305.
Llangyvelach Copper Works, 31, 32, 55.
Llansamlet, 50, 115, 117, 120, 145, 149, 152, 162, 190, 269, 305, 327, 333, 341.
Llewellyn, family, 126.
  John Dillwyn, 161, 163, 182, 269, 292, 301.
  John Talbot Dillwyn, 262, 265, 292, 307.
Local Board of Health, 114, 297-9, 300, 301, 304.
Local government, 85-115, 139, 285-304, 311-19, 335, 342-3.
Lockwood, Morris and Co., 24, 32, 49.
Lower Swansea Valley, 29, 31, 32, 36, 41, 42, 50, 58, 296, 316-7, 321, 323, 326, 327, 330, 333, 339, 341, 342-3, 344.

M

Mackworth, family, 104.
  Sir Humphrey, 23-4.
Maesteg House, 127.
Mansel family, 17, 27, 48, 104, 105.
Mansion House, 198.
Maritime Quarter, 82, 193, 195, 213, 343.
Markets, 5, 8, 15, 21.
Market house, 15, 203.
Matthews, David, M.P., 308.
Mayor, 286, 288, 310.
McKinley Tariff, 43, 54, 74.
Medical Officer of Health, 298.
Melville, George and Andrew, 257.
Members of Parliament, 103, 305-10.
Metal Exchange, 44.
Metal-making, 321.
Methodism, Methodists, 147-51, 153, 154, 162, 176.
Middle classes, 127, 130, 132, 253.
Mond, Sir Alfred, M.P., 308, 309, 325.

Morgan, George, 201.
Morgan, Col. Llewellyn, 250, 262.
Morganite Carbon Company, 333, 339.
Mormons, 154.
Morris Castle, 36, 195.
Morris, Sir Cedric, 188.
Morris family, 32, 37, 58, 116, 126, 188, 196.
  John I, 32, 36, 121, 195.
  John II, 49, 50.
  Robert, 32, 58.
Morriston, 36, 41, 44, 116, 117, 120, 121, 130, 152, 195-6, 269, 271, 300, 310, 323, 326, 327, 332, 340, 341, 347.
  Hospital, 331, 340.
  Orpheus Choir, 271.
  Tabernacl Chapel, 44, 155, 202.
Mortality, 296-7, 304.
Motor cars, 334, 335, 341-2, 346.
Mount Pleasant Chapel, 130, 153, 154, 201.
Mount Pleasant Hospital, 292.
Mowbray family, 5, 6.
Moxham, Glendinning, 203, 207-8.
Mumbles, 107, 119, 263.
  Railway, 334.
Municipal Corporations Act, 1835, 111, 139, 285-6, 304-5, 309.
Murray, W. Grant, 185, 186, 187.
Museums, 302-3.
Music, 253-5, 269, 271-2.
Music Halls, 255-6, 257.
Mynyddbach, 147, 149, 152-3.
  School, 173, 338.

N

Name, Swansea, 1-3.
Nash, Richard ('Beau'), 216-7.
National Eisteddfod, 253-4, 269, 270-1, 273.
National Schools, 158-9, 164, 313.
Nationalization, 334.
Newburgh, Henry de, 3, 5.
  William de, 5, 7, 87.
New Cut, 120.
New Theatre, 247-8.
Nickel industry, 322.
Nixon, John, 178.
Nonconformists, 129-30; see also Dissenters.
Normans, 3-4, 5-6, 86-7.
North Dock, 66, 68, 76, 80, 107, 120, 327, 340, 343.
North Ward, 286.

O

Oil, 78, 83-4, 333.
Olchfa, 152, 172.
  School, 172.
Open spaces, 301-2.
Opera, 251, 255.
Ormond, John, 240.
Oxford Street Schools, 164.
Oystermouth, 119, 162, 177, 189, 347.

P

Palace Theatre, 204-5.
Pantygwydr Chapel, 202.
Parc Wern, Parc Beck, 197.
Parliamentary elections, 104, 105; see also Members of Parliament.
Parry, Joseph, 155.
Pascoe Grenfell and Sons, 38, 120.
Patent fuel, 51, 323.
Patti, Adelina, 206, 269.
  Pavilion, 206.
Paving Commission, -ers, 108-14, 287, 297-8, 304.
Penlan, 336-7.
  School, 172, 338.
Penrice Castle, 191.
Pentre-chwyth, 117, 121, 122.
Pentre Estyll, 152.
Pentre-guinea, 117, 126.
Perry, Alan, 244.
Phillips, Richard Mansel, 49.
Place, Francis, 177.
Plas-marl, 117, 127, 346.
Plas Newydd, New Place, 18-9, 178, 189.
Plaza Cinema, 211, 272.
Politics, 139, 304-10.
Poor Law Amendment Act, 1834, 285, 288, 290-1.
Poor relief, 13, 19-20, 290-4.
Population, 9, 15, 17-9, 25-6, 87, 89, 118, 246, 285-6, 290, 310-11, 314-5, 319, 325-6, 328-9, 336-7, 345, 350.
Port, 5, 8, 12-3, 16-7, 21, 23, 57-84, 88, 105, 106, 107, 129, 333.
Portreeve, 89, 90, 93, 95, 100, 103, 107, 110, 286.
Port Tennant, 66, 120, 126, 333.
Powell, Gabriel, 59-60, 101, 102, 106, 109, 110, 179.
Presbyterians, 146.
Prichard, T. J. Llewelyn, 227.
Prince of Wales Dock, 67, 68, 76, 80, 81.
Public Health, 294-302.
Puritan, Puritanism, 20-2, 26, 130.

Q

Quakers, 130, 146, 154.
Queen's Dock, 76, 81, 327.

R

Races, 249.
Railways, 321, 322, 324, 333-4, 341.
Ratepayers' Group, 310.
Rates, 287, 304.
Recorder, 89, 91, 100, 110.
Rees, Thomas, 156-7.
Reform Acts, 1832, 1867, 1885, 305-6.
Reformation, 20.
Refuse collection, 295-6.
Regattas, 249.
Religion, 145-57, 173-6, 251-3.
Religious Census, 1851, 154.
Report of the Commissioners on Municipal Corporations, 1835, 101, 286.
Restoration, 23, 26.
Richards, Alun, 243.
Richards, Ceri, 186, 188.
Road transport, 328, 333-4, 346.
Robinson, P. F., 197.
Roman Catholics, 154, 165-6, 176, 313.
Romans, 1.
Royal Institution of South Wales, 117, 159, 161, 166, 180, 181, 183, 189, 196, 227-8, 302.
Rugby, 261, 264-5, 266-7, 273-5, 281.
Ruthen, Sir Charles, 207.

S

St Andrew's Chapel, 154, 156, 202.
St David's Church, 166, 200-1.
  shopping centre, 213, 343-4.
St Gabriel's Church, 163, 176, 231-2.
St Helen's, 249, 262-3, 265-6, 273-5, 276-8, 282, 283, 297, 302, 346.
St James's Church, 163.
St John's, Church and parish of, 5, 118, 120, 145, 154, 162, 164, 190, 200, 300, 305.
  Hafod, 164, 200.
St Joseph's Church, 166, 176, 201.
St Mark's Church, 163.
St Mary's, Church and parish of, 108, 118, 145, 162, 164, 174, 189, 200, 290, 300.
St Matthew's Church, 163, 190.
St Paul's Church, Sketty, 163.
St Peter's Church, Cockett, 163.
St Thomas, 118, 120, 122, 140, 143, 154, 163, 263, 305, 329.
Salmon, David, 234.
Samuel, Howell Walter, M.P., 309.

Sandfields, 290.
Sanitary conditions, 296-9.
Savage, Richard, 217-8.
Scandinavians, 1, 3, 4.
Scavenging, 111.
Schools,
  comprehensive, 171-2.
  elementary, 157-9, 164-5, 167, 204.
  secondary, 167-9.
Scott, Clement, 229.
Secombe, Sir Harry, 260.
Seren Gomer, 133, 153, 215.
Service industries, 302, 334-5, 339-40, 342.
Sewerage, sewers, 114, 290, 300, 329.
Shelley, Percy Bysshe, 224.
Shipbuilding, 68-70.
Shipowning, 70-1.
Shipwrecks, 71-2.
Shopping, 340-1, 343-4.
Siemens, Sir William, 47.
Siloh Newydd Chapel, 155, 201.
Simon, Bishop Glyn, 175.
Singleton Abbey, 127, 184, 192, 196.
  Hospital, 212, 340.
Sketty, 37, 115, 118, 152, 231, 263, 329, 337.
  Hall, 127, 190-1, 192.
  Park, 195-6.
Slum clearance, 300-1.
Smith family, 49, 190.
Smith, J. Allan, 163, 164.
Smith, John Warwick, 178.
Smith, William H. ('Waterworks Bill'), 112, 297.
Soccer, 261, 266-7, 274, 282.
South Dock, 66, 76, 80, 82, 118, 295, 301, 327, 341, 343.
South Wales Transport Co., 346.
South Ward, 286.
Squire, Edward B., 163, 164, 174.
Star Theatre, 256-7.
Steel industry, 46, 47, 323, 327, 332, 339.
Steward, 89, 90, 91, 94, 95, 96, 100, 101, 102, 103, 107, 110.
Swansea Airport, 331.
Swansea Amateur Operatic Society, 272.
Swansea and District Male Voice Society, 269.
Swansea Bay City, 322, 347, 355.
Swansea Board of Guardians, 291-4, 310.
Swansea Brewery, 324.
Swansea Canal, 115.
Swansea Castle, 3-4, 6, 9, 189.

Swansea china, 179-80.
Swansea Corporation Act, 1889, 311.
Swansea Cricket and Football Club, 262.
Swansea District (constituency), 143, 306, 307-8.
Swansea Drama Festival, 272-3.
Swansea East (constituency), 308, 309, 310.
Swansea Festival of the Arts, 283.
Swansea Festival Orchestra, 272.
Swansea Herald, 64.
Swansea Hospital, 297.
Swansea Little Theatre, 273.
Swansea Orchestral Society, 271.
Swansea Philharmonic Choir, 271.
Swansea Poor Law Union, 291.
Swansea School Board, 167-8, 313.
Swansea Town (constituency), 143, 306, 307, 308.
Swansea Town Association Football Club ('Swans'), 267-8, 274, 278-9, 281, 282.
Swansea West (constituency), 308, 309.
'Swanzey', 3, 57.

T

Tabernacl Chapel, Morriston, 44, 155, 202.
Tawe, 1, 3, 7, 9, 24, 31, 47, 58, 64, 68, 72, 92, 114, 327, 342, 346.
  Valley, 115-6, 336, 346.
Technical College, 169-70, 171.
Theatre, 248-9, 251, 254-5, 273.
Thomas, David Vaughan, 269, 271.
Thomas, Dylan, 186, 220-1, 224, 229, 235, 236, 237-40, 244, 272, 273.
Thomas, Edward, 234.
Thomas, family (Danygraig), 17.
Thomas, Sir Percy, 210.
Thomas, Thomas, 201.
Thomas, William ('Islwyn'), 215.
Thomas, William, Lan, 139, 206, 301, 302.
Thomas, Wynford Vaughan, 237.
Tillett, Ben, 307.
Tinplate industry, 40-9, 52, 54, 78, 124, 323, 327, 330, 332, 339.
  workers, 137.
Tir John power station, 316, 329.
Tories, 104, 305.
Toshack, John, 281.
Tourism, 341, 344.
Town Clerk, 289, 298.
Town Council, 288.

Town Hall, 100.
Townhill, 95, 96, 109, 209, 245, 287, 294, 326, 329.
Town records, 12, 13.
Townsend, Chauncey, 34, 37, 40, 49.
Trades Council, 137, 140, 142, 307, 310.
Trade Unions, 135-8, 140.
Treasurer, 289, 298.
Treboeth, 124, 300.
Trevivian, Vivianstown, 36, 117, 120-1, 122, 295.
Trewyddfa, 51, 152.
Triniti Chapel, 153, 154, 174.

U

Unitarians, 130, 153, 154, 201.
University College of Swansea, 169-- 71, 212, 317, 335, 340.
Unreformed Corporation, 86-105.
Unwin, Sir Raymond, 209-10, 314, 326-7.
Uplands, 115, 118, 263.
Upper Bank Works, 194-5.
Urban Sanitary Authority, 304.

V

Velindre Works, 332, 339.
Vetch Field, 267, 274, 275, 278-9, 282, 283.
Victoria Park, 302, 316.
Victorian architecture, 198-200, 200-3.
Vivian and Sons, 32, 38, 39, 40, 49, 50, 51, 53, 54, 55, 120, 121.

Vivian family, 32, 38, 126, 163, 164, 249, 269, 313.
  Graham, 184, 196.
  Henry Hussey, M.P., Lord Swansea, 32, 40, 53, 138, 307.
  John, 32, 34, 50.
  John Henry, M.P., 32, 37, 50, 64, 99, 122, 159, 161, 184, 189, 197, 306.
  Odo, 269.
  R. Glynn, 184.

W

Walter Road Chapel, 157.
Walters, Evan, 186.
Waring, Elijah, 218.
Watch Committee, 113.
Watchmen, 113.
Water, water supply, 41, 112-3, 290, 295, 299.
Waterworks Company, 299.
Watkeys, Henry, 226.
Watkins, Vernon, 186, 235-7, 238-9, 240.
Waunarlwydd, 138, 264, 330, 333.
Weaver's Mills, 76, 208, 324.
Webb, Harri, 240-1.
Webber, Vivian W., 230-1, 243.
Welsh Language, 3, 18, 127, 151, 152, 215-6, 253-4, 272-3, 326, 337, 346, 350.
Wesley, John, 150-1.
Wesleyan Chapel, 153-4, 174.
West Cross, 337.
West Glamorgan County Council, 85, 319, 340.
  Hall, 212-3, 340, 342, 343.

West Glamorgan Institute of Higher Education, 187, 335, 340.
Whigs, 104.
Wignall, David, 137.
Williams, David, M.P., 137, 140, 308, 310.
Williams, Foster and Co., 32, 34, 40, 54, 120.
Williams, John, M.P., 307.
Williams, Penry, 178.
Williams, Thomas Jeremiah, M.P., 308.
Williams, William ('Crwys'), 216.
Williams, Williams, Maesygwernen, M.P., 307.
Woods, John Chapman, 229-30, 234.
Worcester, earls and marquesses of, 5, 11, 12, 14, 15, 21, 65.
Workers, working-class, 123-4, 128-9, 130, 131-2.
Workhouse, 292.
Working conditions, 123-6, 128-9.
World War I, 1914-18, 310, 322, 327.
World War II, 1939-45, 79-80, 174, 275, 316, 329-30, 331-2, 336.

Y

York Place Chapel, 201.
Young, William Weston, 179-80.

Z

Zinc industry, 29, 37-9, 322, 327, 333, 338.